THE
LAW
BOOK

THE
LAW
BOOK

DK LONDON

SENIOR ART EDITOR
Gillian Andrews

SENIOR EDITORS
Camilla Hallinan, Laura Sandford

EDITORS
John Andrews, Alethea Doran,
Annelise Evans, Richard Gilbert,
Lydia Halliday, Tim Harris, Victoria Pyke,
Jess Unwin, Rachel Warren Chadd

ILLUSTRATIONS
James Graham

JACKET DESIGN
DEVELOPMENT MANAGER
Sophia MTT

PRODUCER, PRE-PRODUCTION
Gillian Reid

SENIOR PRODUCER
Rachel Ng

SENIOR MANAGING ART EDITOR
Lee Griffiths

MANAGING EDITOR
Gareth Jones

ASSOCIATE PUBLISHING DIRECTOR
Liz Wheeler

ART DIRECTOR
Karen Self

DESIGN DIRECTOR
Philip Ormerod

PUBLISHING DIRECTOR
Jonathan Metcalf

DK DELHI

SENIOR ART EDITOR
Chhaya Sajwan

ART EDITOR
Anukriti Arora

ASSISTANT ART EDITORS
Ankita Das, Adhithi Priya

SENIOR EDITOR
Arani Sinha

EDITORS
Rishi Bryan, Nandini D. Tripathy

ASSISTANT EDITOR
Ankita Gupta

MANAGING EDITOR
Soma B. Chowdhury

SENIOR MANAGING ART EDITOR
Arunesh Talapatra

SENIOR JACKET DESIGNER
Suhita Dharamjit

DTP DESIGNERS
Ashok Kumar, Manish Upreti, Anita Yadav

PROJECT PICTURE RESEARCHER
Aditya Katyal

PICTURE RESEARCH MANAGER
Taiyaba Khatoon

PRE-PRODUCTION MANAGERS
Balwant Singh, Sunil Sharma

PRODUCTION MANAGER
Pankaj Sharma

original styling by
STUDIO 8

SANDS PUBLISHING SOLUTIONS

EDITORIAL PARTNERS
David and Silvia Tombesi-Walton

DESIGN PARTNER
Simon Murrell

First published in Great Britain in 2020
by Dorling Kindersley Limited
DK, One Embassy Gardens, 8 Viaduct Gardens,
London, SW11 7BW

Copyright © 2020 Dorling Kindersley Limited
A Penguin Random House Company
10 9 8 7 6 5 4 3 2 1
001–316472–Sep/2020

A CIP catalogue record for this book
is available from the British Library.
ISBN: 978-0-2414-1019-6

Printed in the United Arab Emirates

For the curious
www.dk.com

CONTRIBUTORS

PAUL MITCHELL, CONSULTANT EDITOR

Paul Mitchell is Professor of Laws at University College London, UK, specializing in legal history, Roman law, and the current law of obligations. His books include *The Making of the Modern Law of Defamation* and *A History of Tort Law 1900–1950*; he is also an editor of *Chitty on Contracts* and *Goff and Jones on Unjust Enrichment*.

PETER CHRISP

Peter Chrisp is a professional author with a particular interest in ancient history. He has written more than 90 books, 25 of them for DK. His titles include *Ancient Greece*, *Ancient Rome*, *Prehistory*, *Crime and Punishment*, and *Chrisp's Crime Miscellany*.

CLAIRE COCK-STARKEY

Claire Cock-Starkey is a writer and an editor with a special interest in Victorian history and current affairs. She has written 12 books, including *The Book Lovers' Miscellany*, *The Real McCoy and 149 Other Eponyms*, and *Seeing the Bigger Picture: Global Infographics*.

FREDERICK COWELL

Frederick Cowell lectures in tort law and human rights law at Birkbeck, University of London. His research interests include the legal obligations of international human rights organizations, the history of the European Convention on Human Rights, and the politics of the International Criminal Court. He has worked as a legal adviser for non-governmental organizations, specializing in international human rights law.

THOMAS CUSSANS

Thomas Cussans, writer and historian, has contributed to numerous historical works. They include DK's *Timelines of World History*, *History Year by Year*, and *History: The Ultimate Visual Guide*. He was previously the publisher of *The Times History of the World* and *The Times Atlas of European History*. Among his other works are *The Times Kings and Queens of the British Isles* and *The Holocaust*.

JOHN FARNDON

John Farndon is the author of many books on the history of science and ideas, and on contemporary issues. He also writes widely on science and environmental issues and has been shortlisted five times for the Royal Society's Young People's Science Book Prize.

PHILIP PARKER

Philip Parker is a historian specializing in the classical and medieval world. He is the author of the *DK Companion Guide to World History*, *The Empire Stops Here: A Journey Around the Frontiers of the Roman Empire*, and *A History of Britain in Maps*, and was a contributor to DK's *The History Book*. He was previously a diplomat working on the UK's relations with Greece and Cyprus and holds a diploma in international relations from Johns Hopkins University's School of Advanced International Studies.

MARCUS WEEKS

Marcus Weeks studied philosophy and worked as a teacher before embarking on a career as an author. He has contributed to many books on the arts, humanities, and popular sciences.

6

CONTENTS

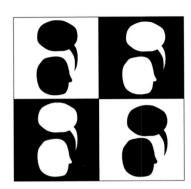

THE RISE OF THE RULE OF LAW
1800–1945

A NEW INTERNATIONAL ORDER
1945–1980

INTRODU

CTION

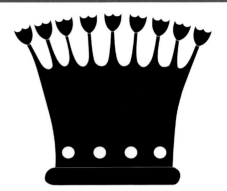
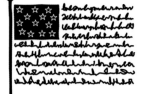

Law is much more than a system of rules governing the conduct of members of society. Its rich complexity stems from its history, how it was created and administered, its function, the way it operates, and its effects.

Around 10,000 years ago, as people began to gather in ever larger settlements, they had to find new ways to live and work together peacefully. Clear laws were needed to settle disputes. The earliest known law code – dating from around 2100 BCE and set down by order of Ur-Nammu, king of Ur, a city in Mesopotamia (now Iraq) – listed commensurate punishments for crimes. Murder, for instance, was punishable by death – an early bid, echoed in many later law codes, to ensure that justice fitted the offence.

From the earliest times, rulers invoked their gods to give laws authority. The Jewish Torah enshrined laws by tradition given to Moses by God. Around 1046 BCE, King Wu of the Chinese Zhou dynasty similarly claimed a divine mandate for his rule. In the 4th century CE, Christianity's Catholic canon law developed into a legal system that has influenced modern civil law and common law, while Islamic Sharia law is based on the word of Allah in the Koran.

New civilizations established legal frameworks for their laws with procedures and officials to ensure compliance. Their philosophers debated the nature of justice and shaped political ideas. In Athens, the ancient Greek city which practised the earliest democracy, reason and a concept of justice as a virtue guided Plato's and Aristotle's theories of law. The early Roman Republic's Twelve Tables explained laws and spelt out citizens' rights. In China, between 476 BCE and 221 BCE, scholars proposed radically different systems – Daoism, Confucianism, and Legalism – ranging in nature from laissez-faire to authoritarian. Each had a lasting impact.

> The end of law is not to abolish or restrain, but to preserve and enlarge freedom.
> **John Locke**
> **English philosopher (1632–1704)**

A large proportion of the law exists to protect members of society and their property, and the enforcement of the law acts as a deterrent as well as ensuring justice. As trade developed, civil laws were drawn up to govern transactions and the conduct of businesses. To facilitate trade between nations, the earliest known maritime law – the *Lex Rhodia* – evolved during Greece's Classical Age (500 BCE–300 BCE).

Punishments and rights

Long after the Greek and Roman civilizations declined, barbaric forms of justice existed in medieval Europe. In the absence of evidence or credible witnesses, alleged offenders (usually the poor) could be tried by ordeal; their innocence gauged by how well they recovered from physical ordeals, such as scalding or burning. Some disputes were settled by trial by combat, a physical fight.

Trial by ordeal was banned by a 13th-century papal decree; trial by combat persisted much longer. Legal systems changed as people beyond a small ruling elite became richer and better educated. Apart from the poorest, ordinary citizens began to acquire greater rights and protections. Chapter 39 of Magna Carta, sealed in 1215, established

the right to justice of every free man, a right later enshrined in the *Habeas Corpus* Act of 1679. In England and Wales, poverty, too, was addressed in the Poor Law Act of 1601, which provided a very basic safety net for those at the bottom of society.

While criminal, property, and commerce laws have existed since ancient times and been steadily adjusted and refined, legislation concerning civil and human rights had to be fought for and even today is not universally adopted. The English Bill of Rights (1688–89) that ensured the power of an elected parliament came in the wake of the English Civil War, the execution of Charles I, and the absolute rule of both Charles II and James II. The Napoleonic Code of 1804 was built around key ideas of The Declaration of the Rights of Man and of the Citizen that emerged at the start of the French Revolution. It took a century of campaigning to abolish most slavery, and bloody protests to secure women's voting rights.

As the Industrial Revolution took shape in the 18th and 19th centuries, workers began to recognize their collective muscle. The UK's Trade Union Act of 1871 gave workers a political voice, and trade unionism gained strength across the globe, prompting better and safer working conditions. In Germany, new laws compelling employers to provide sickness funds for injured workers were passed in 1883 and 1884.

To accept the need for new or revised laws, governments have to be open to change. In more than half of countries with populations of at least 500,000, some form of democratic government has now evolved, with separate branches for the creation, administration, and enforcement of the law by the legislature, executive, and judiciary respectively. Separating the powers in this way guards against the abuse of power and permits each branch to check and balance the powers of the others.

International lawmaking

Global commerce in both goods and services has greatly increased in the past century, requiring rafts of new international legislation. Nations also have to work together to find legal measures to combat spiralling international crime. Organizations such as the United Nations, established to preserve peace after World War II, and trading blocs such as the European Union have extended their remit to found institutions capable of making legally binding regulations regarding matters such as trade, human rights, and international crime. INTERPOL collaborates with the police forces of more than 190 countries to tackle organized crime, terrorism, and cybercrime. A newer area of concern is how measures to protect the environment can be enforced.

This book presents, in roughly chronological order, some of the big ideas that have influenced the law. In each case, it describes the social and political climate that produced them, people who championed them, and the role these concepts have played in shaping the societies they appeared in and others, too. ∎

Laws must be justified by something more than the will of the majority. They must rest on the eternal foundation of righteousness.
Calvin Coolidge
30th US president (1923–29)

THE BEG
OF LAW
2100 BCE—500 CE

INNINGS

Ur-Nammu, **king of Ur**, formulates **the earliest** known **written law code**.

c. **2100** BCE

According to **rabbinic tradition**, Moses receives the Torah, **the foundation of Judaic law**, from God on Mount Sinai.

c. **1300** BCE

Greek merchants from Rhodes, having established long-range trade links, develop **a code of international maritime law** widely adopted across **the Mediterranean**.

500–300 BCE

The first law code of the newly established **Roman Republic** is inscribed on **12 bronze tablets** displayed in the Forum.

c. **450** BCE

c. **1750** BCE

King Hammurabi has a **list of 282 laws inscribed** on a stele in the **centre of Babylon**.

c. **1046** BCE

King Wu establishes the Zhou dynasty in **China**, claiming the **"Mandate of Heaven"** for his rule.

476–221 BCE

During **China's** Warring States period, **legal systems emerge** based on **Confucianism, Daoism**, and **Legalism**.

Humans are a social species. Prehistoric peoples lived in kinship groups and tribes, ruled by elders. Over millennia, as civilizations evolved, different systems of government emerged. Rules of conduct, initially based on customs and religious beliefs, became formalized, and laws were codified. In Mesopotamia (now Iraq), the world's first civilization, Ur-Nammu, king of Ur, issued the first known law code 4,000 years ago.

Religion played a major role in early civilizations and inevitably influenced lawmaking. Laws – especially those governing morality or religious observance – were widely believed to have divine authority. According to Jewish tradition, God gave Moses the Torah, the first five books of the Hebrew Bible which include the Ten Commandments.

These laid the foundations of Mosaic law. The Torah and the later Talmud (a written collection of Jewish oral traditions) are the central sources of Jewish law.

In China, too, rulers claimed they had a divine right to govern. In about 1046 BCE, when Wu, first king of the Western Zhou dynasty, overthrew the ruling Shang dynasty, he declared he had the "Mandate of Heaven", which could be withdrawn if he failed in his sacred duty to rule justly.

Laws for complex societies

Civilizations across the ancient world, in Mesopotamia, Egypt, India, China, Greece, and Rome, established legal frameworks to organize their increasingly large and complex societies, and to ensure the rule of law was properly

administered. To trade with each other, nations also needed mutually accepted rules of commerce. The island of Rhodes, a major mercantile power in the Mediterranean, gave its name to the *Lex Rhodia*, which evolved from around 500 BCE to become the first widely recognized code of maritime law.

As nations became increasingly sophisticated, their thinkers began to consider how their societies might be better organized. In China, from the fifth century BCE, three radically different systems of governing emerged. Confucianism proposed a return to traditional values of virtue and respect, led by example. Daoism advocated the framing of laws in harmony with nature, rather than by a ruler's will, while Legalism imposed authoritarian rule, with harsh

Aristotle outlines his **theory of justice**, based on the idea that laws should conform to **natural law**, which is **universal and unchanging**.

The **customary laws of India** are described in two Sanskrit works, the *Arthashastra* and the *Manusmriti*.

Jurist Domitius **Ulpianus** (Ulpian) writes more than 200 influential **commentaries and treatises on Roman law**.

c. **340** BCE

2ND CENTURY BCE

212–222 CE

348 BCE

286 BCE

70 CE

c. **313** CE

In *Laws*, **Plato** proposes an initial **dictatorship** guided by a **wise legislator** for city-states, before **elected officials** can take charge.

The Roman tribune Aquilius proposes the *Lex Aquilia* to provide financial **compensation** for **wrongful damage to property**.

After **the Second Temple of Jerusalem** is **destroyed**, Jewish people respond with closer observation of the **Torah's laws**.

The **Edict of Milan** decriminalizes **Christian worship** in the Roman Empire, paving the way for the **first systematic collections** of **canon law**.

---

punishment for offences. In the second century BCE, after more than 250 years of conflict during the Warring States period, a Legalist dynasty finally established order, although its severity was soon discredited. Confucianism became the predominant ideology, albeit reinforced with a strict code of law.

From the fifth century BCE, the city-state of Athens had instituted a form of direct democracy, where all adult citizens could participate in government. But in his *Republic* and *Laws*, the Greek philosopher Plato argued for government by the few – a class of "philosopher-kings" in an ideal state, or an initial dictator, guided by a wise legislator. He maintained that only those trained in philosophy were capable of understanding the concepts of government and justice. His pupil

Aristotle advocated a form of constitutional government by the people, and believed that legislation must be in harmony with natural law.

India, by contrast, favoured a strictly hierarchical society, divided into castes, as advocated in the *Arthashastra* and *Manusmriti* of the second century BCE.

Rome and the Church

In about 509 BCE, when the Romans overthrew their tyrannical king, Lucius Tarquinius Superbus, they established the Roman Republic – a constitutional government ruled by two elected consuls. In *c.* 450 BCE, the new Republic published its first written law code – the Twelve Tables, inscribed on 12 bronze tablets – which set out the rights and duties of Roman citizens. As

the Roman Empire expanded, the laws were revised by jurists such as Ulpian but formed the basis of Roman law for a thousand years.

In *c.* 313 CE, Emperor Constantine, a convert to Christianity, issued the Edict of Milan, which proclaimed religious tolerance throughout the Roman Empire, ending the persecution of Christians. In 380 CE, Christianity became the Empire's official religion, and Christian theologians could begin to formulate law based on Christian teachings.

The early canons, derived from disputes about what people should believe, were the foundation of Roman Catholic canon law, the body of law that regulates the organization of the Church and codifies Christian beliefs. Canon law influenced the development of civil law in medieval Europe. ∎

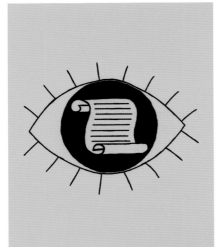

OBSERVE THE WORDS OF RIGHTEOUSNESS

EARLY LEGAL CODES (2100 BCE–1750 BCE)

IN CONTEXT

FOCUS
The first written laws

BEFORE
c. 4000 BCE Uruk, the world's first city, is established in Sumer, Mesopotamia.

c. 3300 BCE Cuneiform, the earliest system of writing, is invented in Uruk.

c. 2334 BCE Sargon of Akkad, a Mesopotamian city-state, conquers Sumer and creates the world's first empire.

AFTER
c. 600 BCE The Book of Exodus echoes Babylonian law by stating "eye for eye" as an element of the law of Moses.

c. 450 BCE The legal basis for retaliation – *lex talionis* – is laid out in the Roman law text, the Twelve Tables.

A round 6,000 years ago in Mesopotamia (now Iraq), the Sumerians, the world's first civilization, began to build cities, such as Uruk and Ur, which came to be governed by an *ensi* (king). For people who lived in small farming settlements, the responsibility to avenge wrongs against individuals had rested on families. In cities, large numbers of unrelated people needed to find ways of living and working together peacefully. Laws were therefore invented to resolve disputes and prevent feuds. When city-states grew powerful enough to form the first empires, they issued laws to control peoples spread across their domain.

Keeping a record

Initially, laws were passed on by word of mouth. Around 3300 BCE, the Sumerians began to record information using a writing system called cuneiform (meaning "wedge-shaped"), which consisted of

symbols etched into clay tablets. The earliest surviving cuneiform set of legal rules, or code, was set down by Ur-Nammu, king of Ur, around 2100 BCE. Each law took the form of a stated crime followed by its punishment – for example, "If a man commits a murder, that man must be killed."

A much more complete code, compiled by Hammurabi, king of Babylon from 1792 to 1750 BCE, was discovered at the start of the 20th century. It is inscribed in cuneiform script on a basalt stele (stone pillar) 2.25 m (7½ feet) high,

The relief at the top of the basalt pillar containing Hammurabi's legal code shows the king standing before Shamash (seated), the Mesopotamian god of justice.

See also: The Ten Commandments and Mosaic law 20–23 ▪ The Twelve Tables 30 ▪ The *Arthashastra* and the *Manusmriti* 35 ▪ Trial by ordeal and combat 52–53

and opens with a prologue, in which the king declares that he had been ordered by the gods "to bring about the rule of righteousness in the land, to destroy the wicked and the evil-doers; so that the strong should not harm the weak". Pillars were set up in Babylonian cities so that all could see and follow the laws.

An eye for an eye

Hammurabi's laws are, like those in Ur-Nammu's code, set out as conditional statements. Number 196 in its list of 282 judgements is "If a man put out the eye of another man, his eye shall be put out". This principle reappeared in the books of Exodus and Leviticus, as part of the Hebrew Torah, and then in Roman law as *lex talionis* (the law of retaliation). Its purpose, however, was not to encourage retaliation but to limit it to fit the offence.

Ur-Nammu's code had a less brutal approach to retribution for violent crime. Each part of the body was given a value in weights of

The ziggurat, a vast stepped pyramid topped with a shrine, was the religious centre of Mesopotamian cities.

silver. Someone who cut off another person's foot, for example, incurred a fine of "ten shekels". This idea of financial penalty – a fine – rather than physical retaliation, is closer to modern ideas on punishment. ▪

> " In future time, through all coming generations, let the king, who may be in the land, ... not alter the law of the land which I have given.
> **The Code of Hammurabi**

Judicial procedures

Court cases recorded on clay tablets show how justice was administered in Mesopotamia. There were no formal court houses or lawyers. Accusers and accused, together with witnesses, appeared before an assembly of local people or city elders – or a panel of three to six judges in more serious cases – and provided oral or written testimony. As today, participants swore a solemn oath to tell the truth. This could take place in a public space, the king's palace, or the city's temple, where the accused swore on a symbol of the local god. In some cases, people confessed because they feared angering the god by swearing falsely.

If a case could not be solved, it became a decision for the gods. The legal solution in Hammurabi's code was a trial by ordeal, where the accused had to leap into the Euphrates River: "If he sink in the river his accuser shall take possession of his house. But if the river prove that the accused is not guilty, and he escape unhurt, then he who had brought the accusation shall be put to death."

The chief god of Babylon, Marduk (centre), representing order, defeats the serpent-like sea deity Tiamat, representing evil and chaos.

THIS SHALL BE AN EVERLASTING STATUTE UNTO YOU

THE TEN COMMANDMENTS AND MOSAIC LAW (*c.* 1300 BCE—6TH CENTURY BCE)

IN CONTEXT

FOCUS
Divine law

BEFORE
c. **1750** BCE King Hammurabi of Babylon writes a law code.

AFTER
c. **1207** BCE An inscription on granite by Pharaoh Merneptah of Egypt is the first reference to Israelites in Canaan, and boasts that "Israel is laid waste".

3rd century BCE The Torah is translated into Greek, entitled *Pentateuch* ("five books").

c. **200** CE Rabbis in Palestine compile a written code of Jewish oral traditions, the Mishnah, which offers further guidance on interpreting the laws in the Torah.

c. **350–550** CE Scholars publish the Gemara, an analysis and elucidation of the Mishnah; the two works form the Talmud.

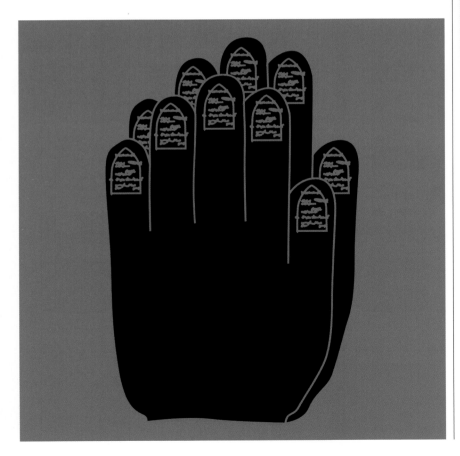

M osaic law is an ancient legal system set out in the Torah, which is the first five books of the Tanakh – the Jewish Bible, known to Christians as the Old Testament. The Torah ("instruction") contains a great number of laws, which are presented as given directly by God to Moses, founder and lawgiver of the Jewish nation. In the legend of the Exodus, described in the Torah, Moses was ordered by God in *c.* 1300 BCE to lead the Israelites out of enslavement in Egypt and take them to the promised land of Canaan. Moses led his people first to Mount Sinai, which he climbed, and there God gave him the Ten Commandments,

See also: Early legal codes 18–19 ▪ The *Arthashastra* and the *Manusmriti* 35 ▪ The Mishnah and the Talmud 38–41 ▪ The origins of canon law 42–47 ▪ The Koran 54–57

as well as many detailed laws covering moral behaviour, religious worship, and every part of daily life. The most important Commandment was the first: "You shall have no other gods before me." The Israelites spent another 40 years in the desert before reaching Canaan, and Moses himself died within sight of it.

This 17th-century painting by French portrait artist Philippe de Champaigne, entitled "Moses with the Ten Commandments", shows the inscriptions on two tablets of stone.

Mosaic law was perceived as part of a covenant, a formal agreement, between God and the Israelites. It was believed that God promised to protect the Israelites and give them the land of Canaan if they obeyed his laws. According to Exodus 19:5, God said: "Now if you obey me fully and keep my covenant, then out of all nations you will be my treasured possession."

Authors of the Torah

The books of the Torah, written in Hebrew, were thought to have been set down by Moses himself. But, from the 18th century, scholars developed a historical approach to reading the Bible, which appeared to show that the stories had been shaped over time by many authors, using different vocabulary and styles. The text includes footnotes inserted by later generations to explain ancient place names and point out evidence for events still visible "to this very day".

Scholars in 19th-century Germany identified four types of source material in the Torah. They were termed E, J, D, and P (Elohist, Jahwist, Deuteronomist, and Priestly), with the earliest material (most of Genesis, much of Exodus, and some elements of Numbers) thought to come from E and J. Source E describes the traditions of the northern tribes, and refers to God by the title "Elohim" ("god"). Source J pertains mainly to the southern Israelite tribe of Judah, and refers to God by his four-letter name YHWH, assumed to be pronounced "Yahweh". »

The five books of the Torah

Genesis
Creation and the Israelites' ancestry from Adam and Eve.

Exodus
Escape from Egypt, and laws including the Ten Commandments.

Leviticus
Laws on sacrifice, priesthood, and ritual purity.

Numbers
The Israelites' 40 years in the desert, and a census of the tribes.

Deuteronomy
Laws on worship, crime, and punishment, delivered by Moses before his death.

The Ten Commandments (Exodus 20)

1. You shall have no other gods before me.

2. You shall not make for yourself an idol and worship it.

3. You shall not misuse the name of the Lord your God.

4. Remember the Sabbath day and keep it holy.

5. Honour your father and your mother.

6. You shall not murder.

7. You shall not commit adultery.

8. You shall not steal.

9. You shall not give false testimony against your neighbour.

10. You shall not covet anything that belongs to your neighbour.

The Book of Deuteronomy, the fifth book of the Torah, is attributed to source D. It is associated with the religious reformation of King Josiah, who ruled the Israelite kingdom of Judah (formed after the northern and southern tribes divided, in c. 930 BCE) in the 7th century BCE. Josiah centralized Jewish worship in the Temple in Jerusalem, and enforced strict monotheism. The northern kingdom, Israel, had been conquered by the Assyrians in 722 BCE, and in Deuteronomy, the history of Israel is rewritten as perceived from Judah.

The latest material, from source P, dates from after the Babylonian king Nebuchadnezzar destroyed the city and Temple of Jerusalem in 586 BCE. He deported the Jewish leaders, including the priests, to Babylon, and there the priests revised the books of Genesis and Exodus, and wrote Leviticus and Numbers. In the Priestly stories, Yahweh was not tied to one place but could accompany the Jews anywhere, including their exile: "I will put my dwelling place among you … I will walk among you and be your God, and you will be my people" (Leviticus 26:11–12).

Mosaic law evolved over time, being updated in response to new circumstances. Yet every new law was presented as having been given to Moses by God at Sinai.

One transcendent God

The early Israelites worshipped other Canaanite gods alongside Yahweh. In the Torah there are many stories of Israelites worshipping Baal, the god of rain and fertility, and Asherah, the mother goddess. Yahweh and the other gods were worshipped at sanctuaries (holy places), often located on hilltops.

The First Commandment, "You shall have no other gods *before me*", could be read to mean that other deities may be worshipped, as long as Yahweh is honoured above them. In the stories attributed to sources J and E, Yahweh appeared in human form, "walking in the garden in the cool of the day" (Genesis 3:8) or visiting Abraham in front of his tent (Genesis 18). However, by the time Deuteronomy was written, God was transcendent, existing beyond the created world, and Judaism was a monotheistic religion. King Josiah, in the course of his religious reformation, removed the Asherah statues from the Temple in Jerusalem, burned them, and destroyed all the hilltop shrines.

Once Judaism became monotheistic, the earlier stories of Israelites worshipping Asherah and Baal were interpreted as examples of regression from Mosaic law. The Babylonian exile was now seen as divine punishment for this.

A nation of priests

During their exile in Babylon, the Jewish priests asserted that God had commanded the Israelites to be a holy people, a nation of priests, so that he could live among them. They were instructed to keep themselves separate from their Babylonian neighbours, by observing strict rules of diet and cleanliness. (The Hebrew word *qadosh*, translated as "holy", literally means "separate".) It was common in the ancient world for priests to observe rules of purity: Egyptian priests, for example, had to bathe in cold water four times a day, and wear papyrus sandals and linen rather than leather or wool. But the idea that a whole nation should follow such laws was unique.

The Jewish rules and rituals are described in detail. Leviticus 11:47 commands the people to distinguish "between the unclean and the clean, between living creatures that may be eaten and those that may not be eaten". Pork, shellfish, and many other foods were forbidden. Those animals that were permitted could be eaten only if they were ritually slaughtered and the blood removed. According to Leviticus 11:39, "If an animal that you are allowed to eat dies, anyone who touches its carcass will be unclean till evening."

Leviticus 14:48–53 describes an elaborate ceremony to purify a house with mould on the walls. A priest should take cedar wood, scarlet yarn,

Speak to the entire assembly of Israel and say to them: Be holy, because I, the Lord your God, am holy.
Leviticus 19:1–2

hyssop, and a live bird, dip them into the blood of a sacrificed bird and some fresh water, and sprinkle the house seven times. "Then he is to release the live bird in the open fields outside the town. In this way he will make atonement for the house, and it will be clean."

Absolute truth

Earlier ancient law codes, such as the Code of Hammurabi, were casuistic – describing procedure in particular cases, from which general principles were derived. In contrast, the Ten Commandments were

apodictic – absolute statements of right and wrong, such as "You shall not murder." Even so, the Mosaic code included many laws that resembled Mesopotamian and Babylonian laws. For example, law 251 in Hammurabi's code states: "If an ox be a goring ox, and it shown that he is a gorer, and [the owner] do not bind his horns, or fasten the ox up, and the ox gore a free-born man and kill him, the owner shall pay one-half a mina in money." Exodus 21:29–30 says that if a bull "has had the habit of goring and the owner has been warned but has not kept it penned up and it kills a man or woman, the bull is to be stoned and its owner also is to be put to death. However … the owner may redeem his life by the payment of whatever is demanded."

Although Mesopotamian kings claimed to rule on behalf of gods, they never claimed that their gods were themselves the authors of the laws. To break a law was to commit an offence against a fellow human, who might choose to pardon the offender. But breaking a law in the Torah was different: it was not just an offence against a fellow human, it was also a sin against God. ∎

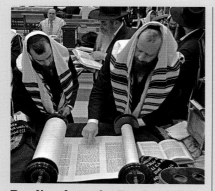

Reading from the Torah scroll is part of the ritual of Jewish prayers. It takes place on certain days, including the Sabbath and Jewish holidays.

The Torah scroll

The scroll that contains the text of the Torah – including the laws given by God to Moses – is the most sacred object in every Jewish synagogue. Each scroll, or *Sefer Torah* (*sefer* means "book", or "written document") is handwritten on special parchment using a traditional quill or reed. The text contains 304,805 Hebrew letters, which have to be written perfectly by a trained scribe. A single mistake would invalidate the entire scroll.

The scroll is kept in a richly ornamented cabinet called the Torah ark. The holiest part of the synagogue and the focal point of prayer, this is built on the wall facing Jerusalem.

Passages from the Torah scroll are read out in the synagogue, usually several times a week. Selected sections are read every Sabbath morning, chosen so that the entire Torah is read over the course of a year. The end of this annual cycle is marked by the festival of *Simchat Torah*.

THE MANDATE OF HEAVEN
ZHOU DYNASTY CHINA (*c.* 1046 BCE—256 BCE)

IN CONTEXT

FOCUS
The right to rule

BEFORE
c. **1600–***c.* **1046 BCE** The Shang, the first Chinese dynasty, rules over much of eastern China. Shang kings create the first Chinese laws. Crimes are punished with the death penalty, mutilation, or imprisonment with hard labour.

AFTER
770–476 BCE Zhou dynastic power is weakened as local rulers compete for supremacy.

476–221 BCE Zhou China breaks up into seven warring states, but Zhou kings continue to play a ritual role until the final king, Nan, is deposed in 256 BCE.

221 BCE The Qin state triumphs, and China is united by Qin Shi Huang, the first emperor of the Qin dynasty.

A round 1046 BCE, King Wu of the state of Zhou overthrew the last king of the Shang dynasty, which had governed China for five centuries. To justify his rebellion, the founder of the new Zhou dynasty appealed to a concept called *tianming* ("Mandate of Heaven"). Wu argued that a king could only govern if he was favoured by heaven. He said that Shang kings had neglected their sacred duties and ruled corruptly, so heaven would transfer its mandate to another dynasty.

Shang kings had derived their royal authority from their supposed ability to communicate with their ancestors through divination. They did this by interpreting cracks made in bones and turtle shells. King Wu and the rulers who succeeded him, including those of later dynasties, now used the Mandate of Heaven to justify their rule.

The duty of kings
Zhou kings believed that they had a duty to rule justly or they risked losing heaven's mandate. This duty is described in the earliest Zhou documents. In the *Kang Gao* (*Announcement to the Prince of Kang*), attributed to Wu, the king gives legal advice to Feng, his younger brother. Feng had been appointed to govern a region of Zhou territory. Wu warns his brother not to let punishments "be warped to agree with [your] own inclinations" and tells him to revere the laws. ∎

> The Mandate is not easy to keep; may it not end in your persons. Display and make bright your good fame ...
> **Ode on King Wen**
> **King Wen (1152–1056 BCE) was King Wu's father**

See also: Early legal codes 18–19 ▪ Confucianism, Daoism, and Legalism 26–29 ▪ Magna Carta 66–71 ▪ The trial of Charles I 96–97

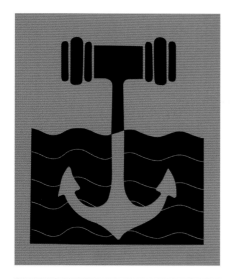

THE LAW OF THE SEA
THE *LEX RHODIA* (500 BCE–300 BCE)

The *Lex Rhodia* (*Law of Rhodes*) is the earliest known code of maritime law. It developed during Greece's Classical Age (500 BCE–300 BCE). The Greek island of Rhodes was one of the wealthiest seafaring states of the eastern Mediterranean. The sea law was so comprehensive that it was adopted by other Greek states and colonies, from Spain to the Black Sea. It also influenced Roman law and provided an agreed accepted method for resolving maritime disputes across the Mediterranean.

Law of jettison
One part of the code that survives, in Emperor Justinian's *Digest* (533 CE), concerns the jettison of cargo by ships in distress and states that, "… if the cargo has been jettisoned in order to lighten a ship, the sacrifice for the common good must be made good by common contribution." This principle of sharing losses, called "general average", still applies in maritime law. Such was the prestige of the *Lex Rhodia* that when the Byzantine Empire issued a new maritime code in c. 700 CE, it was called *Nomos Rhodion Nautikos* (*Rhodian Sea Law*). ∎

The Colossus of Rhodes was one of the Seven Wonders of the Ancient World. Erected in 280 BCE, this huge statue of the sun god Helios greeted sailors entering the harbour at Rhodes.

See also: The *Lex Aquilia* 34 ▪ Ulpian the Jurist 36–37 ▪ The *Lex Mercatoria* 74–77 ▪ The World Trade Organization 278–83

THE ART OF RULING WELL

CONFUCIANISM, DAOISM, AND LEGALISM (476 BCE—221 BCE)

IN CONTEXT

FOCUS
Law and philosophy

BEFORE
***c.* 1046–771 BCE** Kings of the Western Zhou dynasty rule a feudal state, in which regional lords govern on their behalf.

771–476 BCE In the Spring and Autumn period, Zhou kings lose control as regional states fight among themselves. Bigger states conquer smaller ones until only seven are left: Chu, Han, Qi, Qin, Wei, Yan, and Zhao.

AFTER
221 BCE China is unified by the Qin dynasty (221–206 BCE), which imposes Legalism.

141 BCE The Han dynasty (206 BCE–220 CE) makes Confucianism the state philosophy and discredits Legalism.

During China's Warring States period (476–221 BCE), the country was divided into seven rival states, which were constantly at war with one another.

Chinese philosophers responded by developing three competing systems of belief: Confucianism, Daoism, and Legalism. Each took a very different approach to the role of government and law, and each had a lasting influence on Chinese history.

Confucianism

Philosopher Kong Fuzi (551–479 BCE), known as Confucius, looked to traditions to provide social stability. He stressed the importance of the ancient rites (*li*) performed

See also: Early legal codes 18–19 ▪ Zhou dynasty China 24 ▪ Plato's *Laws* 31 ▪ The *Arthashastra* and the *Manusmriti* 35

Three rival philosophies developed during the Chinese Warring States period.

Confucianism:
People can be **taught to be good**. Rulers should govern by **virtue** and **tradition**.

Daoism:
People should live in **harmony** with nature and the Universe. Rulers should **leave people alone**.

Legalism:
People are **self-interested**. Rulers should **deter crime** and **keep people in order** with punishments.

Confucius

Philosopher Kong Qui was born in 551 BCE, into the lower ranks of the nobility in the small eastern state of Lu. He was later known by his followers as Kong Fuzi ("Master Kong"), which led to his Western name Confucius. After spending years at the Lu court, without gaining influence, he travelled from one state to another, hoping to persuade rulers to employ him as a minister. He failed to achieve office, as his ideas seemed idealistic and old-fashioned to the rulers of the time. Yet Confucius continued to spread his philosophy through teaching. His reputation for learning attracted many students, who came to him to study ancient ritual texts, such as the *Book of Rites* and the *Book of Songs*.

Although Confucius wrote no books, after his death in 479 BCE, his teachings were written down by his students in the *Lunyu* ("Conversations"), which is known in the West as the *Analects*.

Key work

c. **500** BCE *Analects*

in honour of ancestors and gods; humaneness or fellow feeling (*ren*); and filial piety (*xiao*), the respect of children for their parents. Confucius argued that filial piety should be extended beyond the family to society as a whole. There were five key social relationships in which each individual had a proper place: ruler to subject, father to son, husband to wife, older brother to younger brother, and friend to friend. In each of these, the superior partner should be like a caring father while the inferior should be respectful and obedient.

Confucius believed that laws and punishments were necessary only in a primitive society, where people did not observe the proper rites. If people were set a good example by those in authority and were educated, they would behave well. Confucius said, "To govern simply by law, and to create order by means of punishments, will make people try to avoid the punishment but have no sense of shame. To govern by virtue, and create order by rites, will not only give them the sense of shame, but moreover they will become good."

Daoism

The key text of Daoism is the *Dao De Jing*, which is attributed to Laozi ("old master"), a possibly mythical teacher from the 6th century BCE. While the text may have been the work of more than one author, its central idea is that people should live in harmony with the natural order of the Universe, called the Dao (Way). The *Dao De Jing* uses water as an example of what this means: "Water is fluid, soft, and yielding. But water will wear away rock, which is rigid and cannot yield. As a rule, whatever is fluid, soft, and yielding will overcome whatever is rigid and hard."

Daoists believed that all social problems would be solved if people lived a simple life and rid themselves of ambition and greed. They shared the Confucian distrust of laws. But unlike Confucians, who thought » that government benefitted society, Daoists defended private life, and wanted rulers to leave people alone. The best way to live was through *wu wei* (action that avoided effort) and the perfect ruler was one who made no laws, imposed no restrictions on his subjects, and whose actions went unnoticed.

As a philosophy of individualism and inaction, Daoism's practical applications for government were limited. Yet it had a lasting influence on later philosophy and religion, especially Chinese Buddhism.

Legalism

The most successful philosophy during the Warring States period was *Fajia* ("standards"), known in the West as Legalism. Legalists believed that people were essentially self-interested, lazy, and ignorant. The way to create social order and a strong state was to deter crime with strict laws and punishments. Even light offences should be punished harshly.

> Do not value goods that are hard to come by, and the people will not steal.
> **Laozi**
> *Dao de Jing*, 4th century BCE

In the 4th century BCE, Legalism was adopted by Shang Yang, chief minister of the western state of Qin. *The Book of Lord Shang*, a compilation of writings by Shang and his followers, attacks the beliefs of Confucianism, saying that reverence for the past and traditions encourage people to criticize their present rulers. Even humaneness and virtue undermine the law.

The Book of Lord Shang argues that wicked people should be in positions of power for two reasons: people's loyalty should be to the laws themselves, not to the people who enforce the laws; and wicked people are likely to report offences because they like to spy on others.

The penalties imposed by Shang Yang were humiliating and painful. They included facial tattooing, mutilation, and public execution in various ways, such as being boiled, quartered, or buried alive. Punishment was also collective, extending to the whole family or clan of an offender. Failure to report a crime was treated as harshly as committing one.

Using Legalism, Shang Yang created a strong authoritarian state and a powerful army of peasants who were conscripted as soldiers. He destroyed the feudal power of the nobility, who were now subject to the same laws as everyone else. When a new ruler whom Shang Yang had previously humiliated

In Qin dynasty China, the philosophy of Legalism was followed strictly, with the law-making emperor at the top of the social pyramid and the slaves at the bottom.

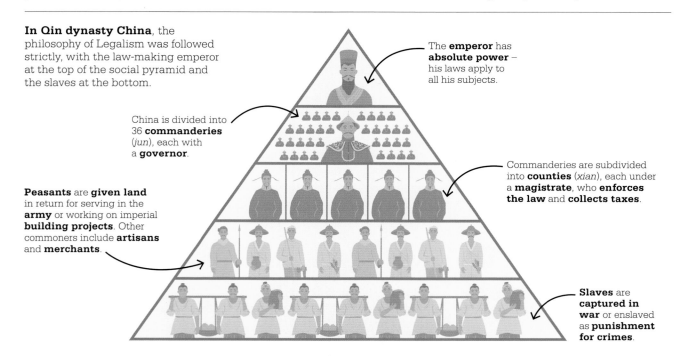

The **emperor** has **absolute power** – his laws apply to all his subjects.

China is divided into 36 **commanderies** (*jun*), each with a **governor**.

Commanderies are subdivided into **counties** (*xian*), each under a **magistrate**, who **enforces the law** and **collects taxes**.

Peasants are **given land** in return for serving in the **army** or working on imperial **building projects**. Other commoners include **artisans** and **merchants**.

Slaves are **captured in war** or enslaved as **punishment for crimes**.

came to power, the minister fell from grace. In 338 BCE, subjected to the same harsh laws he himself had introduced, he was torn apart by chariots, and all members of his family were killed.

Historian Sima Qian (c. 145–86 BCE) wrote that Shang Yang deserved his fate, yet admitted that his policies were effective: "By the end of 10 years, the Qin people were quiet. Nothing lost on the road was picked up and kept, the hills were free of robbers, every household prospered, men fought bravely on the battlefield but avoided disputes at home."

The greatest Legalist philosopher, Han Feizi (c. 280–233 BCE), argued that universally enforced and well-publicized laws benefitted everyone, by bringing order and predictability to life. Legalism made people do things they would avoid otherwise, such as working hard and fighting in wars. If the laws were resented, it was because the people were like infants, who had no understanding of what was good for them.

Qin totalitarianism
The Qin state conquered the other warring states one by one until, in 221 BCE, King Zheng of Qin defeated Qi, the last independent kingdom, and declared himself Qin Shi Huang (First Exalted Emperor of Qin).

> When people are stupid, they are easy to govern.
> **Shang Yang**
> *The Book of Lord Shang*

The Terracotta Army, guarding the tomb of emperor Qin Shi Huang, was intended to protect him in the afterlife. As well as 8,000 warriors, the army includes chariots and horses.

Across China, he imposed Legalism and a unified way of life, introducing standard currency, weights, and measures, and a new, simpler writing system based on a single set of characters. Using forced labour, the emperor built the first Great Wall across the northern frontier, a network of roads, and a vast tomb, where he was later buried with a terracotta army to guard him.

Qin China was a totalitarian state, where every aspect of people's lives was controlled. The emperor ordered a mass burning of books, and according to Sima Qian, he had 460 Confucian scholars buried alive. The first emperor's rule was so harsh that the Qin dynasty lasted just four more years after his death in 210 BCE.

Han reforms
In 206 BCE, Liu Bang, a rebel leader, seized power, founding the new Han dynasty, which created China's First Golden Age. While Legalism had been effective in a time of constant warfare, Confucianism, which promoted social cohesion and loyalty to superiors, seemed more suitable when China was united and at peace. Under the Han, Legalism as a philosophy was discredited, and the harshest punishments were abolished. In 141 BCE, the seventh Han emperor, Wudi, adopted Confucianism as the state ideology. Confucius's *Analects* became a sacred book, memorized by generations of students.

Despite this, China remained an autocratic state, in which Confucianism was backed up by strict enforcement of the law – as one Chinese proverb says, the country is "Confucian on the outside, Legalist on the inside." Confucius's ideal society, where laws and punishments were unnecessary, was never achieved. ∎

THIS SHALL BE BINDING BY LAW

THE TWELVE TABLES (c. 450 BCE)

IN CONTEXT

FOCUS
Codification of Roman law

BEFORE
510/509 BCE Romans drive out their last king and establish a republic. All government positions are held by patricians.

494 BCE After the plebeians threaten to leave Rome, they are granted the right to elect their own officials, called tribunes, to defend their interests and propose laws.

AFTER
390 BCE The original Twelve Tables are destroyed when invading Gauls sack Rome. Copies of the text survive, and it is learned by heart by generations of Roman children.

367 BCE Plebeians finally gain the right to serve as consul, one of Rome's two annually elected heads of state.

In around 450 BCE, the Roman Republic compiled its first written law code, inscribed on 12 bronze tablets displayed in the Forum, Rome's main public space. At the time, the plebeians (commoners) were engaged in a long-running struggle with the small ruling class of patrician (noble) families who held high office and the priests who acted as magistrates and interpreted the laws handed down over time. Plebeians could be punished for offences against laws of which they had no knowledge. As a concession to them, ten patrician magistrates, called decemvirs, were tasked with recording Rome's customary laws. Thanks to the decemvirs' Twelve Tables, Roman citizens now knew some of their more important rights, and could appeal against magistrates' rulings.

A code of civil laws

The Tables dealt with civil law (the law concerning relations between members of society), outlining citizens' rights and responsibilities. It also contained significant provisions about legal procedure, covering summons to court, trials, the role of witnesses, and execution of judgement.

Rome was still an agricultural town, and many of the newly codified laws concerned farming disputes. One law banned marriage between patricians and plebeians but was swiftly repealed. Others were later replaced by updated laws. Yet Romans looked back to the Twelve Tables as the foundation of their legal system. ∎

That single little book of the Twelve Tables … seems to me, assuredly, to surpass the libraries of all the philosophers.
Cicero
Roman statesman (106–43 BCE)

See also: Early legal codes 18–19 ∎ The *Lex Aquilia* 34 ∎ Ulpian the Jurist 36–37 ∎ Magna Carta 66–71

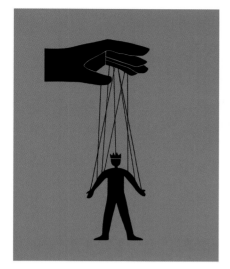

LAW IS MASTER OF THE RULERS

PLATO'S *LAWS* (348 BCE)

Written by Athenian philosopher Plato in the 350s BCE, *Laws* is his last and longest book. His more famous *Republic* had looked at an ideal state ruled by philosopher-kings with no need for laws. In contrast, *Laws* is concerned with the "second-best state", where law is supreme.

The book, set in Crete, is a dialogue between an unnamed Athenian, a Spartan called Megillus, and a Cretan, Clinias. The Cretan is on his way to establish a new city, Magnetes (Magnesia). The three discuss its constitution and the Athenian suggests a code of laws covering every aspect of life.

Plato's theorized city-state combines an authoritarian system with democratic elements. Its laws are first drawn up by a dictator and a wise legislator, who then surrender their powers to elected officials. Every law has a prelude, to persuade the people that it is in their interests to obey it. To stop anyone becoming more powerful than the law, there is a system of checks and balances. The city's

A fresco in the Vatican Museum, Vatican City, depicts Plato (left) with his student Aristotle, who was influenced by his teacher's views on law and government.

officials are subject to the authority of examiners, who check their qualifications and can hold them to account. Plato's doctrine of the sovereignty of law and a mixed government system had a lasting legacy, influencing philosophers from Aristotle to the 18th-century French judge Montesquieu. ■

IN CONTEXT

FOCUS
The sovereignty of law

BEFORE
399 BCE The Greek philosopher Socrates is sentenced to death in Athens, leaving his pupil Plato with a hatred of democracy as mob rule.

***c.* 367–361 BCE** Plato serves as tutor to Dionysius II, the new tyrant of Syracuse, but his attempt to make Dionysus a philosopher-king is a failure.

AFTER
***c.* 330 BCE** In *Politics*, Plato's pupil Aristotle argues that a state should combine democracy and oligarchy (government by the few).

***c.* 130 BCE** The Greek historian Polybius praises the Roman Republic as a successful mixed government system.

1748 In *The Spirit of Laws*, Montesquieu proposes a mixed government system.

See also: Aristotle and natural law 32–33 ■ The Glorious Revolution and the English Bill of Rights 102–03 ■ The US Supreme Court and judicial review 124–29

TRUE LAW IS RIGHT REASON
ARISTOTLE AND NATURAL LAW (*c.* 340 BCE)

IN CONTEXT

FOCUS
Natural law

BEFORE
***c.* 441 BCE** In his tragedy
Antigone, Sophocles suggests
that there are unwritten and
unalterable divine laws.

***c.* 375 BCE** In *The Republic*,
Plato argues that the ideal
community is "established
in accordance with nature".

AFTER
***c.* 1050 CE** Iranian Muslim
scholar Al-Biruni argues that
natural law is the survival of
the fittest, which must be
overcome by divine law,
revealed by Muhammad.

***c.* 1140–50** In his *Decretum*,
Gratian equates natural law
with the laws of the Church.

***c.* 1265–74** Thomas Aquinas
brings together Aristotle's
philosophy and Christian
theology in *Summa Theologica*.

Aristotle distinguished between **natural law** and **conventional laws**.

Natural law is **universal and unchanging**.

Conventional laws **vary according to customs**, over time, and from place to place.

To be just, a law must be based on **more than convention** – it must be in **harmony with natural law**.

In the 4th century BCE, the Greek philosopher Aristotle distinguished between the unchanging, universal law of nature and mankind's conventional laws, which vary from place to place. For a law to be just, he argued, it should be in harmony with natural law.

In his *Rhetoric*, Aristotle cited *Antigone*, a 5th-century tragedy by the Greek playwright Sophocles, as an example of the two laws in conflict. In the play, Antigone breaks the king's edict by holding a funeral for her brother Polyneices. Aristotle observed that in a plea to the king, Antigone justifies breaking his conventional law with an appeal to a higher natural law, which does not belong "to today or tomorrow, it lives eternally: no one knows how it arose".

See also: Plato's *Laws* 31 ▪ Ulpian the Jurist 36–37 ▪ The origins of canon law 42–47 ▪ Gratian's *Decretum* 60–63 ▪ Thomas Aquinas 72–73

> There really is, as everyone senses, something just by nature and common to all.
> **Aristotle**
> *Rhetoric (I.13)*, 4th century BCE

However, Aristotle did not explain how to distinguish natural law from cultural beliefs. Even the example he gave of a natural law – the right to a burial – is not a universal custom. Many societies do not bury the dead, but leave their bodies for carrion birds, who pick the bones clean. It was left to later thinkers to find a rational basis for natural law.

Natural harmony

In *c.* 300 BCE, the Greek philosopher Zeno, the founder of Stoicism, identified natural law with divine reason, which he saw as a purposeful order pervading the cosmos. As part of this cosmos, humans have divine reason within them. By following only reason, rather than emotion, people can live in harmony with natural law.

Because they believed that all human beings shared both divine reason and natural law, the Stoics saw humanity as a community in which all people were equal. The ideal society, in their view, was a world state in which everybody lived together in harmony, following the rule of divine reason.

Centuries later, some Roman jurists, including the renowned Ulpian, early in the 3rd century CE, accepted the Stoic idea that humans were equal in natural law, and that slavery was contrary to nature. Yet they never went so far as to argue that this principle should be put into practice in civil law.

Divine reason

The Roman statesman Cicero was strongly influenced by the Stoics. In *De Republica* (*c.* 51 BCE) he urged that "True law is right reason in agreement with nature … [with] one eternal and unchangeable law … valid for all nations and all times, and … one master and ruler, that is God over us all, for he is the author of this law, its promulgator, and its enforcing judge." While Cicero took the Stoic view of "God" as divine reason, his words resonated with later Christian thinkers, including Gratian – an Italian monk – and Thomas Aquinas. They saw Cicero's description of a universal lawmaker and judge as the Christian God. ▪

> So far as the civil law is concerned, slaves are not considered persons; but this is not the case according to natural law, because natural law regards all men as equal.
> **Ulpian the Jurist**
> *Ad Sabinum (XLIII)*, *c.* 212 CE

Aristotle

The writings of Aristotle – philosopher, scientist, and polymath – shaped the development of ancient and medieval philosophy. Born in 384 BCE at Stagira in Thrace, he went to Athens at the age of 17, where he studied and taught for 20 years at Plato's Academy. After Plato's death in *c.* 347 BCE, Aristotle travelled to Asia Minor. In *c.* 344 BCE, he visited the island of Lesbos in the Aegean, where he made a detailed study of maritime life.

Aristotle was tutor to Alexander the Great for a brief period, then returned to Athens in 335 BCE and founded his own school, the Lyceum. This included a library, a museum, and a map collection. He wrote around 200 books, covering every branch of science and philosophy then known. In 323 BCE, he moved to Chalcis, and died the following year.

Aristotle's work endured in the Islamic world after the fall of Rome, and was revived in the West by Thomas Aquinas.

Key works

Nichomachean Ethics
Rhetoric
Politics

A PERSON IS LIABLE FOR WRONGFUL DAMAGE
THE *LEX AQUILIA* (286 BCE)

IN CONTEXT

FOCUS
Civil law and private property

BEFORE
494 BCE Barred from public office, plebeians set up their own assembly.

***c.* 450 BCE** The Twelve Tables is Rome's earliest written law code.

287 BCE The *Lex Hortensia* gives the Plebeian Assembly the power to make laws without Senate approval.

AFTER
426 CE Emperor Valentinian III's *Lex Citationum* (*Law of Citations*) names five earlier respected jurists (Ulpian, Gaius, Papinian, Paulus, and Modestinus) whose opinions are to guide judges in trials.

529–33 CE Emperor Justinian publishes the *Code*, the *Digest*, and the *Institutions*, which together form a definitive body of Roman law.

The *Lex Aquilia* was a Roman law that provided financial compensation for wrongful damage to property. Named after Aquilius, the plebeian tribune (elected official of ordinary citizens) who framed it, it was one of the first laws drawn up after the Plebeian Assembly was given the power to legislate without seeking approval from the Senate. Plebeians could now gain redress for civil wrongs done by the patricians, the ruling elite who dominated the Senate.

The *Lex Aquilia* described the compensation owed in different scenarios. It stated that if anyone unlawfully killed a slave or livestock, they had to pay the owner its highest value in the preceding year. Another clause covered damage to all types of property, requiring the cost of the damage to be assessed within 30 days and the appropriate sum paid.

Later definition
The *Lex Aquilia* superseded all earlier laws dealing with unlawful damage. Its legacy is the modern legal concept of the "delict" as a civil wrong arising from an intentional or negligent breach of duty of care.

Roman laws were subject to interpretation, but the jurist Ulpian (*c.* 170–223 CE) later reiterated that unlawful damage is that caused "in a blameworthy fashion" – thus including harm through negligence, but not as a result of accident. Ulpian was cited in Emperor Justinian's *Digest* of 533 CE, preserving the *Lex Aquilia*'s legacy for years to come. ∎

If a stone falls out of a cart and … smashes something, the carter is liable to the Aquilian action if he loaded the stones badly.
Ulpian
Justinian's *Digest*, 533 CE

See also: The Twelve Tables 30 ▪ Ulpian the Jurist 36–37 ▪ Gratian's *Decretum* 60–63 ▪ *Donoghue v. Stevenson* 194–95

THE SACRED LAWS OF THE CASTES
THE *ARTHASHASTRA* AND THE *MANUSMRITI* (2ND CENTURY BCE)

IN CONTEXT

FOCUS
The caste system and Hindu law

BEFORE
1500–1200 BCE The *Rig Veda*, the earliest Sanskrit text, is composed in India's tribal society, where *rajas* (rulers) are chosen by chieftains.

1100–500 BCE Hereditary kingdoms appear in northern India, and a fourfold caste system emerges.

AFTER
1794 The *Manusmriti* is translated into English and used by British colonial rulers as a law code for Hindus.

1905 A manuscript of the *Arthashastra*, lost since the 12th century, is rediscovered.

1949 Newly independent India's constitution bans discrimination on the basis of caste, but the issue persists into the 21st century.

T he *Arthashastra* and the *Manusmriti* are two ancient Hindu texts, written in Sanskrit and thought to date from as early as 200 BCE. The *Arthashastra* (*Science of Prosperity*) is a practical guide for kings, offering advice on how to maintain power and create a strong state. The *Manusmriti* (*Recollections of Manu*) is a set of rules or codes, supposedly derived from Manu, mythical founder of the human race. It is more concerned with moral and social behaviour and duties than the *Arthashastra*.

The books portray Indian society divided into four *varnas* (castes), a hierarchy based on ritual purity. The purest were the *brahmins* (priests), followed by *kshatriyas* (rulers and warriors), then *vaishyas* (merchants and farmers) and *shudras* (labourers). It was believed that to be born into a particular caste was a reward or punishment for actions performed in a previous life. Both books forbid mixing between castes. Although neither text functioned as a law code, each describes strict rules and punishments for every part of life.

The *Manusmriti* took on a new significance in the late 18th century, when the British rulers of India interpreted it as a definitive legal code for Hindus, equivalent to Sharia law for Muslims. It was translated into English under the title *Institutes of Hindu Law*, and used to formulate laws for Britain's Hindu subjects. ∎

Dr Bhimrao Ambedkar, seen here on a 1960 postage stamp, was India's first law minister and a prominent campaigner against the caste system.

See also: Early legal codes 18–19 ▪ Confucianism, Daoism, and Legalism 26–29 ▪ The Mishnah and the Talmud 38–41 ▪ The Koran 54–57

WE CULTIVATE THE VIRTUE OF JUSTICE

ULPIAN THE JURIST (*c.* 170–223 CE)

IN CONTEXT

FOCUS
Morality and theory of law

BEFORE
***c.* 450 BCE** The Twelve Tables herald a millennium of codifying Roman law, ending with the *Code* of Byzantine emperor Justinian I in 529 CE.

27 BCE–14 CE Emperor Augustus appoints certain law experts, or jurists, to give legal opinions on his behalf.

1st century CE Two rival law schools flourish in Rome: the Sabinians tend to promote tradition and conservative orthodoxy; the Proculians reasoning and consistency.

AFTER
533 CE Justinian I publishes the *Digest*, a compendium of writings of Roman jurists.

***c.* 1070** Manuscripts of Justinian's legal books are rediscovered in northern Italy, prompting a revival of interest in Roman law and in Ulpian.

Domitius Ulpianus was the most influential jurist of Classical Rome. He wrote prolifically, authoring over 200 books on law in little more than 10 years. His acclaim was renewed many centuries later, in the Middle Ages, when the name "Ulpian" became synonymous with Roman law.

Distinguished career
Ulpian was born in the late second century in the Phoenician city of Tyre, in what is now Lebanon. The nearby city of Berytus (Beirut) was home to the most famous law school of the Roman Empire, and it is possible that Ulpian studied or taught there.

In Rome, Ulpian rose to be a high-ranking official in the imperial government. Early in the third century, he served under Emperor Caracalla as his master of petitions, penning replies to requests made to the emperor. It was after 212 CE, when Caracalla extended citizenship to all free inhabitants of the empire, that Ulpian began to write his own works on law, for the benefit of, among others, the new citizens. In 222 CE, the new emperor, Severus

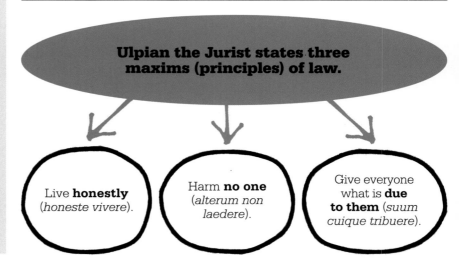

Ulpian the Jurist states three maxims (principles) of law.

Live **honestly** (*honeste vivere*).

Harm **no one** (*alterum non laedere*).

Give everyone what is **due to them** (*suum cuique tribuere*).

See also: The Twelve Tables 30 ▪ Aristotle and natural law 32–33 ▪ The *Lex Aquilia* 34 ▪ The origins of canon law 42–47 ▪ Gratian's *Decretum* 60–63 ▪ Thomas Aquinas 72–73

Ulpian ranked as one of Rome's five most revered jurists, along with Gaius, Papinian, Paulus, and Modestinus. He is depicted here in a French work published in 1584.

Alexander, made Ulpian prefect in command of Rome's Praetorian Guard. However, Ulpian clashed with the soldiers, and in 223 CE they mutinied and killed him.

Priests of law

Ulpian had an exalted view of Roman law, which he considered to be universal, rational, and based on what Aristotle described as "natural law". Ulpian perceived law as "the art of goodness and fairness", of which "we [jurists] are deservedly called the priests. For we cultivate the virtue of justice and claim awareness of what is good and fair."

The above lines form part of a definition of law by Ulpian that was chosen as the opening text of the *Digesta* (*Digest*), a compilation of the interpretations of respected jurists commissioned in the sixth century by Emperor Justinian I. In order to

rationalize Roman law, Justinian directed his legal experts to assess the existing, contradictory body of legislation and produce a definitive version. The result was the *Codex* (*Code*), a comprehensive collection of imperial laws, published in 529 CE. This was followed by the *Digest* and the *Institutiones* (*Institutions*), a textbook for law students, both published in 533 CE.

Much of Ulpian's writing survives in extracts included in the *Digest*. In preparing the work, the compilers often chose Ulpian as their preferred authority – not only because he was one of the last great jurists, and had studied the earlier ones, but also because of the clarity and elegance of his writing, which makes up one-third of the whole text.

The codified system of legal principles expressed in these works of Justinian is a defining feature of

> Law is … the science of what is right and what is unjust.
> **Ulpian the Jurist**

Roman law. In this respect, Roman law forms the basis of civil law, the system widely used today.

Renaissance revival

Despite his prominence in the pages of the *Digest*, Ulpian was largely forgotten until around 1070 CE, when old manuscripts were rediscovered in Italy. Later, in 1583, the *Digest*, the *Code*, and the *Institutions* were printed together under the title *Corpus juris civilis* (*Body of Civil Law*), and became the basis for legal education across Western Europe. ▪

Ulpian was assassinated by the Praetonian Guard in the imperial palace. They struck in the presence of Emperor Severus Alexander and his mother and close adviser, Julia Mamaea.

JUSTICE, TRUTH, AND PEACE

THE MISHNAH AND THE TALMUD (*c.* 200–*c.* 500 CE)

The Talmud ("Study") is a written compendium of Jewish oral laws that govern every part of a devout Jew's life. Made up of the Mishnah and the Gemara, it is the central text of Rabbinic Judaism, which emerged after the Romans destroyed the Temple in Jerusalem in 70 CE, and is the mainstream form of Judaism.

The Romans had ruled Jerusalem and the surrounding province of Judea from the 1st century BCE onwards – at first through client kings, and later through governors. In the 1st century BCE, Judaism divided into rival forms, each taking a different attitude to Jewish law. Temple worship was overseen by

See also: The Ten Commandments and Mosaic law 20–23 ▪ The *Arthashastra* and the *Manusmriti* 35 ▪ The origins of canon law 42–47 ▪ The Koran 54–57

The six seder (orders) of the Mishnah

Zeraim (Seeds)
Prayers, blessings, and the
Torah's agricultural laws
11 tractates

Moed (Festivals)
The Sabbath, Passover, and
other festivals
12 tractates

Nashim (Women)
Rules on marriage, divorce,
and vows
7 tractates

Nezikim (Damages)
Courts, civil and criminal law,
and sayings of the Fathers
10 tractates

Kodashim (Holy things)
Temple worship, sacrifices,
and dietary laws
11 tractates

Tohorot (Purities)
Ritual purity
12 tractates

the Sadducees, aristocratic priests who believed only in the written law outlined in the Torah of Moses. Pharisees, on the other hand, believed in a stricter observance of Jewish law than the Sadducees. They argued that purity laws applied not only to priests, but to the daily lives of all Jewish people.

The Pharisees derived their beliefs from an oral tradition that had accrued over time. In the words of Romano–Jewish historian Josephus: "The Pharisees have delivered to the people a great many observances by succession from their fathers which are not written in the law of Moses; and for that reason it is that the Sadducees reject them." One of the Pharisees' innovations was a belief that, at the end of time, God would resurrect the dead, punish the wicked, and reward the just. The Sadducees rejected this idea of an afterlife.

In 70 CE, following a Jewish rebellion, the Romans besieged and captured Jerusalem, and razed the Temple to the ground. The Sadducees disappeared from history. The loss of the Temple was a catastrophe for Jews – in the ancient world, it was inconceivable to imagine a religion without a temple, and Jerusalem's Temple was the only place on Earth where Jews could offer sacrifices, to atone for sin.

Preserving Judaism
It was largely thanks to Rabbi Yochanan ben Zakkai, a Jewish scholar, that Judaism was able to continue without a temple. He persuaded the Romans to let him re-establish the Sanhedrin, the Jewish high council, in Yavne. Citing Hosea 6:6 in the Torah ("I desired mercy not sacrifice"), Zakkai convinced the Sanhedrin that animal sacrifice (the preserve of temple worship) could be replaced by prayer, study of the law, and benevolence. This was justified in the Talmud with a saying of God to King David: "A single day in which you sit and engage in Torah is preferable to the thousand burnt-offerings that your son Solomon will offer before Me on the altar."

After a second Jewish rebellion in 132–136 CE, Emperor Hadrian expelled all Jews from Jerusalem, which was rebuilt as a Roman city. To preserve Judaism, rabbis compiled a code of laws, written in Hebrew, called the Mishnah »

("Repeating" or "Teaching"). Completed in *c.* 200 CE by Rabbi Judah Ha-Nasi, the book is the oldest part of the Talmud. Based on the oral tradition of the Pharisees, the Mishnah is divided into six seder (orders). These, in turn, are subdivided into between seven and twelve tractates (books), which cover every part of Jewish life. One of these tractates, *Pirkei Avot* (*Sayings of the Fathers*), traced the oral tradition through a line of authorities all the way back to Moses in Sinai.

Building a virtual temple

The subject of the Mishnah's fifth order, Kodashim, was the Temple of Jerusalem. The writers lovingly described every detail of the lost building, and of the sacrificial process. This was so that temple worship could continue to be at the centre of Jewish religious life. According to the Talmud, "He who engages in study of the laws of sacrifice should be regarded as if he had offered up a sacrifice himself." Since 70 CE, Jews have prayed daily for the Temple to be restored by God and for worship to resume there – so study of the Temple was also a

Moses received the Torah at Sinai and transmitted it to Joshua … the elders to the prophets, and the prophets to the Men of the Great Assembly.
Pirkei Avot

way of preparing for the future. Alongside the Mishnah, the Talmud includes the Gemara ("Completion"), a much longer commentary written by later rabbis in Aramaic, which was the everyday spoken language at the time. Two different Gemaras were created; a Palestinian version, compiled between 350 and 400 CE, and a Babylonian one, written between 350 and 550 CE. The latter version is much longer and is seen as having greater authority.

The Gemara is a vast body of diverse material that explores the meaning of the laws outlined in the Mishnah and their application in daily life. Unlike most law codes, it often presents contradictory rulings by rabbis side by side, without deciding between them. Rather than fixing Jewish law, the Gemara enabled it to be studied and argued over, and has been described as the first interactive text.

The Babylonian Talmud (made up of the Mishnah and the Babylonian Gemara) spread widely within the Islamic world, where Jews had a protected status. Following the Muslim conquest of Spain in the

This page of a printed Talmud shows the Mishnah and Gemara in the centre (in larger type), medieval commentaries known as the Tosafot ("Additions") on the left, and Rashi's commentary along with notes by later scholars on the right.

8th century, the city of Córdoba became a centre of Jewish learning. Halakha (Jewish law, derived from the Talmud) influenced the development of Sharia (Islamic law). Unlike Christianity, whose laws were made by councils or synods, Jewish and Muslim laws were derived through scholarship. Both systems regulate every part of daily life, and both combine laws based on a divinely inspired book (the Torah and Koran, respectively) with later oral traditions.

The Talmud on trial

From Spain, the Talmud spread to Christian Europe, where schools were established in major cities. Europe's rulers knew nothing about the Talmud, assuming that Jews only studied the Torah of Moses.

In 1238, Nicholas Donin, a French Jew who had converted to Christianity and became a

O dreadful and terrible day … Sun and Moon are darkened, the heavens shattered, the stars driven away … the Universe mourns.
Hebrew account of the trial of the Talmud

Franciscan friar, denounced the Talmud. He told Pope Gregory IX that the Talmud was offensive and blasphemous, and that without it, the Jews would have converted to Christianity long ago.

On 3 March 1240, King Louis IX of France had every copy of the Talmud in the country seized and brought to Paris, where the book was put on trial for blasphemy. Donin prosecuted, and four leading rabbis defended the Talmud. Donin had found passages referring to a Yeshu (Jesus), a false prophet who was the son of a prostitute and had been justly executed. The rabbis answered that this was not Jesus Christ but another man, saying "not every Louis born in France is king".

The Talmud was condemned and sentenced to be burned. The manuscripts were carried through the streets of Paris in 24 wagonloads to a great bonfire. As a result of this and subsequent public burnings

Yemenite Jews in Jerusalem read and debate the Talmud together. Study of the Talmud was traditionally a male activity, to be undertaken once boys had completed a course of Torah study.

elsewhere in Christian Europe, very few complete manuscripts of the Talmud have survived.

Studying the Talmud

The traditional way to study the Talmud was in male-only pairs. Students read a page, and argue over its meaning. As the Gemara explains, "when Torah scholars study together, they sharpen one another." Today, women also explore the book, in yeshivas (Jewish schools dedicated to the study of the Talmud, the Torah, and other religious texts). People now read the Talmud online, too, using live streaming or video conferencing, and websites offer to find students a *havruta* ("learning partner").

In 1923, Meir Shapiro, a Polish rabbi, suggested that Jews around the world should study the Talmud collectively, at the rate of one page a day. This idea was embraced, and tens of thousands of Jews began to read the book together. It took seven and a half years for them to read the Talmud, a cycle first completed in February 1931. The 13th cycle ended in 2020. Today, around 350,000 Jews take part in the collective reading. ∎

Rashi

Born in Troyes in northern France in 1040, Rabbi Shlomo Yitzaki, known as Rashi, was the most influential Talmudic commentator in history. As a young man he studied in the yeshiva at Worms in Germany. At the age of 25, he returned to Troyes and became a rabbi, while also working as a winemaker. He founded a yeshiva of his own five years later.

Rashi wrote extensive commentaries on both the Torah and the Babylonian Talmud. His writing was clear and concise, and he analysed the text phrase by phrase. Although he wrote in Hebrew, he explained the meaning of obscure words in French. Rashi died in 1105 in Troyes.

Ever since the Babylonian Talmud was first printed in the 1520s, every copy of the work has included Rashi's commentary on the inner margin of each page.

Key works

c. **1070–1105** *Commentary on the Torah*
c. **1070–1105** *Commentary on the Talmud*

WALK IN THE WAY OF RIGHTEOUSNESS

THE ORIGINS OF CANON LAW
(*c.* 313–380 CE)

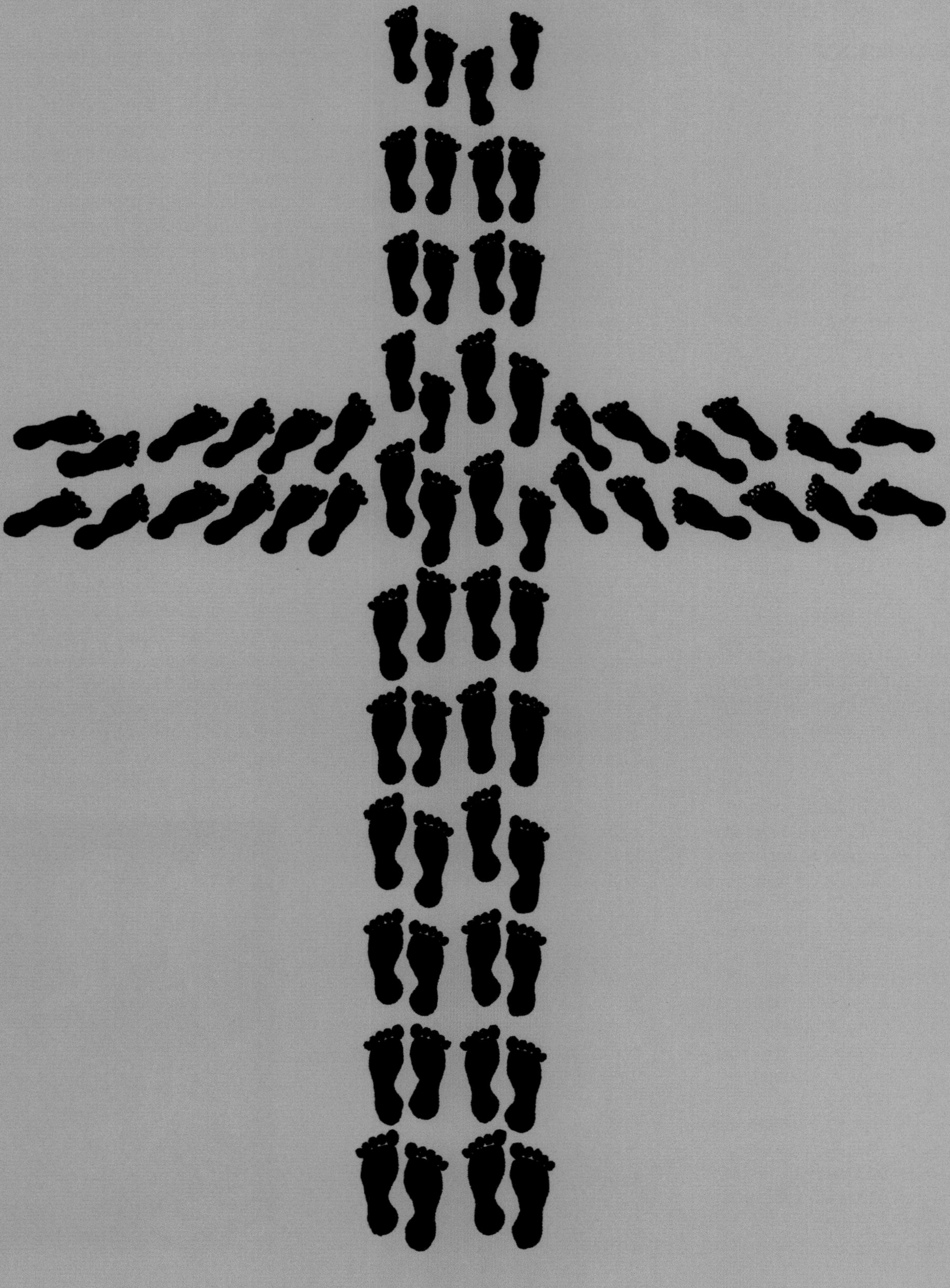

Roman Catholic canon law is the world's oldest continually functioning legal system. It has its origins in the first years of Christianity, but has over the past two millennia been adapted to reflect political, economic, social, and cultural changes as well as religious ones. The word "canon" derives from the Greek *kanon*, meaning a straight rod, or rule. Early canons were primarily concerned with theology and developed from debates about what people should believe.

The first followers of Jesus Christ were Jews who followed Mosaic law (Hebrew laws ascribed to Moses in the Old Testament).

They believed that Christ's 12 apostles ("messengers") had received the Holy Spirit – the third member of the Christian Holy Trinity. Saul of Tarsus, later known as Paul (*c.* 5–67 CE), also claimed to be an apostle on the basis of a vision of Christ. In *c.* 48 CE, one of the first theological disputes in the new Christian Church was resolved at a meeting of its leaders, the Council of Jerusalem. Paul, backed by the apostle Peter, argued that Gentiles (non-Jews) who believed in Jesus could be Christians without first becoming Jews or following Mosaic law. The Council circulated a canon to this effect.

Leadership and beliefs

The Christian communities founded by Paul and his companions were led by *episkopoi* ("overseers"), or bishops, assisted by *diakonoi* ("servants"), or deacons. They presided over rituals, such as communion (a holy meal of bread and wine in memory of Christ's death), and baptized converts. In the early years of the Church, Christians were able to select their own local bishops and deacons.

As Christianity spread, the authority of the bishops increased. They appointed presbyters ("elders"), or priests, to perform rituals on their behalf. In the late 1st century, Bishop Clement of Rome claimed to belong to an unbroken line of bishops going back to St Peter. He argued that bishops of churches founded by apostles, such as his own, had apostolic authority for their canons. In *c.* 100 CE, Bishop Ignatius of Antioch, another church

Paul's dramatic conversion on the road to Damascus turned him from a persecutor of Christians into one of the most influential Christian missionaries.

founded by apostles, wrote, "We should look upon the bishop even as we would upon the Lord himself."

Bishops issued canons to govern local church organization and ritual, and their followers' behaviour, but primarily to dictate what people should believe. Doctrine had never been important in earlier religions, but Christianity was different, offering salvation to the faithful and damnation to those who held incorrect beliefs. Serious offences such as heresy (opinions contrary to those of the Church leadership) and blasphemy (insulting the sacred) were disciplined by "anathema" – a punishment excommunicating, or expelling, the offender from the Christian community. Less serious offences were punished with exclusion from communion.

Another way to control belief was through texts. In the 2nd century, the bishops assembled a fixed set of holy books to stand alongside the Mosaic Old Testament. This New Testament included only books and letters thought to have been written by apostles or their companions. When various Gnostic and other

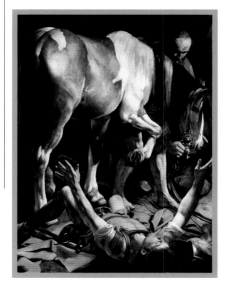

See also: The Ten Commandments and Mosaic law 20–23 ▪ Aristotle and natural law 32–33 ▪ The Koran 54–57 ▪ Gratian's *Decretum* 60–63 ▪ Thomas Aquinas 72–73

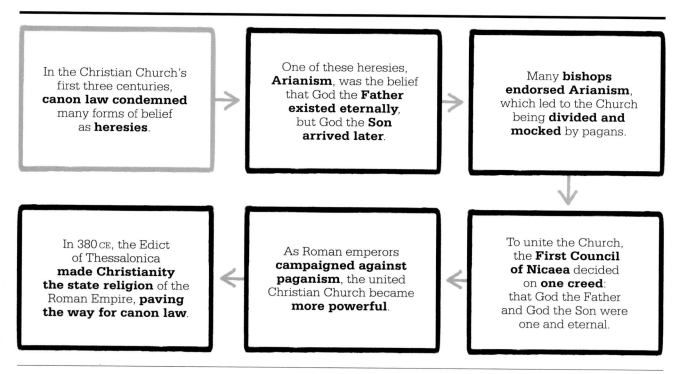

In the Christian Church's first three centuries, **canon law condemned** many forms of belief as **heresies**.

One of these heresies, **Arianism**, was the belief that God the **Father existed eternally**, but God the **Son arrived later**.

Many **bishops endorsed Arianism**, which led to the Church being **divided and mocked** by pagans.

To unite the Church, the **First Council of Nicaea** decided on **one creed**: that God the Father and God the Son were one and eternal.

As Roman emperors **campaigned against paganism**, the united Christian Church became **more powerful**.

In 380 CE, the Edict of Thessalonica **made Christianity the state religion** of the Roman Empire, **paving the way for canon law**.

sects challenged this apostolic authority, the Church condemned their writings as heretical.

Persecution of Christians

Christians refused to make sacrifices to Roman gods or the emperor and so, in the early years, most Romans viewed Christians with suspicion and hostility. They suffered a series of sporadic persecutions, beginning in 64 CE, under Emperor Nero. Despite this, by the 3rd century, Christians had become a visible minority throughout the empire, and the persecution increased dramatically.

In 250, Emperor Decius ordered everyone except Jews to make sacrifices to Roman gods or face death. Some Christians submitted, and were called *lapsi* ("lapsed"). After the persecution ended, the Church had to decide whether the lapsed could be readmitted. In 251, Bishop Cyprian of Carthage held a synod (council) of bishops, which ruled that the lapsed should be judged according to individual guilt. A second synod in Rome confirmed the ruling later that year. The Church was now deciding its law by a majority vote of bishops in synods. The greatest persecution took place under Emperor Diocletian in 303–05 and continued to a lesser extent for several years under his successor Galerius in the Eastern Roman (Byzantine) Empire (separated from the Western Empire in 285).

In the early 300s, 19 Spanish bishops held a synod at Elvira (now Granada in Spain), where they issued canons regulating the behaviour of believers. One canon forbade baptized women from marrying Jews, pagans, or heretics.

Communion, even on the deathbed, was denied to anyone who sacrificed in a pagan temple, and to adulterous wives. Bishops, priests, and deacons had to be celibate or they were removed from office. The canons of Elvira were binding only over churches that took part in the synod. The practice of permanent clerical celibacy spread to other churches in the Western Roman Empire, but it was interpreted more loosely in the Eastern Roman Empire, where priests were allowed to marry.

The Edict of Milan

In 312, Constantine I, a recent convert to Christianity, became ruler of the Western Roman Empire. The following year, together with Eastern Roman Emperor Licinius, he issued the Edict of Milan, which for the first time gave freedom of worship to Christians. It also ordered the » restoration of property that had been confiscated from Christians during Diocletian's persecution.

In 324, Constantine became sole ruler of the Roman Empire. Although Christianity was not yet the state religion, under Constantine's rule bishops assumed the rank, dress, and duties of civic authorities. The emperor, who was constantly attended by bishops, gave the bishop of Rome an imperial palace, later called the Lateran Palace – the precursor to the Vatican. He also issued several edicts that gave the Church power to enforce its canons.

Constantine decreed that any Christian in a civil lawsuit with a fellow Christian could transfer the case from a secular court to the arbitration of a bishop. According to the historian Eusebius, Constantine also "put his seal on the decrees of bishops made at synods, so that it would not be lawful for the rulers of provinces to annul what [the bishops] had approved, since the priests of God were superior to any magistrate". Another imperial decree banned heretics from assembling to worship and handed over their property to the Church. Constantine's defeat of Licinius

> Let us free our life
> from errors and
> with the help of the
> mercy of God, let us direct it
> along the right path.
> **Constantine I**
> **Letter to the**
> **Numidian Bishops, 330 CE**

had taken place at a time when there was a major split in the Church over the nature of Jesus Christ. It began in Alexandria, where a priest called Arius argued that while God the Father had existed for all time, the Son came later and had a beginning in time, and was therefore subordinate to the Father. Alexander, bishop of Alexandria, denounced Arius as a heretic. Yet many bishops and leading Christians supported Arius, and the argument spread

throughout the empire. This quarrel delighted pagans, who exploited it to mock Christian beliefs.

The Council of Nicaea

Constantine, who had no interest in theology, was horrified to see the Church divided and mocked by pagans. To unite the Church, he summoned the first universal synod of bishops, which met at Nicaea, in what is now Turkey, in 325. It was described as an ecumenical council, because bishops came from "the whole world" (*oikoumenikós* in Greek). More than 250 bishops attended what became known as the First Council of Nicaea, which was overseen by Constantine.

The Council rejected Arianism (the views expressed by Arius) and adopted the Nicene Creed, a statement of belief declaring that the Father and Son were "of one substance" and that the Son had been born of the Father "before all ages". Two dissenting bishops were exiled along with Arius, whose writings were burned. The Council also issued a number of canons on matters including the date of Easter and the organization of the Church's hierarchy. The bishops

Constantine the Great

The first Christian emperor, Constantine I, was born *c.* 272 CE. He became ruler of the Western Roman Empire in 312 after winning a civil war against the previous emperor, Maxentius (*c.* 276–312 CE). Before the decisive Battle of the Milvian Bridge, Constantine had a dream in which he was told to decorate the shields of his soldiers with a Christian symbol, the chi-rho (the first two letters of Christ in Greek). Following his victory, Constantine saw the Christian God as his personal patron and did all he could to spread his religion.

In 324, Constantine became sole ruler of the Roman Empire after defeating the Eastern emperor Licinius. In 330, he transferred the imperial capital from Rome to Byzantium, founding a new Christian city, Constantinople (now Istanbul). Constantine had formerly worshipped Sol Invictus, ("unconquered Sun"), the official sun god of the Roman Empire and patron of the army. For a few years after his conversion, Constantine continued to show Sol Invictus on his coins, and was only baptized a Christian on his deathbed in 337.

The First Council of Nicaea was attended by bishops from all parts of the Roman Empire, including Britain and Persia. The Eastern bishops formed the majority at the Council.

of provincial capitals (known as metropolitans) were given authority over the other provincial bishops. However, the bishops of Rome, Antioch, and Alexandria were set above all the rest. The canons agreed at the First Council of Nicaea were binding on every church, but they still did not apply to all the emperor's subjects because Christians remained a minority in the Roman Empire.

Later Roman emperors campaigned against paganism, and the Christian Church grew increasingly powerful. Christianity finally became the state religion in 380, when Emperor Theodosius I issued the Edict of Thessalonica, which ordered everyone in the empire to become Christian. Anyone who refused was judged to be "demented and insane". The Church was now able to burn almost all heretical writings. The Edict of Thessalonica was so significant that it was listed in

529 as the first item in Emperor Justinian's comprehensive collection of imperial laws, the *Codex Justinianus*.

Canon law is imposed

In 381, Theodosius held a second ecumenical council, which took place in Constantinople. This reaffirmed the Nicene Creed as the only legitimate statement of Christian belief. The Council also added a new clause, which said that the Holy Spirit "proceeded from" the Father. Now everyone in the Roman Empire, except Jews, had to obey canon law: they had to go to church, follow fasts, and believe in the Nicene Creed. Canon law would continue to develop alongside civil law as a separate legal system, eventually with its own courts, judges, and coercive penalties.

For almost 700 years, there was a single Christian Church, but that changed in the 11th century when Pope Benedict VIII added the word

filioque ("and the Son") to the Nicene Creed, arguing that the Holy Spirit proceeded from the Son as well as the Father. In 1054, this led to the Great Schism between the western Roman Catholic and eastern Greek Orthodox churches when the latter refused to adopt the new wording. Although the Orthodox Church has a collection of early canons (the Pedalion, or "Rudder"), it does not have the Catholic Church's full code.

As the body of Catholic canons grew, various attempts were made to put them into some sort of order, culminating in the writings of a 12th-century monk called Gratian. In his *Concordia discordantium canonum* (later known as Gratian's *Decretum*), Gratian analysed and organized around 3,800 texts on ecclesiastical discipline. With this work, canon law became a legal science, distinct from theology and worthy of study in its own right. ∎

> Canon law is a unique phenomenon ... because of the unique nature of the Church: a society of divine origin by its institution, yet human in its bearers of authority.
> **Stephan Kuttner**
> **German historian**
> **(1907–96)**

LAW IN T
MIDDLE
500—1470

THE
AGES

The **Koran**, a record of divine **revelations** to the **Prophet Muhammad**, forms the **basis of Islamic law**.

Imam al-Bukhari's authoritative collection of *hadith*, along with others, provides **guidance** for Islamic *qadis* (judges) and *muftis* (legal scholars).

The Domesday Book, a comprehensive **survey of landownership** in England, helps to **centralize power under the monarchy**.

Gratian's *Decretum* becomes the **definitive** reference for **canon law** in the Roman Catholic Church.

632   *c.* **840**   **1086**   *c.* **1140–1150**

529–533   **8TH CENTURY**   **1066**   *c.* **1088**

The Eastern Roman (Byzantine) Emperor Justinian publishes a series of **works of Roman law**, the *Corpus juris civilis* (*Body of the Civil Law*).

Imam Abu Hanifa establishes the first of the great **Islamic law schools**.

William the Conqueror introduces **trial by combat** to England, to settle **property and land disputes**.

Europe's **first university** is established in Bologna, Italy. At first, it teaches only **canon and civil law**.

Even after the Western Roman Empire collapsed, the Roman Catholic Church remained a predominant cultural and political power in Europe throughout the Middle Ages. It had a monopoly on the dissemination of written texts – and the knowledge they contained – before the advent of printing, and consequently exercised a significant influence on government and the law. However, this period also saw struggles between the Church and monarchy, and between the monarchy and its citizens, for control of the law.

Meanwhile, in Arabia in the 7th century, the Prophet Muhammad founded the religion of Islam. He told of a divine revelation of the words of God, which he began preaching in Mecca in 610, and continued until his death in 632.

His followers collected the texts of the revelations in the Koran. The Prophet was also a skilled military and political leader, uniting warring tribes under a single constitution and amassing an army. Within a century of his death, Islam had spread from the Arabian Peninsula as far as South Asia and North Africa to create the Islamic Empire.

Codifying religious law

The Islamic Empire developed a sophisticated legal system that was inspired by Muhammad's example and based on study of the Koranic text. Muhammad's disciples had also recorded many *hadith* – sayings and actions ascribed to the Prophet and his family and companions. These *hadith*, once they had been verified by Islamic judges and legal scholars, provided commentary and

interpretation of the Koran. Together with the Koran, *hadith* became the basis for what was to become Sharia, or Islamic law.

The Roman Catholic Church also formulated its own laws, known as canons; they governed the beliefs and behaviour of mainly the clergy at first, but later of the congregation too. The Italian legal scholar Gratian was the first to compile the canons into a comprehensive treatise, called *Decretum Gratiani*. It was the first of six texts collected into the *Corpus juris canonici*, which was completed by the 14th century and became the definitive reference of canon law.

Islamic and Christian scholars also incorporated ideas from the Classical Greek philosophers, such as the concept of natural law, into their cultures. Gratian in his *Decretum* said that natural law

English common law
(customary law based on
precedent) is **defined in
a treatise** commissioned
by King Henry II from
his chief minister,
Ranulf de Glanvill.

**Trials by
ordeal** are
abolished in
England by King
Henry III.

In his *Summa
Theologica* (*Theological
Treatise*), Thomas
Aquinas says **human
law** may be **unjust** if it
conflicts with **eternal,
divine, or natural law**.

1187–89   **1219**   **1265–1274**

1166   **1215**   **1225**   **13TH–15TH CENTURY**

The Assize of Clarendon
extends the power of
the English Crown with
assize courts and
makes use of **trial by
ordeal** and **jurors** in
trial procedures.

English King John
signs **Magna Carta**,
a charter of rights
affirming that the
monarch is **not
above the law**.

King Henry III reissues
England's **Magna
Carta**, which binds
the **king to observe
the law** and **protects
all men** from royal
abuse of power.

A customary **law
among merchants**,
the *Lex Mercatoria*,
evolves as a form of
**self-regulation of
international trade**.

is "the law common to all nations".
Influenced by Aristotle, Italian
theologian Thomas Aquinas
examined the concept of law itself,
especially the differences between
the ecclesiastical laws of the
Church and civil law, which was
not concerned with Church affairs.
He identified different types of law,
from God-given divine and eternal
laws, to the natural law that exists
universally, and laws devised by
humans. His view that all types of
law should conform to overarching
natural law influenced legal thought
for centuries to come.

The law and the state

England's legal system was an
example of the important changes
that took place in the medieval
period. Until the Norman invasion
of 1066, Saxon rulers had enforced a
hybrid of Viking and Christian laws,
with summary justice and harsh
punishments. The new Norman
king, William the Conqueror, took
control of land ownership in a new,
feudal system. To do this, he made
a detailed inventory of his realm, in
the Domesday Book – a record that
would later supply precedents in
property law cases.

A significant innovation in the
12th century in England was the
introduction of assize courts. These
were convened from time to time in
towns and cities, presided over by
travelling judges. Assizes wrested
control of the law from the Church
and bolstered the idea of a common
law. They also required local jurors
to give evidence and, after trial by
ordeal fell into disuse, to judge guilt
in a precursor of the jury system.
Another landmark in English law
came in 1215, when the barons
negotiated a deal with King John,
recorded in a document later called
Magna Carta. The king agreed that
he would no longer act outside the
law. The document also promised
that every "free man" should
have access to the law through
travelling assizes and could not
be arrested or punished save by
established legal procedure.

While medieval Europe largely
functioned under a dual system
of civil and canon law, merchants
had a greater influence on
European society from the 13th
century onwards, instigating
new commercial laws and even
international agreements. These
would prove vital to the further
development of trade between
nations and maintained their
relevance until the modern era. ∎

IS GOD A JUST JUDGE?

TRIAL BY ORDEAL AND COMBAT (6TH–12TH CENTURY)

IN CONTEXT

FOCUS
Establishing guilt

BEFORE
***c.* 1750 BCE** The world's oldest known legal code, the Code of Hammurabi, includes the use of trial by ordeal.

AFTER
1215 Pope Innocent III bans clergy involvement in trials by fire and water.

1219 The general use of trials by ordeal is abolished under English King Henry III.

1396 The Battle of the Clans, one of the last mass trials by combat, takes place in Perth, Scotland.

16th–17th century In Europe and Colonial North America, ordeal by water is used in witch-hunts, where sinking is taken to be proof of innocence.

1819 Trial by combat is abolished in the UK.

Judging legal cases by ordeal developed from the law codes of the Germanic peoples, which emerged in the 6th century CE after the fall of the Roman Empire. The practice arose where defendants and plaintiffs were not able to satisfy other modes of proof, such as providing a sufficient number of witnesses to swear to their version of the facts. Where a defendant was unable to provide witnesses, or was considered to be untrustworthy, the chieftain or designated judges could resort to ordeal.

Water and fire

Several forms of ordeal became common in England and mainland Europe. Ordeal by hot water was first mentioned in the Salic Laws of the Franks (*c.* 507–11). The accused had to retrieve a stone from boiling water by dipping his hand into it. (The depth of the water depended on the severity of the crime.) The hand was bound and unwrapped three days later; if it had healed, the accused was deemed innocent. Ordeal by iron involved walking on red-hot irons or coals and examining the wound to see if it had festered or healed. Under the ordeal of the cross, the defendant and plaintiff were made to stand with their arms outstretched; the first one to drop his arms lost the case.

Guilty parties often paid a fine or fled rather than face an ordeal. The innocent – believing they would suffer no injury – submitted. The clergy who administered the ordeals understood this and did not wish the innocent to suffer, so they often cheated; "boiling" water would be merely hot, for example.

Trial by combat

While trials by ordeal were usually administered to the lower classes, wealthy parties made more use of trial by combat – effectively, judicial duels – as a mode of proof. This was

If then they do not give the oath, let him go to the threefold ordeal.
Woodstock Code of King Æthelred, 997

See also: Early legal codes 18–19 ▪ The Domesday Book 58–59 ▪ The Assize of Clarendon 64–65 ▪ Magna Carta 66–71 ▪ The trial of Charles I 96–97 ▪ The Salem witch trials 104–05

because in some systems they were permitted to hire champions to fight for them, and because, at least in English law, trial by combat was available in respect of rights to land, which only the wealthy would have. Common in western Europe from at least the 9th century, the practice was imported into England after the Norman Conquest in 1066.

The rules of engagement for trial by combat varied in different countries. In England, each side agreed the rules under the supervision of the judge, who determined if the case could be decided this way, and gauntlets were exchanged to symbolize that a challenge had been accepted. The combat lasted until one participant was killed, mortally wounded, or cried out "craven" to halt the fight. If the defendant was the loser, he suffered the original penalty for his crime and perhaps additional loss of property. If the plaintiff lost, he had to cede the case and pay a fine.

Disuse and abolition

In 1215, Pope Innocent III banned the clergy from practising trials by fire and water. Four years later, King Henry III banned the general use of trial by ordeal in England. Trial by combat gradually fell into disuse, and concerns about the practice paved the way for jury trial. By 1819, when trial by combat was removed from the UK statute book, it had become an antiquarian legal curiosity. ▪

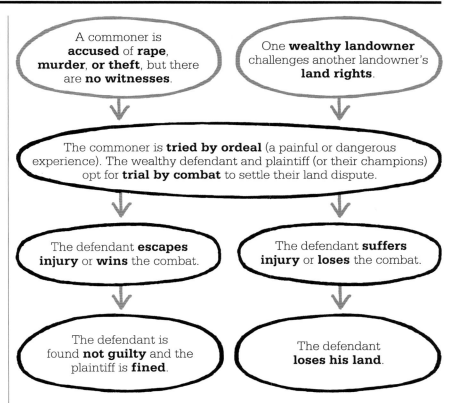

A commoner is **accused** of **rape, murder, or theft**, but there are **no witnesses**.

One **wealthy landowner** challenges another landowner's **land rights**.

The commoner is **tried by ordeal** (a painful or dangerous experience). The wealthy defendant and plaintiff (or their champions) opt for **trial by combat** to settle their land dispute.

The defendant **escapes injury** or **wins** the combat.

The defendant **suffers injury** or **loses** the combat.

The defendant is found **not guilty** and the plaintiff is **fined**.

The defendant **loses his land**.

Two bishops (wearing mitres) judge a duel between two knights in medieval France, where the last trials by combat took place in 1386.

A DIVINE LAW AND A TRACED-OUT WAY

THE KORAN (632)

IN CONTEXT

FOCUS
Divine law

BEFORE
610–632 CE The Prophet
Muhammad receives the
divine revelation of the Koran.

AFTER
c. **660 CE** The first *qadis* or
Islamic judges are appointed.

8th century Abu Hanifa
founds one of the first schools
of Islamic jurisprudence.

c. **840 CE** Muhammad al-
Bukhari compiles a definitive
collection of *hadith*.

c. **900 CE** "The gates of *ijtihad*"
are declared closed by Islamic
legal scholars, ending the
practice of independent
reasoning by judges.

I slamic law arose from a
religious revolution. The
divine revelation that the
Prophet Muhammad received in
the early 7th century CE had at its
core the oneness of God. It also
brought unity to the Arabian
Peninsula, which had been fractured
both religiously, between Jewish
and Christian communities and
pagan worshippers of many gods,
and politically, between large
numbers of nomadic desert tribes
and more settled coastal states.

Although the pre-Islamic
period was later characterized
as *al-Jahiliyya*, an age of
ignorance, it was not entirely
without law. Customary law
governed the contracts made by
merchants trading in coastal and
oasis towns – among them the
family of Muhammad, from Mecca.

See also: The Ten Commandments and Mosaic law 20–23 ▪ The *Arthashastra* and the *Manusmriti* 35 ▪ The Mishnah and the Talmud 38–41 ▪ The origins of canon law 42–47 ▪ Gratian's *Decretum* 60–63 ▪ Thomas Aquinas 72–73

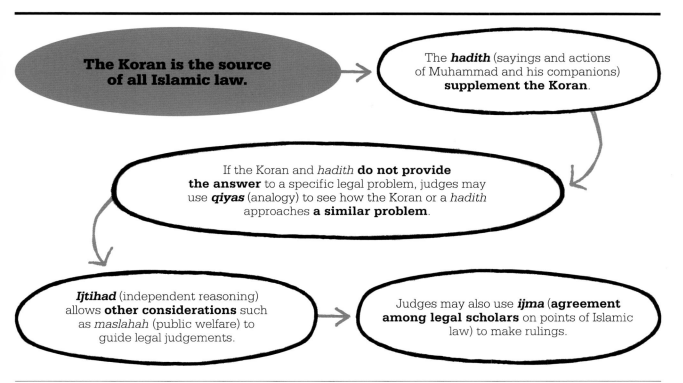

The **Koran is the source of all Islamic law.**

The **hadith** (sayings and actions of Muhammad and his companions) **supplement the Koran**.

If the Koran and *hadith* **do not provide the answer** to a specific legal problem, judges may use **qiyas** (analogy) to see how the Koran or a *hadith* approaches **a similar problem**.

Ijtihad (independent reasoning) allows **other considerations** such as *maslahah* (public welfare) to guide legal judgements.

Judges may also use **ijma (agreement among legal scholars** on points of Islamic law) to make rulings.

In the desert interior, blood-feuds were moderated by negotiations for compensation between the offended parties.

Once the followers of Islam, the new religion Muhammad preached, fled persecution in Mecca and found refuge in Yathrib (now Medina) in 622 CE, they rapidly grew from a small group of companions into a community (*umma*) of several thousand, and needed a law to govern them. This was contained in the Koran (or Qur'an), the sacred book of Muhammad's revelations, which was first compiled in 632 CE. Held to be the literal word of God, it was both unchangeable and sacred, and the guidance and commandments it contained – such as the obligation to pray five times a day and to be charitable to the poor – form the Sharia (or "right path"), which is the bedrock of the principles of Islamic law.

Sources of Islamic law

The Koran is not a formal legal document. Although there are principles within the Koran that can be applied to situations not directly mentioned in its text, it lacks a means to interpret it. Within a century of Muhammad's death in 632 CE, Islam had spread from the Arabian Peninsula across large parts of the world, including South and Central Asia, North Africa, and Spain. The huge increase in the number of followers made it even more important that a consistent Islamic legal framework was developed. Consequently, a system of Islamic jurisprudence, or *fiqh*, grew up, accelerated by the appointment of *qadis* or Islamic »

Imam al-Bukhari (see p.56), who compiled one of the most authoritative collections of *hadith*, is buried at this mausoleum in Uzbekistan. It is an important pilgrimage site in Islam.

A 9th-century Kufic manuscript of a section of the Koran on parchment. Kufic calligraphy is the oldest Arabic script and was the main script used for early copies of the Koran.

judges under the Umayyad dynasty from the 660s CE onwards. They were aided in their deliberations by *muftis*, legal scholars who delivered *fatwas*, or opinions on matters of religious law.

Among the first matters to be determined was the precise status of the *sunna*, the body of social and legal practices that guided the Muslim way of life. Islamic law was often based on *hadith*, or sayings and actions of the Prophet, his family, and his companions, but these did not have the same status as the divine word of the Koran itself.

Guidance for judges

Legal scholars traced back the chain of transmission of these *hadith*, discarding those they discovered to be not well-founded. A popular compilation of *hadith* by the scholar al-Bukhari in the mid-9th century is said to have reduced them to a core group of 2,762.

Egyptian jurist al-Shafi (d. 820) elaborated a process to help *qadis* navigate through this difficult terrain. He said they should first examine the Koran, and if the answer to the legal problem was not found there then consider the *hadith*. If these did not cover

the matter, or were found to be contradictory, a *qadi* was permitted to exercise *qiyas*, or the use of analogy, to find a similar circumstance that was dealt with in the Koran or a *hadith*. If even this was not enough, then it was permitted to seek *ijma*, or scholarly consensus, which required the examination of the opinion of legal scholars. The whole process of reason was known as *ijtihad*, which allowed for other considerations. These factors included *istishab* ("continuity"), by which if a matter had always been considered permissible (or forbidden), it continued to be so, and *maslahah* (public interest), through which the welfare of the community as a whole could be taken into account in a judicial decision.

In the 10th century, scholars began to rule that all the main legal issues had been determined and that, at most, analogy might be needed to decide new matters in the light of old decisions. Formal legal schools of *fiqh*, notably those founded by Abu Hanifa, Malik ibn Anas, al-Shafi, and Ibn Hanbal, gave rise to the Hanifi, Maliki, Shafi, and Hanbali judicial schools, which are still the most important for Muslims

today. The Islamic community had split in the 7th and 8th centuries over the question of the succession to Muhammad. The majority Sunni group adhered to the five caliphs, or heads of Islamic communities, who had followed the Prophet and then their Abbasid and Umayyad successors. The minority Shia held that the leadership should have gone through the line of Ali, Muhammad's son-in-law. As well as minor differences in ritual, the Shia have their own jurisprudence schools, such as the Zaidi and Jafari, which lend more weight to the independent reasoning of the religious hierarchy (such as Iran's ayatollahs) than the *taqlid* ("imitation") of past decisions, which became more predominant in the Sunni schools.

Crime and the law

Islamic law differentiates between matters that are compulsory (*fard*), recommended (*mandub*), neutral (*mubah*), reprehensible (*makruh*),

Whoever treads a path seeking knowledge, Allah will make easy for him the path to Paradise.
Ibn Majah
Compiler of *hadith* in 9th-century Iran (824–c.887)

Suleiman the Magnificent was sultan of the Ottoman Empire when it was at its strongest, from 1520 to 1566. He was the most powerful leader of the Islamic world in the 16th century.

or forbidden (*haram*). Punishments are prescribed for the last two categories. Some types of serious crime, including murder and sexual violations, known as *hudud*, had severe punishments laid down in the Koran and the *hadith* (such as the cutting off of thieves' hands, or the stoning of adulterers). However, the evidential requirements for these were greater. For most crimes, two male witnesses (or one male and two female) were required, but for adultery, four adult male witnesses were needed.

Partly because it could be difficult to find sufficient witnesses, many aspects of criminal law were transferred to state courts under the Abbasids in the 9th century (at roughly the time that *taqlid* supplanted *ijtihad* as the core of legal reasoning). Although family and property law remained the domain of religious judges, this established a long-running tension between secular and religious law in Islamic societies. Whereas once the religious hierarchy made – or at least made judgements upon – the law, secular rulers now legislated. These included the Ottoman sultans, such as the 16th-century sultan Suleiman the Magnificent, who built up a body of administrative law, or *kanuni*.

Sharia law today

The idealized view of the Islamic state had been one ruled by Islamic law, based on the Koran, *hadith*, and a partnership between the caliph, the clergy, and *qadis*. In countries where Muslims are a minority, this balance clearly cannot hold, but there have been calls for governments to recognize the authority of Sharia courts to decide on religious matters. This has proved controversial because it has been viewed by some as the subordination of national law to Islamic religious law.

In Muslim-majority countries such as Pakistan, pressure has grown for Sharia law to have a role

> Stand out firmly
> for justice,
> as witnesses to Allah.
> **Koran 4:135**

within the secular national legal framework. In extreme cases, such as the Taliban regime in Afghanistan, this has led to Sharia being taken to be the only source of legal legitimacy. On the other hand, in some countries the law has been seen as oppressive towards certain sections of society, such as women, and there has been pressure to reform. In Saudi Arabia, for example, it was recognized that forbidding women to drive was based more on traditional cultural practice than Islamic law. The struggle to define and interpret the laws governing the world's two billion Muslims continues. ∎

Abu Hamid al-Ghazali

Born in Tabaran, Iran, in 1058, al-Ghazali was appointed head of the Shafi *madrasa* (educational institute) in Baghdad in 1091, where he taught for five years. He wrote more than 70 works and was later regarded as a *mujaddid*, or renovator of the law, whose interpretations were treated with particular respect.

Al-Ghazali condemned loyalty to leaders who claimed their own secret revelation of the Sharia, denouncing this as heretical. This denunciation was aimed at the Assassins, an Islamic sect that regularly sent assassins to kill opponents. He lectured until at least 1110 and died the following year.

Key works

Late 11th century *The Revival of the Religious Sciences*
c. **1105** *The Alchemy of Happiness*

NO YARD OF LAND WAS LEFT OUT

THE DOMESDAY BOOK (1086)

F ollowing his invasion of England in 1066, William the Conqueror, now King William I, made frequent visits to his home duchy of Normandy, leaving writs (written instructions) in his absence. However, the wholesale change of landownership that had followed the conquest had not been well documented, risking legal and administrative chaos. William desired a fuller account of his new royal demesne (landed property) in England and – being in urgent need of money – he needed to ascertain the total yield of rents.

Compiling Domesday
In December 1085, the king sent out commissioners to establish who owned each estate and each one's productive value (even down to the number of ducks on the land). In each area, a sworn jury of local landowners and villagers reported to the commissioners. The findings were then gathered into summaries and returned to Westminster Palace. There they were bound together in 1086 into the first draft of what we now know as the Domesday Book (the book was as binding as the Christian Day of Judgement, or "Doomsday").

William died in 1087, before he put the Domesday census to use, but it was of huge value. Virtually all of England had been mapped administratively and lordship and land-holding were now inseparable, reflecting the new political structure.

The king's land
Before the Norman Conquest, English property law had presumed that the land had no single owner, such as a king. So individuals had been able to own a parcel of land

This most powerful king sent his justices through every shire ... of England, and caused an inquiry to be made by sworn inquest how many hides ... there were in each village, and what livestock.
Henry of Huntingdon
English historian
(*c.* 1088–*c.* 1157)

See also: The *Lex Aquilia* 34 ▪ Gratian's *Decretum* 60–63 ▪ Magna Carta 66–71 ▪ The Venetian Patent Statute 82–85 ▪ The Treaty of Tordesillas 86–87 ▪ The Statute of Anne 106–07

William of Normandy **conquers England** and **confiscates land** from the Anglo-Saxon aristocracy.

↓

He **keeps one-sixth** of the land for himself and **distributes** the rest to **noble tenants-in-chief**, who **own land in return for services** to him.

↓

The **Domesday Book commissioners** are sent out to **compile lists of the nobles' estates** and their values.

↓

The results of the Domesday survey **provide a legal basis for land-holding** across the whole country.

The Norman Conquest

William had become Duke of Normandy in 1035, aged just eight years. In 1066, he crossed the English Channel to claim the crown, which he believed the Anglo-Saxon King Edward the Confessor had promised to him. He defeated Edward's successor, King Harold, at the Battle of Hastings, earning the name of William the Conqueror.

William brought an army of around 7,000 knights and men-at-arms. After defeating Harold, he needed to control the English population of more than two million people, to quash a series of revolts, and to ward off the threat of invasion by the Danes. So he rewarded his Norman followers with English land, much of it taken from Anglo-Saxon nobles. By the 1080s, the native land-holding aristocracy had been decimated. The Domesday Book documented that revolution in land-holding.

King Harold is said to have been killed by an arrow in the eye at the Battle of Hastings, shown in this scene from the Bayeux Tapestry.

absolutely. Furthermore, an individual could have acquired private property by occupying land with no recorded owner. William's new form of land-holding swept away these traditional rights.

Noble tenants-in-chief were now enfeoffed (given a fief, or land with its peasants and the income it provided) by the king on certain conditions – principally military service or rent. The new tenants-in-chief received something like legal title to their land for the first time; they in turn granted portions of their fiefs to subtenants.

No one save the king now held land in their own right and the former free men of the Anglo-Saxon period became tenants, including some (known as villeins) who were tied to their land and were not allowed to leave it.

Domesday and the law

The Domesday Book, with unrivalled levels of detail on land-holders, was used in legal cases involving title, paving the way for precedents of title to become a cornerstone of English property law. Information such as the number of "hides" (the land needed to support one household) on each estate was used as late as 1193. The value of its detail waned over time, but the Domesday Book has stood as a foundational text of the English legal and political system for 900 years. ▪

AN ACCUSATION CANNOT BE REPEATED

GRATIAN'S *DECRETUM* (MID-12TH CENTURY)

IN CONTEXT

FOCUS
Canon law

BEFORE
325 Emperor Constantine convenes the first major council of the Christian Church at Nicaea (now Iznik, in Turkey).

380 Thedosius I issues the Edict of Thessalonica, making Christianity the state religion of the Roman Empire.

529 Emperor Justinian publishes his *Code*, an important source of canon law.

1100 Flemish priest Alger of Liège publishes the *Liber de misericordia et justitia* (*Book of Mercy and Justice*), from which Gratian borrows texts.

AFTER
1234 The *Liber extra* is published under the authority of Pope Gregory IX.

1917 The publication of a new code of canon law finally replaces Gratian's *Decretum*.

As the Christian Church grew in strength during its first centuries, and particularly after it emerged under Emperor Constantine from the shadows of persecution in 313 CE, it needed a law to govern it. The relatively small number of rules that could be derived from the New Testament had to be supplemented with a more detailed framework. This was required to govern both the behaviour of the Church hierarchy itself, and those areas such as

See also: The Ten Commandments and Mosaic law 20–23 ▪ Aristotle and natural law 32–33 ▪ The *Lex Aquilia* 34
▪ Ulpian the Jurist 36–37 ▪ The origins of canon law 42–47 ▪ Thomas Aquinas 72–73

A stained-glass window in Worms Cathedral, Germany, depicts Burchard of Worms. His *Liber decretorum* was one of the most significant collections of canon law before Gratian's.

The inconsistency of canon law mirrored that of Roman civil law, alongside which it had developed, where successive pieces of imperial legislation sat alongside a mass of juristic writing to produce a legal framework that was both incomplete and contradictory.

Compiling canon law
Attempts were made early on to bring some form of order to this chaos, beginning with the *Apostolic Canons*, assembled in the early 6th century by Dionysius Exiguus, a scholar who worked for Pope John I in Rome. This brought together canons of a number of Church councils on issues such as the date on which Easter ought to be celebrated.

The 9th and 10th centuries brought a new sense of urgency to attempts to gather together the vast body of canon law. This era of the *jus antiquum* ("old law") saw the compilation of collections such as the *Libri duo de synodalibus causis et disciplinis ecclesiasticis* (*Two Books Concerning Synodical Causes and Church Discipline*) by German abbot Regino of Prüm in 906, and the *Liber decretorum* (*Book of Decretals*) by German bishop Burchard of Worms, which was compiled around 1020. The *Liber decretorum*, in particular, gathered together previous ecclesiastical decisions about penance, such as whether a man needed to commit penance for killing on the battlefield, and whether

marriage and family life where the Church authorities felt they had a greater claim than the civil law.

The canon law (law relating to the Christian Church) that developed in the centuries after Constantine had a piecemeal nature. The decisions of a series of Christian councils, such as the First Council of Nicaea in 325 CE – many of them concerned with Church discipline, such as forbidding priests to live with women to whom they were not related – were supplemented by ad hoc decretals (decrees concerning points of canon law).

A lack of consistency
Only in the very particular case of monastic rules – such as those of St Benedict, written in the early 6th century – was there a consistent set of regulations governing all aspects of religious life. And there was very little in the way of legal reasoning to justify those regulations that had been clearly decreed.

the penance should be more severe if he killed without the command of a legitimate ruler.

Despite the production of such compilations, by the early 12th century there was still no systematic treatise that attempted to make coherent sense of the broad body of canon law in the way that Justinian's *Corpus juris civilis* (*Body of the Civil Law*) had done for Roman civil law (see box, p.62). The *Concordia discordantium canonum* (*Harmony of Discordant Councils*) by the Italian legal scholar Gratian filled this gap. It consisted of three parts, dealing with questions of Church administration, ecclesiastical organization, and the sacraments, and it cited authorities as diverse as Church councils, papal decretals, Roman imperial rescripts (written replies from emperors to legal queries), and the works of 7th-century Spanish encyclopedist Isidore of Seville.

Little is known about Gratian, the author of the collection, later known as the *Decretum Gratiani* (*The Decretum of Gratian*). He may have been a Benedictine monk, or possibly a bishop, but »

> Justice is the firm and continuous desire to render to everyone that which is his due.
> **Justinian**
> Roman emperor (*c.*482–565)

Roman civil law

By the 4th century CE, Roman civil law consisted of multiple ad hoc imperial decrees and extensive juristic writings. Some attempts had been made to bring order to the morass of imperial legal decrees – most notably in 438 CE, in the *Code* of Theodosius.

A more successful reform was achieved by Emperor Justinian, who established a legal commission tasked with finding all valid laws and weeding out those which were defunct, defective, or contradictory. In 529, he published his *Code*, valid throughout the Eastern Roman Empire. Four years later, he authorized the publication of the *Digest*, a summary collection of the writings of jurists through previous centuries. The *Institutions*, a basic handbook for law students (also published in 533), completed the *Corpus juris civilis*, which was later to prove such a useful source for Gratian.

Justinian was emperor of the Eastern Roman (Byzantine) Empire from 527 to 565. He tried, with some success, to reconquer the lost western half of the Roman Empire.

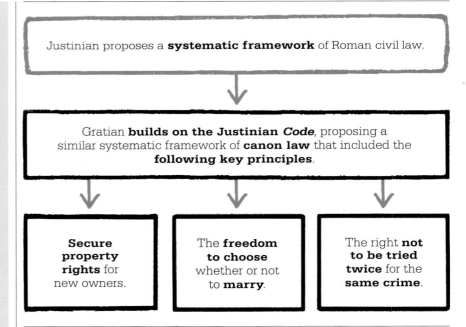

Justinian proposes a **systematic framework** of Roman civil law.

↓

Gratian **builds on the Justinian *Code***, proposing a similar systematic framework of **canon law** that included the **following key principles**.

↓ ↓ ↓

Secure property rights for new owners.

The **freedom to choose** whether or not to **marry**.

The right **not to be tried twice** for the **same crime**.

---

the only reliable information about him relates to a legal case in Venice in 1143 in which he was cited as an authority by the papal legate (a clerical representative of the Pope). It seems likely that Gratian was associated with the prestigious legal school in Bologna. Despite only scant information about his life, the impact of the *Decretum* itself was enough to secure Gratian the title of "Father of Canon Law".

The *Decretum* was written in two stages, some time after 1139 and then around 1150. (Some scholars argue there are two versions of the *Decretum*.) The first part of the work is divided into 101 subsections; the second deals with 36 particular questions; and the third addresses matters related to the sacraments.

Gratian adopted a systematic approach throughout, appealing to earlier authorities as models and using reason to resolve problems. He used the *Corpus juris civilis* as an invaluable source of Roman law, and from 1150 he drew in particular

on Justinian's *Digest*, using it to illustrate issues such as the effect of adoption on the prohibited degrees of marriage and divorce within a family. In other areas, such as rules on the behaviour of clergy and the payment of tithes, which did not have precedents in Roman law, Gratian had to derive rules from the Bible, Church councils, and papal decretals.

Intent, double jeopardy, and marriage

In several areas in particular, Gratian's formulation of Church law established rulings that would have far-reaching implications for the Church. In the second part of the *Decretum*, for example, he devotes a chapter to the subject of land property rights, which was an issue of grave importance to the Church as a major landowner. The problem was that Church land had often been "alienated" – leased or allowed to be used by a new owner. The latter, or a third party who the land was passed on to, might have come into possession of the land through illegitimate means, or their title might be otherwise defective. Gratian addressed this issue. He carried over a precedent from Roman civil law such that if the acquisition had been in good faith – even if technically not legal – then the new owner's right to the property could not be challenged by the previous owner (in this case, the Church) after a period of 40 years. This represented a ten-year extension to the period a civil landowner had to claim his rights from a new owner.

Gratian's *Decretum* also helped establish the principle of double jeopardy, in which a person cannot be tried twice for the same crime. He took as his starting point a passage from the Book of Nahum in the Old Testament that "God does not judge twice in the same matters". Despite this, in certain cases the ecclesiastical courts still permitted a civil case to be taken to deprive a cleric of their position, and a separate criminal case on the same matter.

Gratian's sections on marriage helped solidify the notion that consent for marriage should be freely given, and that no one should be coerced into marriage. Even so, on the question of whether a man, having taken monastic vows, is subsequently permitted to change his mind and marry, Gratian finds the matter so difficult that he cites no fewer than 40 previous authorities, and eventually concludes that a simple vow of chastity cannot be broken.

The body of canon law

Gratian's *Decretum* inaugurated an era of ecclesiastical law, known as the *jus novum* ("new law"), in which canon law became regularized and the subject of intense academic study. As early as the 1140s, glossators – writers who provide glossaries or commentaries on other authors' works – had begun to provide supplements to the *Decretum*; work that would still be ongoing in the 16th century.

The *Decretum* was one of six works – including the *Liber extra* of the Spanish canon Raymond of Peñafort (approved by Pope Gregory IX in 1234), the *Liber sextus* (1298) of Pope Boniface VIII, and the *Clementines* (1317) of Pope

Canon law dominated in areas to do with family life, marriage, and sexual morality. In this illustration from Gratian's *Decretum*, a woman has been condemned to wear a chastity belt.

Clement V – that together formed the *Corpus juris canonici* (*Body of Canon Law*). This was the main source of canon law until the Roman Catholic Church's 16th-century Council of Trent, which clarified Catholic doctrine in the face of Protestant criticism. Even after this time, the *Corpus juris canonici* remained an important influence in the law of the Christian Church until 1917, when a revised code of canon law was promulgated by Pope Benedict XV. In 1959, Pope John XXIII established a papal commission to undertake a new revision, and this took effect in 1983, comprising 1,752 canons (rules or principles), divided into seven books.

Although it had never been formally recognized by the Church, Gratian's *Decretum* has been an essential legal text in universities for more than 750 years, making it one of the most influential legal works of all time. ∎

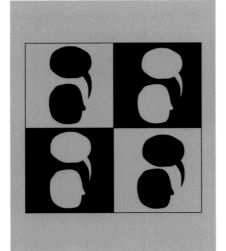

SPEAK THE TRUTH

THE ASSIZE OF CLARENDON (1166)

IN CONTEXT

FOCUS
Trial by jury

BEFORE
1154 Henry II (1133–89) is crowned king of England.

1164 The Constitutions of Clarendon give secular courts power over canon law in many matters, including trial and punishment of criminal clergy.

AFTER
1170 The Inquest of the Sheriffs replaces 21 sheriffs (mostly barons, or hereditary nobles) with royal appointees, to stop corruption of the courts.

1176 The remit of juries and punishments are extended by the Assize of Northampton.

1215 The Fourth Lateran Council forbids clergy from taking part in trials by ordeal.

1353 A statute by Edward III forbids service on both a trial jury and jury of presentment.

England's **itinerant justices** tour the country.

⬇

Local **juries** of free men (men who are not legally tied to a master or plot of land) **inform justices** of suspected murderers, rapists, and thieves.

⬇

Justices determine whether the **accused** should be **tried by ordeal** by water.

⬇

Guilty defendants have their **property seized** and a **foot amputated**. Even **innocent** defendants of ill repute may be **exiled**.

Henry II inherited an English kingdom in which law and order had broken down during the Anarchy (1135–53), the civil war between Henry's mother, Matilda, and his predecessor, King Stephen. Henry also had to face the challenge of canon law – a parallel legal system of ecclesiastical, or

Church, justice. In 1163, he received a report that the ecclesiastical, rather than royal, courts had tried more than 100 churchmen for murder since 1154.

The growing assertiveness of the papacy also threatened Henry's authority and his courts. Henry needed to regain control of the law:

See also: Early legal codes 18–19 ▪ Trial by ordeal and combat 52–53 ▪ Gratian's *Decretum* 60–63 ▪ Magna Carta 66–71 ▪ The trial of Charles I 96–97 ▪ The Glorious Revolution and the English Bill of Rights 102–03

Trial by cold water, shown here in the 9th-century *Codex Lambacensis*, a manuscript of church rules, involved dropping the accused into a pond, lake, or river. If he sank, he was innocent.

a first step was to restrict the Church courts' ability to punish the clergy. Then Henry held a council at Clarendon Palace, Wiltshire, in 1166. The resulting series of laws, called the Assize of Clarendon, ordered "justices in eyre" (justices travelling periodic circuits) to take royal justice out of London to the provinces.

Visits by justices in eyre had begun under Henry I (r. 1100–35), but had long since fallen into disuse. The Assize of Clarendon added a new condition: 12 free men from each "hundred" (land large enough to support 100 households) or four from each "vill" (part of a hundred and roughly equivalent to a village) were to sit on a jury of presentment.

The role of jurors

In a jury of presentment, the jurors had to report, on oath, to the justices on local suspects for the most serious crimes – murder, rape, and theft. Jurors did not have to decide on a suspect's guilt: if the person had been apprehended committing the crime, his or her guilt could be presumed.

The Assize of Clarendon had also replaced the previous practice of compurgation, by which the accused could prove innocence by producing a sufficient number of witnesses to swear to it. Trial by cold water now became the prime legal process of proof in criminal trials; it had earlier been used only on lower classes. Those found guilty by the ordeal faced a fine, confiscation of property, and the amputation of a foot; even those found innocent could be exiled if they were of ill repute. Large numbers of accused simply fled rather than face the ordeal, but their property could still be seized.

The Assize of Northampton in 1176 added arson and forgery to offences to be dealt with by justices in eyre. Penalties became harsher, with the guilty suffering amputation of a hand as well as a foot.

Evolution of the jury

When the Fourth Lateran Council (a Roman Catholic synod in Rome) in 1215 forbade clerics from taking part in trials by ordeal, such trials were discounted as a practical method of determining guilt. Juries were now asked to judge whether defendants were innocent or guilty. This new role created a conflict of interest with the role of a jury of presentment, so in 1353 a statute of Edward III forbade a person from sitting on both forms of jury.

As well as the grand assizes (courts) set up by the Assize of Clarendon, petty assizes had also evolved to deal with special cases such as land disputes – they had juries of 12 men. Other measures followed, such as Clause 39 of the 1215 Magna Carta, which forbade the seizure of a free man's land without judgement by his peers.

The use of juries, begun by the Assize of Clarendon, gradually extended until trial by jury became established and a hallmark of the British legal tradition. Henry's reforms also laid the basis for common law (law applied to all). ▪

The lord king wills that those who ... be absolved by the law, if they have been of the worst repute ... shall abjure the king's lands.
The Assize of Clarendon

TO NONE WILL WE DENY OR DELAY RIGHT OR JUSTICE

MAGNA CARTA (1215)

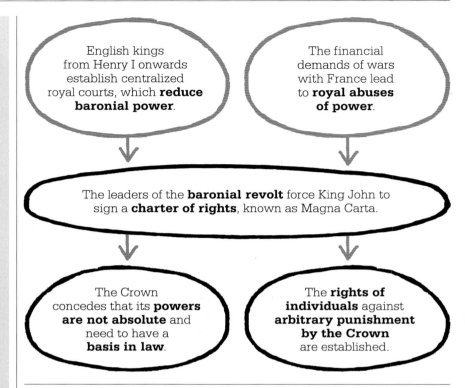

English kings from Henry I onwards establish centralized royal courts, which **reduce baronial power**.

The financial demands of wars with France lead to **royal abuses of power**.

The leaders of the **baronial revolt** force King John to sign a **charter of rights**, known as Magna Carta.

The Crown concedes that its **powers are not absolute** and need to have a **basis in law**.

The **rights of individuals** against **arbitrary punishment by the Crown** are established.

The monarchs of medieval England had a problem. The feudal system instigated from 1066 by William I was breaking down. Under this system, barons (nobles) were the superior "vassals", who swore allegiance to the Crown, provided fighting men, and paid dues to the king in return for his protection and land (called fiefs or fiefdoms). Barons, too, had vassals – often trusted knights – who swore fealty (allegiance) to their lord and sometimes oversaw their lands. Below them were peasants – tenant farmers who might be free men but were mostly "villeins", legally tied to the lord. At the system's base were serfs, who were owned by the lord. Serfs and peasants had no rights.

From the 1190s, the revenue that a king could raise from feudal dues and his own estates was wholly inadequate to fund the wars pursued to defend the land England held in France. The king extorted increasing funds from his barons, who became ever more embittered.

Legal abuses under John

England's justice system was in need of reform. The legal processes that had suited earlier kings were under severe strain by the 12th century. Henry II's reforms provided the nucleus of a central court system and the beginnings of a codification of common law (see box, p.70). The reforms, however, limited the power of the barons' local courts, and the concessions offered by the reforms could be abused or withdrawn at will by a less enlightened king – notably John, who acceded to the throne in 1199.

A series of disastrous military expeditions in France ended with the loss of Normandy in 1204 and left John critically short of money. To finance a new army, he turned to wholesale abuse of feudal dues. Scutage (a cash levy in lieu of military service) was increased and raised even when no service was required. The royal courts of law grew more powerful and were used to levy fines on questionable grounds. The dues exacted when a baron inherited his position and land rose enormously. The sums extorted from barons to avoid the "king's displeasure" also escalated. Both contributed to an increase in the royal revenues to £145,000 in 1211 (around 10 times more than had been typical in the 1190s).

Another war in France from 1214 to 1215 squandered the money and eroded any residual goodwill among the barons. There was a contractual

See also: The Domesday Book 58–59 ▪ The Assize of Clarendon 64–65 ▪ The trial of Charles I 96–97 ▪ The Glorious Revolution and the English Bill of Rights 102–03 ▪ The US Constitution and Bill of Rights 110–17

The English Church shall be free, and shall have its rights undiminished, and its liberties unimpaired. […] This freedom we shall observe ourselves …
Magna Carta, Chapter 1

element to medieval English kingship; the monarch's authority was considered a contract with his people. His feudal vassals had a right to renounce their fealty if the king broke his side of the bargain.

A dispute with Pope Innocent III worsened the situation. When John rejected the Pope's candidate, Stephen Langton, for Archbishop of Canterbury, the Pope issued an interdict that banned church services in England. In 1209, he excommunicated John. The ban on religious services was deeply felt and further tested the barons' loyalty.

The barons' revolt
John finally capitulated to the Pope, but in 1215 he faced a serious baronial uprising. The rebels gathered in the north and marched towards London. Under pressure from Archbishop Langton to avoid a bloody confrontation, John agreed to negotiations. He met the barons on 15 June in a field beside the Thames at Runnymede in Surrey. They presented the Articles of the Barons, which sought to prevent

almost every royal abuse of power that had occurred during John's reign. John assented and set his seal on the document.

The Great Charter
In 1218, the new document was named Magna Carta (Latin for "Great Charter"). Today, it is revered as a foundation document for modern democracy and the rule of law, but when it was issued, it was a conservative contract, primarily intended to protect the barons' legal rights against royal encroachment.

The charter's 63 chapters begin by confirming (at Archbishop Langton's insistence) that the English Church should be free from royal interference, and should have its rights "undiminished". Much of the rest of the charter dealt with baronial grievances. Chapter 2 laid down that heirs of an earl or baron should pay the Crown no more than £100 to take up their inheritance. Chapter 18 stipulated that a widow

could not be forced to remarry against her will (as wealthy widows often were, to those favoured by the king). Chapter 12, which forbade the raising of scutage except by "common counsel of our kingdom", challenged the king, but had little immediate force as John chose the members of his royal council. Chapter 16 summarized the nobility's major grievance against their monarch by stating that no one should be compelled to do greater service "for a knight's fee" (scutage) than was legally due.

Other chapters had more profound consequences. Chapter 18 laid down that certain assizes should be held by a travelling committee of two justices and four knights in each county at least »

King John signs Magna Carta at Runnymede – a site used for assemblies since ancient times. In reality, the king used the Great Seal to mark his assent to the document.

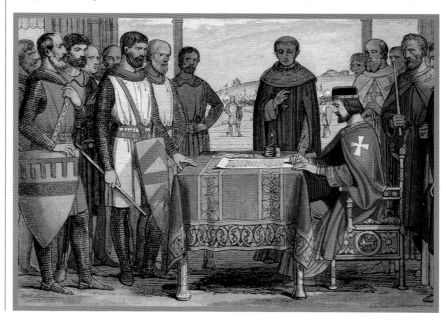

four times a year, providing speedier access to justice for all. Previously, the only guaranteed legal sittings had been those of the court established in 1178 at Westminster. Chapter 39 was even more significant as it included rights later enshrined in the *Habeas Corpus* Act of 1679. It stated that no free man could be arrested, imprisoned, dispossessed, exiled, outlawed, or in any way victimized except by the "lawful judgement of his peers" or by the law of the land. The following chapter affirmed that the right to justice could not be bought, refused, or delayed. By accepting Chapters 39 and 40, the king swore for the first time to be bound by the law.

Early survival

The barons knew that John would try to renege on the charter. As a precaution, Chapter 61 stated that should the king break the agreement, a committee of 25 barons could hold him to account. John could not accept such an assault on his authority, and in August he secured a papal bull (a public decree from the Pope) allowing him to revoke the charter. This prompted the First Barons' War, as a group of barons, supported by a French army, rose up against the king. When John died, in October 1216, his heir, Henry III, was just nine years old and in no position to challenge the barons as John had. Most of the warring barons quietly defected back to the government side, and by 1217 the rebellion had collapsed.

The charter was first reissued in 1216 when Henry III acceded to the throne and again in 1218 when it was named Magna Carta. The 1225 reissue expanded the coverage of the charter's protection from "all free men" to "all men". It did not explicitly offer women the same protection, although some have since argued that, at this time, "men" could mean "people".

The 1225 reissue was regarded as definitive and incorporated into law. It marked the transition of the rights it included from common law (laws developed on the basis of previous rulings) to statute law passed by a legislature. Edward I confirmed this with his 1297 reissue. The 13th century also saw legal consolidation in the common law. After Ranulf de Glanvill (see box, below) had paved the way, another treatise, *De legibus et*

Magna Carta was issued in Latin – the legal language of the day. Some 17 copies survive, including ones at Salisbury and Lincoln cathedrals, and the Bodleian Library in Oxford.

consuetudinibus Angliae (*On the Laws and Customs of England*), attributed to cleric and jurist Henry de Bracton, developed the subject in around 1235. This treatise also introduced the idea of *mens rea* (criminal intent) and formulated a theory of kingship inspired by Magna Carta, stating that a king was a rightful monarch only if he obtained and exercised power in a lawful manner. Under Edward III, laws known as the Six Statutes expanded the protection Magna Carta offered; they included explicit statements of the right not to have goods or chattels seized (1331) and that of all men to have access to due process of law if accused (1368).

Reinforced by Parliament

The 13th century marked the birth of parliamentary democracy. Over time, the king's right to appoint whom he wished to his royal council of administrators and advisers was eroded. A further baronial revolt against Henry III led

Ranulf de Glanvill and the common law

One of the earliest authoritative texts on common law was the *Tractatus de legibus et consuetudinibus regni Angliae* (*Treatise on the Laws and Customs of England*), attributed to Ranulf de Glanvill and written between 1187 and 1189. Born around 1112, Glanvill was the Justiciar of England – Henry II's chief minister from 1180 to 1189.

An independent judiciary had begun to emerge. In 1178, an ordinance established that five judges should sit in Westminster to hear suits – the origins of the Court of the King's Bench. Their decisions, the precedents that such decisions set, and the reference to earlier customary law marked the emergence of English common law. The treatise, which the king had commissioned to help establish peace in turbulent times, clearly defined the legal processes of the day.

Dismissed and imprisoned by Richard I in 1189, Glanvill died on a crusade in Palestine in 1190.

> By our spontaneous and good will, we have given and conceded ... to all our kingdom, these below written liberties.
> **Henry III**
> **1225 reissue of Magna Carta**

to the Provisions of Oxford in 1258. These placed the government in the hands of a committee of 15 barons and a parliament (made up largely of nobles) summoned three times a year. The system soon collapsed, but a revolt in 1264 led by Simon de Montfort (the Second Barons' War), led to the calling in 1265 of the first parliament to include representatives not just of the wealthy elite, but of all the people. It included two burgesses (representatives) from each large town and two knights from each shire.

By the 14th century, this body was exerting its rights under Chapter 12 of Magna Carta, interpreting it to mean that the king could not raise any tax without first seeking Parliament's consent. The charter's influence waned during the 15th century as the Tudor monarchy strengthened. In the 17th century, however, it became a highly

King John's assent to Magna Carta was marked in 1957 by this memorial at Runnymede on land leased by the American Bar Association (ABA). Its president William Hubbard declared the charter "an enduring worldwide symbol of liberty and the rule of law".

effective shield for parliamentary rights against the power of the Stuart kings during the English Civil Wars that resulted in the execution of Charles I, the exile of Charles II, and Cromwell's rule.

A broad, lasting influence

In the late 18th century, Magna Carta's defence against royal tyranny resonated with the American colonists' struggle for independence from British rule. The wording of the US Constitution in 1789 and the later Bill of Rights was influenced by the limitations on the arbitrary power of a ruler that Magna Carta had established more than 500 years earlier.

In Britain, by the 19th century, much of Magna Carta had become obsolete. From 1828 onwards, most of its provisions were removed from the statute book. Only four of its chapters are still in force today – the first, on the liberties of the English Church; Chapter 13 on the privileges

> The democratic aspiration is no mere recent phase in human history. It was written in Magna Carta.
> **Franklin D. Roosevelt**
> **32nd US president (1933–45)**

of the City of London; and Chapters 39 and 40 on the right to trial according to the law, and the forbidding of arbitrary seizures by the Crown. For these two chapters Magna Carta is still perceived as the cornerstone of British legal rights, and a turning point in constitutional government and human rights. ■

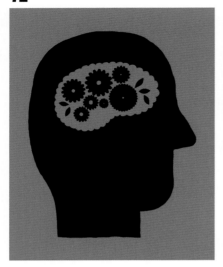

EVERY LAW IS ORDAINED TO THE COMMON GOOD
THOMAS AQUINAS (c. 1225–1274)

IN CONTEXT

FOCUS
Natural law

BEFORE
54–51 BCE Cicero's *De Republica* discusses ideas of natural law and natural right.

388–95 CE St Augustine tries to reconcile Christian teaching and natural law in *De libero arbitrio* (*On Free Will*).

c. 1140–50 Gratian's *Decretum* describes natural law as "the law common to all nations".

AFTER
1323 Thomas Aquinas is canonized by Pope John XXII.

1689 English philosopher John Locke's *Two Treatises on Government* argues that natural law existed in our original state of nature, before the rise of governments.

1948 The Universal Declaration of Human Rights sets out fundamental rights that are common to all nations.

People have the **faculty of reason** and seek to **live in a virtuous way**.

→

People discover natural laws **embedded in nature** and **through divine commands**.

↓

Immutable and universal, **natural law** enables people to live in a **good and moral way**.

←

Natural law takes precedence over **manmade laws**, which are **subject to change** and **can be unjust**.

As legal theory developed from antiquity onwards, a series of philosophical questions particularly troubled scholars. Central among these were three conundrums: from where did law arise, could laws be applied universally, and were there moral grounds on which laws could be disobeyed? Endeavouring to solve these problems, the theory of natural law held that there was an overarching law whose principles were embedded in nature itself – and, according to philosopher and theologian Thomas Aquinas, were dictated by divine command. The idea maintained that to be just, human laws – those of a nation state, for example – must conform to the principles of natural law.

Reason and virtue
Natural law theory originated with Greek philosophers such as Aristotle in the 4th century BCE, who in his *Politics* described law as reason and part of mankind's rational attempt to organize society well. The Roman statesman and lawyer Cicero in the 1st century BCE argued that the best way to achieve happiness was through living a life of virtue and that natural law, framed in

See also: The Ten Commandments and Mosaic law 20–23 ▪ Aristotle and natural law 32–33 ▪ The origins of canon law 42–47 ▪ Gratian's *Decretum* 60–63

> Reason in man is rather like God in the world.
> **Thomas Aquinas**
> *Summa Theologica*, 1265–74

accordance with nature, made this possible. By the early Middle Ages, Christian writers such as St Augustine had developed this idea further to conclude that laws contrary to natural law were unjust and might not need to be obeyed.

In the 13th century, these strands were gathered together and refined by Aquinas, whose *Summa Theologica* (*Theological Treatise*) included a key section on natural law. He distinguished between four types of law. Eternal law transcends everything and touches upon God's divine plan and order for the Universe, while divine law concerns creation and the path to salvation. Natural law is the link between mankind and God, made possible by humanity's ability to reason and perceive good.

At the bottom of Aquinas's hierarchy of laws is human law, which is created according to particular circumstances and can,

unlike natural law, easily be modified. Even this, according to Aquinas, should conform to the dictates of natural law – and if it does not, it may be deemed unjust.

Natural law and justice

Aquinas believed that both natural law and human law aimed at the common good, but sometimes this produced surprising – and to modern eyes unfounded – results. He deemed slavery, for example, to be in accordance with natural law, supporting a divinely ordained social hierarchy. However, he thought it legitimate to conform to the spirit, rather than the letter, of natural law if this prevented a greater evil.

Aquinas's ideas of natural law remained influential after his death, providing defences of the right to overthrow tyrants and for theories of a "just war". They flowered anew in the 20th century with the notion of universal norms contained in the Universal Declaration of Human Rights. And they continue into the 21st century with appeals to "natural justice" as a means to oppose unjust government laws. ▪

In his *Summa Theologica*, a page of which is shown here in a 13th-century decorated manuscript, Thomas Aquinas cites Christian, Muslim, Hebrew, and pagan sources.

Thomas Aquinas

The Catholic Church's most influential medieval theologian, Aquinas was born in Fossanova between Naples and Rome, in *c.*1225, to a family of minor nobility. Against their wishes, he became a Dominican friar aged 20. Studying in Paris under theologian Albertus Magnus, he rapidly rose to prominence and was appointed regent master of theology there in 1265.

In 1265, Aquinas was summoned to serve as papal theologian, establishing a Dominican training school at Santa Sabina in Rome, where he began to compose the *Summa Theologica* as a manual for students. He was called back to Paris in 1268, but in 1272 he returned to Italy to found his own school in Naples. There he had an ecstatic vision, which caused him to cease writing, leaving the *Summa* unfinished at the time of his death in 1274.

Key work

1265–74 *Summa Theologica* (*Theological Treatise*)

THE MERCHANT'S COMPANION

THE *LEX MERCATORIA* (13TH–15TH CENTURY)

IN CONTEXT

FOCUS
**International
commercial law**

BEFORE
c. **700 CE** Rhodian Sea Law
combines various existing
laws and customs to form
a body of maritime law.

c. **1010** The *Tavole Amalfitane*
is the first body of maritime
law to be recognized
throughout much of the
Mediterranean.

AFTER
1622 English merchant and
free trade advocate Gerard de
Malynes' *Consuetudo vel Lex
Mercatoria* is a clear exposition
of merchant law.

1940 UNIDROIT is set up,
providing an arbitration forum
for private commercial cases
and beginning a new era for
the *Lex Mercatoria*.

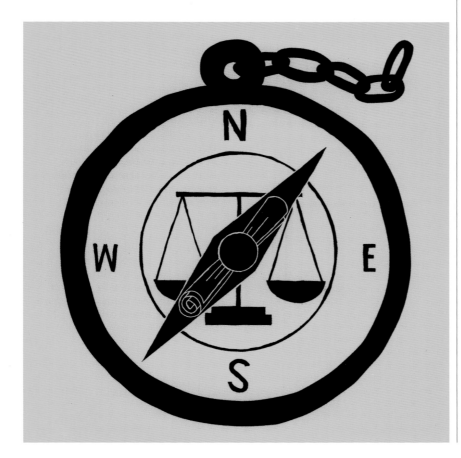

The problem of which law
should regulate merchants
who trade internationally
is as old as commerce itself. Greek,
Phoenician, and Roman traders
all developed systems of what
was essentially private law – not
regulated by the state – to resolve
disputes and enhance confidence
in trading networks that relied
on trust.

The Romans in particular
developed a means to regulate
dealings between Roman citizens
and those who were not subjects
of the empire. This *jus gentium*
("law of people") had its origins in
the 3rd century BCE and became
redundant after the collapse of the

See also: The *Lex Rhodia* 25 ▪ Blackstone's *Commentaries* 109 ▪ The United Nations and International Court of Justice 212–19 ▪ The World Trade Organization 278–83

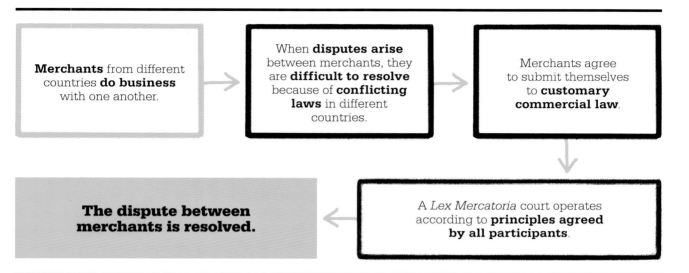

Merchants from different countries **do business** with one another.

When **disputes arise** between merchants, they are **difficult to resolve** because of **conflicting laws** in different countries.

Merchants agree to submit themselves to **customary commercial law**.

A *Lex Mercatoria* court operates according to **principles agreed by all participants**.

The dispute between merchants is resolved.

empire in the 5th century CE, with its dissolution into a series of barbarian successor states, each with its own territorial laws. From the 9th century onwards, however, there was economic growth in parts of northern Europe and commerce revived as a result. Trading centres such as Dorestad, in the Netherlands, flourished. To the south, Arab pirates had made Mediterranean trade dangerous but after their bases were captured in the 11th century, maritime trading republics such as Amalfi, Pisa, Genoa, and Venice, in Italy, helped to boost commerce.

With the increase in trade came an increase in disputes. Merchants who disputed the quality of the goods they had received from foreign traders – or who were trying to recover the value of goods lost at sea by a careless carrier – had little recourse to the regular legal systems. International treaties between states may have covered the treatment of merchants in general, but they did little to help in particular cases. Law courts –

where they existed – tended to be slow, bureaucratic, and inflexible. The solution was an early form of self-regulation – a customary law that was developed among merchants over several centuries, known by the 13th century as the *Lex Mercatoria* (Mercantile Law, or Law of Merchants).

Voluntary acceptance
The *Lex Mercatoria* was followed voluntarily by the mercantile community, with no state mandate, although individual nations did also pass laws affecting commerce.

Extensive maritime networks carried much of Europe's high-value trade, so it is not surprising that maritime law emerged as the forerunner of fully developed mercantile laws. As early as the 8th or 9th century, codes such as Rhodian Sea Law (which was introduced by the Byzantine Empire across the Mediterranean) had gathered together customary maritime rules. The growth of trading cities in Italy accelerated the process. Some laws gained widespread acceptance, such as the 11th-century *Tavole Amalfitane* (Amalfi Tables), whose 66 articles were observed across the western Mediterranean. Italian city-states such as Genoa and Venice had their own maritime trading laws, introduced in 1186 and 1258, respectively. The first such code in northwest Europe was the »

The Hanseatic League, whose seal is shown here, regulated maritime trade throughout much of northern Europe. Established in 1356, it maintained its role until the 17th century.

Rôles d'Oléron (Law of Oleron), which was adopted near La Rochelle, France, in 1160, and was later more widely accepted.

By the early 13th century, northern European ports such as Hamburg had codes to combat piracy. The Hanseatic League was a trading organization formally established in 1356 as an umbrella under whose protection merchants from many towns around the Baltic Sea and further afield could trade.

These codes soon came to have sections dealing with matters not purely to do with trading at sea, such as the repayment of debts and the freedom of foreign merchants from *aubaine*, the right of rulers to seize the property of foreigners when they died. The rise of great trading fairs – such as those in Leipzig and Frankfurt, in Germany, or Troyes and Lagny, in France – in the 11th–13th centuries increased the need for regulations to determine relations between merchants from different states. This was especially relevant since these fairs often fell under the direct jurisdiction of a local lord, and outside the protection of royal laws. Merchants needed more confidence that their rights (and their goods) would be protected.

In England, as elsewhere, the *Lex Mercatoria* was recognized as an expedient way of resolving disputes and encouraging foreign trade. In 1303, King Edward I issued the *Carta Mercatoria* (*Merchant Charter*), which granted foreign merchants freedom to trade, exempted them from certain regulations, and enjoined officials "to do speedy justice … according

> And this Law of Merchants … ought in regard of commerce to be esteemed … as the Law of the Twelve Tables.
> **Gerard de Malynes**
> *Consuetudo vel Lex Mercatoria*
> (*The Custom or Law Merchant*), 1622

to the Law Merchant". Cases involving foreign traders were heard in the Court of King's Bench, not by the regular crown-appointed judiciary but by expert assessors or jurors. These were chosen by the parties themselves and judged cases according to the *Lex Mercatoria*, rather than the laws of England.

Merchant courts

Throughout Europe, the merchant courts that emerged to administer the *Lex Mercatoria* included the Civil Rota in Genoa, the Curia Maris in Pisa, and the Consolat del Mar in Barcelona. Officials with specialist knowledge of trading customs and norms administered these courts, starting with the Sea Consuls of Genoa in 1206. This system assured merchants that disputes could be resolved satisfactorily and swiftly. In turn, this assurance fostered the use

A depiction of 14th-century Venice shows it to be a bustling city with boats in the harbour and merchants on the quay. It was one of the first ports to have its own maritime trading laws.

of financial instruments such as promissory notes for payment, which the merchants could now trust would be honoured, or if necessary enforced, by the courts.

As voluntary bodies, the merchant courts had more in common with modern arbitration rather than formal judicial courts. However, their very flexibility and the lack of uniformity in the rulings they made raised troubling issues. They operated under few general legal principles and even those principles that seemed to be universal, such as that of "earnest" (a part-payment made to seal a contract), were subject to variance.

Since merchants could petition for cases to be considered under whichever legal system they chose, this could lead to further disputes between parties. There were cases where Antwerp merchants trading with merchants in London refused to submit to the law of London, while the authorities in Ypres insisted that any merchants trading there did so under the law of Ypres. National governments were also concerned

Spain's *Book of the Consulate of the Sea* is a collection of maritime customs that contributed to the development of the *Lex Mercatoria* in the Middle Ages. This edition was printed in 1523.

The new *Lex Mercatoria*

An intensification of trade and the proliferation of independent legal jurisdictions fuelled by 20th-century decolonization brought a growing awareness of the need to ensure international commerce was not strangled by legal impediments.

In 1940, UNIDROIT, the International Institute for the Unification of Private Law, was set up to harmonize private commercial law and establish generally agreed principles for international contracts. Similar to the original *Lex Mercatoria*, its guidelines are not mandatory and only apply where parties opt to follow them. The rise of other international organizations such as the United Nations has led to a parallel growth in mechanisms to resolve legal conflicts. These include UNCITRAL, the UN Commission on International Trade Law, whose Vienna Convention (1988) seeks to remove legal barriers to world trade by setting in place mutually accepted rules on, for example, breach of contract.

that foreign merchants were able to gain undue advantage by appealing to judgement under the *Lex Mercatoria*. The English Parliament sought to subsume it under the common law. As early as 1353, King Edward III established staple ports in England, Wales, and Ireland, where specific goods (or "staples") could be traded. These ports had their own courts, administered by the Crown, to rule on commercial disputes. Even so, a court chaired by Bishop Robert Stillington in 1473 could still assert that foreign merchants should be judged according to the *Lex Mercatoria*. That position gradually began to shift in the 17th century, when champions of common law such as jurist Edward Coke fought for its supremacy.

By the 1760s, Lord Chief Justice William Murray, Earl of Mansfield, declared that there was no such separate body of law as the *Lex Mercatoria*. The 1809 edition of jurist William Blackstone's *Commentaries on the Laws of England* reinforced the view that merchant practices were covered by the law of the land and that the *Lex Mercatoria* no longer had force.

State law takes over
Across Europe, as national judiciaries and legislatures grew stronger, they no longer tolerated the existence of competing types of law within their jurisdictions. Commercial law codes enacted by individual states took the place of the *Lex Mercatoria* – among them the French *Code de Commerce* in 1807 and the German *Allgemeines Deutsches Handelsgesetzbuch* in 1861. And yet, although the *Lex Mercatoria* seemed moribund, it was not entirely dead.

During the 20th century, when the volume of international trade soared, there was a new wave of private commercial law for dealings between private individuals that do not involve the state (see box, above). Born over a millennium ago, as Europe rebuilt itself after the fall of Rome, the *Lex Mercatoria* still remains relevant in the field of international trade. ∎

EMPIRE ENLIGHT

1470–1800

AND
ENMENT

The Venetian Patent Statute establishes the **first codified patent system** in the world.

1474

The English and Welsh Poor Law Act provides **support for the "settled" poor** through parishes and local taxation.

1601

Astronomer Galileo Galilei is **tried for heresy** by the Catholic Church for saying that Earth is not the static centre of the Universe.

1633

During the English Civil War, Parliament establishes the High Court of Justice to **try King Charles I for treason**.

1649

1494

After Columbus returns from the New World, Spain and Portugal sign the Treaty of Tordesillas, **dividing ownership of the world** between them.

1625

In *De Jure Belli ac Pacis* (*On the Law of War and Peace*), Hugo Grotius champions **diplomacy in international law**.

1648

The Peace of Westphalia establishes the **principle of national sovereignty** and reinforces the principle of **diplomatic means** to secure peace.

17TH CENTURY

Slave codes in the Caribbean and North America classify slaves as the **property of their owners**.

At the end of the 15th century, enormous cultural and political changes started to take effect in Europe, ushering in the age known as the Renaissance. Nation states began to assert their independence and found prosperity through trade and empire-building. The Catholic Church's authority was challenged as these changes shifted the emphasis from religion to natural laws inherent in humans.

One of the major mercantile powers to emerge was the Republic of Venice, which introduced commercial laws, such as the Patent Statute, to protect the interests of its traders. Spain and Portugal were the most ambitious powers, seeking routes across the Atlantic to Asian markets as an alternative to the overland Silk Road. After Christopher Columbus stumbled across the Americas on his voyages of discovery, the two Iberian states negotiated a deal, the Treaty of Tordesillas, in which they effectively divided the world into two hemispheres, awarding Spain the lands to the west, and Portugal those to the east. These claims were indicative of the prevalent attitude that the world was there to be "discovered" – and conquered and exploited – by the new European trading nations. The Protestant Reformation of the 16th century was a further challenge to the authority of the Church.

International order

Trading and territorial disputes led to battles between the countries vying for dominance, and in the 17th century steps were taken to establish an international rule of law. In 1625, Dutch scholar Hugo Grotius wrote the treatise *On the Law of War and Peace*, which championed human reasoning and cooperation in international affairs. This was then played out in 1648 in the Peace of Westphalia, which brought an end to the Thirty Years' War and established a precedent for diplomatic negotiations to protect national sovereignty. A century later, the basis for truly international law was laid by Swiss diplomat Emmerich de Vattel in *The Law of Nations*.

The Americas, and parts of Africa and Asia, soon became colonies of European empires, providing seemingly endless resources. But it was not only goods that were being traded. To provide labour in the colonies

In the "Glorious Revolution", William of Orange and his wife, Mary, accept the English throne and accede to a **Bill of Rights**.

The principle of **authors' copyright** is enshrined in UK law in the Statute of Anne.

William Blackstone's *Commentaries on the Laws of England* lays out **English common law** in a comprehensive and accessible form.

In France, the Declaration of the Rights of Man and of the Citizen sets down the principle that **all people are equal under the law**.

↑ **1688–89**   ↑ **1710**   ↑ **1765–69**   ↑ **1789**

1692   **1758**   **1787**   **1791**

↓ More than 200 people are **accused of witchcraft** and 19 condemned to death on spurious evidence at the Salem witch trials in Massachusetts.

↓ In *The Law of Nations*, Emmerich de Vattel lays the foundations for **countries to cooperate under international law**.

↓ Delegates meet in Philadelphia to frame the **Constitution of the United States**, ratified by all states by 1790.

↓ **Ten amendments**, collectively known as the **Bill of Rights**, are added to the US Constitution.

---

of the Americas, slaves were transported from Africa in their hundreds of thousands, a practice given legal justification in the West Indian and American slave codes, which treated slaves as "chattel" – the property of their owners.

Reason above faith

Europe's new prosperity fostered intellectual and scientific enquiry, leading, in the late 17th and 18th centuries, to the Enlightenment, or "Age of Reason". The Catholic Church still wielded considerable power, which it exercised in trying to quash "heretics" such as Galileo Galilei for their scientific theories. Its authority, however, was severely undermined, as was the notion of the divine right of kings and a monarch's authority over the people. Enlightenment theorists promoted rational thought over religious faith, and progress, liberty, and tolerance over the old political order's deference to Church and monarchy, instead advocating constitutional government to protect the rights of citizens.

The first signs of this movement appeared during the English Civil War (1642–51), with the trial and execution in 1649 of King Charles I and the subsequent establishment of the Commonwealth. In 1689, the introduction of a Bill of Rights as the English Parliament's condition for accepting the rule of King William and Queen Mary then confirmed the power of the law over the supremacy of the monarchy.

Inspired by the changes in the political order, English philosopher John Locke argued for a government that protects the liberty and rights of its citizens. This cause was readily taken up elsewhere, including in the American colonies, which were growing resentful of their British rulers and sought independence under a more democratic and fairer government.

When America declared its independence in 1776, it asserted the rights of all men to life, liberty, and the pursuit of happiness. This establishment of the concept of rights as central to the code of law, was then embodied in the 1787 Constitution of the United States of America. France similarly overthrew its oppressive rulers in 1789, to install a government by the people and for the people, with its ideals of *liberté*, *égalité*, and *fraternité* embodied in the Declaration of the Rights of Man and of the Citizen. ■

PROTECTION FOR ANY INGENIOUS DEVICE

THE VENETIAN PATENT STATUTE (1474)

IN CONTEXT

FOCUS
Patent law

BEFORE
500 BCE Chefs in Sybaris in Greece are said to have been granted a year's monopoly on dishes they have invented.

1421 The first known patent on an invention is issued to Filippo Brunelleschi in Florence.

1449 English king Henry VI issues John of Utynam a monopoly on stained glass manufacture.

AFTER
1624 The Statute of Monopolies, which allows patents to be granted for noteworthy inventions, becomes law in England.

1790 The US Patent Act gives inventors an exclusive patent for 14 years.

The Venetian Patent Statute of 1474 marks the true beginning of modern patent law (the law protecting new inventions). Established in the Republic of Venice, it was not the first example of patent protection, but it was the first to establish a comprehensive system that applied to all inventions.

In the early 15th century, the city-states of Renaissance Italy were thriving, and the different states vied to come up with new ideas in the arts, science, and technology. Inventions, after all, could earn money and status. But if ideas could be copied easily the instant they came off the

See also: The *Lex Mercatoria* 74–77 ▪ The Statute of Anne 106–07 ▪ The Federal Trade Commission 184–85
▪ The WIPO Copyright Treaty 286–87

The dome of Florence's cathedral was built without a central support. Its innovative design includes an inner and outer shell, with interlocking arches to prevent the dome from expanding.

a patent can be transferred both during the life of the patent-holder and after; and a patent is lost if it is not used within a certain time, or if the invention a patent refers to is proven not to be the first of its kind after all. Each of these criteria underpins modern patent law.

Ingenious contrivances

In colloquial language, the Venetian statute provided protection for "any new and ingenious device, not previously made". It declared confidently that Venice had the "most clever minds, capable of devising and inventing all manner of ingenious contrivances". It then asserted that these clever minds would only exert themselves to make things that would benefit the city if their ideas were protected. »

In Venice … they reward and cherish every man that brings in any new art or mystery whereby the people may be set to work.
Sir Thomas Smyth
Discourse on the Common Weal of this Realm of England, 1581

drawing board, these benefits would be lost – and there would be no incentive for inventors to spend their time and money developing ideas, let alone sharing them with others.

Patents for invention

As trading networks expanded across Europe and commercial and political rivalry between Italy's city-states grew, it became clear that inventors needed to be protected by recognizing their ownership of an idea. Ideas had to become property. Inventors had to be given an exclusive legal claim, so that others might not copy inventions without their permission. And so the idea of patents slowly emerged.

The first known patent was issued in Florence in 1421. The recipient was the architect Filippo Brunelleschi, famous for designing the dome of Florence's cathedral, although his patent was not for an architectural innovation but for a special barge to carry building materials to the cathedral via the

River Arno. Unfortunately, in 1427, Brunelleschi's craft sank on its first voyage. The idea of patents was abandoned for a while in Florence, but guilds of craftsmen and artists wielded considerable power at the time, and members' "ownership" of their own ideas and innovations was protected by the private rules of these guilds.

The Venetian Patent Statute

It was in Venice that the idea of legal patents really emerged. The city first began issuing one-off individual patents, similar to the one awarded to Brunelleschi in Florence. Then, on 19 March 1474, Venice's governing Senate issued the first general patent law. This landmark statute established a system that would protect inventors by the free registration of patents.

The Venetian system had most of the features associated with patents today: an invention must in some way be useful; the term of a patent is limited to a fixed number of years; the right to use

Monopolies have too much power over the market and damage trade, but **inventors** need some way of **protecting their intellectual property**.

Monopolies should be banned, and **useful inventions** should be granted **exclusive rights for a limited time**.

This will motivate **clever minds** to create more **new and ingenious inventions**.

And so the statute provided that any creator whose invention was turned into a practical device should have the sole right over that invention for up to 10 years. Anyone who made an illegal copy would be compelled to destroy it and pay a fine of 100 ducats. This would be about $15,000 in today's terms, so the statute was clearly meant to be taken seriously.

With this legislation, Venice became the first state to develop a continuous and consistent system for the protection of inventions. For the first time, there was a proper legal framework of intellectual property rights. In other words, knowledge could be "owned", giving people an incentive to develop the skills and techniques to invent – confident that if their work was successful, their right to earn money from it would be guaranteed.

This argument is at the heart of capitalist thinking. It assumes that without the potential rewards of financial gain, people will not bother to create or invent. The strategy clearly worked in Venice: by the end of the 15th century, the city's commercial prominence was unmatched in Europe. It had become a centre for technological development and stood at the hub of a trading empire stretching across the Mediterranean Sea and as far as India and Central Asia. When French writer and diplomat Phillipe de Commynes visited Venice in 1495, he declared it to be "the most triumphant city I have ever seen".

Venice in demand
If the number of patents granted is anything to go by, the Venetian statute was a great success. In the period 1474–1600, 621 patents were awarded, an average of five each year. Another 605 were granted in the following century.

Venetian products were very much in demand, and as Venetian merchants and artisans moved

The Barovier Cup was created as a wedding gift in about 1470 by master glassworker Angelo Barovier, who first discovered how to produce the clear glass that made Murano famous.

away from the city and settled elsewhere in Europe, they took the idea of patents with them, keen to protect their products from being copied, which would dilute their brand and profits. In 1551, for example, a Venetian glassmaker called Theseo Mutio was the recipient of the first patent awarded in France, for making glass "according to the manner of Venice". Venetian glassware (produced on the island of Murano) was hugely popular, and Venetian glassmakers in Antwerp and Germany were also awarded early patents. In 1565, Italian engineer Jacopo Aconcio was awarded the first patent to be granted for innovation in England – for machines powered by water wheels (see box, top right).

Exclusive rights
In England, the idea of patents on inventions was extended to include exclusive rights to sell particular products or skills – in other words, monopolies. As early as the 14th century, licences called "letters of protection" had been granted to foreign craftsmen and inventors to encourage them to come to England. In 1331, John Kempe, a Flemish weaver, had been a beneficiary, and in 1449,

King Henry VI granted a 20-year monopoly on the making of stained glass to John of Utynam, who had been invited to England from his native Flanders to make stained glass windows for Eton College.

Ninety years later, King Henry VIII's secretary Thomas Cromwell granted a 20-year monopoly on growing silk to Venetian silk merchant Antonio Guidotti in an attempt to persuade Venetian silk-makers to come to England. The practice of granting monopolies had became popular with English monarchs because they could charge heavily for the privilege. Consequently, more and more industries came into the realm of exclusive rights, including even such basics as salt and starch.

By the end of the 16th century, the stranglehold of monopolies had become so extreme that they provoked bitter resentment. In 1601, the English Parliament forced Queen Elizabeth I to hand over the power to regulate monopolies and eliminate some of the most restrictive ones. A Committee of Grievances, led by senior judge and politician Sir Edward Coke, was set up to bring monopolies

The first English patent

The first patent granted in England was to Venetian engineer Jacopo Aconcio. Originally from northern Italy, Aconcio had moved to Strasbourg. There, he was recruited by Sir William Cecil, who was Queen Elizabeth I's secretary of state. Aconcio came to England in 1559 to bring Venetian engineering expertise to improve English fortifications at a time when Elizabeth's regime was very vulnerable. He went on to

review and redesign some of the fortifications at Berwick Castle, on the England–Scotland border.

Just a few months after his arrival, Aconcio applied for a patent for a variety of machines using water wheels, and for furnaces for dyers and brewers. In his patent application, he argued that, "those who by searching have found out things useful to the public should have some fruit of their rights and labours". Aconcio's patent was granted in 1565.

under control. And yet Elizabeth's successor James I continued to issue patents that established monopolies.

As anger rose, James I promised to abolish the three worst monopolies, but Parliament had had enough. In 1621, Coke introduced a Statute of Monopolies, which became law three years later, in a trail-blazing assertion of business interests in opposition to the absolute power of an English monarch.

The Statute of Monopolies

Coke's Act made all past, present, and future patents and monopolies in England null and void. It also ordered that patents could not be used by the Crown for farming out the administration of justice and criminal law to private individuals and companies – asserting that only Parliament could do this.

There was one key exception to the voiding of all patents. This section preserved, crucially, the patent on original inventions. But

the exclusion lasted only 14 years, so inventors could be granted a patent giving them exclusive rights for 14 years if they were "the true and first inventor". Patents could also be granted for any entirely new method of manufacture. Although it was more than a century before the courts developed a coherent way of implementing patent law, the Statute of Monopolies was a landmark in England's evolution from a feudal to a capitalist economy. And its provisions – doubtless influenced by the Venetian Patent Statute – have shaped patent laws ever since. ∎

The King himself should be under no man but under God and the Law.
Sir Edward Coke
Institutes of the Lawes of England, 1628–44

English barrister, judge, and politician Sir Edward Coke's Statute of Monopolies, which only permitted patents to be granted for truly new inventions, became law in 1624.

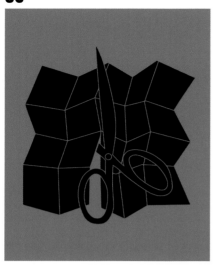

A BOUNDARY FROM POLE TO POLE
THE TREATY OF TORDESILLAS (1494)

IN CONTEXT

FOCUS
International law

BEFORE
2100 BCE The Mesopotamian city-states of Lagash and Umma mark a boundary between them on a stone slab.

387 CE The Peace of Acilisene divides Armenia between the Sassanian Persian and Eastern Roman (Byzantine) empires.

1266 The Treaty of Perth divides jurisdiction over the Northern Isles between Norway and Scotland.

AFTER
1739 By the Treaty of El Pardo, Spain and Britain resolve their dispute about American navigation and trade.

1750 The Treaty of Madrid redraws the boundaries of the Spanish and the Portuguese colonies in South America.

1885 At the Berlin Conference, European leaders divide Africa among themselves.

Portugal and Spain both claim to have **discovered**, and therefore to **own**, new **territories**.

⬇

To **avoid a costly war** between these two rival Catholic empires, Pope Alexander VI is asked to **arbitrate**.

⬇

The Treaty of Tordesillas **divides the world** into Spanish and Portuguese sectors.

When explorer Christopher Columbus landed in Lisbon, Portugal, on his return from the New World in 1492, he unleashed a centuries-long diplomatic row between Spain and Portugal, the world's first great colonial powers. Columbus had been sent on his voyage by the joint rulers of Spain, Ferdinand II of Aragon and Isabella I of Castile, but it was the Portuguese king, John II, who was first to hear of the historic discovery.

No European powers at the time considered it relevant that all the regions they "discovered" were already long known and inhabited by Indigenous Peoples. For the new arrivals, "discovery" meant ownership. Portugal, by virtue of its pioneering voyages – its navigators had already explored the coasts of West Africa and India – assumed for itself a natural right to claim "undiscovered" territories. Columbus's announcement to King

See also: The Domesday Book 58–59 ▪ The *Lex Mercatoria* 74–77 ▪ The Peace of Westphalia 94–95 ▪ Vattel's *The Law of Nations* 108 ▪ The Treaty of Versailles 192–93 ▪ The Helsinki Treaty 242–43

Christopher Columbus lands in the West Indies, on an island he named San Salvador. Believing they had reached east Asia, Columbus and his crew dubbed the locals "Indians".

John II that he had discovered a New World on behalf of the king's Spanish rivals was a bombshell.

John sent a threatening letter to King Ferdinand and Queen Isabella, claiming that under the 1479 Treaty of Alcáçovas and the 1481 papal bull (a sacred decree with the force of law) all lands south of the Canary Islands – and therefore all the lands discovered by Columbus – belonged to Portugal. John also announced that he would despatch a fleet to make good the Portuguese claim.

The papal bull
Aware of Portugal's naval might, Ferdinand and Isabella appealed to the Pope, Alexander VI, knowing they would get a sympathetic hearing since Alexander was a fellow Spaniard. He responded with what now seems a breathtaking statement of European self-belief, issuing a papal bull that divided the entire world, by this time known to be round, into two halves. The line ran from pole to pole, north to south through the Atlantic Ocean, 100 leagues (about 550 km / 345 miles) west of the Azores and Cape Verde, and crossed through what is now the easternmost tip of Brazil. All land to the west of the line not already ruled by a Christian monarch would henceforth belong to Spain and everything to the east would belong to Portugal.

The Pope's solution inflamed tensions, as each country sought to move the boundary line further east or west. Finally, in 1494, diplomats from Spain and Portugal met in the Spanish town of Tordesillas and came up with a deal – the Treaty of Tordesillas. This upheld the division of the world in half, but Portuguese naval prowess meant the boundary was pushed west by 270 leagues.

The treaty's new line was drawn at approximately 46°30'W by modern calculations. At that time, no one had any way of calculating longitude accurately, so it was inevitable that there would be disputes. And while dividing the world in half north–south down the Atlantic, it did not specify whether the line continued around the world to divide the Pacific as well.

South America divided
Despite its huge shortcomings, the treaty proved surprisingly effective. It left Portugal in control of the route around Africa to India until it was supplanted later by the British. It also gave Portugal control of Brazil, when six years later Pedro Álvares Cabral landed there while sailing south through the Atlantic en route to India. Some historians maintain that, at the time of Tordesillas, the Portuguese already knew of this huge eastward bulge of South America and kept quiet about it. Whatever the truth, its legacy was to give Portugal the riches of Brazil, while Spain exerted its influence over the whole of the rest of South and Central America, dominating what is now called Latin America. ▪

This boundary ... shall be drawn ... at a distance of three hundred and seventy leagues west of the Cape Verde Islands.
Treaty of Tordesillas

ALL GOVERNORS SHALL KEEP EVERY POOR PERSON

THE POOR LAWS (1535, 1601)

IN CONTEXT

FOCUS
Social welfare

BEFORE
1351 The English Parliament's Statute of Labourers requires that everyone able to work must do so.

1388 The Statute of Cambridge differentiates between "sturdy" and "impotent" beggars.

1494 The Vagabonds and Beggars Act states that "vagabonds, idle, and suspected persons" should be punished.

AFTER
1662 The Act of Settlement allows for the exclusion of outsiders from a parish.

1696–98 In Bristol, the Corporation of the Poor opens England's first two workhouses.

1834 The Poor Law Amendment Act introduces purpose-built workhouses, run by "unions" of parishes.

1948 The National Assistance Act abolishes the old Poor Law and ensures relief to all aged over 16 and "without resource".

The 1601 English and Welsh Poor Law Act was one of the first attempts in the world to establish a national legal framework to deal with poverty. Building on various laws that had been enacted since the mid-14th century, it established the precedent that there must be laws for tackling the personal and wider economic outcomes of poverty, and that the fate of paupers could not be left to chance and charity.

See also: Aristotle and natural law 32–33 ▪ The origins of canon law 42–47 ▪ Thomas Aquinas 72–73 ▪ The Workers' Accident Insurance System 164–67 ▪ The Universal Declaration of Human Rights 222–29

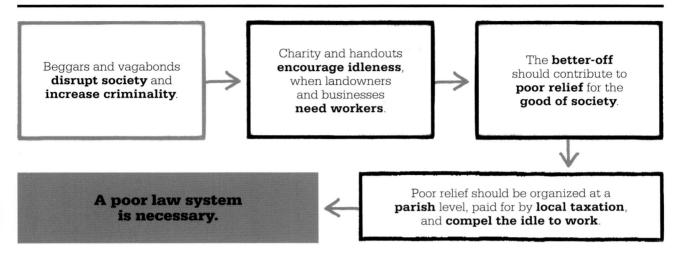

Beggars and vagabonds **disrupt society** and **increase criminality**.

→

Charity and handouts **encourage idleness**, when landowners and businesses **need workers**.

→

The **better-off** should contribute to **poor relief** for the **good of society**.

↓

Poor relief should be organized at a **parish** level, paid for by **local taxation**, and **compel the idle to work**.

←

A poor law system is necessary.

The Act did not establish a person's legal right to support in the face of hardship, but it did confirm that those who administer laws have a legal obligation to provide support, paid for through taxation. The idea of central responsibility for the poor became the legal root for the state welfare systems that grew from the late 19th century in Germany, the UK, and other countries.

A labour shortage
The pressure for poor laws dated back in part to the aftermath of the Black Death of 1348–50. The plague killed 30–40 per cent of people in England, leading to severe labour shortages. In 1351, the English Parliament passed the Statute of Labourers, which aimed to keep all able-bodied people in work and at pre-plague wage levels. Labourers, however, saw the demand for labour as a way to move where they wanted, and earn higher wages.

A 1349 manuscript shows the burial of Black Death victims. Sweeping in from Asia, the plague killed more than 20 million people in Europe.

In 1388, Parliament countered with the Statute of Cambridge, which restricted the movement of workers, including beggars deemed to be "sturdy", in order to keep them working cheaply for their overlords. In return, the statute imposed on local administrations, known as "hundreds", the responsibility for providing some basic relief for the "impotent poor", those deemed incapable of working. And so a two-pronged approach to poor relief emerged. On the one hand, poor laws aimed to support the needy; on the other, they were a cudgel to impel the poor into low-wage work.

Beggars and vagabonds
The "sturdy" – those considered fit for work – could not escape labour. Under the 1536 Act for Punishment of Sturdy Vagabonds and Beggars, anyone wandering far from their home parish without a job was considered a "vagabond" and »

Economic pressures in Tudor England

Grain prices more than tripled between 1490 and 1569, then increased by another 73 per cent between 1569 and 1609, making bread more expensive.

Agricultural and building labourers and skilled craftsmen saw their wages decline by about 60 per cent over the course of the 16th century.

Between 1536 and 1549, the dissolution of monasteries (and of guilds and hospitals run by religious orders) ended the traditional sources of charity and poor relief.

subject to harsh penalties, such as whipping, the severing of an ear, and eventual execution.

Further legislation in the 16th century added to the severity of punishment and forced vagabonds to take the first job on offer, however dreadful. Disabled beggars who refused to do work in their own homes were sent for punishment to a "house of correction".

Leaning on the parish

During the Tudor period (1485–1603) the population of England increased dramatically, which, together with rising prices and rock-bottom wages, left more and more people unable to support themselves. Also, Henry VIII's dissolution of the monasteries, whereby he stripped them of their wealth and property, meant that the poor could no longer fall back on the Church for charity. With the system close to collapse, the Poor Law Act was introduced in 1601 to

Economic pressures in the 16th century led to a growing number of beggars on Tudor streets. Punishments such as whipping and – for repeat offenders – hanging, became common.

provide a comprehensive framework for the legal provision of the poor. The law was primarily aimed at helping the "settled" poor – those who found themselves out of work through no fault of their own – and punishing beggars and vagabonds. It bought together all the previous poor law legislation into a single act.

Although the law applied to the whole of the Tudor kingdom, its provisions were applied locally rather than nationally, through 15,000 local parishes. Each parish had to levy a poor rate or tax from property owners to raise money to provide for the needy. Two unpaid parish "overseers" were elected annually to set the poor rate, collect it from property owners (fining those who did not pay), and then dispense money or food to those who needed it – or compel them to work. The law also placed a legal obligation on parents and children to look after each other. Elderly parents, for example, should be looked after by their children.

The law crystallized the idea that the whole of society suffers if the poor suffer. It became the norm to levy a universal tax to provide money to support the poor and vulnerable. The better-off no longer supported the poor out of charity alone. Instead, it was a legal obligation for everyone who could afford to pay the tax to do so.

Dividing up the poor

The 1601 Act established two kinds of relief – "outdoor" and "indoor". Outdoor relief was the most common and allowed poor

Bridewell Prison, depicted in 1720. At this time, it housed petty criminals and pauper apprentices as well as vagrants and others deemed to be the "idle" poor.

Bridewell Prison

The original "house of correction", Bridewell Prison in London started life as Bridewell Palace, one of the homes of Henry VIII. In 1553, Edward VI, Henry's son, gave the decaying palace to the City of London Corporation to be used as an orphanage and a place of "correction" for "disorderly" women – that is, prostitutes. By 1556, part of the site had become Bridewell Prison. After the 1601 Poor Law Act, it became the template for the idea of the "short, sharp shock" for those unwilling to work, or guilty of minor crimes. Bridewell combined prison, hospital, and workhouse, where inmates were forced to carry out hard labour. Regular punishments included public whippings twice a week.

Bridewell was the model for future houses of correction, which in turn were often referred to as a "Bridewell". The prison burned down in the 1666 Great Fire of London but was quickly rebuilt and remained in use until the 1860s.

people to stay in their homes. They were then given money, known as a "dole", or help in kind, such as clothes or food. Indoor relief compelled the homeless poor into almshouses (charity-run houses), orphanages, or houses of correction, where people would be set to work.

The poor who were "lame, impotent, old, blind", and therefore unable to work, were provided either with outdoor relief or a place in an almshouse or hospital. The able-bodied poor with no home might be sent to a "house of industry" – the prototype for the later workhouses – where they were provided with raw materials and made to work. Conditions in these places were deliberately kept harsh, in order, it was argued, to act as a deterrent to falling into poverty and relying on public support.

Vagabonds and the "idle" poor (those branded as unwilling to work) were sent to a house of correction, which was a much harsher option. Here, they were forced into hard labour, such as beating hemp plants to make rope.

The effectiveness of the Poor Law Act's provisions varied hugely from parish to parish. Some parishes were generous to the poor, while others were mean, and many tried to pass on their responsibility by shifting poor people to other parishes. The 1601 Act did, however, establish the precedent of providing a basic level of support for people in the direst poverty, and for more than two centuries this was the one safety net for those at the bottom of society.

Punishment of poverty

Despite the principle of charity at its core, the poor law system was a double-edged sword. It aimed to punish poverty as much as to support it, and to be harsh enough to prevent a reliance on poor relief.

The issue of poverty as a crime came to the fore as the Industrial Revolution began in Britain in the late 18th century and city populations grew. Industrialists needed workers for their factories, and labourers were required to work the land in order to feed the increasing numbers. Philosopher, jurist, and social reformer Jeremy Bentham was particularly insistent that poor relief should be framed to discipline and punish slackers. Meanwhile, political economist David Ricardo argued that any kind of poor relief undermined "the iron law of wages", in which wages were paid according to demand.

These ideas paved the way for a new Poor Law Act in 1834, which ended outdoor relief, replacing it with a system of workhouses, where tough conditions were imposed to act as a deterrent. The workhouse was the stuff of nightmares, as depicted so vividly by Charles Dickens in his novel *Oliver Twist*. It took more than 100 years of campaigning before workhouses were abolished and replaced with a modern welfare system in 1948. ∎

[The 1834 Poor Law Amendment Act] announces to the world that in England poverty is a crime.
Benjamin Disraeli
UK prime minister
(1868, 1874–80)

PEACE IS GLORIOUS AND ADVANTAGEOUS
GROTIUS'S *ON THE LAW OF WAR AND PEACE* (1625)

Dutch philosopher and jurist Hugo Grotius (1583–1645) has been credited as the "father of international law" due to his influential 1625 work, *De Jure Belli ac Pacis* (*On the Law of War and Peace*). Grotius was a proponent of the theory of natural law, which he saw as unalterable and universal. He believed that natural law derived from natural rights and human reason, and therefore could not be changed by God or organized religion.

Grotius applied these ideas to international relations, arguing that legal principles exist naturally and should underpin all dealings between nations. He believed that nations should have equal rights and sovereign status, and that states should be subject to the same laws as individuals. In his view, grievances between states should be resolved diplomatically, and war should be waged only if no other solution can be found. Grotius also developed a system of principles to govern international relations in times of war and peace.

Hugo Grotius's views were coloured by the bloodshed taking place during his lifetime, especially the Eighty Years' War and Thirty Years' War.

War had previously been seen as a legitimate political tactic, as popularized by Florentine politician Niccolò Machiavelli (1469–1527). Grotius argued that war is only acceptable if it is just – for instance, if a country faces an imminent threat and uses force that is proportionate to the threat. His insistence that diplomatic efforts should be made to avoid war laid the foundation for our modern notion of international law. ∎

See also: The Peace of Westphalia 94–95 ▪ Vattel's *The Law of Nations* 108 ▪ The Geneva Conventions 152–55 ▪ The Hague Conventions 174–77

THY GRAVE ERROR AND TRANSGRESSION
THE TRIAL OF GALILEO GALILEI (1633)

olish astronomer Nicolaus Copernicus published his book *On the Revolutions of the Heavenly Spheres* in 1543. He put forward the theory that Earth orbits the Sun (which became known as heliocentrism), contrary to the then-accepted view that the Sun rotates around a stationary Earth (geocentrism).

Heliocentrism challenged both the natural philosophy of Aristotle and the traditional ideas of the Catholic Church. Copernicus's theory was widely dismissed as far-fetched, but in 1616, respected Italian astronomer Galileo Galilei revived it. As a result, the Church banned him from teaching or defending heliocentric ideas. Galileo was warned not to espouse anything other than the accepted Church view that Earth was the centre of the Universe.

Heliocentric theory
Galileo continued his studies and in 1632 published *Dialogue on the Two Chief World Systems*, which once again discussed the heliocentric

theory. The Church brought Galileo before the Roman Inquisition in 1633. Galileo admitted no wrongdoing but accepted a plea bargain in which he agreed not to promote heliocentrism. He was found guilty of heresy, put under house arrest, and had his book banned. It was not until 1822 that the Catholic College of Cardinals accepted that the heliocentric theory could be true. In 1992, Galileo was finally cleared of heresy. ∎

The proposition that
the sun is immovable in the
centre of the world ... is
absurd, philosophically false,
and formally heretical ...
**Indictment against
Galileo Galilei, 1633**

See also: Aristotle and natural law 32–33 ▪ The origins of canon law 42–47
▪ Gratian's *Decretum* 60–63 ▪ The Salem witch trials 104–05

A TURNING POINT IN THE HISTORY OF NATIONS

THE PEACE OF WESTPHALIA (1648)

IN CONTEXT

FOCUS
International law

BEFORE
1555 The Peace of Augsburg allows each prince within the Holy Roman Empire to decree his state's religion.

1568 The 17 provinces of the Low Countries rebel against Philip II of Spain, beginning the Eighty Years' War.

1618 The Thirty Years' War erupts, between Protestant and Catholic states within the Holy Roman Empire.

AFTER
1919 The Treaty of Versailles officially ends World War I and creates many new nation states from the territory of former empires, including Habsburg Austria-Hungary.

1920 The League of Nations (the precursor of the United Nations, or UN) is established.

By the mid-17th century, the Holy Roman Empire (made up of territories in central and western Europe and at this time ruled by the Habsburg dynasty) had been plagued by conflict for decades, resulting in famine and instability throughout the region.

The Thirty Years' War (1618–48) began when Holy Roman Emperor Ferdinand II attempted to enforce

At the Battle of Lützen in Saxony in 1632, the Protestant king of Sweden, Gustavus II Adolfus, was killed fighting the forces of Ferdinand II. Eight million people died in the Thirty Years' War.

religious uniformity on the empire by suppressing Protestantism and promoting Catholicism. Many Protestant states rebelled, forming the Protestant Union and setting up a rival emperor, Frederick V.

This religious war morphed into a conflict of dynastic ambitions, which pitted the Habsburgs of the Holy Roman Empire against ascendant Bourbon France and the growing military might of Sweden. Meanwhile the Eighty Years' War (1568–1648) between Spain (also ruled by the Habsburgs) and the provinces of the Low Countries, which sought independence,

See also: Grotius's *On the Law of War and Peace* 92 ▪ Vattel's *The Law of Nations* 108 ▪ The US Constitution and Bill of Rights 110–17 ▪ The Hague Conventions 174–77 ▪ The United Nations and International Court of Justice 212–19

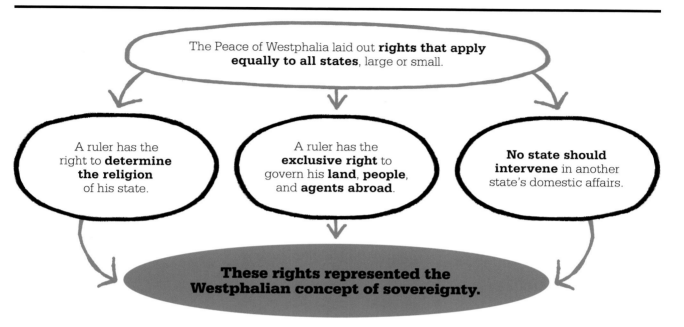

The Peace of Westphalia laid out **rights that apply equally to all states**, large or small.

A ruler has the right to **determine the religion** of his state.

A ruler has the **exclusive right** to govern his **land, people,** and **agents abroad**.

No state should intervene in another state's domestic affairs.

These rights represented the Westphalian concept of sovereignty.

rumbled on. The two conflicts were hugely disruptive to the whole region and, by the mid-17th century, all parties were ready to seek peace.

Negotiating peace
After 194 states took part in lengthy negotiations from 1644 to 1648, two treaties, together known as the Peace of Westphalia, were signed in the cities of Osnabrück and Münster. All states agreed to uphold the 1555 Peace of Augsburg principle of *cuius regio, eius religio* ("whose state, his religion"), whereby a ruler could decide the religion of his own state or principality. The Peace of Westphalia extended this right, so that most subjects who did not follow the state religion had the right to practise their own faith.

Crucially, the treaties laid out the concept of exclusive sovereignty of each state over its own lands, people, and agents aboard. They redrew the map of Europe, granting

sovereignty to around 300 German principalities, and recognizing the independence of Switzerland from Austria and the Dutch Republic (made up of seven northern Low-Countries provinces) from Spain.

The Westphalian legacy
International law has its roots in the principle of Westphalian sovereignty, which outlines that each state has sovereignty over its own lands and that other states should not interfere in another country's domestic affairs. (Even so, some historians argue that while the principle grew from the Peace of Westphalia, it was not overtly described in the treaties themselves.) The notion that all states, no matter what their size, are equal under international law also stems from the Peace.

The Westphalian concept of sovereignty developed further in the 18th and 19th centuries, becoming

a key tenet of international relations. The modern international system, enshrined in the UN Charter (1945), requires that no state interfere in another's domestic affairs. Recent globalization has seen a decline in sovereignty's status and some now argue for intervention in state affairs to avert humanitarian crises. ▪

The first attempt to institutionalize an international order ... on a multiplicity of powers ...
Henry Kissinger
American diplomat (1923–)
on the Peace of Westphalia

TYRANT, TRAITOR, MURDERER

THE TRIAL OF CHARLES I (1649)

IN CONTEXT

FOCUS
Parliamentary authority

BEFORE
1215 Magna Carta lays out the rights and liberties of English subjects.

1236 The term "parliament" is first used by the Crown, in reference to King Henry III's council of advisers.

1628 The Petition of Right reasserts the rights laid out in Magna Carta.

AFTER
1660 The monarchy is restored when Charles II returns from exile in France.

1689 The Bill of Rights circumscribes the powers of the monarch and defines the rights of the English Parliament.

1792 King Louis XVI of France is tried by the French National Convention on charges of tyranny, and is executed the following year.

Charles I rules as an **absolute monarch** based on the **divine right of kings**.

→

Parliament argues for **a greater say** in government.

↓

The Civil War sees the **Parliamentarians defeat the Royalists**.

←

Parliament declares itself the **supreme power** and puts Charles on trial.

↓

The High Court of Justice **finds the king guilty of treason** for waging war on his own people.

The trial of King Charles I was unprecedented in English (and European) history as the first time a monarch faced trial for treason. Charles I subscribed to the traditional doctrine of the divine right of kings, believing that the monarch was chosen by God and was therefore subject to no earthly authority (such as Parliament). He also argued that his power should be absolute and that only he should be allowed to pass laws. This position put him at odds with Parliament, which at that time was convened or dissolved as the king saw fit, but had for many years pushed for greater influence. In 1641, when, against the wishes of Parliament, Charles raised an army to deal with a rebellion in Ireland, it was seen as an affront to Parliament's power. Events came

See also: The Assize of Clarendon 64–65 ▪ Magna Carta 66–71 ▪ The Glorious Revolution and the English Bill of Rights 102–03 ▪ The Declaration of the Rights of Man 118–19 ▪ The Universal Declaration of Human Rights 222–29

This portrait of Charles I is by Flemish artist Anthony Van Dyck, who became principal painter to the king in 1632. Charles was passionate about art, and commissioned many royal portraits.

to a head on 3 January 1642, when Charles attempted to arrest five Members of Parliament, and the Speaker of the House defied him.

Civil wars and trial

A series of three civil wars from 1642 to 1651 ended in triumph for the Parliamentarians under Oliver Cromwell, albeit at a cost of 200,000 lives. Charles was placed under arrest in 1646, and in 1648 Parliament was purged of any members opposed to putting the king on trial, resulting in what became known as the Rump Parliament. Supported by Cromwell's New Model Army (a reformed army with improved military resources), the Rump declared itself the supreme power, with authority to pass laws without the backing of the monarch or the House of Lords.

One of the Rump's first acts was to pass an ordinance on 1 January 1649 setting up a High Court of Justice to try Charles on charges of waging war on Parliament and against his own people. There was no precedent in English law to try a king, and so Dutch lawyer Isaac

Dorislaus, who wrote the indictment, based it on an ancient Roman law that a military body (or government) had the right to overthrow a tyrant.

The trial began on 20 January 1649, but without the full support of the judiciary – of the 135 men nominated to sit in judgement, only 68 attended. Charles repeatedly refused to accept the validity of the court, arguing that a parliament that had been purged of opposition could not claim to represent the people. On 27 January, he was found guilty of being a tyrant, a traitor, a murderer, and an enemy to England, and was sentenced to death. He was publicly executed at Whitehall, London, on 30 January.

Monarchy restored

The execution of Charles I allowed Oliver Cromwell to take power as Lord Protector – serving as both

I do stand more for the liberty of my people, than any here that come to be my pretended judges.
Charles I

head of state and the head of the government from 1653 to 1658. However, the new regime did not bring political stability, as Cromwell clashed with his parliament and was heavily reliant on the army for support, and public disaffection grew. When Cromwell died in 1658, his son, Richard, succeeded him as Lord Protector, but soon resigned. In 1660, Charles II was restored to power. Those who had committed regicide by signing Charles I's death warrant were put to death. ▪

The Petition of Right

The difficult relationship between Charles I and his parliament is exemplified by the 1628 Petition of Right issued by Parliament. This stemmed from the "forced loan" that Charles had pushed through after Parliament refused his request to grant a tax to fund war with Spain. The forced loan meant Charles's subjects were compelled to "gift" the Crown money or face imprisonment. Parliament saw this as going against Magna Carta, and so drafted the Petition of Right to reassert the rule of law and to confirm the rights of free men and Parliament. The format of the petition was crucial, in that it reasserted existing rights as opposed to creating new ones.

Charles reluctantly agreed to the petition, recognizing that he needed Parliament's support to raise any further taxes. He went on to ignore it in principle – but the fact that the Crown had accepted the petition gave it the same constitutional importance as Magna Carta itself.

ALL SLAVES SHALL BE HELD TO BE REAL ESTATE

SLAVE CODES (1661–18TH CENTURY)

IN CONTEXT

FOCUS
Law codes, slavery

BEFORE
1619 The first African slaves are landed in North America, in the colony of Virginia.

AFTER
1865 Slavery ends in the United States but is replaced with the "black codes".

1954 The US Supreme Court declares that school segregation on racial grounds is unconstitutional.

2000 Alabama is the last American state to lift the ban on interracial marriage.

2013 The US Supreme Court overturns the last remaining restrictions on African American voting rights.

A year before the *Mayflower* carried 102 colonists from England to New England in 1620, a Dutch ship, the *White Lion*, landed further south at Point Comfort, Virginia. On board were 20 African slaves, the first to arrive in North America. By the end of the century, more than 20,000 slaves had been imported, and by the time of the US Declaration of Independence in 1776 the slave population was nearly half a million.

Many Europeans had come to America to find freedom and make a new start. Others were there to exploit the profits to be made from growing crops such as tobacco, rice, and indigo. The harvesting and processing of these crops required labour on a large scale,

See also: The US Constitution and Bill of Rights 110–17 ▪ The Declaration of the Rights of Man 118–19 ▪ The Abolition of the Slave Trade Act 132–39 ▪ The Universal Declaration of Human Rights 222–29 ▪ The Civil Rights Act 248–53

Slaves in the US in 1790

The US held its first national census in 1790. The population was counted in all 13 states, plus the districts of Kentucky, Maine, and Vermont. "Slaves" were listed separately from "free white males" and "free white females". No slaves were counted in Massachusetts or Maine, which had unofficially abolished slavery. By 1840, the slave population had tripled.

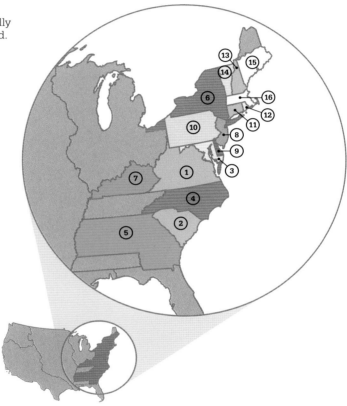

State/district	Slaves	Slaves as % of state population
1. Virginia	292,627	39%
2. South Carolina	107,094	43%
3. Maryland	103,036	32%
4. North Carolina	100,572	26%
5. Georgia	29,264	35%
6. New York	21,324	6%
7. Kentucky	12,430	17%
8. New Jersey	11,423	6%
9. Delaware	8,887	15%
10. Pennsylvania	3,737	<1%
11. Connecticut	2,764	1%
12. Rhode Island	948	1%
13. New Hampshire	158	<1%
14. Vermont	16	<1%
15. Maine	0	0%
16. Massachusetts	0	0%

Total US population	**3,893,635**
Slave population in US	**695,280**
Percentage of slaves in US	**18%**

which could not be provided by the settlers or the Indigenous population. African slaves had already proved their worth in the South American and West Indian colonies of the Spanish, Dutch, Portuguese, and English, so it followed that they would provide the necessary labour for the new plantations of North America.

In the 17th and 18th centuries, slaves were imported across the southern and eastern North American seaboard, with most shipped to the South, where they were set to work on plantations. Once the invention of the cotton gin in 1793 transformed the speed with which cotton seeds could be separated from fibres, slaves were tied to the cotton plantations that spread across all Southern states.

Master and slave

Despite enduring backbreaking work and poor conditions, slaves rarely rebelled. The prospect of rebellion, however, terrified the slaves' masters, and as slave numbers grew, so the American colonies set up policing rules, or codes, to keep slaves under control. Virginia, the largest slave-owning colony, introduced its first slave statute in 1639, declaring that, "All persons except Negroes are to be provided with arms and ammunitions or be fined."

In 1661, the English colony of Barbados in the Caribbean went further. Here, newly planted sugar estates were proving highly » profitable and owners were taking on ever more slaves to work them. The colony passed "an act for the better ordering and governing of Negroes", which for the first time enshrined in law the subjugation of plantation slaves to the will of their masters. Other Caribbean colonies, such as Jamaica and Antigua, and all Southern American colonies followed suit, establishing their own official slave codes. Virginia took the lead by following the Barbados model and in turn influenced the codes of Maryland, North Carolina, South Carolina, and Georgia.

Less than human

As well as providing an escalating scale of punishment for a slave who offered "violence to any Christian", the 1661 Barbados slave code set out another purpose – to "protect [slaves] as we do men's other goods and chattels". Under the guise of looking after the interests of slaves, the aim of the code was to ensure a master's total control. As "chattel", slaves were part of his personal property, to be bought and sold like

> Slaves are generally expected to sing as well as to work.
>
> **Frederick Douglass**
> **Human rights leader and former slave (1818–95)**

animals, rather than afforded rights as individual human beings. A Virginia code of 1705 went beyond "chattel", replacing it with the term "real estate". This made slaves the property not only of the master, but also of his descendants.

Masters could enforce slave codes in many ways. Whipping, branding, and imprisonment were common. Killing was rare because slaves only had value while alive, although there was no punishment for a master who overstepped even that mark. According to another 1705 Virginia code, any master who killed a slave while "correcting" that slave "shall be free of all punishment … as if such accident had never happened". Later laws applied some restrictions on the actions of slave owners, but even if a master were found guilty, often the best the slave could hope for was to be sold to someone kinder.

Limiting basic freedoms

With the growth of Southern cities, such as Charleston, in South Carolina, and Lyndhurst, in Virginia, opportunities for labour increased and owners began to hire out slaves for profit. Such slaves had to carry a permit or wear a copper slave tag to prove they had their owners' permission to travel. In New York and elsewhere, harsh penalties were imposed if slaves walked the streets at night or congregated together.

Until the 1830s, a slave could be taught to read or write, but after the Nat Turner slave rebellion in 1831 (see box, opposite), most slave states banned such teaching. In Virginia, statutes passed in 1831 and 1832 even banned education for freed slaves. Slaves had no legal right to get married but were often allowed to do so. Many owners believed that married slaves were more likely to be settled and less likely to rebel. Slave marriages also produced more children and so boosted slave numbers. Any married slave, however, had to be prepared for the break-up of a family when at any time a wife, husband, or child might be sold to another owner.

R UN away from the subscriber in *Albemarle*, a Mulatto slave called *Sandy*, about 35 years of age, his stature is rather low, inclining to corpulence, and his complexion light; he is a shoemaker by trade, in which he uses his left hand principally, can do coarse carpenters work, and is something of a horse jockey; he is greatly addicted to drink, and when drunk is insolent and disorderly, in his conversation he swears much, and in his behaviour is artful and knavish. He took with him a white horse, much scarred with traces, of which it is expected he will endeavour to dispose; he also carried his shoemakers tools, and will probably endeavour to get employment that way. Whoever conveys the said slave to me, in *Albemarle*, shall have 40 s. reward, if taken up within the county, 4 l. if elsewhere within the colony, and 10 l. if in any other colony, from

THOMAS JEFFERSON.

In a newspaper notice of 1769, future US president Thomas Jefferson offers a reward for the capture of a slave. Most of America's Founding Fathers, like Jefferson, were slave owners.

A 19th-century woodcut shows African American slaves picking cotton. Huge demand for the fibre from textile manufacturers fuelled the high number of plantation slaves.

Keeping control over slaves and their personal relationships also helped to maintain racial purity. Male owners often took sexual advantage of their female slaves, but the codes made it plain that the responsibility for any resulting offspring rested not with the father, as established in English common law, but with the mother. A Virginia slave code of 1662 stated that "all children born in this country shall be held bond or free only according to the condition of the mother". This committed any child of a slave mother, including one born mixed race, to a life of slavery.

Slave codes also stamped out all prospects of settled relationships between races. In 1664, Maryland passed the first "anti-amalgamation" law to prevent marriage between races, and other American colonies soon followed suit.

Internal slavery

In 1807, President Thomas Jefferson signed the legislation that officially ended the US slave trade. But that did not mean an end to slavery, or even the slave codes. As the external slave trade dried up, the slave market within the US intensified, alongside a boom in the growing of cotton. Slave women were encouraged to "breed", with girls as young as 13 being cajoled into motherhood to provide more slave children.

By the time the American Civil War broke out in 1861, there were still 15 slave states in the US, all of which had slave codes. Even when the war officially ended slavery in 1865, "black codes" were developed in Southern states to limit the freedoms of former slaves and keep them on low wages. It took another century, and the passing of the 1964 Civil Rights Act, for the descendants of African American slaves to finally begin to enjoy the same legal rights as the descendants of white slave owners. ∎

Nat Turner's rebellion

The bloodiest American slave rebellion took place in 1831. It was led by Nat Turner, born a slave in 1800 in Southampton, Virginia. By his twenties, he had become a spiritual leader among his fellow slaves and was persuaded by a series of visions that God was preparing him for a great battle. A solar eclipse early in 1831 was, for Turner, the sign that he should plan a rebellion, and on 21 August he set out with six other slaves to attack plantations. As they moved from farm to farm, killing at least 55 white people, the rebels grew to around 75 strong. Their goal was to reach the town of Jerusalem but they were soon broken up by 3,000 state militia.

Turner went on the run but was captured and hanged, and 55 of his fellow rebels were executed. White mobs soon went on a killing spree among slaves, but received no punishment. Afterwards, both Virginia and neighbouring North Carolina imposed even harsher slave codes.

After hiding in woods for six weeks, slave leader Nat Turner was captured on 30 October 1831 by farmer Benjamin Phipps and executed on 11 November.

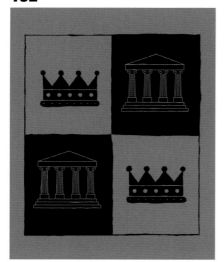

THE RIGHTS AND LIBERTIES OF THE SUBJECT

THE GLORIOUS REVOLUTION AND THE ENGLISH BILL OF RIGHTS (1688–89)

IN CONTEXT

FOCUS
Constitutional monarchy

BEFORE
1215 England's Magna Carta limits the monarchy's power.

1649 Parliament establishes the High Court of Justice to try Charles I for treason.

1681–85 Protestant Charles II dispenses with Parliament to rule as an absolute monarch.

1685 Catholic James II succeeds Charles II.

AFTER
1701 The Act of Settlement ensures that only a Protestant can sit on the English throne.

1789 The French National Assembly approves the Declaration of the Rights of Man and of the Citizen.

1791 The US Bill of Rights is passed; partly inspired by the English Bill of Rights, it guarantees the rights of individuals and of US states.

By the time James II was crowned in 1685, England had long been riven by religious and political tensions. During the English Civil War of 1642–51, James's father, Charles I, had been executed in 1649, when Parliament had declared itself the supreme governing power. Although the monarchy had been restored in 1660 under James's older brother, Charles II, in an uneasy compromise,

questions still remained about the balance of power between monarch and Parliament, and about the religious direction of the country. James II was openly Catholic and, for a largely Protestant country such as England, this was problematic.

The strain began to show when in 1687 James issued a Declaration of Indulgence – a royal proclamation giving religious freedom both to Catholics and to Protestants who did not conform to the Church of England. Incensed by protests at his perceived attack on the established Church, James dissolved Parliament in July. In June 1688, while the king prosecuted seven defiant bishops, his Catholic wife, Mary of Modena, gave birth to a son and heir to the throne – fuelling fears of a long line of Catholic monarchs and an end to England being a Protestant country.

The Glorious Revolution
As civil war now seemed imminent, a group of politicians wrote to Dutch Protestant ruler William of Orange,

William III and Mary II, shown in an engraving, after ascending to the English throne as joint monarchs – titles granted by agreement with Parliament, rather than by the divine right of kings.

See also: Magna Carta 66–71 ▪ The trial of Charles I 96–97 ▪ The US Constitution and Bill of Rights 110–17 ▪ The Universal Declaration of Human Rights 222–29

In an **absolute monarchy**, the king or queen has **complete control of the nation**.

In a **constitutional monarchy**, the **power of the king or queen is limited** by and shared with an elected parliament.

The **Bill of Rights** effectively took England from an absolute monarchy to a **constitutional monarchy**.

who was already married to James's daughter, Mary. They asked him to come to England to defend the faith.

When William of Orange landed in England in November 1688 and began marching his army towards London, support for King James fell away. James soon realized that his position was untenable and within a month fled to France. He had, in effect, abdicated his throne and handed it to William and Mary in a bloodless revolution – known as the Glorious Revolution.

For redress of all grievances, and for the amending, strengthening and preserving of the laws, Parliaments ought to be held frequently.
The English Bill of Rights

Parliament convened in January 1689 and offered the crown jointly to William and Mary. The new monarchs signed a Declaration of Rights in Parliament, which was formally passed as the Bill of Rights.

The Bill of Rights
By ensuring the power of an elected Parliament under a constitutional monarchy, the Bill of Rights protected the freedoms of English citizens. It condemned James's misdeeds; ordered that sessions of Parliament be held frequently; required Parliament's consent for a monarch to rule, raise taxes, or suspend laws; guaranteed freedom of speech in parliamentary debates; and barred Catholics from the throne. It also banned the raising of an army in peacetime without the consent of Parliament.

Together with the 1701 Act of Settlement, the Bill of Rights gave Parliament absolute sovereignty over all and any other government institutions and over succession to the throne, separating Parliament's powers from those of the Crown. In so doing, the Bill paved the way for the constitutional monarchy and parliamentary democracy that Britain has today. ▪

Natural rights

The politicians who drafted the Bill of Rights were greatly influenced by the embryonic Enlightenment movement, most notably by English philosopher and scholar John Locke (1632–1704), and by the concept of natural rights.

Since ancient times, thinkers such as the Greek philosopher Aristotle had advocated that natural law, a universal code of behaviour and rights, could not be denied by any legal system. Locke took up the baton. He believed in natural rights: that all men are naturally free and equal and have a right to life, liberty, and property.

Locke rejected the idea of the divine right of kings and absolute monarchy. He argued that a parliament should hold a central role in governing a country, as part of a social contract with its people. This implied that, if the people believed that a government failed to represent their interests adequately, it should be replaced – an idea that would soon support revolution.

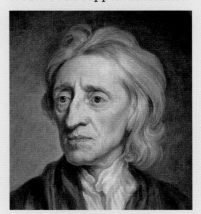

John Locke inspired thinkers in Europe's Enlightenment and the Founding Fathers who drafted the US Declaration of Independence.

THOU SHALT NOT SUFFER A WITCH TO LIVE
THE SALEM WITCH TRIALS (1692)

IN CONTEXT

FOCUS
Due process

BEFORE
1486 The German treatise *Malleus Maleficarum* (*The Hammer of Witches*) advises using torture to get confessions and advocates the death penalty for those convicted.

1581–93 The Trier Witch Trials in Germany, one of the largest witch trials in Europe, sees some 368 people executed.

1662 At a witch trial in Bury St Edmunds, England, spectral evidence is ruled as admissible.

AFTER
1697 Massachusetts governor William Stoughton calls for a day of prayer and atonement for events in Salem.

1711 Massachusetts reverses 22 verdicts of the convicted (the remaining nine are exonerated in 1957 and the state officially apologizes for the trials).

Mass hysteria leads to the imprisonment of **more than 200 suspected witches** in Salem.

Trials begin in May 1692 with the use of **spectral evidence** (from dreams or visions), resulting in **19 people** being found guilty and **put to death**.

After local governor William Phips's wife is **questioned over witchcraft**, he instigates a court that **does not allow spectral evidence**.

Only three further people are found guilty, and by May 1693 all **remaining prisoners are released**.

In January 1697, Judge Samuel Sewall makes a **public apology** for the trials.

The Devil and his recruitment of witches had long been perceived as a threat across Europe. Between 1300 and the end of the 1600s, tens of thousands of people (mostly women) were put to death as witches across the region, often confessing to their "crime" after sustained torture. Although they began many years after the witch panic had swept Europe, the trials in Salem, Massachusetts in 1692 saw 19 people hanged and more than 200 accused in a case of mass hysteria. The trials rested on similar issues to those of the past: scapegoating vulnerable people.

When a local minister's daughters began having fainting fits and acting strangely, it seemed

See also: The origins of canon law 42–47 ▪ Trial by ordeal and combat 52–53
▪ The trial of Galileo Galilei 93 ▪ *Miranda v. Arizona* 254–55

A somewhat fanciful engraving from *c.* 1892, depicting the Salem witch trials taking place in a courtroom, with a woman conjuring power and a man passed out on the floor.

clear to the highly religious community in Salem that it must be the work of the Devil. The girls accused three local women of witchcraft: a slave named Tituba; a poor elderly woman, Sarah Osborne; and a homeless beggar, Sarah Good. The women were arrested and Tituba, perhaps hoping to save herself, confessed to meeting with the Devil. This set off a chain of accusations over the coming months and increasing numbers of arrests.

The trials
With the jails filling up, local governor William Phips set up a special court of Oyer and Terminer (meaning "to hear" and "to decide") to start hearing cases. The judges had no formal legal training. On 27 May 1692, the first of the trials went ahead, and local gossip Bridget Bishop was found guilty of witchcraft and was later hanged. Preacher Cotton Mather commented: "There was little occasion to prove the witchcraft, it being evident and notorious to all beholders." The

court was criticized for allowing spectral evidence (see box, right), but the trials continued, and over the next few months a further 12 women and six men were found guilty and put to death.

One of the accused, 81-year-old Giles Corey, refused to enter a plea so he could not be tried. In a medieval practice known as *peine forte et dure* (French for "hard and forceful punishment") he was laid under a wooden board which was weighted down with stones until he could not breathe, in an attempt to extract a plea or a confession. After two days, Corey died.

Recognition of injustice
When Phips's own wife was questioned over witchcraft, he scrapped the court of Oyer and Terminer and instigated a Superior

Evidence at the Salem witch trials

The key evidence used in most of the cases at Salem was spectral evidence – testimony from victims who told of seeing an apparition of the accused witch while they were suffering a fit. After some debate, it was decided that this constituted valid evidence because a person must give the Devil permission to take their form, indicating that the accused had entered into a pact with the Devil.

The judges in Salem used the precedent of a witch trial in Bury St Edmunds, England, in 1662, during which spectral evidence was ruled admissible by judge Sir Matthew Hale. Further evidence used to convict witches included finding ointments or books of the occult in their homes; the fits of the victims ceasing when touched by the accused; or the discovery of a "witches' teat" – a mark on the body.

Court of Judicature, which did not allow spectral evidence. Only three of the 56 people subsequently accused were found guilty. This seemed to stem the flow of accusations and by May 1693 all those still in prison were released.

In January 1697, the General Court instigated a day of fasting and reflection to atone for the mistakes made, and a key judge, Samuel Sewall, publicly apologized. This marked a growing recognition of the injustice of these trials and of the disproportionate punishments employed. A dark episode in American history, the Salem witch trials are a reminder of the importance of due process in protecting innocent people. ∎

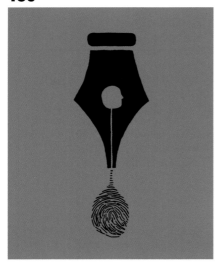

THE AUTHOR SHALL HAVE THE SOLE RIGHT OF PRINTING
THE STATUTE OF ANNE (1710)

In the Middle Ages, when trained scribes painstakingly hand-copied manuscripts for monasteries, universities, and the wealthy elite, the right to copy was not an issue. All changed in around 1440, when German goldsmith Johannes Gutenberg invented the printing press. Using movable metal type, presses could produce multiple copies of a text cheaply and quickly for a new readership.

By 1500, 1,000 presses had produced about 8 million books in Western Europe. William Caxton brought the first printing press to England in 1476. Printers realized they would suffer if other printers sold copies of the same book, and sought to establish copyright to protect their commercial interests.

The royal hand

In England, King Henry VIII decreed in 1538 that the Court of Star Chamber must approve all new books before publication – a bid to prevent any considered subversive or heretical. His daughter Queen Mary went further, by assigning the right to print books solely to the Stationers' Company, a publishing trade guild. Each book had to be entered by a guild member in the Stationers' register, giving them exclusive printing rights – the author simply received a small fee.

The rebel parliament that would eventually overthrow King Charles I abolished the Star Chamber in 1640, but its restrictive monopoly persisted through the Stationers. It provoked the poet John Milton to pen his angry polemic *Areopagitica*

William Caxton reads a page from his printing press in Westminster, London. The first book known to have been printed on it was *The Canterbury Tales* by Geoffrey Chaucer.

See also: The *Lex Mercatoria* 74–77 ▪ The Venetian Patent Statute 82–85 ▪ The *Madame Bovary* trial 150 ▪ The Federal Trade Commission 184–85 ▪ The WIPO Copyright Treaty 286–87

> If a book can be **copied by anyone**, why would an author or a bookseller **make the effort to write or publish** it?

> But if **no one else** can ever **make a copy** of a book, the **spread of knowledge is blocked**.

> So the author and bookseller must be **protected by copyright**, but for a **limited period**.

---

in 1644, one of the most forthright defences of the right to freedom of expression ever written.

In the 17th century, as scientists including Isaac Newton made new discoveries and figures such as English philosopher John Locke challenged old ways of thinking, the Stationers' stranglehold began to look outdated. When its exclusive licence lapsed in 1694, strenuous efforts by the Company to persuade Parliament to restore the licence failed – until they cited authors' right to protect their work from being copied – their "copy right". In 1710, Parliament passed the Statute of Anne (named after the British queen of the time).

The right to copy

The Statute of Anne gave exclusive rights to the Stationers' Company for all the books they published, but only for a number of years. Most significantly, it was the first Act to protect authors by granting them and those to whom they had assigned rights exclusive right of publication of existing works, for 21 years, until 1731. For new works, the same right ran for 14 years from publication, with another 14 years if the author was still living. The Stationers had to buy the rights to publish a new book from the author.

Booksellers or authors had to send a copy of the book to a few recognized libraries, known as "legal deposit libraries". This practice, which began in 1610 when diplomat and scholar Sir Thomas Bodley created the Bodleian Library in Oxford, England, continues today. ▪

Hold! You crafty ones, strangers to work, and pilferers of other men's brains! Think not rashly to lay your thievish hands upon my works.
Albrecht Dürer
German painter and engraver (1471–1528)

The battle of the booksellers

Despite the Statute of Anne, the Stationers' Company insisted that they still had exclusive rights on books. In particular, they did not accept that, under natural law as applied on the European continent, their rights on new books should expire.

For more than half a century, in the "battle of the booksellers", the Stationers mounted legal challenges against booksellers who were printing what the Stationers claimed were pirate copies. Finally, in 1774, the matter came to a head in the House of Lords in the case of *Donaldson v. Becket*.

Alexander Donaldson, a printer and bookseller, sold cheap reprints of books after their copyright expired. The Stationers claimed that under common law they had perpetual copyright to the books. The Lords ruled that the issue of copyright was one of statute, not common law, and upheld the Statute of Anne's provision that copyright had a limited term.

A GRAND SOCIETY OF NATIONS
VATTEL'S *THE LAW OF NATIONS* (1758)

IN CONTEXT

FOCUS
International law

BEFORE
1625 Dutch statesman Hugo Grotius's *On the Law of War and Peace* is published. It is regarded as the first book on international law.

1648 The Peace of Westphalia ends the Thirty Years' War between Protestant and Catholic Europe, and establishes state sovereignty as a fundamental cornerstone of international relations.

1749 Christian Wolff publishes *The Law of Nations*.

AFTER
1776 The US Declaration of Independence, partly inspired by Vattel's *The Law of Nations*, is signed.

1920 The League of Nations is established in the aftermath of World War I, with the aim of maintaining global peace.

Swiss diplomat Emmerich de Vattel (1714–67) wrote the first widely accessible treatise on international law. He was inspired by Enlightenment philosophers, such as Germans Gottfried Wilhelm Leibniz and Christian Wolff, and their work on natural law and international politics. Wolff's 1749 publication *Jus Gentium* (*The Law of Nations*) contained key ideas, but its Latin text and complex arguments made it impenetrable to a wider audience. Vattel decided to take Wolff's ideas on what duties nations owe to each other and create his own work as a practical guide for statesmen.

A national blueprint
With its mixture of philosophical arguments and practical politics, Vattel's *The Law of Nations, or Principles of the Law of Nature, Applied to the Conduct and Affairs of Nations and Sovereigns* was well received following its publication, in French, in 1758. Vattel argued that like individual people, nations should be free and independent, and able to enjoy that liberty without interference from a foreign power. Nations must also accept, however, that they are underpinned by a common concern for each other, and are obliged to work together, particularly through the free flow of commerce.

American colonists fighting taxes imposed from Britain were drawn to Vattel's theories. They proved a major influence on the 1776 Declaration of Independence and the US Constitution (1787). ∎

> The natural society of nations cannot subsist, unless the natural rights of each be duly respected.
> **Emmerich de Vattel**
> *The Law of Nations*

See also: Grotius's *On the Law of War and Peace* 92 ▪ The US Constitution and Bill of Rights 110–17 ▪ The United Nations and International Court of Justice 212–19

THE MOST IMPORTANT BOOK IN THE HISTORY OF COMMON LAW
BLACKSTONE'S *COMMENTARIES* (1765–69)

IN CONTEXT

FOCUS
Common law

BEFORE
1166 King Henry II issues the Assize of Clarendon, a series of legal reforms that lay the basis of English common law.

1215 The seminal document of English common law, Magna Carta, is signed.

1689 The English Bill of Rights is passed by Parliament.

AFTER
1771–72 An American edition of Blackstone's *Commentaries* is published in Philadelphia to great interest.

1787 The US Constitution – the founding legal document of the United States – is signed.

1871 *A Selection of Cases on the Law of Contracts*, by American jurist Christopher Columbus Langdell, supplants the *Commentaries* as the key US law textbook.

William Blackstone's *Commentaries on the Laws of England*, a systematic work describing every aspect of English common law, was pivotal in fostering a wider understanding of law. Blackstone began to lecture on common law at the University of Oxford in 1753, the first time this had occurred in Britain. His lectures were popular due to his clear explanations of complex legal issues. Between 1765 and 1769 he published these lectures in four volumes: *Of the Rights of Persons*; *Of the Rights of Things*; *Of Private Wrongs*; and *Of Public Wrongs*.

Blackstone's book made English common law, with its huge body of statutes and judgements, much more accessible. It was used well into the 19th century as a foundation text at law schools in Britain, the US, and throughout the Commonwealth.

Revolutionary impact
The book's portable format was especially useful in America, where frontier lawyers often lacked the

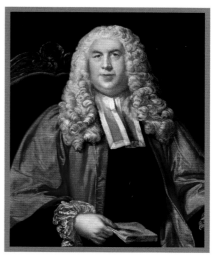

Sir William Blackstone (1723–80), an English barrister, judge, and politician, gave practical, logical, and accessible guidance to English common law.

resources to check legal precedents. Now they could refer to Blackstone's succinct *Commentaries*. His promotion of the idea that the law should protect people, their property, and their liberty resonated in revolutionary America and in the drafting of the US Constitution. ■

See also: Magna Carta 66–71 ■ The Glorious Revolution and the English Bill of Rights 102–03 ■ The US Constitution and Bill of Rights 110–17

THIS CONSTITUTION SHALL BE THE SUPREME LAW OF THE LAND

THE US CONSTITUTION AND BILL OF RIGHTS (1787, 1791)

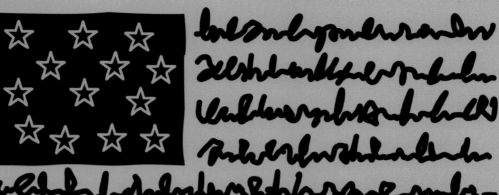

IN CONTEXT

FOCUS
Constitutional government and citizens' rights

BEFORE
1215 Magna Carta promises rights and protections for all "free men" in England.

1689 England's Bill of Rights limits the monarchy's power and sets out individuals' rights.

1776 The Second Continental Congress of 13 American colonies adopts the Declaration of Independence, cutting all political ties with Britain.

AFTER
1789 The Declaration of the Rights of Man and of the Citizen sets out civil rights in France.

1791 Poland creates the first modern national constitution in Europe.

1803 *Marbury v. Madison* establishes the principle of judicial review, giving the US Supreme Court the power to interpret the Constitution.

1948 The UN's Universal Declaration of Human Rights (UDHR) affirms individual rights worldwide.

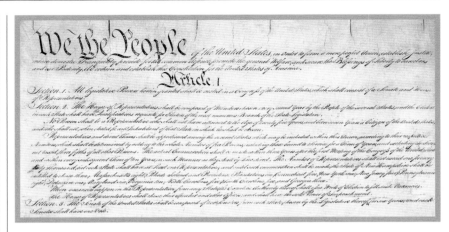

W ritten in the summer of 1787, the Constitution of the United States is the oldest national constitution. Ancient Greek city-states had their own written constitutions, but the US Constitution was the first to set out a framework for governing modern nations, and has inspired national constitutions ever since.

The process began in 1786, when New York lawyer and politician Alexander Hamilton wrote a report calling for a convention (later known as the Constitutional Convention), to address the inadequacies of the Articles of Confederation – the agreement between the 13 colonies, ratified in 1781, that served as an early constitution.

From war to independence
The Articles had been drafted in 1776–77 during the American Revolution, waged by the colonies to fight off British rule. At this time, the Continental Congress was the governing body of the colonies. The Delegates to the First Continental Congress initially met in 1774 to organize a response to the Coercive Acts that Britain had imposed to punish those who resisted taxation. The colonists' resentment of "taxation without representation" became a call to arms. In 1775, when the Second Continental Congress convened, the war was underway. On 4 July 1776, the Congress adopted the Declaration of Independence, drafted by Thomas Jefferson (its main author), John Adams, and Benjamin Franklin – three of the Founding Fathers who had united the colonies and led the revolt against Britain.

The first page of the US Constitution famously begins with the words "We the People of the United States, in order to form a more perfect Union, establish Justice … ".

Among the Declaration's provisions were that the united colonies "ought to be Free and Independent States". The Articles had reflected this, creating a confederation of 13 sovereign states. By 1786, however, three years after the Treaty of Paris confirmed America's independence, Hamilton and several other Founding Fathers recognized that the sovereignty of each state was weakening the power of the national government, leaving it unable, for instance, to tax the population, or enforce requests for troops. To replace the Articles, they wanted a constitution that could bind the confederation of states together.

Fierce debate
The Constitutional Convention took place in Philadelphia between May and September of 1787. The 55 delegates represented all states except Rhode Island, which opposed a stronger central government. George Washington, who had led the Continental Army in the American Revolution, was elected convention president.

See also: Magna Carta 66–71 ▪ The Glorious Revolution and the English Bill of Rights 102–03 ▪ The Declaration of the Rights of Man 118–19 ▪ The US Supreme Court and judicial review 124–29 ▪ The Universal Declaration of Human Rights 222–29

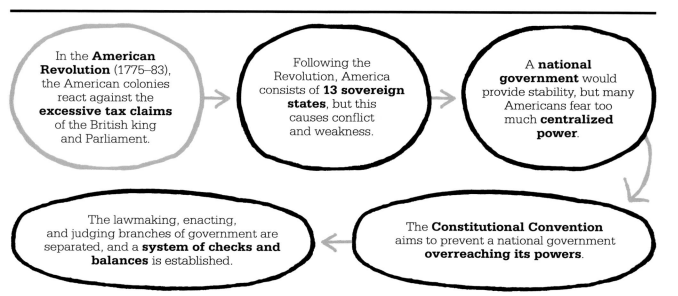

In the **American Revolution** (1775–83), the American colonies react against the **excessive tax claims** of the British king and Parliament.

Following the Revolution, America consists of **13 sovereign states**, but this causes conflict and weakness.

A **national government** would provide stability, but many Americans fear too much **centralized power**.

The **Constitutional Convention** aims to prevent a national government **overreaching its powers**.

The lawmaking, enacting, and judging branches of government are separated, and a **system of checks and balances** is established.

Like Rhode Island, other states feared that a federal government might overstep its powers and worried, too, about how they would be represented in Congress, the national legislature. Delegates from larger states wanted the number of representatives to reflect the size of their population; those from smaller states wanted equal representation.

The slavery question also came to the fore. Northern states, some of whom had already abolished slavery, strongly favoured complete abolition, but states in the South were determined to ensure that slavery remained legal. So divisive was the issue that it was excluded from the Constitution and left to individual states to decide.

The Great Compromise
On the question of representation, the delegation from Virginia, which included Edmund Randolph and James Madison, set the agenda. The 15 resolutions of their Virginia Plan, which Randolph put to delegates,

outlined a wholly new structure of government based on a bi-cameral (two chamber) legislature, limited terms, and rotation of office, along with other bodies to act as checks and balances. The number of representatives from each state would depend on their economic power or their population.

While larger states agreed to the idea, small states did not. William Paterson of New Jersey countered with a plan to give each state an

Liberty, when it begins to take root, is a plant of rapid growth.
George Washington
1st US president (1789–97)

equal voice in Congress. After a heated debate, delegates agreed a proposal from Roger Sherman of Connecticut to create two chambers – the Senate, where each state has equal representation, and the House of Representatives, in which representation is based on a state's population. This solution was dubbed the Great Compromise. Under the plan, each state would be able to appoint two senators to serve six-year terms in the Senate. In the House of Representatives, seats would be held for two years, and the number each state had would be based on its population and reassessed every 10 years.

In a further debate, conference delegate James Wilson proposed that the president should be elected directly by the people. However, the majority of delegates decided that the general populace knew little about politicians outside their own states and would therefore be too ill-informed to make a valid choice. They agreed instead that the »

The three branches of the US government

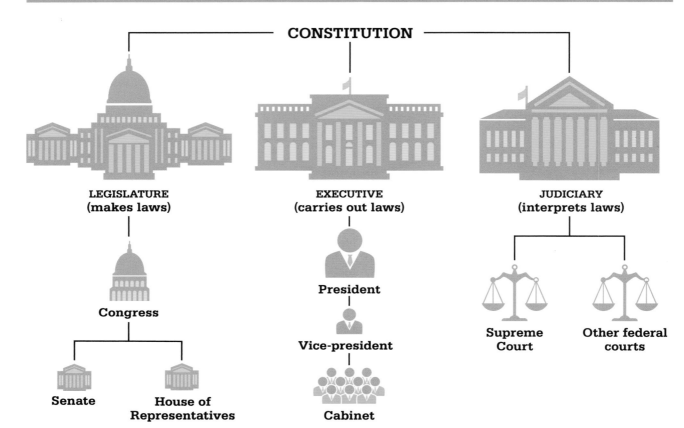

The US Constitution separated the powers of government into three branches: the legislature, the executive, and the judiciary. The legislature makes laws; the executive enacts them; and the judiciary interprets them and punishes lawbreakers. The divisions prevent any one branch gaining too much power, as the other two can act as a brake.

president should be elected indirectly by "electors" chosen by each state – the Electoral College. States have the same number of electors as they do members in the two chambers of Congress.

With all issues resolved and set down, the Committee of Style, led by James Madison, finally produced the first draft of the Constitution.

Separation of powers

The Constitution is concise – just over 4,000 words long. Yet it provided the basis for a complex machinery of government that now employs millions of people. Much of its complexity stems from the desire of those early delegates to separate the branches of government, limiting the authority of each with a system of checks and balances designed to avoid the abuse of power. They had fought the War of Independence to challenge the tyranny of centralized power, so were naturally nervous about a new central government. Indeed, many states only agreed to ratify the Constitution if they could be sure they would have some guarantee of protection against the new government's power.

As a result of these concerns, the US government is divided horizontally between lawmakers (the legislative body: Congress), law enacters (the executive: the office of the president), and law interpreters (the judiciary: the Supreme Court); and also vertically between federal, state, and local governments.

Signed and ratified

The draft Constitution (written out by clerk Jacob Shallus for a fee of $30) was finally presented to the delegates in September 1787.

At the Pennsylvania State House (now Independence Hall), 39 delegates signed the Constitution in September 1787. The Declaration of Independence had been signed there 11 years earlier.

Washington was the first to sign, followed by 38 other delegates. The next step was for at least nine of the 13 states to ratify the draft. After much haggling, the ninth state, New Hampshire, ratified in June the following year, and it was agreed that the Constitution would come into effect in March 1789.

At the end of April 1789, George Washington was elected the first US president. In February 1790, the Supreme Court sat, and the first US Congress met a month later. The government was finally fully functional. At the end of May, Rhode Island, the last of the 13 states to ratify, came on board.

Protecting rights
Ratifying the Constitution had proved difficult. Many delegates had argued that it failed to protect political rights, such as freedom of religion and speech, and demanded that a Bill of Rights be added before they agreed to sign. In a 1788 letter to Thomas Jefferson, Madison suggested that the Constitution alone, by creating a just and proper government, should be enough

to guarantee the protection of fundamental rights. Gradually, however, Madison warmed to the idea of a Bill of Rights, partly for pragmatic reasons and partly because he could see its merits.

In 1789, as a member of the new House of Representatives, Madison proposed 19 amendments. Twelve were agreed and 10 were added to the Constitution as the Bill of Rights, adopted in 1791.

Since then, remarkably few other amendments to the Bill have been added. Thousands have been proposed, but only 17 accepted, partly because of the system of checks and balances. Changes to the Constitution not only have to pass through both houses of Congress; at least three-quarters of the states must also ratify them.

English roots
The new Constitution of the United States was a groundbreaking and historic document. The framers, however, were not trying to create something wholly revolutionary. In their determination to fashion a system that could curb the power of an overambitious government, many saw a parallel with the

Let our government be like that of the solar system. Let the general government be like the sun and the states the planets, repelled yet attracted …
John Dickinson
Delaware representative (1732–1808)

balance of power achieved by English legislation to protect the rights of Parliament against the threat of royal tyranny. The US replaced monarchy with a president elected for fixed terms, but in other respects the Constitution had much in common with the British system that the US had rebelled against a decade earlier. At first, it was even proposed that the president should be addressed as "Your Highness". »

The Bill of Rights

Influenced by forerunners such as England's Magna Carta in 1215 and Bill of Rights in 1689, the US Bill of Rights is a collection of individual rights reinforced by limitations on federal and state governments. It comprises the first 10 amendments to the Constitution, enshrining rights such as freedom of speech and religion, the right to remain silent, and the right to keep and bear arms. Also included are protections for those accused of crimes, such as the right not

to be imprisoned without due process of law and not to be tried twice for the same offence (double jeopardy). As axioms of government, the amendments have a binding legal force. Congress cannot pass laws that conflict with them; states could initially, but now cannot legislate against most of their guarantees.

More citizens were covered by the Bill's protection when slavery was abolished in 1865, and in 1868 when, under the Fourteenth Amendment, those born or naturalized in the US became American citizens.

Central to the machinery of government laid down by the Constitution was the concept of parliament that had evolved over centuries in England. With the development of the cloth industry and emergence of a new merchant class in the 15th century, widening prosperity had meant more people had a stake in how kings and lords operated, especially in the way they raised money from taxation.

The population's demands for a say in government had reached a pinnacle in the English Civil War in the 1640s, when Charles I, accused of waging war on his people, was executed by the will of Parliament. The subsequent republic of the Commonwealth under Oliver Cromwell soon collapsed, and the monarchy was restored in 1660, but the turbulent period had sowed the seeds of democracy and the shift of power from the king towards Parliament. This was reinforced in 1689, after the Glorious Revolution when the Catholic king James II was compelled to abdicate, and William and Mary from Holland were invited to rule on condition that they accepted a Declaration of Rights. Translated by Parliament into a Bill of Rights, it formally set

> Whenever any Form of Government becomes destructive … it is the Right of the People to alter or to abolish it, and to institute new Government.
> **US Declaration of Independence**

down the rights and liberties of British subjects, and was a model for the later US Bill of Rights.

Enlightened thinking

The leading framers of the Constitution were highly educated men. They were deeply aware of new currents in philosophical and political thought that had developed in Europe during the Enlightenment, particularly the ideas of John Locke in England and Jean-Jacques Rousseau and Charles Montesquieu in France. Both Locke and Rousseau argued strongly for people's natural

rights, while Montesquieu proposed a separation of legislative, judicial, and executive powers to prevent the despotism he abhorred in the French monarchy. Locke had maintained there must be a "social contract", whereby people, who are by nature free and equal, agree to be ruled and have some of their choices limited in order to live harmoniously with others. Those who rule, however, must protect the people's rights and promote the public good.

Locke's ideas were echoed in the opening words of the US Declaration of Independence and its "self-evident" truths that all men are created equal and endowed with certain unalienable rights, including "Life, Liberty and the pursuit of Happiness"; and that to secure these rights, governments should derive their powers from the "consent of the governed".

Locke also believed in majority rule. This and the consent of the governed, would become the central planks of democracy, while both Locke's and Montesquieu's thoughts on the separation of powers were key to shaping the US Congress.

Republic v. democracy

The Constitution is sometimes seen as the starting point of modern democracy. It begins with the words, "We the People … ", but this was not a ringing endorsement of the democratic ideals expressed so stirringly by President Abraham Lincoln in 1865, when he spoke of "government of the people, by the people, for the people". The Founding Fathers framed the Constitution to be the "supreme Law of the Land" and the basis of

George Washington – the first person to sign the Constitution – is inaugurated as the first US president at Federal Hall, New York City, on 30 April 1789.

> Don't interfere with anything in the Constitution. That must be maintained, for it is the only safeguard of our liberties.
> **Abraham Lincoln**
> 16th US president (1861–65)

a republic that primarily championed its people's liberty and rights. Many considered elections only as a means to an end, a way of keeping government in check, rather than part of some great democratic ideal.

Madison, the chief architect of the Constitution, argued that it was a republic they were creating, not a democracy. Here, Madison was talking of a democracy such as that of ancient Athens, where all adult citizens had to play an active role in government, which was plainly impractical for a nation such as the US. For him, the key difference was that a republic works by the delegation of government to a small number of people elected by the rest. In 1820, Scottish philosopher James Mill proclaimed such a system of representation to be "the grand discovery of modern times". His son John Stuart Mill declared it to be the "ideal type of a perfect government".

What the three men were all describing is now the standard model of democracy, where the people elect representatives to govern and create laws. The gradual shift of Western governments towards this model during the 19th century was, however, perhaps less for its perceived benefits than because other systems had failed.

A work in progress

The delegates at the Constitutional Convention knew the document they had agreed to was a historic achievement, but not perfect. At the Convention's close, Benjamin Franklin, aged 81, looked at the half-sun symbol on Washington's chair and declared it was "a rising and not a setting sun", adding that the Constitution with all its faults was the very best they could obtain.

The 1787 Constitution could not produce a government that truly represented the entire nation. It did not set out voting rights; at first, only male property-owners could vote at all. The Fifteenth Amendment gave African American men the right to vote only in 1870. In 1919, the Nineteenth Amendment gave women the right to vote; the first states to give Native Americans the vote did so in 1924. Yet, by defining a government system empowered by the people, while limiting its powers in order to protect citizens' basic rights, the Constitution set a pattern for modern democratic government that is now the norm across much of the world. ■

> To live under the American Constitution is the greatest political privilege that was ever accorded to the human race.
> **Calvin Coolidge**
> 30th US president (1923–29)

James Madison

Born in 1751, on Belle Grove Plantation in Virginia, Madison was the oldest of 12 children. He graduated from Princeton and was soon involved in the politics of the American Revolution, becoming a member of both the Virginia House of Delegates and the Second Continental Congress. He was one of the more prominent Founding Fathers of the United States.

After the war, Madison led the work on the creation of the Constitution. He sponsored the amendments that make up the Bill of Rights and was one of the first leaders of the House of Representatives. Madison was elected fourth president of the United States, serving from 1809 to 1817 at the very peak of the political edifice he had helped to create. When he left office in 1817, he retired to his Virginia tobacco plantation, and died there in 1836.

Key works

1787 Speeches at the Constitutional Convention
1787–88 Articles in *The Federalist*

MEN ARE BORN AND REMAIN FREE AND EQUAL IN RIGHTS
THE DECLARATION OF THE RIGHTS OF MAN (1789)

IN CONTEXT

FOCUS
Human rights

BEFORE
***c.* 1750 BCE** In Mesopotamia, the Code of Hammurabi lists basic rights and punishments.

539 BCE Cyrus the Great decrees religious tolerance for his conquered subjects in Babylon.

1215 England's Magna Carta is signed by King John.

1776 The Virginia Declaration of Rights influences the US Declaration of Independence.

AFTER
1948 In the wake of the atrocities of World War II, the United Nations' Universal Declaration of Human Rights (UDHR) defines rights worldwide.

1950 The European Convention on Human Rights (ECHR) draws on the UDHR, enforcing individual rights across Europe.

The Declaration of the Rights of Man and of the Citizen was a landmark statement of human rights. It emerged at the start of the French Revolution, and laid down the principle that by law all men are equal, with equal rights to liberty, private property, safety, and freedom from oppression. This idea has shaped the modern world.

The events that gave rise to the Declaration started in May 1789, when King Louis XVI was compelled by financial crisis and widespread agitation to reconvene the Estates General, the legislative assembly, after a gap of 175 years. The Estates General comprised three groups, or estates – the clergy, the nobility, and the people – and Louis insisted that each group had a single vote. This meant that the two elite estates, the clergy and the nobility, would always outvote the people.

The National Assembly
On 17 June 1789, the enraged "Third Estate", the people, declared a separate National Assembly to make laws themselves. Locked out of the official assembly hall, they convened on the Royal Tennis Court instead. Here, they resolved to set out the principles by which France would be governed. A fundamental principle was that, for "the good of all", the Assembly would govern only with the consent of the people.

For this reason it was necessary to define the rights of every citizen, and so the Declaration was drafted, initially by the Marquis de Lafayette, in consultation with American

All men are equal and **no man has a right to rule over any other**.

But men may choose to **give the power to rule** to the monarch and the government.

So the monarch and the government **rule on behalf of the nation** and only **by the consent of the people**.

See also: The Glorious Revolution and the English Bill of Rights 102–03 ▪ The US Constitution and Bill of Rights 110–17 ▪ The Napoleonic Code 130–31 ▪ The Universal Declaration of Human Rights 222–29

statesman Thomas Jefferson. The draft was presented to the Assembly on 11 July 1789, and after revision it was accepted six weeks later.

The document was inspired by the ideas of the Enlightenment developed in France in the previous half-century. The new philosophy of Montesquieu, Rousseau, and Voltaire challenged the idea of the rule of a monarch by divine right, asserting a law of the rights of men derived not from religious authority but by rational thought.

Articles of the Declaration

In 17 articles and a preamble, the Declaration describes individual and collective rights for all men. The preamble emphasizes the principle that rights are "natural, inalienable, and sacred". It also guarantees freedom of speech, freedom of the press, and freedom of religion.

The first article contains the heart of the Declaration, stating that "Men are born and remain free and equal in rights. Social distinctions can be founded only on the common good." The second article asserts that the primary duty of government is to look after the rights of man – his rights to liberty, property, safety, and resistance to oppression. The third states that the government's authority depends on the consent of all. Article Four explains that liberty means the freedom to do anything that does no harm to others, while Article Five says the government can ban only those actions that are harmful to society. Article Six states that laws are the expression of the general will of the people.

The rest of the text goes on to define many rights that we now take for granted, including the principle that people are innocent until proven guilty. Indeed, these ideas, which seemed so radical at the time, are now so much a part of the fabric of the democratic world that to us they seem to be plain common sense.

Active and passive citizens

Despite the moral authority of the Declaration and its championing of equality, it conferred rights only on

> A woman has the right to mount the scaffold. She must possess equally the right to mount the speaker's platform.
> **Olympe de Gouges**
> **The Declaration of the Rights of Woman, 1791**

"active" citizens. These were French free men over the age of 25 who paid a certain level of tax (in effect, property owners). Women, poor men, and slaves were "passive" citizens. But, as the Revolution progressed, they too demanded to be included. In 1790, Nicolas de Condorcet and Etta Palm d'Aelders called for the National Assembly to recognize women's rights. Their appeal was rejected – prompting playwright Olympe de Gouges to write her Declaration of the Rights of Woman and of the Female Citizen. "Woman is born free and remains equal to man in rights," she claimed.

The original Declaration also inspired the first successful slave uprising, by slaves in the French colony of Saint-Domingue; now Haiti. Slavery was abolished in France and its colonies in 1794. ▪

The Tennis Court Oath was sworn by the National Assembly of the Third Estate on 20 June 1789. They vowed "not to separate" until a written constitution had been established for France.

THE RISE
RULE OF
1800—1945

OF THE
LAW

The **US Supreme Court** is given the power of **judicial review**, allowing it to rule on any breach of the Constitution.

The **Abolition of the Slave Trade Act** abolishes the slave trade in British colonies and on British ships.

Under the **Metropolitan Police Act**, a state-run police force is established in London, UK.

The first of the **Geneva Conventions** is agreed by European powers, establishing a set of rules to prevent suffering during war.

 1803   **1807**   **1829**   **1864**

1804   **1822**   **1863**   **1871**

Napoleon Bonaparte commissions an overhaul of France's legal system, resulting in a new civil code, the **Napoleonic Code**.

The UK is the first country to pass a law **preventing cruelty to farm animals**, which is extended in 1849 to all domestic animals.

The Republic of **Venezuela** becomes the first nation to **abolish the death penalty** for all crimes.

The **Trade Union Act** secures the legal status of trade unions in the UK and protects their funds from embezzlement.

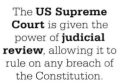

The spirit of the Age of Reason of the 18th century led to fundamental changes in how society was organized: the French and American revolutions overthrew the old established order, and new nation states were created, with laws and constitutions that upheld the values of democracy, liberty, and human rights. Through the 19th century, more and more countries adopted similar models of government, espousing the same values. But a key factor involved in the changes within society was the Industrial Revolution, which started in 18th-century Britain and went on to shape the modern world.

With industrialization came capitalism, and while political power had been transferred from monarchies and aristocracies to parliaments, the owners of the new industries held the economic reins. The rural peasant class shrank, to be replaced with a class of city-dwelling factory workers, no longer in thrall to landowners but instead reliant on industrialists for their livelihood.

Changing societies

The governments and laws of the new era's nation states had to evolve to reflect the changing nature of the societies within them, recognizing the rights of all their citizens. There was a gradual move towards more liberal legislation, protecting the interests of workers and consumers, as well as ensuring that businesses could continue to bring prosperity in a fair market economy.

Fresh from revolution, the US and France were among the first to rise to the challenge of creating legal systems fit for the modern world.

The principle of citizens' rights was written into the US Constitution, but further legislation was needed to protect the people from abuses of power. A major step was to grant the Supreme Court the power of judicial review, so it could exercise the necessary checks and balances on other branches of government. At much the same time, France began to draw up its new civil code, which became a model for many other nations' civil codes.

British parliamentary and legal systems were well established, and evolved more slowly to the demands of industrialized society. But with the formation of the Metropolitan Police Force by an Act of Parliament, the UK created a policing model fit for modern cities, with uniformed officers under a central command given powers to enforce the law.

German chancellor Otto von Bismarck proposes a compulsory **insurance scheme to protect workers** injured in industry.

↑

1881

Women in New Zealand are the first to win the **right to vote**; elsewhere, they do not win suffrage until well into the 20th century.

↑

1893

US president Woodrow Wilson creates the **Federal Trade Commission** to regulate businesses and **protect consumers**.

↑

1914

In the **Treaty of Versailles** following World War I, the victorious Allies impose **punitive measures** on Germany.

↑

1919

1890

↓

The **Sherman Antitrust Act** is passed by the US Senate, banning anti-competitive cartels and monopolies.

1899

↓

The first Hague Convention proposes an international **set of rules of war**, and founds international humanitarian law.

1918

↓

Following the 1917 Revolution, Vladimir Lenin delivers a **new Russian constitution**, establishing a state ruled by the workers.

1935

↓

The **Nuremberg Laws** lay down the Nazi policy of German citizenship, effectively defining Jews as "non-persons".

The UK also led the way in creating laws to protect the rights of workers and trade unions in the latter part of the 19th century, while in the US, regulation of large corporations was introduced in the Sherman Antitrust Act to protect customers from unscrupulous businesses. As mass production and consumerism grew, it became clear that legislation was needed to ensure businesses met certain production standards, and the "snail in the bottle" case brought against ginger-beer manufacturer David Stevenson in 1932 became a landmark in the law of negligence.

Human rights

By the 19th century, the rights of citizens were a core principle of most legal systems, but recognition of basic human rights took far longer. The UK was first to ban the slave trade in its colonies and on its ships, but the complete abolition of slavery was slow in being achieved. Despite the good intentions of documents such as France's Declaration of the Rights of Man, all men were not yet seen as equals, even by the law – and women were certainly not regarded as deserving of equal rights, the majority of countries denying them the vote until after World War I.

While the "Jim Crow" laws sanctioning segregation in the US were blatantly discriminatory, an even more flagrant form of racism was made law in Nazi Germany. The humiliating terms imposed on Germany in the Treaty of Versailles, and the consequent economic depression, triggered a backlash that made the Jews scapegoats, stripped of their rights as citizens.

Meanwhile, in Russia, the world's first socialist state was founded, with its leader Vladimir Lenin promising a fairer and more equal society. This became the model for other communist states, which at one point in the 20th century accounted for about a third of the world's population, and stood in stark opposition to the liberal capitalism of the Western world.

At an international level, the effects of industrialization were also felt in the nature of modern warfare, with unprecedented levels of casualties prompting a series of Geneva Conventions on the conduct of war. These were complemented by the Hague Conventions, agreeing the rules of warfare, limiting the use of certain weapons, and laying the foundations for international humanitarian law. ■

JUSTICE UNDER THE CONSTITUTION

THE US SUPREME COURT AND JUDICIAL REVIEW (1803)

IN CONTEXT

FOCUS
US federal law

BEFORE
1787 The text of the new US Constitution is agreed, making the judiciary a "third branch" of government.

1789 Congress passes the Judiciary Act, which sets out some of the Supreme Court's powers.

AFTER
1857 In *Dred Scott v. Sandford*, Chief Justice Roger Taney rules that the word "citizens" in the Constitution does not refer to black people. This much-vilified decision is later overturned by the Fourteenth Amendment.

1973 In *Roe v. Wade*, the Supreme Court rules that the Constitution protects the right of a woman to seek an abortion.

The Supreme Court is the highest federal court in the US. It was specified by the Constitution and signed into force by President George Washington with the Judiciary Act of 1789. This decreed that the Court would have six judges (also known as justices). Nominated by the president and confirmed by the Senate, they usually hold office for life (until they retire or die), and their salary cannot be decreased during their term. In this way, the justices are kept independent of government.

Although the US Constitution provided for the Supreme Court to exist, it did not codify (write down in law) its powers and prerogatives. Rather, the Court's powers have, over time, been defined by its own rulings. One such power is that of judicial review.

Judicial review allows the Court to decide whether a legislative act (produced by Congress), executive act (produced by the president), or judicial act (produced by a lower court) violates the Constitution. This provides an essential system of checks and balances, ensuring limitations on the powers of each of the three branches of government. The Supreme Court, therefore, has the final word on any constitutional conflict: a unique role in US government.

Marbury v. Madison
The appointment of the fourth chief justice, John Marshall, in 1801, was pivotal for the Supreme Court. More robust than previous chief justices, Marshall was keen to assert the Court's power and political autonomy. His opportunity came in 1803, when a case was brought by William Marbury.

In 1801, outgoing Federalist president John Adams had passed an act that allowed him to nominate a number of new judges, including Marbury. (The Federalists and the Democratic-Republicans were the first US political parties.) The government of the new president, Democratic-Republican Thomas Jefferson, was unhappy with so many Federalist appointees, who would advance a nationalistic

---

The Supreme Court has an official seal, which is kept in the custody of the Clerk of the Court. It contains a number of symbols, each representing different and important elements of the Court's authority. The seal differs from the coat of arms of the United States in only one respect: the single star at the base, beneath the tail of the eagle.

The single star represents the creation of "one Supreme Court" by the US Constitution in 1789.

The eagle's head represents the president. Its nine tail feathers symbolize the nine judges of the Supreme Court.

The shield resembles the flag of the United States. Its 13 stripes represent the 13 original states.

The motto on the scroll in the eagle's beak reads *E pluribus unum*: "Out of many, one".

A constellation of 13 stars symbolizes the emergence of the US as an independent nation.

The olive branch in the eagle's right talon represents peace. The eagle's gaze is turned towards this side.

A sheaf of arrows held in the eagle's left talon symbolizes war, showing that the nation is always in readiness for war.

See also: The US Constitution and Bill of Rights 110–17 ▪ The exclusionary rule 186–87 ▪ *Miranda v. Arizona* 254–55 ▪ *Roe v. Wade* 260–63

> The judicial Power of the United States shall be vested in one supreme Court, and in such inferior Courts as the Congress may from time to time ordain and establish.
>
> **US Constitution**
> **Article III, Section 1**

agenda and shift the balance of power towards the judiciary. As a result, Marbury did not receive his commission. He took secretary of state James Madison to court, asking that the Supreme Court issue a writ of mandamus (an order to a lower court or official to fulfil their public duty) to compel Madison to grant the commission.

Chief Justice Marshall delivered his verdict against Marbury. He agreed that Marbury was legally entitled to his commission, but declared that the Supreme Court did not have the power to issue the writ of mandamus – because, in requiring the Supreme Court to do so, Congress had expanded the original jurisdiction of the Court, and this was in violation of the Constitution. This ruling positioned the Constitution as the supreme law of the land and the Supreme Court as the body that interpreted it. It defined the power of judicial review, setting a precedent that has stood the test of time.

Marshall has been praised by commentators for his deft handling of the case. His strategic decision built on the existing concept of judicial review – which, while not written into law, had been accepted by most framers of the Constitution as necessary. (Founding Father Alexander Hamilton wrote in 1788 that "the Constitution ought to be preferred to the statute, the intention of the people to the intention of their agents".) Marshall, in his ruling, explained that by creating a written constitution the US had defined the limits of powers for the different departments of government, and that the Constitution would mean nothing "if these limits may, at any time, be passed by those intended to be restrained".

The impact of this fairly obscure case was immense. While ensuring that the original jurisdiction of the Supreme Court was not expanded, Marshall had, as a result, centred its focus on appellate jurisdiction: the power of the Court to review, amend, or overrule the decision of a lower court. This asserted the power of the Supreme Court as a co-equal branch of government. »

> It is emphatically the province and duty of the judicial department to say what the law is.
>
> **John Marshall**
> *Marbury v. Madison*, 1803

John Marshall

Born in Virginia in 1755, John Marshall was the eldest of 15 children. He served during the American Revolutionary War, then left the army in 1780 to study law. He quickly gained a reputation for measured decisions, and soon became involved in government. He was a strong advocate for the ratification of the new US Constitution: this replaced the Articles of Confederation, which had lacked provision for a judicial or an executive branch of government.

In 1800, Marshall became secretary of state under John Adams. A year later, he was appointed chief justice of the Supreme Court – a position he held until his death in 1835. In this role he presided over numerous key cases that, over time, defined the powers of the Court. These included *McCulloch v. Maryland* (1819), in which Marshall ruled that the federal government had the right to open a national bank, and *Cohens v. Virginia* (1821), which established that the Supreme Court had jurisdiction to rule on all state court judgements that challenged the Constitution.

The **US Constitution** is the **supreme law** of the land.

The Constitution **balances power** across the **legislative**, **executive**, and **judicial** branches of government.

Judicial review is the **power** of the Supreme Court to **interpret and uphold the Constitution**.

The **Supreme Court** represents the **judicial branch** of government.

Marshall may be best known for this ruling, but during his tenure as chief justice he also presided over other important innovations. One example was the shift to an Opinion of the Court presented as a majority decision, in contrast to the former method of seriatim decisions, in which each judge delivered their own separate opinion.

Put to the test

Although *Marbury v. Madison* was the watershed case that established the Supreme Court's power of judicial review, it was just the start of a long process of clarification. During its early years, the Court heard numerous cases that served to define more clearly the parameters of this power. Each ruling gave greater legitimacy to the Supreme Court as arbiter of the Constitution, and confirmed the right of the Court to review the constitutionality of laws passed by lower courts and by the legislative branch or the executive branch of government.

However, the principle was not without its opponents. President Andrew Jackson, for example, who held office from 1829 to 1837, was a proponent of the departmental theory of government, which argued that each branch of government possessed the right to interpret the Constitution. Jackson put a number of cases to the Supreme Court that served to challenge John Marshall's perception of the Court's role. In 1832, he even defied the decision of the Court in *Worcester v. Georgia*: a ruling that laid the foundations for the principle of tribal sovereignty. Jackson circumvented the ruling,

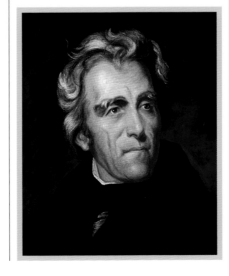

allowing the forced relocation of the Cherokee people from their lands to continue. (This chapter in US history, in which more than 60,000 Native Americans were compelled to leave their ancestral lands and walk thousands of kilometres to designated "Indian territory", is known as the Trail of Tears.)

Judicial review was also put to the test in *Lochner v. New York* (1905). The state of New York had, in 1895, passed the Bakeshop Act, which ruled that bakers, who often worked in poorly ventilated spaces and as a result suffered from lung problems, should not be forced to work more than 10 hours a day or 60 hours a week. Bakery owner Joseph Lochner, after being prosecuted for contravening this law, challenged the Act. The Supreme Court ruled by a majority of 5-4 that the Act was indeed a violation of the due process clause of the Fourteenth Amendment. This clause effectively

President Andrew Jackson famously disregarded the Supreme Court's ruling in *Worcester v. Georgia* (1832). He is said to have declared: "Marshall has made his decision; now let him enforce it!"

> The opinion of the judges has no more authority over Congress than the opinion of Congress has over the judges, and on that point the President is independent of both.
> **Andrew Jackson**
> **7th US president (1829–37)**

states that the government should not interfere unduly with the rights of an individual. The ruling argued that bakers should have a "right" to negotiate working contracts without the interference of the state, and that the Bakeshop Act was therefore unconstitutional. Judicial opinion was divided on whether the decision represented the Court defending the Constitution or promoting economic and business interests.

Detractors of judicial review argue that it is a role the Supreme Court has taken upon itself, and that nowhere has this power of legislative supremacy been overtly described. For this reason, its legitimacy has often been called into question. In many countries (Canada, Australia, and the UK, for example), legislation on contentious issues, such as same-sex marriage or abortion, is decided after parliamentary debate by elected representatives. In the US, issues can be debated in Congress, but the decision of Congress may ultimately be upheld only by the judges. The idea that elected legislatures are to be held to account by unelected judges is, to some, an affront to democracy itself.

Latterly, judicial review has been seen as increasingly important in the protection of civil rights, since the Supreme Court can strike down laws that it believes violate the rights of an individual. For example, in *Brown v. Board of Education of Topeka* (1954), the Supreme Court overturned state laws that allowed the existence of racially segregated schools. And in 2015, the Court ruled that the Fourteenth Amendment requires that all states must legalize same-sex marriage. While these progressive rulings have been held up as examples of the value of judicial review, many scholars point out that, should a president nominate a number of conservative judges to the Supreme Court (as President Trump has done), the balance of power could swing to a more conservative agenda – with the effect that landmark rulings, such as *Roe v. Wade*, which legalized abortion, could be challenged. ∎

The present Supreme Court building, in Washington, DC, opened in 1935. Until then the Court had no permanent home, meeting in various locations over the previous 146 years.

EVERY FRENCHMAN SHALL ENJOY CIVIL RIGHTS
THE NAPOLEONIC CODE (1804)

IN CONTEXT

FOCUS
Law codes, civil rights

BEFORE
6th century CE The *Corpus juris civilis* of Roman law provides a foundation for civil law across much of Europe.

1215 England's Magna Carta includes a number of civil and human rights.

1791 The first 10 amendments to the US Constitution of 1787 form the Bill of Rights.

AFTER
1881–83 Egyptian politician Youssef Wahba translates the Napoleonic Code into Arabic.

1896 Germany promulgates its own Civil Code, which also influences those of Japan (1896), Switzerland (1907), Turkey (1926), and others.

2012 The Commission supérieure de codification recommends that French legal codes are no longer updated.

The leaders of the French Revolution (1789–1799) recognized the urgent need for an overarching legal code for France. Historically, differing customary laws had developed across the French regions. To complicate matters, marriage and family life came under separate canon law (laws made by the Roman Catholic Church), and other laws had been created by royal decree. This had resulted in a confusing array of conflicting legislation, and many feudal lords had secured exemptions. To consolidate its power, the new National Assembly set up a special commission to overhaul the legal system and establish a civil code for the whole nation based on the Revolution's key principles.

Napoleon takes charge
When the Revolution descended into the murderous chaos known as the Reign of Terror, General Napoleon Bonaparte seized power in 1799. Elected as First Consul in 1800, he quickly took control of the special commission charged with overhauling France's laws. The commission met more than 80 times over the next four years to formulate the Napoleonic Code, with Napoleon frequently overseeing the discussions.

The Revolution had paved the way for the new Code by abolishing the monarchy, suppressing the power of the Church and medieval trade guilds, and creating a new French national identity. The Code

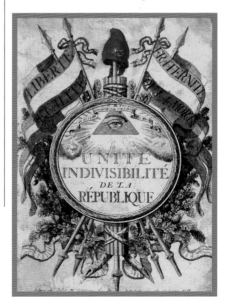

The Napoleonic Code is based on the French Revolution's ideals of liberty, equality, and fraternity in a united France, spelt out on the banners and shield of this 1792 Revolutionary poster.

See also: The origins of canon law 42–47 ▪ Magna Carta 66–71 ▪ The US Constitution and Bill of Rights 110–17 ▪ The Declaration of the Rights of Man 118–19

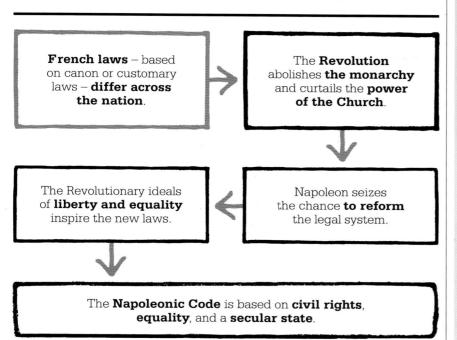

French laws – based on canon or customary laws – **differ across the nation**.	The **Revolution** abolishes **the monarchy** and curtails the **power of the Church**.
The Revolutionary ideals of **liberty and equality** inspire the new laws.	Napoleon seizes the chance **to reform** the legal system.

The **Napoleonic Code** is based on **civil rights**, **equality**, and a **secular state**.

Napoleon Bonaparte

Born in 1769 in Corsica, Napoleon was educated in France from the age of nine, later attending a military academy in Paris. He forged a successful military career, rising through the ranks and, in 1795, he played a major role in suppressing rebels opposed to the National Convention, the first government of the French Revolution. In 1799, however, he took advantage of the power vacuum to seize control in a coup d'état.

Napoleon crowned himself emperor in 1804 and launched a series of military campaigns to expand the French Empire, conquering swathes of continental Europe and ousting Spain as a colonial power in much of Latin America. In 1812, he was forced to abdicate after a disastrous invasion of Russia but returned to power in 1815. After defeat by the British at the Battle of Waterloo, Napoleon was exiled to the island of St Helena, off the western coast of Africa, where he died in 1821. He left behind numerous letters, speeches, addresses, and proclamations to his troops, some of which were collected and published.

was built around key Revolutionary ideas – the principles of civil liberty (basic human rights and freedoms under the law), equality, and a secular state where people had the right to religious dissent. By making all (male) citizens equal before the law, it sought to end primogeniture (the eldest son's right to inherit property), hereditary nobility, and class privilege. It protected men's property rights, but women were legally subordinate to fathers or husbands. The Code divided civil law into property and family law, and codified criminal and commercial law. A new freedom to form contracts without government interference was also included.

An enduring influence

The Napoleonic Code was highly influential. Countries under the control of France in 1804, including Belgium, Luxembourg, and parts of Germany and Italy all introduced it, as did a number of Latin American countries. Its influence is also evident in the law codes of some Middle Eastern nations. In many countries that adopted it, the Code, although updated and revised, is still the cornerstone of civil laws today. ▪

My real glory is not the forty battles I won … What nothing will destroy, what will live forever, is my Civil Code.
Napoleon Bonaparte

LET THE OPPRESSED GO FREE

THE ABOLITION OF THE SLAVE TRADE ACT (1807)

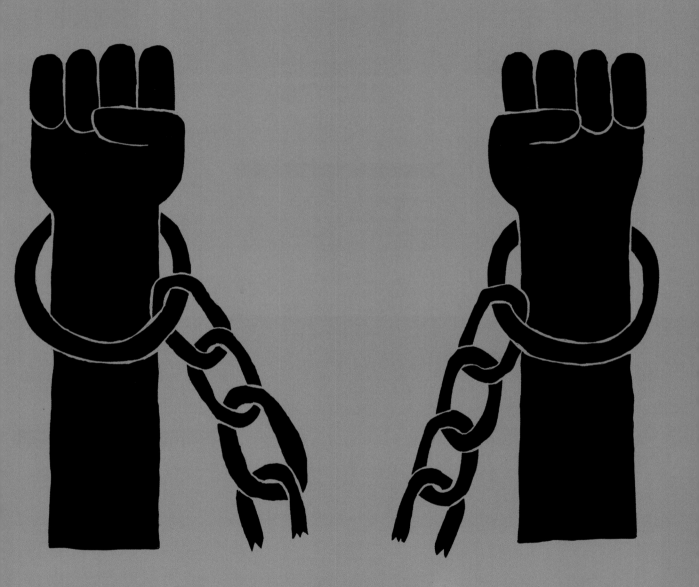

How does the slave differ from his master, but by chance?
Thomas Clarkson
An Essay on the Slavery and Commerce of the Human Species, 1786

Slavery is a system that treats people as property to be owned and controlled, with no regard for their rights as human beings. It existed in some form in almost every ancient civilization, from Egypt and India to China and Rome, and has persisted through medieval to modern times. Slavery was a major industry in Europe from the 16th to the 18th centuries, until protests against the trade's atrocities became widespread.

The trade triangle

In medieval Africa, slaves had been traded between countries or tribes and to supply Islamic countries in Arabia. Portuguese and Spanish navigators discovered the African slave markets in the mid-15th century and a slave trade triangle began to emerge in the 16th century. European ships took goods to Africa's west coast to exchange for slaves. The ships crossed the Atlantic, on the Middle Passage, to sell their human cargoes in South America (especially Brazil) or the Caribbean, mostly to plantations. Then tobacco, sugar, molasses, rum, and later cotton, filled the ships for the homeward voyages.

Conditions during the 8,000-km (5,000-mile) Middle Passage were horrific. Sickness was rife, due to brutal treatment, scarce food and water, and acute overcrowding. By 1867, *c*. 2.5 million of 10–12 million Africans had died on ships during the Middle Passage.

White European slavers (slave traders) portrayed slaves as savages to dehumanize them. They even painted themselves as saviours, and Africans as lucky to be taken to better lives in the New World. Slavers made huge profits and those involved became rich and powerful. In Britain, the West India Lobby of slavers and plantation owners included MPs, who incited fears that restricting the trade would aid Britain's rivals, such as France.

By the 17th century, Britain, the Netherlands, France, and Denmark had become major players in the transatlantic slave trade, to furnish their respective colonies with labour. Britain controlled two-thirds of the trade, supporting slavers with laws such as a series of Trade and Navigation Acts.

Slaves as property

In 1677, the solicitor-general's ruling that "negroes" be classified as property under the Trade and Navigation Acts was confirmed by the *Butts v. Penny* case of the same year. Slave owners could now use property law to claim for lost or "damaged" slaves, reducing them to mere commodities.

Many plantation owners brought slaves back to Britain to work as servants. Over the years, a number of slaves had escaped from their masters and appealed to the courts for their freedom, most notably in the case of *Somerset v. Stewart*. James Somerset was a slave who had been brought to England by his owner, Charles Stewart, and had

I cannot say this case is allowed or approved by the law of England; and therefore [the slave] must be discharged.
William Murray, 1st Earl of Mansfield
Somerset v. Stewart ruling, 1772

See also: Slave codes 98–101 ▪ The US Constitution and Bill of Rights 110–17 ▪ The US Supreme Court and judicial review 124–29 ▪ The Universal Declaration of Human Rights 222–29 ▪ The Civil Rights Act 248–53

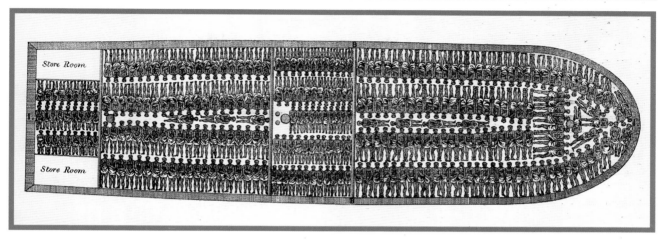

escaped. He was recaptured and put on a boat bound for Jamaica to be resold. Abolitionist Granville Sharp took up his case and Lord Mansfield, the lord chief justice, issued a writ of *habeas corpus* (an order to bring a person under arrest before a judge or court to decide whether the detention is lawful). Somerset duly appeared before the Court of King's Bench.

Lord Mansfield ruled in 1772 that, although slavery was allowed in the colonies, a slave in England

A replica of *Zong*, the ship from which slaves were thrown to ease overcrowding, took part in events in London in 2007 to mark 200 years since the Abolition of the Slave Trade Act.

was subject to English law. As no English law permitted Somerset's recapture and forcible shipping to Jamaica, he had to be freed. The judge tried to make a ruling that freed Somerset without setting a precedent, but the case was a watershed moment in the abolitionist movement. It was widely seen as outlawing slavery in Britain, allowing other slaves to plead for their own freedom.

In Britain, growing opposition to the slave trade was fuelled in part by atrocities such as the *Zong* massacre. In 1781, due to severe overcrowding on the slave ship *Zong*, Captain Luke Collingwood commanded 132 sick slaves to be thrown overboard. (If any slaves died of sickness, insurers would not pay compensation, but would do so if the slaves had been killed to safeguard the ship.) In law, slaves were viewed as commodities rather than people, so it was treated

The slave ship *Brookes* became notorious in 1788 when abolitionists published an engraving of the appalling, yet legal, conditions onboard, including its crammed lower deck.

as a disputed insurance claim rather than as mass murder. Such rank injustice brought many more people to the abolitionist cause.

Abolitionist campaigns

In 1787, 12 activists founded the Society for Effecting the Abolition of the Slave Trade at a printing shop in London. They included Thomas Clarkson, who had recently published an influential essay condemning slavery. The society's many women supporters – ten per cent of its subscribers in the first year were women – included prominent abolitionists Quaker poet Mary Birkett Card, evangelist Hannah More, and feminist philosopher Mary Wollstonecraft.

To inform popular opinion on the arguments against slavery, the society's network of campaigners produced pamphlets, hosted talks, and secured signatures on petitions. The goal was abolition »

Olaudah Equiano

Kidnapped as a child of about 11 from his Nigerian home, Olaudah Equiano was shipped across the Atlantic, ending up in the plantations of Virginia. He was sold to a Royal Navy officer, Lieutenant Michael Henry Pascal, who renamed him Gustavus Vassa (after a 16th-century Swedish king).

Equiano spent eight years at sea and, while with Pascal, learnt to read and write and was baptized in 1759. He was later sold on to Philadelphia merchant Robert King, who allowed Equiano to trade a little for himself. Within three years, in 1766, he was able to buy his freedom. He worked on ships for the next 20 years, then settled in London in 1786, where he became involved in the abolitionist movement.

In 1789, Equiano published his autobiography, one of the first books by a black African writer. It was hugely popular and Equiano toured around the country to tell his story. He died in London in 1797.

Key work

1789 *The Interesting Narrative of the Life of Olaudah Equiano, or Gustavus Vassa, the African*

of the slave trade because it seemed more achievable than the outright outlawing of slavery. The campaign quickly gained momentum. In 1788, in just three months, more than 100 anti-slavery petitions were delivered to Parliament.

One of the campaigners' key concerns was to give a voice to the Africans themselves, by providing evidence and testimonies from escaped slaves, and from sailors of slave ships, as well as accounts from freed slaves such as Olaudah Equiano (see left). He was literate, charming, and a Christian convert (which mattered in a fervently Christian society). Such stories helped to rehumanize Africans in the eyes of the public and forced it to face the brutal reality of slavery.

The idea of human rights

Revolutions in America (1775–83) and France (1789–99) made the late 18th century a period of political turmoil. Such popular movements highlighted the concept of human rights and inspired people to engage with activism. However, the threat of revolution made the British Parliament cautious. As the abolitionist movement grew in strength, it began to be portrayed

Is one half of the human species, like the poor African slaves, to be subject to prejudices that brutalize them … ?
Mary Wollstonecraft
A Vindication of the Rights of Woman, 1792

as "radical". This frustrated early efforts in Parliament to end slavery: anti-slavery bills were repeatedly blocked by the vested interests of those who profited from slavery and feared a collapse of the old order.

Unable to vote, let alone stand for election, women were largely barred from taking an active role in politics at this time, but activists such as Hannah More and Mary Wollstonecraft used their influence and writings to effect change. The burgeoning women's rights movement saw the oppression of women reflected in the plight of African slaves and often equated the two issues in their campaigns.

Slave revolts

While abolitionists were lobbying the British Parliament, slaves in the Caribbean were taking matters into their own hands. In Jamaica, the Maroons – escaped slaves and their descendants – had fought British colonialists for years and in 1739

Emotive designs, such as this by British potter Josiah Wedgwood in 1787, were used on medallions and other items, to support the abolitionist cause.

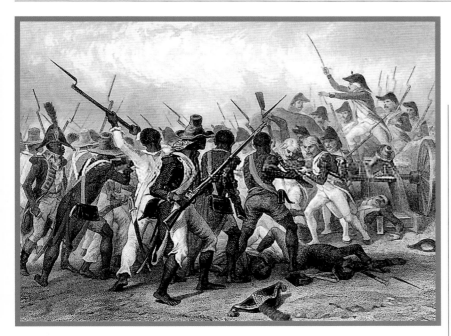

In the Haitian Revolution, slaves fought in a series of battles with French troops (shown here), as well as with British and Spanish colonialists, between 1791 and 1804.

Despite widespread public support for abolition, Parliament did not allow an outright ban on slavery until the 1830s. The economic climate had changed: British-run Caribbean sugar plantations were now much less profitable than those in Brazil and Cuba. So British merchants pressed for free trade and an end to the Caribbean monopoly of the British sugar market.

The 1833 Slavery Abolition Act freed only those aged under six years; older slaves became "apprentices", compelled to work for their former owners for a number of years. The territories controlled by the British East India Company, for example Ceylon (now Sri Lanka), were also exempt, but slavery was otherwise outlawed across the British Empire.

America and slavery
Slavery was key to the economy of the Southern colonies of America, where slaves were used to do the gruelling work on plantations of cotton and other cash crops that »

won a settlement of land. In the French colony of Saint-Domingue on the western end of the island of Hispaniola, slaves began an armed revolt in 1791. Toussaint L'Ouverture, a freed slave and skilful soldier, played a leading role in the struggle for control of Saint-Domingue and its neighbour, Santo Domingo (later the Dominican Republic).

The uprisings eventually won Saint-Domingue, now called Haiti, its independence from France in 1804, making it the first country to be governed by former slaves. These early slave revolts inspired other slaves in the Caribbean to take agency in the fight for freedom.

Parliament's ban
From 1787, British parliamentarian William Wilberforce became a leading abolitionist and strove for 20 years to bring anti-slavery bills before Parliament. Despite great public support, politicians were unwilling to vote for an outright ban on slavery, fearing it would harm British business interests.

In 1806, abolitionist James Stephen advised Wilberforce to change tack and introduce a bill to stop Britons from trading slaves with foreign territories. As Britain was at war with France, the bill was presented as a patriotic effort to harm French interests and was passed. However, as Wilberforce hoped, it caused a collapse in the British slave trade and paved the way for the 1807 Abolition of the Slave Trade Act. Passed with a majority of 114 to 15 in the House of Commons, the 1807 Act made it illegal to engage in slave trading in the British Empire or to carry slaves in any British ship, but did not compel the freeing of all slaves. That became the goal of the next phase of the abolition campaign.

The Royal Navy patrolled the coast of Africa to enforce the ban on trading slaves. Between 1807 and 1860, it stopped many British vessels and liberated over 150,000 slaves, but enforcing the Act was a huge task. Rogue British merchants often evaded it by operating under other countries' flags.

A trade founded in iniquity, and carried on as this was, must be abolished …
William Wilberforce
Speech to Parliament, 1789

thrived in the warm, humid climate. In the North, where different crops were grown, fewer slaves were used to work the land.

Many in the North favoured abolition and, during the American Revolution (1775–83), they equated British rule with the practice of slavery. The North–South divide on slavery became so intense that the two sides could only agree the US Constitution in 1787 by omitting the slave trade issue from its articles. Yet, in 1788, the ratified Constitution had clauses that guaranteed the rights to repossess

any "person held to service or labor", effectively acknowledging the institution of slavery across the US, which would continue for eight more decades.

In 1839, the case of the slave ship, *La Amistad*, galvanized opinion. Two Spanish plantation owners had sailed from Cuba with 53 slaves, who broke free and ordered the owners to sail to Africa. After sailing off course, the ship and slaves were impounded as salvage in Connecticut. A two-year legal battle involving Spain ended with the US Supreme Court ruling

the Africans were not property, but free persons who had been illegally kidnapped and brought to Cuba.

Dred Scott v. Sandford
Since 1643, various Acts had compelled the return of escaped slaves to their masters. The 1850 Fugitive Slave Act included fines for anyone interfering in rendition of slaves and forced citizens to aid in their recapture. Some Northern states issued their own laws to try to nullify its impact.

In 1856, the US Supreme Court heard the *Dred Scott v. Sandford* case. Dred Scott was born a slave, but his owners had lived for a time in Wisconsin and Illinois, where slavery was outlawed, before they returned to Missouri, a slave state. So Scott applied to the court to be set free, with his wife Harriet.

In 1857, Chief Justice Roger B. Taney ruled against Scott, stating that all people of African descent, slaves or not, were "beings of an inferior order", not US citizens, so could not bring a suit in a federal court. This controversial ruling was a factor in igniting the American Civil War (1861–65) between the North and the slave-owning South.

Neither slavery nor involuntary servitude ... shall exist within the United States, or any place subject to their jurisdiction.
US Constitution, Thirteenth Amendment

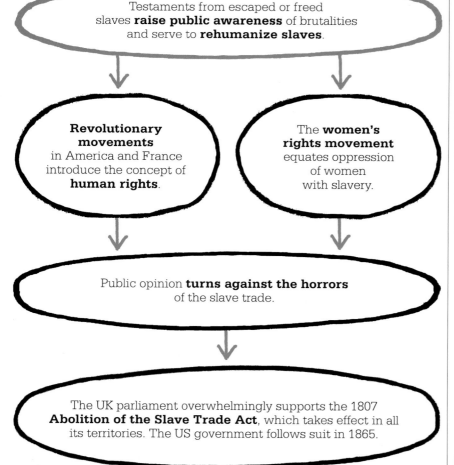

Testaments from escaped or freed slaves **raise public awareness** of brutalities and serve to **rehumanize slaves**.

Revolutionary movements in America and France introduce the concept of **human rights**.

The **women's rights movement** equates oppression of women with slavery.

Public opinion **turns against the horrors** of the slave trade.

The UK parliament overwhelmingly supports the 1807 **Abolition of the Slave Trade Act**, which takes effect in all its territories. The US government follows suit in 1865.

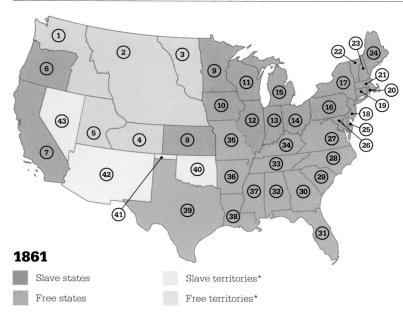

1861

- Slave states
- Free states
- Slave territories*
- Free territories*

Key:

1. Washington Territory
2. Nebraska Territory
3. Dakota Territory
4. Colorado
5. Utah
6. Oregon
7. California
8. Kansas
9. Minnesota
10. Iowa
11. Wisconsin
12. Illinois
13. Indiana
14. Ohio
15. Michigan
16. Pennsylvania
17. New York
18. New Jersey
19. Connecticut
20. Rhode Island
21. Massachusetts
22. Vermont
23. New Hampshire
24. Maine
25. Delaware
26. Maryland
27. Virginia
28. North Carolina
29. South Carolina
30. Georgia
31. Florida
32. Alabama
33. Tennessee
34. Kentucky
35. Missouri
36. Arkansas
37. Mississippi
38. Louisiana
39. Texas
40. Indian Territory
41. Neutral strip
42. New Mexico Territory
43. Nevada Territory

* Territory: region directly ruled by federal government

Slave states numbered 15 in 1861 at the start of the Civil War, up from 8 in 1789, but were now outnumbered by 19 Free states. At the war's end, slavery was banned in all US states and territories.

	1789	1800	1821	1837	1846	1858	1861
Slave states	8	9	12	13	15	15	15
Free states	5	8	12	13	14	17	19

President Abraham Lincoln's advocacy of abolition strengthened the more the Southern Confederacy threatened the Union (Northern States of America). In 1863, his Emancipation Proclamation declared free all slaves in rebellious states. It did not apply to slave states loyal to the Union, but did allow black men to enlist. After the Union's victory, the Thirteenth Amendment was ratified in 1865, abolishing slavery across the US and setting more than four million slaves free.

Limited rights

After the Civil War, President Andrew Johnson was keen to allow Southern states to set their own laws, provided that they recognized the Thirteenth Amendment and repaid their war debts. When the Southern states began passing laws, called "black codes", that restricted the rights of freed slaves, many in the North were outraged.

In 1866, Congress passed the Civil Rights Act: anyone born in the United States had the right to citizenship and equality before the law. Congress then took control of reconstruction in the South and took care to enforce the Fourteenth Amendment, which granted equal protections under the Constitution to former slaves. In 1870, Congress adopted the Fifteenth Amendment, which guaranteed that a citizen's right to vote could not be denied "on account of race, color, or previous condition of servitude".

Although slavery was officially abolished, in the Deep South a practice called "peonage" persisted into the 1920s. African Americans who had been convicted (often on false charges) were sent to work in dangerous workplaces, such as brick factories, plantations, and mines, to "pay off" their fines. This trapped workers in a cycle of unpaid work and mounting debt. The 1964 Civil Rights Act banned racial segregation and employment discrimination, which had been used in the South to stop black people exercising their freedoms.

Slavery today

Debt-slavery continues in the 21st century. Britain passed the Modern Slavery Act in 2015 to outlaw such practices as compelling migrant workers to work to pay off human traffickers. However, despite a raft of similar legislation, vulnerable people continue to be exploited across the world, with up to 45 million people effectively enslaved. ∎

PURITY, ACTIVITY, VIGILANCE, AND DISCRETION

THE METROPOLITAN POLICE ACT (1829)

The ancient Egyptians, Greeks, and Romans all had a loose form of policing for maintaining public order and keeping watch at night. In medieval England, the Anglo-Saxons took this idea further with the Statute of Winchester in 1285, which directed all citizens to keep the king's peace, making policing a collective responsibility. These and other early forms of policing did not extend to investigating or prosecuting crimes, such as theft or assault, which were considered to be private matters between individuals.

See also: Trial by ordeal and combat 52–53 ▪ The Assize of Clarendon 64–65 ▪ The abolition of the death penalty 151 ▪ INTERPOL 220–21 ▪ The Federal Witness Protection Program 259 ▪ Megan's Law 285

> It is much better to prevent even one man from being a rogue than apprehending and bringing forty to justice.
> **John Fielding**
> *An Account of the Origin and Effects of a Police Set on Foot etc, 1758*

In 1361, the Justice of the Peace Act created a network of justices of the peace (JPs, or magistrates) across England, to enforce order with the aid of part-time, unpaid constables and watchmen who were elected and later appointed by the local JP. They were also to be supported by the public, for example, if someone shouted "Stop, thief!" the public were expected to pursue and apprehend the accused person until a constable or watchman arrived to arrest them.

From the 16th century, wealthy merchants began to group together to pay for private "thief-takers", known as stipendiary police, who would recover stolen items for a fee – but this system benefitted only the rich and was open to corruption. Deterrents were the main method of enforcing law and order in the 17th century, and even minor misdemeanours such as stealing could be punished by death. Since this brutal form of justice impacted most on the poor, social campaigners began to call for reform.

The Bow Street Runners

In the 18th century, the long-running British system of constables began to fail as many of the better-off people selected to serve *pro bono* (without payment) bought their way out of the responsibility, complaining that it took them away from their own affairs. As a result, the position often went to those without a job – the old, the sick, or the poor – who struggled to carry out their duties.

In 1749, magistrate and author Henry Fielding, along with his brother John, established the Bow Street Runners, a small team of salaried police working from London's Bow Street Magistrate Courts. They did not patrol the streets but could serve writs or pursue criminals on behalf of the court. The initial six constables were paid by central government, and used organized methods of dealing with crime. However, they were not a preventative force since they could only act after a crime had been committed. Despite being limited to a small area of London, the idea of the Bow Street Runners as a professional police force proved influential.

Calls for reform

By the late-18th century, London was booming, crime levels were soaring, and the military were often called in to quell rioting. Magistrate Patrick Colquhoun pushed for police reforms in his *A Treatise on the Police of the Metropolis* (1796) and later called for efficient and highly motivated policemen with strong moral values. Colquhoun's theories were tested in 1798 when he took charge of the newly created Marine Police (which later became the Thames River Police). This salaried »

The Bow Street Runners, London's first salaried police force, shown in their blue coats, apprehending two men identified by a third as muggers who had made a career of robbing travellers.

Policing begins as a social **obligation of all citizens**.

→

Privately paid, or stipendiary, police receive **fees for making arrests**, and are open to **corruption**.

→

Capital punishment for even minor crimes is widely used in an effort to **deter crime**.

↓

Unpaid local constables are **ineffectual** in the face of **soaring population and crime** in London.

←

Reformers promote the idea of **preventative policing**.

←

Robert Peel establishes the Metropolitan Police in 1829 as a **professional force** focusing on **crime prevention**.

---

force was groundbreaking in that they took part in regular patrols – this visible deterrent proved successful as crime on the river dropped notably.

The government resisted growing calls for a similar model to be rolled out across Britain's cities as the cost would likely require a rise in taxes – never a popular move. Also, the dominant political ideology of the time argued for light state intervention, which seemed at odds with an organized police force run by the state. It was likewise feared that a standing police force would be open to corruption or misuse for political ends.

The weaknesses in allowing the army to handle law and order were laid bare in the excessive use of force that resulted in the Peterloo Massacre of 1819 in Manchester. Huge, but peaceful, crowds of protestors calling for parliamentary reform were charged by armed soldiers, resulting in 18 deaths and many injuries. The public were outraged and Parliament, fearing more violence, knew it had to act.

Creating a new police force

Politician Robert Peel led the call for police reform in London, which by the 1820s had a booming population and a crime rate to match. While chief secretary in Ireland, Peel had been inspired by the success of Dublin's police force. As home secretary, he focused on pushing through legislation to create a similar police force for London, arguing that lack of law and order in the capital was creating instability. By 1829, he had gained enough support for the Metropolitan Police Act to be passed.

The Metropolitan Police Act created a full-time professional police force for the London area that answered to the home secretary. Constables wore uniforms to make them easily identifiable, in blue

Use of heavy-handed armed forces led to the 1819 Peterloo Massacre in Manchester, where peaceful demonstrators were calling for parliamentary reform.

> The primary object of an efficient police is the prevention of crime: the next ... detection and punishment of offenders ...
> **Richard Mayne**
> **British justice of the peace**
> **(1796–1868)**

rather than the army's red, and were unarmed. Police constables (known as "bobbies" or "peelers" after Robert Peel) were paid more than a labourer but less than a skilled worker and, to stem corruption, they were no longer allowed to take fees for recovering stolen goods. Until 1897, constables were banned from voting in elections, to show that they had no political allegiance.

The new police force was the first to prioritize crime prevention, patrolling streets and keeping order by working with the local community. At first, people were hostile; they felt that uniformed officers telling them what to do was too much state interference in their daily lives. However, as crime levels across London began to fall, public opinion started to shift.

Going nationwide

By 1835, many newly formed local councils were appointing paid constables. The Rural Constabulary Act of 1839 allowed counties to establish their own police forces. Professional forces slowly spread across Britain, each overseen by a centralized command with power derived from the law itself –

Parliament. The County and Borough Police Act of 1856 then required all British towns and counties to establish their own police forces. By 1900, there were 181 police forces across Britain, but communication between them was scant, so many country forces were amalgamated into regional police forces to foster greater cooperation in policing across the nation.

Adopting the British model

Many Commonwealth countries and the US based their police forces on the British model, which focused on crime prevention and community ties and was viewed as less open to corruption than municipal police forces in continental Europe. The first centralized municipal US police force was formed in 1838 in Boston, with New York following soon after in 1845. However, the US police system soon diverged, as it became decentralized and based on local communities – often with strong ties to local politics, making some forces open to corruption.

Today Britain's police service has expanded its remit to include crime detection, undercover policing, anti-terrorism, and fighting cybercrime. Yet, at its root, it is still based on the 1829 principle that the police and the public are synonymous. ■

> The police are the public and the public are the police.
> **Metropolitan Police's General Instructions, 1829**

Robert Peel

Father of modern policing, son of a wealthy industrialist and baronet, Sir Robert Peel was born in 1788 and educated at Harrow and Oxford University. He entered the UK Parliament as a Conservative MP in 1809 and held a number of important roles, including chief secretary for Ireland from 1812 to 1818. But it was as home secretary from 1822 that Peel was to leave his mark, instigating prison reform and establishing the Metropolitan Police.

Peel later served twice as prime minister, in 1834–35 and 1841–46. In 1846, he successfully repealed the Corn Laws (trade restrictions and tariffs designed to protect domestic grain producers) to free up grain to send to Ireland and relieve the potato famine there. He also introduced the Factory Act of 1844, restricting the number of hours women and children could be made to work in factories. This, coupled with the Mines Act of 1842 – which banned women and children from working in the mines – was significant in the reform of Victorian working practices. He died in 1850, after a fatal fall from his horse.

ALL CONTRACTS BY WAY OF GAMING SHALL BE NULL AND VOID
THE GAMING ACT (1845)

IN CONTEXT

FOCUS
Gambling regulation

BEFORE
1254 King Louis IX bans gambling in France, in the first of many such edicts.

1541 In England, the Unlawful Games Act outlaws pastimes deemed distracting to the public, such as dicing tables, card tables, bowls, and tennis.

AFTER
1853 The Betting Act makes it illegal to use any premises for betting in the UK.

1910 The state of Nevada is one of the last in the US to ban casino gambling.

1931 The first casino opens in Las Vegas after the Nevada authorities legalize gambling due to its economic benefits.

2005 The UK Gambling Act makes wagers legally enforceable, ushering in an era of liberalized gambling.

Gaming and betting **grow in popularity** in the 18th century.

Increasing numbers of **legal cases** are brought to **recover gambling debts**.

The 1845 Gaming Act makes gaming contracts null and void.

Gambling debts are **no longer legally recoverable** in the courts.

Gaming (playing games of chance, such as dice) and wagering (placing a bet on an expected outcome) have long presented a dilemma to legislators. Often decried as a moral scourge by politicians and religious leaders, gambling has been variously prohibited – due to the financial ruin and negative social effects it often brings – or legalized, in order to regulate it, protect participants, and tax it to boost state coffers.

Although certain new games were, in theory, outlawed in 1541 in England, with the aim of preventing the public from neglecting their archery practice, the prohibition was

See also: The Cruelty to Animals Act 146–47 ▪ *Hadley v. Baxendale* 148–49 ▪ The International Convention Against Doping in Sport 304 ▪ The Match-Fixing Task Force 306–07 ▪ The Open Internet Order 310–13

Aristocrats play dice at Crockford's gentlemen's club in London, 1843. William Crockford, a former fishmonger, made a vast fortune from the gambling losses of his club's members.

not practical to enforce. Gambling was ever-popular, in many countries and cultures. In Britain, by the dawn of the Georgian era, in the early 18th century – a time of rapid social and economic change – it was booming. Wagers were legal and enforceable under common law. Placing bets on boxing matches, bear-baiting, and cockfighting was popular with the working class, while the aristocracy favoured dice or card tables.

Legislation was introduced not as a response to the moral concerns of social reformers, but due to the increase in gambling disputes being handled by the overstretched courts. The Gaming Act of 1845 ruled that gaming contracts were "null and void", making gambling debts legally unenforceable.

Changing the rules

The 1845 Act did not make wagers illegal. However, it stated that court actions seeking to recover "any sum of money or valuable thing" related to wagers would no longer be permitted – effectively removing gambling from the jurisdiction of

the law courts. The legislation was criticized as overly paternalistic and at odds with the principles of free choice. Why, libertarians asked, should people be discouraged from placing a wager of £10 on a sporting event, when they could just as easily lose a stake of £10 by investing it in the stock market?

One effect of the new Act was to deter professional bookmakers (whose rising numbers had stoked the growth of problem gambling in the late 18th century) from allowing punters to make wagers on credit. A punter who had lost a bet could no longer be forced by law to pay money owed. So bookmakers began to take cash bets, spurring a growth in cash-betting houses. The 1853 Betting Act suppressed betting houses and forced bookmakers to take their business onto the streets: a practice that was later outlawed by a further Act in 1906.

Liberalizing legislation

In the early part of the 20th century, gambling went underground in the UK, and was controlled by criminal

gangs. In 1949, a Royal Commission was tasked with investigating betting, lotteries, and gaming. Its conclusions resulted in the 1960 Betting and Gaming Act, which permitted licensed betting shops on Britain's high streets, making gambling more widely accessible.

In the 21st century, the UK government decided that gambling should no longer be seen as morally dubious, but encouraged in the same way as other leisure sectors due to its economic potential. The 2005 Gambling Act boosted the industry by regulating online gambling and removing planning obstacles to opening new betting shops. It also restored the legal enforceability of wagers that had been removed by the 1845 Act, and created the Gambling Commission to regulate commercial gambling. ▪

No Suit shall be brought or maintained in any Court of Law or Equity for recovering any Sum of Money or valuable Thing alleged to be won upon any Wager …
Gaming Act, 1845

BOUND TO DO NO INJURY TO FELLOW-CREATURES
THE CRUELTY TO ANIMALS ACT (1849)

IN CONTEXT

FOCUS
Animal welfare law

BEFORE
1764 In "Bêtes" ("Beasts"), an entry in his *Dictionnaire Philosophique*, Voltaire argues that animals are sentient.

1822 The first national law against animal cruelty is passed, in the UK.

1835 Revised British animal cruelty laws ban cockfighting and bull- and badger-baiting.

AFTER
1911 The Protection of Animals Act extends cruelty laws to cover all animals.

2006 The UK Animal Welfare Act makes owners responsible for ensuring their animals have a suitable environment and diet, and protection from injury, disease, and suffering.

2019 In the US, extreme animal cruelty becomes a federal crime.

Historically, people had viewed animals either as wild forces of nature, imbued with magical or even demonic powers, or as property. By the 17th century, some people had begun to recognize that animals needed legal protection from unnecessary suffering. In 1635, the Parliament of Ireland passed an "Act against Plowing by the Tayle, and Pulling the Wooll off Living Sheep" to prevent the Gaelic Irish practices of attaching a plough to a horse's tail and tearing wool from a sheep's back. In New England, too, the Massachusetts Body of Liberties (1641), one of the first legal codes in America to set out people's rights and responsibilities, included rules against "Tirranny or Crueltie" towards domestic animals – any specifically kept "for man's use".

In the 18th century, as the ideas of the Enlightenment gathered pace in Europe, there was a growing

---

The **Enlightenment** promotes the idea that **animals feel** and **therefore suffer**.

Christians feel a growing **moral duty** to **prevent the suffering** of animals.

Legal protection is initially extended only to **economically important** farm animals.

Lobbying by the **Society for the Prevention of Cruelty to Animals** increases **public awareness of animal suffering** and the Cruelty to Animals Act passes.

See also: The "Vivisection Act" 163 ▪ The Endangered Species Act 264–65 ▪ The World Network of Biosphere Reserves 270–71 ▪ The Kyoto Protocol 305

> Our treatment of animals – of creatures wholly subject to our control, may be regarded as an accurate criterion of our humanity towards our own species.
> **Elizabeth Heyrick**

philosophical debate about whether animals were sentient (able to feel). Philosophers Voltaire and Jean-Jacques Rousseau in France, and Jeremy Bentham in England, all wrote about animals' capacity to suffer physical pain or even have feelings. Gradually, thinking about the mistreatment of animals in terms of economic loss for an animal's owner shifted to the idea of treating animals kindly for their own sake.

A duty to protect

As consensus grew that people had a duty to protect animals, British Quaker philanthropist Elizabeth Heyrick launched a campaign in 1809 against bull-baiting and later battled for the protection of all farm animals. In 1822, the UK became the first country in the world to pass an animal welfare law. Known

Bull-baiting, setting dogs on a tethered bull, had been popular at fairs until the 1840s. Those who opposed it were also concerned about the gambling and fighting that accompanied such events.

as Martin's Act, after the MP and animal rights campaigner Richard Martin, it legislated against cruelty to farm animals such as cattle, sheep, mules, and horses. Heyrick's campaign continued with the publication of *Cursory Remarks on the Evil Tendency of Unrestrained Cruelty* in 1823, which targeted the cruel goading of animals before slaughter at Smithfield, London, the UK's largest meat market.

The Society for the Prevention of Cruelty to Animals was set up in 1824 and became a powerful lobbying force, attracting greater public support to the cause. In 1835, animal cruelty laws were updated to ban cockfighting, and bull- and badger-baiting, and to include protection for animals such as dogs and cats.

By the 1840s, public opinion had swung firmly in favour of greater protection for animals. Animal cruelty prosecutions increased, especially those involving knackers' yards, where horses awaiting slaughter were often denied food or water. In 1849, the Cruelty to

Animals Act was passed, which banned all animal baiting and fighting, and prevented the beating or overworking of domestic animals and any transportation of animals that caused them harm. Anyone breaking the law – or causing or procuring someone else to break animal cruelty laws – could be fined.

A wider debate

It was not until 1911 that the Protection of Animals Act granted protection to "all animals", although this still excluded wild animals, animals eaten as food, and those used in scientific experiments. Once it was widely accepted that animals could suffer, those excluded areas also began to be discussed.

In the UK, the Hunting Act of 2004 banned the hunting of wild animals (such as foxes) with dogs, and the Animal Welfare Act of 2006 made owners responsible for their pets' welfare. In the US, for the first time, the PACT (Preventing Animal Cruelty and Torture) Act of 2019 made extreme animal cruelty a federal (national) crime. ▪

THE DAMAGES SHOULD BE FAIRLY CONSIDERED
HADLEY V. BAXENDALE (1854)

IN CONTEXT

FOCUS
Contract law

BEFORE
531 CE The *duplum* ("double") rule in Roman law under Byzantine emperor Justinian I states that the amount of damages should be limited to twice the contract obligation.

1839 In the *Blanchard v. Ely* case, a US court cites French civil law as a precedent for the rule of foreseeability in awarding damages in breach of contract cases.

AFTER
1949 An English court rules that "reasonably foreseeable" means "ordinary" but not "extraordinary" loss of profits, in *Victoria Laundry (Windsor) Ltd v. Newman Industries Ltd*.

1980 The United Nations Convention on Contracts for the International Sale of Goods sets out an internationally agreed rule of foreseeability.

According to the **Hadley v. Baxendale** ruling, **damages for breach of contract** can be recovered in either of these two circumstances:

Where the loss could **reasonably be considered to arise naturally** from the breach.

Where the loss could reasonably have been **contemplated by both parties** when the contract was made.

The ruling of an English court of appeal in the 1854 case of *Hadley v. Baxendale* proved to be influential in the development of modern contract law. The case hinged on whether a defendant in breach of contract can be held liable for damages arising from a loss of earnings incurred as a result of the breach if the defendant was not made aware of such a possibility when the contract was signed.

Joseph and Jonah Hadley were proprietors of the City Steam-Mills in Gloucester, which processed grain. The crankshaft of the mill's steam engine had broken and had to be replaced. While it was out of action, the mill had to shut, losing the brothers business, so they urgently required a replacement.

The Hadleys ordered a new crankshaft from engineers W. Joyce & Co. in Greenwich, London, and contracted the carriers Pickford & Co. (owned by Joseph Baxendale) to take the broken crankshaft to the manufacturers the next day so that a new one could be cast. Although a clerk at Pickford & Co. assured the brothers' servant that, if sent by

See also: The *Lex Aquilia* 34 ▪ The *Lex Mercatoria* 74–77 ▪ The Napoleonic Code 130–31 ▪ The Workers' Accident Insurance System 164–67 ▪ *Salomon v. Salomon & Co. Ltd* 178–79 ▪ *Donoghue v. Stevenson* 194–95

Sir Edward Hall Alderson, the judge in the *Hadley v. Baxendale* case, was a Baron of the Exchequer, an appeal court which dealt with matters of equity. His many rulings helped shape commercial law in the 19th century.

Hadley v. Baxendale is still, and presumably always will be, a fixed star in the jurisprudential firmament.
Grant Gilmore
American law professor (1910–82)

noon, the broken crankshaft would be delivered the next day, the carriers did not send it for seven days. This delayed the completion of the new crankshaft by five days, forcing the closure of the mill for five days longer than anticipated.

As well as losing business during the additional five days, the Hadleys had to buy in flour for some of their customers and pay wages to employees who were unable to work until the crankshaft was repaired. To recover their losses they took Baxendale to court.

The rule of foreseeability
Initially the jury at Gloucester Assizes found in favour of the Hadleys and ordered Baxendale to pay them £25. Baxendale appealed to the Court of Exchequer, arguing that he had not known the Hadleys would suffer profit losses if the delivery of the crankshaft was delayed. Appeal judge Baron Sir Edward Hall Alderson agreed and ordered a new trial of the case.

In his ruling, Alderson made two points which have become key precedents in contract law in the UK and the US. He stated that

Baxendale could only be liable for losses that were reasonably foreseeable. He added that the Hadleys' case would have had some merit only if, when the contract was made, they had mentioned to Baxendale the special circumstances – that the mill could not operate without a crankshaft and, to secure the new one, the broken one had to be delivered urgently to W. Joyce & Co.

It was a landmark ruling because it created the first defined rule for the limitations on damages for a breach of contract. It was swiftly taken up as a principle by British and US courts, and forms the basis of the US law of contract damages. In 1888, for instance, the US Supreme Court ruled that the Western Union Telegraph Company was not liable for losses suffered by George F. Hall of Iowa when his

These special circumstances were never communicated by the plaintiffs to the defendants.
Baron Alderson
Hadley v. Baxendale ruling

message about buying petroleum was delayed. The judgement hinged on whether the damages claimed for were foreseeable. The court concluded that they were not and awarded Hall only the cost of transmitting the delayed message.

Lasting impact
Later cases have refined the rule of foreseeability. In *Victoria Laundry (Windsor) Ltd. v. Newman Industries Ltd.* in 1949, the Court of Appeal awarded the laundry damages for Newman Industries' failure to deliver a boiler on time, ruling that losses as a result of having no boiler were "reasonably foreseeable". It excluded a higher level of damages for the laundry's loss of "particularly lucrative dyeing contracts" as these could not have been foreseen.

The principle of foreseeability established in *Hadley v. Baxendale* remains significant. Parties to a business contract now routinely include a simple limitation of liability clause so that they can avoid a legal dispute over what losses each ought to have foreseen. ▪

WHO CAN CONDEMN THE WOMAN IN THIS BOOK?

THE *MADAME BOVARY* TRIAL (1857)

IN CONTEXT

FOCUS
Censorship

BEFORE
1571 In France, the Edict of Gaillon is issued to prevent undesirable works being published.

1803 Napoleon decrees that every book must be submitted to the Commission of Revision.

1852 Napoleon III introduces strict press censorship.

AFTER
1857 French poet Charles Baudelaire goes on trial for obscenity in his collection *Les Fleurs du Mal*; the court bans six poems.

1921 *Ulysses*, by Irish novelist James Joyce, is banned in the US after it is judged obscene.

1960 In the UK, the publisher of *Lady Chatterley's Lover* by D.H. Lawrence is tried under a new obscenity law, and acquitted.

France in the 1850s was under the authoritarian rule of Napoleon III, who had seized power in 1851. He was the nephew of Napoleon Bonaparte and, like his uncle before him, he restricted press freedom and exerted censorship over literary works. This was in an effort to curb the individualism that had sprung up during the French Revolution (1789–99) and was thought harmful to the unity of the French Republic. In 1857, when Gustave Flaubert published his first novel – *Madame Bovary* – about a bored housewife who embarks on a series of affairs, he was indicted on charges of "outraging public and religious morals and good manners".

The literary realism of the novel, in which Emma Bovary's desires, extravagance, and adulterous actions receive no moral censure from the narrator, led to concerns that male readers might be aroused and female readers led astray. However, the way in which Flaubert implied impropriety without overtly describing it made it difficult for the censors to build a compelling case. As a result the trial only lasted a day, and Flaubert was acquitted.

Obscenity laws across the globe have since been used to restrict the public's access to books that are deemed morally reprehensible, such as *Ulysses* by James Joyce, which was banned in both the UK and the US. Ironically, the main impact of such trials is that the works they intended to suppress went on to become bestsellers. ∎

Emma Bovary is shown here on her death bed, having committed suicide by swallowing poison after her former lovers refuse to help her pay her debts.

See also: The trial of Galileo Galilei 93 ▪ The Statute of Anne 106–07 ▪ The WIPO Copyright Treaty 286–87 ▪ The Open Internet Order 310–13

TO TAKE A LIFE IS REVENGE, NOT JUSTICE
THE ABOLITION OF THE DEATH PENALTY (1863)

Historically, the death penalty is the ultimate punishment, seen as both a deterrent and a just method of retribution. The first recorded capital punishment laws are found in the Code of Hammurabi (*c.* 1750 BCE), which imposed death for 25 crimes in ancient Babylon. By the 18th century, more than 200 crimes were punishable by death in Britain, and public executions were a spectacle across Europe.

Those in favour of the death penalty often invoked the ancient principle of *lex talionis* (law of retaliation) – "an eye for an eye". This form of retaliatory justice argues that the punishment should mirror the crime, so that anyone taking a life should lose their own. The counter-argument against the death penalty emerged with the Age of Enlightenment in the 18th century, when philosophers argued that executions were themselves a legitimized form of murder.

Support for the abolitionist argument against the inhumanity and hypocrisy of state-sanctioned executions grew, but it was slow to take hold. While the Republic of Venezuela abolished the death penalty in 1863, by 1900 just three countries had followed suit. Today there is a steady shift away from capital punishment; more than 100 countries have abolished it entirely, others have partially abolished it or barely use it, but more than 50 nations (including the US) still retain the death penalty. ∎

[It] seems so absurd to me that the laws ... to dissuade citizens from murder, order a public murder.
Cesare Beccaria
Italian jurist, politician, and philosopher (1738–94)

See also: The trial of Charles I 96–97 ▪ The Universal Declaration of Human Rights 222–29 ▪ The European Convention on Human Rights 230–33

EVEN WAR HAS RULES

THE GENEVA CONVENTIONS (1864, 1906, 1929, 1949)

IN CONTEXT

FOCUS
International law

BEFORE
1337–1453 During the Hundred Years' War, Richard II and Henry V of England and Charles VII of France each try to codify military discipline.

1863 Abraham Lincoln adopts the Lieber Code on the ethical treatment of civilians during the American Civil War.

AFTER
1977 Two protocols are added to the Geneva Conventions; one covers internal conflicts.

1998 The Rome Statute agrees to establish the International Criminal Court in The Hague, in the Netherlands.

1999 Yugoslav president Slobodan Milošević is the first sitting head of state to be charged with war crimes.

The Geneva Conventions comprise four treaties adopted between 1864 and 1949 and are based on the principle of public international law that is applicable to armed conflicts. The Conventions lay out a minimum standard for the humane treatment of both combatants and civilians who become victims of war, to ensure that life is respected.

The idea for an internationally agreed set of rules to prevent suffering during war was first proposed in 1862 by Henry Dunant, a Swiss businessman. Dunant had travelled to northern Italy to request water rights for a business venture from Napoleon III of France, who

See also: The Peace of Westphalia 94–95 ▪ The Hague Conventions 174–77 ▪ The United Nations and International Court of Justice 212–19 ▪ The Universal Declaration of Human Rights 222–29 ▪ The International Criminal Court 298–303

was engaged in the Second War of Italian Independence. By chance, Dunant arrived just as the Battle of Solferino, one of the bloodiest battles of the 19th century, was coming to an end. Almost 5,000 soldiers are known to have died, with more than 23,000 wounded and many others missing. The suffering and neglect on the battlefield affected Dunant so strongly he was inspired to write *A Memory of Solferino*, in which he not only described the horrors of war but also proposed suggestions as to what he saw as the solution – an international, volunteer-led group to take care of the wounded.

Dunant's clarion calls for an international body to protect the victims of war led the *Société genevoise d'utilité publique* (Geneva Society for Public Welfare) to appoint a committee of five, including Dunant, to explore whether this idea was viable. The group met for the first time in Geneva early in 1863 as the International Relief Committee for Injured Combatants (IRCIC). The IRCIC convened a conference in Geneva in October that year. Delegates from 16 states and four philanthropic organizations took part. They agreed initial resolutions on the humanitarian treatment of wounded combatants.

First Geneva Convention

In 1864, at another Geneva conference, the earlier resolutions were agreed as the First Geneva Convention for the Amelioration of the Condition of the Wounded in Armies in the Field, which was later abbreviated to the First Geneva Convention. Its key provisions were: protection from capture of all injured and sick soldiers; impartial treatment of all captured combatants; protection for all civilians providing aid to the wounded; and recognition of the symbol of the red cross on a white background as identifying people and equipment covered by the »

At the Battle of Solferino in 1859, many wounded and dying soldiers were shot or bayonetted to death rather than receiving medical treatment as they lay on the battlefield.

Henry Dunant

Born in Geneva in 1828, Henry Dunant devoted much of his life to humanitarian issues. In 1859, while travelling in Italy, he witnessed the terrible aftermath of the Battle of Solferino. Horrified by the treatment of the injured, he campaigned for the creation of a neutral body to help those wounded on the battlefield. His work led to the creation of the International Committee of the Red Cross and the First Geneva Convention in 1864.

Later, Dunant became bankrupt and was shunned by Genevan society, but that did not stop him from continuing to campaign on humanitarian issues, including the idea for a universal international library and the codification of rules concerning prisoners of war. After some years in obscurity, Dunant was recognized in 1901 as the first recipient of the Nobel Peace Prize, yet died in poverty in 1910.

Key work

1862 *A Memory of Solferino*

The Lieber Code

Henry Dunant was not the first to see the need for a code of conduct for the battlefield. Francis Lieber was a German–American academic who had fought for Prussia during the Napoleonic Wars and was injured at the Battle of Waterloo in 1815. During the American Civil War (1861–65), he became aware of the mistreatment of civilians, spies, and escaped slaves and saw the need for a code of ethics. The Lieber Code was adopted by US president Abraham Lincoln in 1863 and was the first modern codification of the laws of conflict. It was legally binding and not merely issued as advice.

The Lieber Code explicitly banned "taking no quarter" (which amounted to killing prisoners of war). It also emphasized the need to treat civilians in an ethical and humane fashion. Although it was not always adhered to, it served as a blueprint for the Hague Conventions of 1899 and 1907, and was the inspiration for most later war regulations.

agreement. By the end of 1867, all the key European powers had ratified the agreement and the United States signed up in 1882. The IRCIC body was renamed the International Committee of the Red Cross (ICRC) in 1875. It became the neutral body that actively assisted the wounded on the battlefield.

In 1899, delegates from 26 nations met in The Hague, in the Netherlands, and agreed to strengthen international law covering the conduct of warfare. The delegates adopted the Hague Convention, which was largely based on the Lieber Code. The Hague Convention incorporated the First Geneva Convention, agreed to establish a Permanent Court of Arbitration, and extended protection to cover marked hospital ships, shipwrecked soldiers, and combatants at sea.

In 1906, the Swiss government arranged a conference of 35 states to agree a Second Geneva Convention. This further extended protection for those captured or wounded in battle and recommended the repatriation of prisoners of war (which finally became mandatory in 1949). The Third Geneva Convention, agreed in 1929, extended the provisions again, notably to include the fair treatment of prisoners of war.

World War II's impact

Despite being a signatory to the Convention of 1929, the German state was responsible for horrific acts within civilian concentration camps and military prison camps before and during World War II (1939–45). These abuses included torture, human experimentation, and genocide on an unprecedented scale: six million Jews died in the Holocaust, and up to 11 million other civilians and prisoners of war died under Nazi rule. Although the worst offender, Germany was far from alone among nations in ignoring the Geneva Conventions.

The barbarity of World War II demonstrated that the existing Conventions were not strong enough. The war crimes had been so abhorrent that they damaged the entire international community. The ICRC was the driving force behind extending protection to cover civilians and toughening up the enforcement of the Conventions. Its proposals were agreed at an International Red Cross Conference in Stockholm in 1948.

The following year, the Fourth Geneva Convention was agreed at a conference in Geneva attended by delegates from 64 nations. Whereas

Among those incarcerated at the Nazi concentration camp of Auschwitz in World War II were 230,000 children. Mostly Jews, more than 1.1 million men, women, and children died here.

> The Second World War has shown that the Geneva Conventions would be incomplete if they did not also ensure the safety of civilian populations.
> **Max Petitpierre**
> **Swiss politician**
> **(1899–1994)**

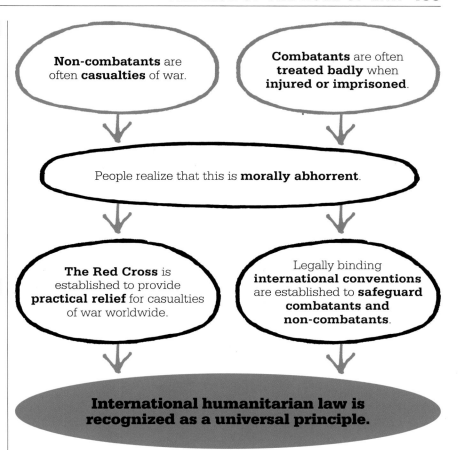

Non-combatants are often **casualties** of war.

Combatants are often **treated badly** when **injured or imprisoned**.

People realize that this is **morally abhorrent**.

The Red Cross is established to provide **practical relief** for casualties of war worldwide.

Legally binding **international conventions** are established to **safeguard combatants and non-combatants**.

International humanitarian law is recognized as a universal principle.

previous Conventions had concerned themselves almost entirely with combatants, the scope in 1949 was much broader, in that the delegates considered the treatment of civilians. They agreed provisions, or articles, covering the treatment of the sick and wounded, children, and workers; repatriation; a ban on imprisonment without trial; and the maintenance of medical and hospital services.

Article 3 of the Convention is considered especially important because it covers "conflicts not of an international character". It stipulates that those taking no active part in hostilities are always to be treated humanely, and prohibits the torture of prisoners, the taking of hostages, and sentencing without due process.

Updating the Conventions

The Fourth Geneva Convention entered into force in 1950 and became the basis of international humanitarian law. It has been ratified by 196 countries to date, making it universally applicable. In 1977, two additional protocols were added to supplement the Geneva Conventions. One prohibits indiscriminate attacks on civilians, cultural artefacts, places of worship, and the natural environment. The other extends the scope of protection during "internal" conflicts to include those fighting occupation, colonial rule, or racist regimes. Any conflict between signatory nations when no war has been declared is also included in the protocols.

The international community is obliged to locate and bring to trial those responsible for war crimes, which are the most serious breaches of the Geneva Conventions. In 2002, the International Criminal Court was established in The Hague to deal with these crimes, which can be summarized as: wilful killing; torture; the extensive destruction of property not justified by military necessity; compelling a prisoner of war to serve in the forces of a hostile power; the denial of a fair trial for a prisoner of war; unlawful transfer or confinement; and hostage-taking.

Modern challenges

In recent years, as terrorism has become more common, some commentators have asked why states should comply with the Geneva Conventions when terrorists expressly flout them. This facet of modern conflict, in particular, has made the Conventions ever more difficult to enforce. The ICRC is carefully addressing how they can be better applied in these challenging new situations. ∎

THE RIGHTS OF EVERY WORKER

THE TRADE UNION ACT (1871)

IN CONTEXT

FOCUS
Employment law

BEFORE
1799, 1800 The Combination Acts passed during the Napoleonic Wars make strike action illegal in Britain.

1824 UK Parliament repeals the Combination Acts as the power of trade unions grows.

1868 The Trade Unions Congress (TUC) is established, in Manchester.

AFTER
1886 The American Federation of Labor (AFl), a national federation of craft unions, is founded in Ohio.

1900 The UK Labour Party is established.

1901 The first international trade union organization is established.

1906 The Trade Disputes Act is passed in the UK.

Key legislation passed in the UK in the late 19th and early 20th centuries helped protect trade unions and, as a consequence, shifted the balance of power somewhat in favour of workers and away from employers.

Those who established the first trade unions believed that any worker–employer negotiation is heavily weighted in favour of the employers because they have the economic power and influence. Unless there is a severe skills shortage, the individual worker has very little bargaining power and therefore can easily be

See also: The *Lex Mercatoria* 74–77 ▪ *Hadley v. Baxendale* 148–49 ▪ The Workers' Accident Insurance System 164–67 ▪ The Sherman Antitrust Act 170–73 ▪ The Triangle Shirtwaist Factory fire 180–83

Has not the working man as much right to preserve and protect his labour as the rich man has his capital?
George Loveless
Tolpuddle Martyr (1797–1874)

The **Industrial Revolution** draws hundreds of thousands of workers into **new factories**.

Factory workers are **paid badly** and work **long hours**.

New **machines replace** skilled artisans.

Workers begin to organize themselves into unions, using **collective action to make demands**.

Frederic Harrison's **Minority Report** argues that trade unions should **not be prosecuted** for acts that would be **legal** if they were **committed by an individual**.

The **legal status** of trade unions is **protected** by the 1871 Trade Union Act.

exploited. Trade unions were formed to redress this disparity by creating organized groups of workers to collectively bargain with their employer.

From the 17th century, groups of skilled workers began forming small trade unions in Britain. In the 18th century, as the effects of the Industrial Revolution began to be felt, with machines and factories replacing hand-made goods, disputes between factory owners and workers became more common. As a result of this disaffection, more trade unions were formed. The government saw these workers' movements as a threat to the economic order.

Early challenges
Britain's first major strike was that of the weavers of Calton, Scotland, who withdrew their labour in protest at a pay cut. The strike was broken only when soldiers shot six weavers dead. The Combination Acts of 1799 and 1800 served to make strike action illegal, which hampered the burgeoning trade

unions and dissuaded many workers from joining. Although the Combination Acts were repealed in 1824, a number of punitive laws against trade unions still existed and in 1834 six agricultural workers who formed a trade union in the Dorset village of Tolpuddle were arrested and transported to Australia as punishment. The case of the "Tolpuddle Martyrs", as they came to be known, reflected the government's continued hostility towards trade unions.

An additional challenge to trade unions came from the civil courts. Trade unions were

mostly loose groupings of skilled tradespeople who, in order to join, were required to resign some of their individual bargaining rights in favour of collective interests. British courts saw this as restraining individual freedom of contract, which was unlawful and therefore made trade union rules unenforceable in practice.

However, as the economy picked up in the 1850s and 1860s, and railway workers and engineers became increasingly important to the continued industrialization of the country, trade unions began to gain strength once again, pressing for »

In industrial cities such as Sheffield, UK, thousands of workers were at the mercy of unscrupulous employers in the 19th century. Trade unions sought to give them greater collective strength.

better working conditions and collecting funds for members in distress. At this time, two incidents brought the legal status of trade unions into focus. The first was the case of *Hornby v. Close* (1867), in which it was ruled that because a trade union restrains competition, it cannot be protected from embezzlement by the laws that apply to friendly societies (mutual associations formed for cooperative banking). This meant that trade unions were at great risk of having their funds stolen by untrustworthy members. The second incident was a spate of violence in Sheffield carried out by trade unionists against non-union members.

As a result of these two incidents, in 1867 the government set up the Royal Commission on Trade Unions to investigate their legal status but could not agree on an outcome. A Majority Report offered little in the way of legal changes, but a Minority Report,

During the Great Railroad Strike of 1877 in the United States, more than 100,000 workers fought for the right to organize in a trade union. The strike was broken by soldiers and police.

championed by lawyer and historian Frederic Harrison, argued for trade unions to get legal protection from criminal and restraint-of-trade laws.

Global movement

Towards the end of the 19th century, as the Industrial Revolution gathered pace beyond Britain, trade unions began gaining strength across the globe. In the United States, craft guilds had existed on a local level since the 18th century and labour reform movements sprang up from the 1860s onwards, to campaign

for better working conditions. But it was not until 1886 that the first national trade union, the American Federation of Labor (AFl), was established. In Germany, trade unionism was initially suppressed by Otto von Bismarck's anti-socialist laws, but once these had been repealed the Free Association of German Trade Unions was established in 1897. Similarly in France, the formation of trade unions was illegal until 1884, after which time they flourished. The growth in trade unions was reflected by the creation of the International Secretariat of National Trade Union Centres (ISNTUC) in 1901, the first global trade union body, which helped to develop and support new union federations around the world.

Legalizing trade unions

In the UK, the Liberal government of William Gladstone opted for Harrison's Minority Report and pushed forward with the 1871

The 1889 London Dock Strike

A labour leader addresses dockers during the London dockworkers' strike of 1889.

By the 1880s, unskilled British manual workers were becoming increasingly dissatisfied with poor pay, dangerous working conditions, and long hours. Trade unions had previously largely only represented skilled workers but low-skilled workers saw the power of collective bargaining and they too began to organize.

In 1889, dockworkers in London went on strike over pay, demanding a rate of sixpence an hour (known as the "docker's tanner"). All levels of dockworkers were included in the action and it is estimated that up to 130,000 went on strike, bringing the docks to a standstill for five weeks. As a result of this mass industrial action, the dock owners agreed to the majority of the workers' demands, thereby bringing the strike to a close. The success of the dockers' strike inspired many more unskilled workers to join trade unions, swelling their collective membership in the UK to over 2 million by 1899.

Trade Union Act. This mitigated the common law of restraint of trade (any action that prevents free competition in the market), which had previously made trade union rules impossible to enforce. Although the Trade Union Act secured the legal status of trade unions and protected their funds from embezzlement this did not mean the government supported industrial action – it also passed the Criminal Law Amendment Act, which made picketing illegal. Trade unions were now legal but anyone taking industrial action could still be legally penalized, leaving them as vulnerable to prosecution as before.

Other changes were taking place, however. In 1867, 1 million working-class men won the right to vote, and the 1874 election saw two working men elected to Parliament for the first time. Now that they had a political voice, working people no longer had to rely on sympathy from the liberal middle classes to further their agenda. Growing political activism within the working class was echoed in the establishment of the Trades Union Congress (TUC) in 1868. The TUC quickly grew in membership and one of its first campaigns was to lobby against

the Criminal Law Amendment Act – its repeal in 1875 handed back to workers the power to strike.

In 1901, however, the Taff Vale Railway Company of South Wales took the Amalgamated Society of Railway Servants (ASRS) to court after the railway workers went on strike for better pay and union recognition. The employers demanded compensation for the days lost to the strike but the ASRS argued that as a trade union it was neither a corporation nor an individual and therefore could not

The purposes of any trade union shall not ... be deemed to be unlawful so as to render any member of such trade union liable to criminal prosecution.
Trade Union Act

be held liable. The judge disagreed and ruled against the ASRS, meaning that unions could now be sued for taking strike action. As a result, unions could no longer afford to strike.

The Trade Disputes Act

Many workers, who felt that the Taff Vale judgement was unfair, joined the recently formed Labour Party, and between 1900 and 1906 the number of Labour MPs rose from two to 29. The 1906 general election returned a Liberal government and many more Labour MPs, who had campaigned to overturn the ruling. As a result, the Trade Disputes Act was passed in 1906: trade unions could no longer be sued for taking strike action. They flourished in the UK until the 1980s when a Conservative government, hostile to the trade unions, reduced their power after the mineworkers' strike of 1984–85.

Globally, about 350 million workers are organized into trade unions, but labour rights are under pressure as the digital economy sheds unskilled workers and global trade relies greatly on cheap, unregulated labour in the developing world. ∎

THE NORDIC NATIONS ARE BRANCHES OF A TREE
SCANDINAVIAN COOPERATION (1872)

IN CONTEXT

FOCUS
Legislative harmonization

BEFORE
11th–13th century Regional laws begin to be codified across Scandinavia – for example, the Gulathing's law in Norway (11th century) and the law of Jutland (1241) in Denmark.

AFTER
1880 The first joint Nordic law on bills of exchange is issued.

1901 The Nordic Civil Law Commission is established.

1940s Legislative cooperation among Nordic nations extends to include criminal law.

1952 The Nordic Council is established to encourage cooperation between the parliaments of member nations.

1962 The Helsinki Treaty of cooperation between Nordic nations is signed.

1995 Finland and Sweden join the European Union.

The Scandinavian or Nordic countries of Sweden, Denmark, and Norway have fostered cooperation in the forming of their laws since the end of the 19th century, with Finland and Iceland joining later. This legislative harmony has been one of the most successful aspects of Nordic cooperation, serving as a prime example of the benefits of comparative law and continuing to produce a number of agreed statutes each year.

Scandinavian solidarity
Historically there has always been close interplay between the Nordic nations. Between 1524 and 1814, Denmark and Norway were joined in a union and, following the efforts of King Christian V, enjoyed a very similar legal code. Likewise, Sweden and Finland were united as one country until war with Russia severed them in 1809. By then, however, a feeling of kinship existed among the Scandinavian nations, and it was believed that unity should be encouraged.

This pro-Scandinavia feeling was channelled towards creating greater uniformity in Nordic law as this would not only be of practical

King Christian V of Denmark and Norway created a similar legal code for each of the two nations – Danish Law (1683) and Norwegian Law (1687) – based on their existing laws.

use, but would also recognize the region's historical and cultural ties. In 1872, the Scandinavian nations entered into an agreement whereby representative lawyers from each country would meet frequently in order to find common ground on legislation and the administration of justice. Groups of lawyers or representatives from law schools

See also: The *Lex Mercatoria* 74–77 ▪ The Helsinki Treaty 242–43 ▪ The World Trade Organization 278–83

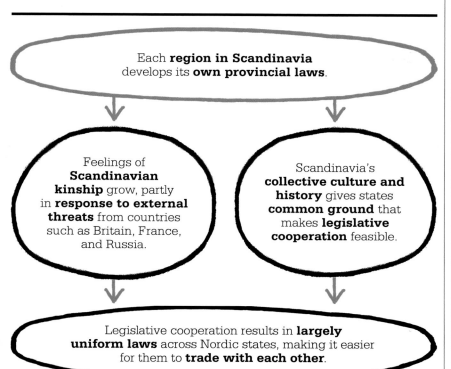

Each **region in Scandinavia** develops its **own provincial laws**.

Feelings of **Scandinavian kinship** grow, partly in **response to external threats** from countries such as Britain, France, and Russia.

Scandinavia's **collective culture and history** gives states **common ground** that makes **legislative cooperation** feasible.

Legislative cooperation results in **largely uniform laws** across Nordic states, making it easier for them to **trade with each other**.

have since assembled every three years to suggest areas of law on which the Nordic countries might cooperate. Judges, legal scholars, and attorneys then discuss the practicalities of creating joint legislation on the issue at point.

The focus of the meeting in 1872 was on contract law, and the first suggested piece of legislation was a unification of the laws on bills of exchange. This legislation was eventually completed in 1880.

Nordic Contracts Acts
Contract law proved the most fruitful area in which to cooperate, and from 1915 a series of Nordic Contracts Acts were passed that created shared legislation regarding contract formation and voidability (the circumstances in which a

contract may be set aside). As a result, there is now a near-uniform law of contracts across Scandinavia. Even so, the committee system in which each idea must be debated among experts in order to harmonize such laws across the region has, at times, proved ineffectual.

Unified laws can take a long time to be agreed and sometimes no consensus can be reached – for instance, when each nation believes its own legal precedent is superior to that of others. However, the harmonization of laws between the Nordic states has been largely successful, and has enabled greater cooperation and trade. Today, there is uniform legislation in the fields of contract, commerce, nationality, and family law. ■

Comparative law

The study of different legal systems by comparing and contrasting them is known as comparative law. To this end, legal systems are categorized into families, allowing nations whose laws have similar historical roots to be grouped together. In the era of globalization, comparative law has become more important as trade is conducted between countries with different legal systems. This has inspired calls for greater harmonization of laws worldwide. Likewise, with the formation of the European Union (EU), attempts have been made to achieve greater legislative cooperation among EU member states.

The rise of comparative law in the 20th century was confirmed in 1924 with the creation of the International Academy of Comparative Law in The Hague. The academy promotes comparative law through numerous reports and international conferences. Nordic legislative cooperation is seen as a positive example of comparative law in action.

There exists no "they and we", only "us". Solidarity is and has to be indivisible.
Olof Palme
Prime minister of Sweden (1969–86)

EVIL CUSTOMS OF THE PAST SHALL BE BROKEN OFF
THE CHARTER OATH (1868)

IN CONTEXT

FOCUS
Constitutional law

BEFORE
1603 The Edo Period (of rule by the Tokugawa shogunate) begins, closing Japan to foreigners for more than 250 years.

1854 Commodore Matthew Perry intimidates Japan into allowing some US ships and consuls into Japan, paving the way for future trade.

1867 The shogun resigns in favour of Emperor Meiji, ending the Tokugawa shogunate.

AFTER
1890 A Japanese parliament, called the Diet, becomes the first elected national assembly to be created in Asia.

1946 After Japan's catastrophic intervention and defeat in WWII, Emperor Hirohito reissues the Charter Oath and states that he is not a living god.

During the long Edo Period, Japan's feudal society was ruled by a dynastic series of shoguns (military dictators). It was an era of economic growth and stability, but strict laws kept Japan closed to all foreigners. By the mid-19th century, many Japanese, resentful of the rigid feudal system and influenced by Western ideas, called for the ultra-conservative regime to modernize.

In the face of political agitation and armed rebellions, the shogun's grip on power faded; he resigned in 1867. Emperor Meiji came to power soon after and the Meiji Restoration ushered in an era of modernization.

Signalling a new direction
In 1868, statesmen Yuri Kimimasa, Fukuoka Takachika, and Kido Takayoshi drafted the Charter Oath, paving the way for the modernizing of Japan under a parliamentary constitution. The Oath's five articles laid out the key aims: to set up deliberative assemblies; break down feudal systems; allow every citizen the right to pursue "his own calling"; leave behind harmful old customs; and open up Japan to international ideas and trade.

The Oath is seen as the first constitution of modern Japan, and as pivotal as similar charters were for other nations. Japan was at last able to move towards a more open society with an elected parliament. ∎

Emperor Meiji proclaimed the Charter Oath, also known as the Imperial Oath, at his coronation in 1868. Aged 15, he was keen to "stand upon a similar footing with the most enlightened nations".

See also: Magna Carta 66–71 ▪ The US Constitution and Bill of Rights 110–17 ▪ The Declaration of the Rights of Man 118–19 ▪ The Russian Constitution 190–91

IT IS JUSTIFIABLE, BUT NOT FOR DETESTABLE CURIOSITY

THE "VIVISECTION ACT" (1876)

During a British Medical Association meeting in Norwich in 1874, French physiologist Eugene Magnan injected a dog with absinthe, to show the effects of alcohol, and the dog died. A prosecution under the Cruelty to Animals Act by the Royal Society for the Prevention of Cruelty to Animals (RSPCA) failed (Magnan had returned to France), but the case gained public support and proved that existing legislation on vivisection (experiments on live animals) was inadequate.

Scientists and animal cruelty campaigners supported tighter legislation for opposing reasons: scientists sought protection from prosecution whereas campaigners wanted to stop cruelty to animals.

Regulating experimentation

In 1875, a British Royal Commission recommended amending the 1849 Cruelty to Animals Act, to cover vivisection. When the new bill went before Parliament, lobbying by the medical establishment resulted in a watered-down version (commonly known as the "Vivisection Act") being passed in 1876. Anyone carrying out vivisection now would need a licence and experiments all had to be medically justified and could no longer be done in public.

The Act balanced research needs and animal safety, but both sides felt it did not go far enough. It was a landmark piece of legislation, however, as the first in the world to regulate the use and treatment of live animals in medical research. ∎

Whether the practice be useful or useless, we ask you to reflect whether it be morally lawful.
Frances Power Cobbe
Irish animal rights activist
(1822–1904)

See also: The Cruelty to Animals Act 146–47 ∎ The Endangered Species Act 264–65 ∎ The World Network of Biosphere Reserves 270–71 ∎ Euthanasia 296–97

THE STATE WILL CARE FOR THE VICTIMS OF INDUSTRY

THE WORKERS' ACCIDENT INSURANCE SYSTEM (1881)

IN CONTEXT

FOCUS
Employment law

BEFORE
1838 In Prussia, legislation is passed that requires railway companies to compensate those injured at work.

1880 The UK Employers' Liability Act enables some workers to seek compensation for workplace injuries resulting from the negligence of others.

AFTER
1897 In the UK, the Workmen's Compensation Act introduces a system of no-fault compensation for industrial injuries.

1911 Germany expands the workers' insurance scheme to cover nearly all workers for death, disability, and sickness.

1935 In the US, a system of work-based health insurance is introduced with the Social Security Act.

As the Industrial Revolution accelerated across 19th-century Europe and the US, more and more people moved from farming to employment in manufacturing and construction. The mechanization of agriculture and industry made work more hazardous and injuries increasingly common. Social reformers saw that a system was required to provide compensation for work-related injuries and deaths.

From the mid-19th century, in Britain and other industrialized countries, aid organizations called "mutual" or "friendly" societies emerged. These allowed groups

See also: The Trade Union Act 156–59 ▪ The Triangle Shirtwaist Factory fire 180–83 ▪ *Donoghue v. Stevenson* 194–95 ▪ The Whistleblower Protection Act 274

Otto von Bismarck

Born in 1815, near Berlin, Otto von Bismarck became prime minister of Prussia in 1862, and gained a reputation as an authoritarian leader. He deftly exploited regional rivalries, annexing territory in Denmark and Germany and provoking war with France, to engineer the 1871 unification of 26 small states and duchies into the German Empire, with Prussia at its core. The ruler of the new empire, Wilhelm I, rewarded Bismarck by making him Germany's first chancellor. He became known as the "Iron Chancellor".

Bismarck worked to create a stable Germany with a strong national identity. He achieved this partly by campaigning against the rise of socialism and also the influence of the Catholic Church. To consolidate the position of Germany against the growing threat of Russia and France, Bismarck negotiated an alliance with Austria-Hungary in 1879.

Despite Bismarck's many efforts to discredit the Social Democrats in Germany, the party won a large number of seats in the 1890 election, and he resigned in disgust. He died at his country estate in 1898.

The Götze & Hartmann engineering factory in Saxony, eastern Germany, employed at least 2,700 workers by 1870. Highly industrialized, Saxony was a hotbed of German socialism.

of workers to pay each week into a fund that paid out if they became sick, disabled, or died. The funds were based on local communities or specific workplaces – those who lived or worked in an area that had no mutual society were not covered. Anyone injured at work who was not a member of a mutual society could sue an employer for compensation, but only if the victim was wealthy enough to afford a lawyer. Proving liability against a large company was almost impossible. As a result, many people injured at work who could no longer support their family resorted to begging or were forced into a public institution, such as a workhouse or even a prison.

When the German Empire was formed in 1871, its heavy industries, such as engineering and steelmaking, rapidly expanded. The rights of workers became a pressing social issue as business owners grew increasingly rich, while their employees worked long hours in often dangerous conditions. Growing unrest among German industrial labourers proved fertile ground for the champions of socialist ideals, such as equal rewards and state protection for workers in industry.

Bismarck leads the way

In 1875, German socialists formed the Socialist Workers' Party (SAP, which, 15 years later, became the Social Democratic Party, SDP). Some members of the party supported Karl Marx's aim of achieving socialism through revolution. The highly conservative chancellor of Germany, Otto von Bismarck, saw this as a threat to his power, and in 1878 he passed the Anti-Socialist Law, which banned any meeting that aimed to spread social democratic views, and suppressed socialist »

The power unleashed by the steam hammer, invented by Scottish engineer James Nasmyth in 1838, increased output but also made conditions much more dangerous for industrial workers.

newspapers. The law did not have the intended effect, however, as the SAP still won nine seats in the Reichstag (the German parliament) in the July 1878 election, giving it a continued voice in national affairs.

To neutralize the popularity of the socialists, Bismarck decided to champion some radical workers' protection legislation. In 1881, he put forward the Workers' Accident Insurance scheme. This obliged industrial employers to contribute to a private insurance scheme that would pay out to workers in the event of factory accidents. The policy was based on the socialist ideal of worker protection, although Bismarck refuted this, preferring to focus on the economic benefits of increased productivity from a healthy and obedient workforce.

A system of welfare

At first there was opposition to the scheme in the Reichstag, but, after winning an election in October 1881, Bismarck was able to return to the programme. In doing so, he would make Germany the first country to create a national workers' welfare system.

In 1883, the first piece of legislation was passed. The Health Insurance Act stated that both employers and employees should subscribe to "sickness funds", which provided those injured at work with sick pay and the costs of medical treatment for up to 13 weeks. The employer paid one-third of the fund costs; the employees two-thirds. Contributions to the scheme and benefits paid were based on levels of income.

The Accident Insurance Act, which followed in 1884, covered injured workers beyond 13 weeks. The new funds were financed entirely by employers, and workers no longer had to prove the liability of the company. Instead, a compulsory insurance scheme covered all employment-related injuries. At first, only workers in mines, shipyards, and manufacturing industries could benefit, but between 1885 and 1901 this was expanded to other areas of employment, including transport, agriculture, and the military.

The welfare policy was promoted as being of benefit to the German economy, in that it supported a healthy and productive workforce, but it also conferred the economic

advantage of reducing levels of emigration. Fewer Germans now wanted to move to places like the US, because at home they enjoyed greater protection from their state-mandated health insurance.

Other nations follow suit

The German system of workers' protection was widely admired and seen as a positive social reform. Between 1897 and 1907, a number of European countries, including Austria, Sweden, and France, enacted similar laws.

In Britain, the growing number of work-based accidents led to calls from workmen's associations for a change in the law to protect employees. The result was the 1880 Employers' Liability Act, which entitled industrial manual workers to compensation for an accident caused by the negligence of a non-manual supervisor. However, the worker still had to prove who was responsible for the injury, which complicated any claims.

Those who are disabled from work by age and invalidity have a well-grounded claim to care from the state.
Wilhelm I
German emperor (1797–1888)

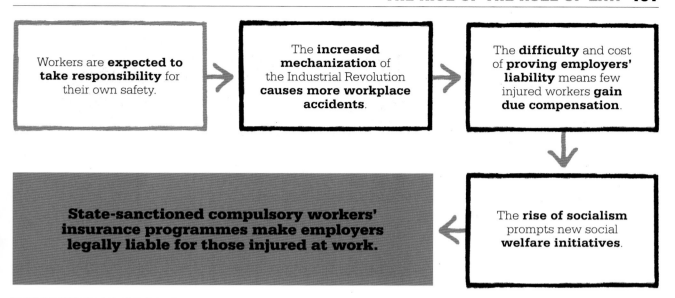

Workers are **expected to take responsibility** for their own safety.

The **increased mechanization** of the Industrial Revolution **causes more workplace accidents**.

The **difficulty** and cost of **proving employers' liability** means few injured workers **gain due compensation**.

State-sanctioned compulsory workers' insurance programmes make employers legally liable for those injured at work.

The **rise of socialism** prompts new social **welfare initiatives**.

The passing of the 1897 Workmen's Compensation Act rectified this problem by allowing those injured at work to receive compensation so long as they could prove that the injury occurred on the job. This gave British workers the same rights as those enjoyed by workers in Germany.

American legislation

The US, like Europe, experienced a rise in the number of workplace accidents corresponding to huge industrial growth. In 1898 and 1899, American legislators ordered a number of inquiries into European accident liability and compensation schemes, and concluded that a system based on the German model would be feasible. In 1908, Congress passed the Federal Employers' Liability Act (FELA). It applied only to railroad workers, but was the first piece of national legislation based on legally entitled compensation for the victims of workplace accidents.

Although inspired by the German model, FELA differed in that it still required the worker to prove the fault of the employer. However, the legislation did water down the defence of contributory negligence, previously open to employers, in which the employee could be denied payment if their actions were deemed to have even partially contributed to the accident.

Soon afterwards, individual states began to introduce workers' compensation schemes. Wisconsin was the first, in 1911, and over the next decade the majority of states followed suit. Unlike FELA, these

It is a reproach to our civilization that any class of American workmen, should ... be subjected to a peril of life and limb as great as that of a soldier.
Benjamin Harrison
23rd US president (1889–93)

state-wide laws did allow for no-fault compensation; however, they were voluntary only, as compulsory participation laws had been judged unconstitutional. This changed in 1917, when, in *New York Central Railroad Co. v. White*, the US Supreme Court ruled that compulsory requirements were permitted under the US Constitution. US states could now compel the creation of workers' compensation schemes, and by 1948 all states had introduced compensation laws whereby injured workers no longer had to demonstrate that the employer was at fault.

Although the compensation system adopted by US states was based on the German scheme, on a national level the US lagged behind Europe in the provision of universal rights for workers. It was not until 1935 that the Social Security Act introduced an old age pension and workers' unemployment and disability benefits. Also, while in Europe the German model developed into state-sponsored healthcare, in the US a system based on private health insurance was preferred. ∎

NO NECESSITY COULD JUSTIFY KILLING

THE QUEEN V. DUDLEY AND STEPHENS (1884)

IN CONTEXT

FOCUS
Criminal law

BEFORE
1600s Six English sailors who killed and ate a compatriot, with his agreement, are cleared of his murder in the "Saint Christopher case".

1841 In the US, a court finds crewman Alexander Holmes guilty of manslaughter after he threw up to 16 people overboard to prevent a lifeboat from sinking.

AFTER
1971 British lawyer and judge Lord Denning rules that "necessity" does not mean squatters may trespass.

2018 A Massachusetts judge sets a legal precedent when she rules that environmental activists could employ the defence of necessity to justify their climate-change protest over a fracked gas pipeline.

When the *Mignonette*, a 16-m (52-ft) English yacht, was wrecked during a storm around 2,575 km (1,600 miles) off the Cape of Good Hope, South Africa, in July 1884, her crew – Tom Dudley, Edwin Stephens, Edmund Brooks, and cabin boy Richard Parker – escaped in a lifeboat. After 20 days with very little food and water, in order to save themselves, Dudley and Stephens decided to kill and eat Parker, who had fallen into a coma.

The Dudley and Stephens case was widely reported in the media. This image, based on a sketch by Stephens himself, appeared in the *Illustrated London News*.

A few days later, the surviving men were rescued and transported home to Falmouth, on Britain's southwest coast, to be put on trial.

The story gained substantial coverage in the Victorian press, and public opinion was in favour of acquittal; many were convinced that there had been no option but for the men to kill and eat Parker. Due in part to the strength of public opinion, it was felt important that the trial go ahead and the principle of necessity be tested. The judge, Baron Huddleston, asked the jury to return a "special verdict" that would ensure a panel of judges could make a ruling. They ruled that there was no common-law defence of necessity in a murder charge and handed down the death penalty, with a recommendation for clemency.

Dudley and Stephens served six months in prison when their sentences were commuted by the Crown. This case set the precedent that the killing of an innocent, even in the event of extreme hunger, has no defence in English law. ∎

See also: The Ten Commandments and Mosaic law 20–23 ▪ The *Lex Rhodia* 25 ▪ The abolition of the death penalty 151 ▪ The exclusionary rule 186–87

WHERE WE ARE IS OUR PROPERTY

THE ST CATHERINE'S MILLING CASE (1888)

IN CONTEXT

FOCUS
The land rights of Indigenous Peoples

BEFORE
1763 King George III's royal proclamation states that Indigenous Peoples have title to their land; the Crown must handle treaties that cede land.

1867 The British North America Act makes the federal government responsible for the interests of Indigenous Peoples and their lands in Canada.

AFTER
1982 The Constitution Act of Canada recognizes existing Indigenous or treaty rights.

1992 In Australia, the Mabo Decision rejects the concept of *terra nullius* ("empty land" that is not legally owned before it is colonized) and grants land title to the people of Murray Island.

2010 Canada signs the United Nations Declaration on the Rights of Indigenous Peoples.

The St Catherine's Milling case was a landmark in the law relating to the land rights of Indigenous Peoples following colonization. In 1888, the St Catherine's Milling and Lumber Company wanted to cut timber around Wabigoon Lake in Ontario, Canada and obtained a licence to do so from the federal government. The Ontario government, however, claimed that it owned the land where the timber stood, and the company should therefore have obtained the licence from it. The case rested on whether a treaty between the federal government and the Indigenous Peoples living on the land had transferred ownership of that land. This could only have happened if the Indigenous Peoples had owned the land in the first place.

The case was heard by four courts, eventually reaching the Privy Council in London, England. Each court held that the land had not been owned by the Indigenous Peoples, but for different reasons. The trial judge used what is now acknowledged to be racist language,

... there is no Indian title at law or in equity. The claim of the Indians is simply moral and no more.
Oliver Mowat
Premier of Ontario (1872–96)

saying that "as heathens and barbarians", the Indigenous Peoples had no right of ownership. The Privy Council was more restrained, saying that Indigenous Peoples' rights were only to use and enjoy land, not to own it. No Indigenous People had the chance to give evidence in the case. Canadian law now recognizes that Indigenous Peoples have (and had) rights very similar to ownership rights over land, but the fight is far from over. ∎

See also: Magna Carta 66–71 ▪ The Treaty of Tordesillas 86–87 ▪ The Peace of Westphalia 94–95 ▪ The United Nations and International Court of Justice 212–19

FREE AND UNFETTERED COMPETITION

THE SHERMAN ANTITRUST ACT (1890)

IN CONTEXT

FOCUS
Commercial law

BEFORE
1776 Scottish economist Adam Smith's *The Wealth of Nations* defines competition as the absence of legal restraint on trade.

1882 Standard Oil combines several companies across the US into one large trust under chairman John D. Rockefeller.

1889 Canada passes the first competition statute, which addresses price-fixing and monopolies.

AFTER
1890 The McKinley Tariff Act raises import duty to protect American companies from foreign competition.

1911 The US Supreme Court rules that Standard Oil is an illegal monopoly and orders it to break up.

I n the United States in the late 19th century, a number of large "trusts" were formed. Trusts are created when business owners combine several different ventures into one overarching company. A trustee (or sometimes multiple trustees) is then appointed to work in the interests of the trust. By creating such bodies, companies are able to band together and collaborate to control the market by fixing prices and restricting competition. This puts a huge amount of power and wealth into the hands of just a few corporations and suppresses competition. One of the most powerful trusts in the US

See also: The *Lex Mercatoria* 74–77 ▪ *Hadley v. Baxendale* 148–49 ▪ *Salomon v. Salomon & Co. Ltd* 178–79 ▪ The Federal Trade Commission 184–85

America's first commercial oil well was built in Pennsylvania in 1859 and saw the start of an oil boom in the country. At the boom's peak, the city was producing a third of the world's oil.

was formed in 1882, when a number of oil refiners across the country combined to form the Standard Oil trust. This allowed the company to control the price and supply of oil while, at the same time, dodging corporate regulations and state-level taxes. The rise of trusts stifled competition and was seen as a bad deal for ordinary consumers.

Federal legislation

As the number of American trusts grew in the 1880s, legislators began to see a need to control the situation and to break up monopolies. (A monopoly is a market's sole supplier of a specific product.) Several state-wide antitrust laws were passed, but long-distance communications opened up by the telegraph and rail travel made it easier for large

trusts to work across a number of states. Nationwide, federal laws were now required. From 1888, Senator John Sherman of Ohio began working on a federal antitrust law that could curb the power of trusts to control the market. The bill went through a number of iterations and revisions, and when it was passed in 1890, it retained very little of Sherman's original wording, but was still named in his honour.

Banning monopolies

The Sherman Antitrust Act was the first federal bill to make anti-competitive acts illegal, and it forms one of the most important statutes in US competition law. It ensured that combinations (two or more businesses working together) or trusts that restrained trade between states or foreign nations were outlawed. The Act included provisions against price-fixing, the rigging of bids, or the exclusion of competition, and outlawed the creation of monopolies. »

If we will not endure a king as a political power, we should not endure a king over the production, transportation, and sale of any of the necessaries of life.
John Sherman
Speech to US Congress, 1890

John Sherman

Born in 1823, John Sherman served in both the House of Representatives and the Senate and held the positions of secretary of the treasury and secretary of state. Known as the "Ohio icicle" due to his cold demeanour, Sherman was keenly interested in financial matters, and as a senator he helped redesign the US monetary system after it was ravaged by the effects of the American Civil War (1861–65).

In 1884 and 1888, Sherman tried for the Republican presidential nomination but failed to garner sufficient support. It was said that Sherman's dislike of his rival for the presidential nomination Russell A. Alger in part inspired the creation of his antitrust legislation. Alger had a large interest in the Diamond Match Company, which, like Standard Oil, was especially hated by the public because it had a monopoly over a daily necessity: the match. Sherman saw the Antitrust Act as an opportunity to damage Alger. He died at his home in Washington, DC, in 1900.

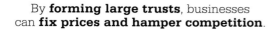

By **forming large trusts**, businesses can **fix prices and hamper competition**.

Large trusts **work across states**, revealing the **weaknesses of state-based laws**.

The **unfettered success** of a few large trusts **limits consumer choice** and undermines **public faith in business practices**.

The Sherman Antitrust Act is passed. This federal law prevents large corporations dominating commerce in the United States.

The key aim of the Act was to protect the core Republican value of free enterprise. However, some legal commentators criticized the lack of detail in the law, pointing out that antitrust laws should focus on *bad* monopolies, not *all* monopolies. This lack of detail in the Act ultimately proved beneficial because it allowed the US judiciary to interpret and enforce it, refining its meaning in law. In 1898, in the case of *United States v. Addyston*

Every person who shall monopolize … any part of the trade or commerce among the several States, or with foreign nations, shall be guilty of a felony.
Sherman Antitrust Act, Section 2

Pipe & Steel Co., the Addyston Pipe Company was accused of "working in agreement". Several companies would band together when work was being contracted out, and between them they decided which should bid lowest and therefore win the tender. By so doing, they were effectively controlling the fee paid for the job.

The Supreme Court judged that Addyston Pipe and Steel was restraining trade. This set the "rule of reason" precedent, whereby only those restraints of trade that are deemed "unreasonable" are considered a violation of the Sherman Act. Reasonable restraint of trade would apply to a company that had created a monopoly through building a superior product or technology; such an action would not break antitrust laws.

Standard Oil
The power of the Sherman Antitrust Act was again used in 1911 to force the break-up of Standard Oil, which at that time controlled 90 per cent of the United States' oil production. Standard Oil had struck deals with rail companies, guaranteeing them

the rights to transport substantial amounts of oil each day in return for a huge discount on the transport rates. The Supreme Court ruled that this violated the Sherman Act "on the ground that it is a combination in unreasonable restraint of inter-State commerce". This furthered the concept of "unreasonable restraint" in competition law. As a result of the ruling, Standard Oil was broken up into 34 smaller companies, putting an end to its monopoly.

Upgrading the Act
The Sherman Act contained several loopholes that related to anti-competitive mergers and acquisitions. Additionally, Congress was concerned that by leaving the definition of "reasonable restraint of trade" loose, it required the courts to repeatedly make decisions on a case-by-case basis. As a result, in 1914 Congress amended the Sherman Act with the Clayton Act. One of the key measures of the Clayton Act was to tighten up the laws for mergers and acquisitions, legislating against mergers that would hamper competition and create a monopoly.

The Federal Trade Commission is based in Washington, DC. It moved to its headquarters in 1938, and the building is famed for its Art Deco sculptures and reliefs.

At the same time, the Federal Trade Commission Act was passed, widening the scope of competition law to ban "unfair methods of competition" and unfair acts that affect commerce. This was designed to protect the consumer by making sure businesses did not make false claims about their products or mislead the consumer. The Act also established the Federal Trade Commission to regulate business and oversee antitrust law, and made it clear that any violation of the Sherman Act would also violate the Federal Trade Commission Act.

The historic Sherman Act, Clayton Act, and Federal Trade Commission Act continue to form the cornerstone of US antitrust laws today and have proved a blueprint for effective competition laws across the globe. Europe did not collectively tackle competition laws until 1957, when the Treaty

Though American businessmen may sometimes complain about the interpretation or administration of [antitrust] laws, we know that – like spinach – they are good for us.
Henry Ford II
American businessman (1917–87)

of Rome created the European Economic Community (as the European Union was initially known). With the founding of the Common Market in 1992, it became necessary to make sure roughly the same competitive opportunities existed throughout Europe, agreeing regulations that applied across all member states of the European Union.

The validity of existing antitrust legislation came under scrutiny in 1998 when the US Department of Justice (DOJ) filed antitrust charges against Microsoft. The DOJ argued that the way in which Microsoft bundled its web browser Internet Explorer into its operating system made it difficult for consumers to run other browsers on a Windows computer. This, they stated, was effectively a monopoly that hampered fair competition.

Digital dominance

The DOJ eventually won its case, and Microsoft was ordered to split into two companies. However, on appeal the ruling was amended, and the company was allowed to stay whole.

The high-profile case may not have affected Microsoft's dominance, but competition in the shape of Mozilla Firefox and Google Chrome saw Microsoft lose its market majority. Some argued that this proved that the market corrects itself, making antitrust laws redundant. However, the continued growth of large technology firms such as Google and Facebook has raised fresh questions over digital monopolies and the need for more regulation. ∎

When Microsoft fell foul of American antitrust laws in 1998 over bundling its web browser with its operating system, the company argued they were both part of the same product.

THE LAWS, RIGHTS, AND DUTIES OF WAR

THE HAGUE CONVENTIONS (1899, 1907)

IN CONTEXT

FOCUS
International law

BEFORE
1863 The Lieber Code sets out rules of conduct for the military during the American Civil War.

1864 The first Geneva Convention protects the wounded and non-combatants during conflict.

1868 The St Petersburg Declaration proscribes the use of certain types of weapon.

AFTER
1954 The Hague Convention on the Protection of Cultural Property is signed, focusing solely on the protection of cultural heritage during war.

1993 The UN approves the Chemical Weapons Convention, which outlaws the production, stockpiling, and use of chemical weapons.

The Hague Conventions were the first international treaties laying out the customs and rules of warfare. They were agreed at international peace conferences convened in The Hague in the Netherlands in 1899 and 1907. The background to the agreements was the increasingly brutal and far-reaching scope of war in the 19th and early 20th century. The balance of power across Europe and beyond had been destabilized. As nation states grew, they vied for territory, raw materials, and trade. Nations assembled powerful armed forces, and an armaments race developed, particularly involving Britain,

See also: The Geneva Conventions 152–55 ▪ The Nuremberg trials 202–09 ▪ The United Nations and International Court of Justice 212–19 ▪ The Universal Declaration of Human Rights 222–29 ▪ The International Criminal Court 298–303

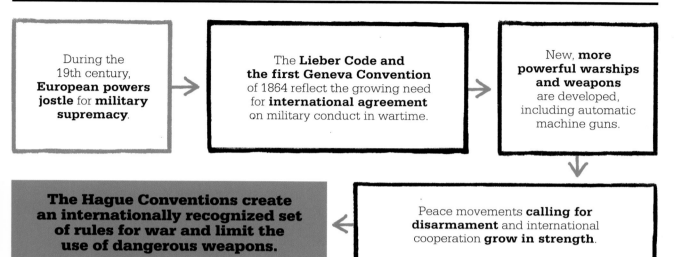

During the 19th century, **European powers jostle** for **military supremacy**.

The **Lieber Code and the first Geneva Convention** of 1864 reflect the growing need for **international agreement** on military conduct in wartime.

New, **more powerful warships and weapons** are developed, including automatic machine guns.

The Hague Conventions create an internationally recognized set of rules for war and limit the use of dangerous weapons.

Peace movements **calling for disarmament** and international cooperation **grow in strength**.

France, Germany, and Russia. Under Otto von Bismarck (1815–98), newly unified Germany adopted militarism – the idea that a state should use its armies to aggressively advance its national interests.

First steps

In 1863, during the American Civil War (1861–65), President Abraham Lincoln issued the Lieber Code, the first attempt to establish the rules of war. The Code was formulated by political philosopher Francis Lieber and was widely admired.

In the aftermath of the bloody Franco-Prussian War of 1870–71, the Code inspired Tsar Alexander II of Russia to hold a conference of European states in Brussels in 1874 to draft an international version. The aim of the conference, which was attended by representatives

from 15 nations, was to find a way of restoring the fragile balance of power in Europe and define terms of engagement for future warfare. It agreed codes that covered the obligations of occupying powers; defined who should be recognized as combatants; established rules for bombardments and sieges; and stated the duty of nations to treat prisoners of war humanely. The

conference laid the foundations for the later development of international humanitarian law at the Hague Peace Conference in 1899.

Since Britain, Germany, and Spain did not wish to be bound by the Brussels Declaration, it was not ratified. After this failure, the Institute of International Law (IIA), which had been founded in 1873, studied the draft agreement and »

The Battle of Fort Wagner was one of many bloody episodes in the American Civil War. It was fought in 1863, the same year that President Lincoln issued the Lieber Code.

came up with additional proposals. The IIA included these in *The Laws of War on Land*, a manual that was approved at a conference in Oxford in 1880. Although it believed that an international treaty was unrealistic at the time, it appealed to governments to adopt the codes as national law. The Lieber Code and *The Laws of War on Land* laid the groundwork for the creation of a truly international codification of the rules of war.

Multilateral agreement

As the arms race accelerated, particularly between Britain and Germany towards the end of the 19th century, so peace movements gained wider support. In 1891, the International Peace Bureau was formed. Based in Berne, Switzerland, it campaigned for world peace and promoted arbitration and disarmament. The development of modern, more deadly weaponry had changed the nature of conflict, and peace campaigners and even some

Delegates at the first Hague Peace Conference included representatives from China, France, Germany, the Russian Federation, Great Britain, Spain, and the United States.

heads of state believed that limits should be placed on the most destructive weapons.

It was against this backdrop that the first Hague Conference was proposed by Tsar Nicholas II of Russia. Convened in The Hague in 1899, it was attended by delegates from 26 nations. The main aims of the conference were to control the arms race and negotiate disarmament, codify the rules of war, and find a way to peacefully resolve international disputes without resorting to war.

Although it failed to agree a programme for disarmament, the conference ratified three treaties and some additional declarations – together, these formed the first of the Hague Conventions. They included important rules on the conduct of war, forbidding the execution of surrendered enemy combatants; the use of projectiles containing poison gas; the launch of explosives from balloons; the use of bullets that expand in the body (dumdums); and attacks on undefended towns or villages.

The conference also agreed to create the Permanent Court of Arbitration in The Hague. This was the first international institution to provide legal solutions for disputes

between states. More than 50 nations ratified the first Hague Convention and, alongside the Geneva Conventions, it served as the foundation of international humanitarian law.

A further conference was called by US president Theodore Roosevelt in 1904, but it had to be delayed due to the war between Russia and Japan. It was finally convened in 1907, when 43 states met. No major changes were made to the provisions of the 1899 Convention, but they were improved to incorporate warfare at sea, for

example. The British attempted to secure a limitation on naval armaments, but Germany rejected this proposal. Although the Hague Conventions were the first multilateral treaties to clarify the rules of war, they were seriously flawed. In particular, neither of them laid out specific penalties for states that violated them. Until the creation of the International Criminal Court (ICC) in The Hague in 2002, it was up to individual states to prosecute for breaches of the Conventions, but states might be unable or unwilling to prosecute.

Two world wars

A third peace conference was planned for 1914 but it was delayed indefinitely due to the outbreak of World War I. The war resulted in many catastrophic breaches of the Conventions – from Germany invading Belgium without warning to the widespread use of poison gas on all sides.

Even greater abuses took place in World War II, including the Holocaust (the worst genocide in history), the carpet bombing of

> The sad reality is that, over the centuries, many works of art have been lost and cultural sites damaged or destroyed in war.
> **International Committee of the Red Cross**
> Statement on the 1954 Hague Convention for the Protection of Cultural Property

The German city of Dresden in ruins after heavy bombing raids in 1945 destroyed its historic centre, including many sites of cultural value, and killed about 25,000 residents.

cities, and the widespread torture and execution of prisoners of war. The United States, Soviet Union (USSR), UK, and France oversaw the establishment of the Nuremberg trials in 1945–46. These military tribunals applied the provisions of the Hague Conventions to try and sentence the political, military, judicial, and economic leadership of Nazi Germany.

The rules of the Hague Conventions are now considered to be binding on all states, even if they have not directly signed up to them. Although the Conventions had been blatantly flouted during both world wars, the international community recognized the value of international systems of law. This created a space for diplomacy and new international bodies, notably the United Nations, founded in 1945.

In 1954, the Hague Convention for the Protection of Cultural Property in the Event of Armed Conflict was ratified. This is designed to protect cultural heritage, including archeological sites, works of art, and scientific collections. Its roots lay in the ruins of World War I, when Russian artist and writer Nicholas Roerich, appalled by what he had witnessed, campaigned for the protection of sites of scientific and artistic importance. The Roerich

Pact had been agreed by the Pan-American Union in 1935, but the devastation of World War II reinforced the need for an international treaty to protect cultural property.

The 1954 Convention has since been ratified by 133 states and is overseen by the United Nations Educational, Scientific and Cultural Organization (UNESCO). In 1996, four non-governmental organizations established the International Committee of the Blue Shield, which is the cultural equivalent of the Red Cross, to promote the ratification of the 1954 Convention.

Prosecuting war crimes

The Hague Conventions still form the cornerstone of the rules of war. Allegations of war crimes can now be tried by the ICC. In 2012, the court delivered its first verdict when it found D.R. Congo militia leader Thomas Lubanga guilty of war crimes and sentenced him to 14 years imprisonment. It is currently investigating alleged war crimes in 11 countries. ∎

A SEPARATE LEGAL PERSONALITY

SALOMON V. SALOMON & CO. LTD (1896)

In the 19th century, Britain was a leading industrial, financial, and corporate global power. Lawmakers were keen to govern the explosion in economic activity with a just framework for company law. The 1844 and 1856 Joint Stock Companies Acts (see box, right) and the 1862 Companies Act made it progressively easier to form a joint-stock company (one that is owned by shareholders). The Acts consolidated the principle in law of a "separate legal personality" (SLP): where an incorporated business or company had an identity legally distinct from those who created or financed it; sole proprietors or partnerships did not have this protection. Limited liability, first introduced in 1855, depended on the notion of a SLP and was key to encouraging enterprise, since it removed responsibility from any individual or group that owned or invested in a business for any losses the business incurred.

In 1892, Aron Salomon, a London bootmaker and sole proprietor, formed a new, limited company. His wife and five children held one £1 share each, and he kept 20,001

An incorporated limited company is a **separate legal entity** from those who **own or invest in it**.

Company owners or shareholders are **not responsible** for losses incurred by the company often **beyond their initial investment**.

Creditors cannot sue company owners or shareholders, only the limited company.

See also: *Hadley v. Baxendale* 148–49 ▪ The Sherman Antitrust Act 170–73 ▪ The Triangle Shirtwaist Factory fire 180–83 ▪ The Federal Trade Commission 184–85

Robert Lowe

Widely acclaimed as "the father of modern company law", barrister and Liberal politician Robert Lowe was born in 1811. He served as vice president of the Board of Trade in Britain in 1855–58 and it was chiefly due to him that critical revisions of the 1844 Joint Stock Companies Act were passed in an Act of the same name in 1856.

The 1844 Act had created a regulatory framework enabling companies – which until that point could only be incorporated by royal charter – to register as legal trading entities with Companies House, a new governmental agency. Although the 1844 Act had given companies much more flexibility, it did not allow for limited liability of shareholders.

The Joint Stock Companies Act of 1856, championed by Lowe, made limited liability available to any company with seven shareholders. It also, as importantly, helped raise levels of confidence in corporate activities. The law lords' verdict on *Salomon v. Salomon & Co. Ltd* would have been unthinkable without him. Lowe was made Viscount Sherbrooke in 1880 and died in 1892.

shares, so it had the legal minimum of shareholders. He then sold his business to the limited company for a hefty £39,000, £10,000 of which was issued to Salomon as a debenture (a loan secured against company assets). The company went into liquidation in 1893, with debts of £7,773 to be borne by its unsecured creditors (those owed money but with no assets in the company against which to claim).

The court case

Aron Salomon launched his case, *Salomon v. Salomon & Co. Ltd*, as a secured creditor claiming the company's remaining funds. The liquidator claimed Salomon was not due any money because he had fraudulently overvalued the business and was therefore liable for the company's losses.

Both the High Court in 1893 and the Appeal Court in 1895 found against Salomon, on the grounds that the price he had received for his bootmaking business was excessive. They also ruled that the incorporated company was a "mere scheme" to allow Salomon to carry on his business with the benefit of limited liability and to gain priority over unsecured creditors if it failed. Lastly, the courts held that the other shareholders were tokens, used to create what was effectively a one-man limited-liability company.

The High Court and Court of Appeal rulings were rejected in 1896 by the highest British court, the House of Lords. The law lords' literal interpretation of company law, and assertion that "everyone was entitled to limited liability", fuelled concerns that the unscrupulous might manipulate limited liability. However, the central role of limited liability as "the unyielding rock" of British company law was upheld. The law lords – Lord Halsbury among them – also rejected the idea that shareholders must be independent of each other.

Subsequent court rulings have distinguished between legitimately incorporated businesses that cease trading and ultimately leave large

The motives of those who took part in the promotion of the company are absolutely irrelevant in discussing what those rights and liabilities are.
Hardinge Giffard, Lord Halsbury
British law lord (1823–1921)

unpaid debts that the directors and shareholders are not liable for, and companies created in an attempt to evade an existing obligation of the company's creator, where the creator still has to pay. By 1900, the British corporate model based on limited liability had been adopted in much of the West, but with some national variations. ▪

FACTORIES ARE LITERALLY DEATH TRAPS

THE TRIANGLE SHIRTWAIST FACTORY FIRE (1911)

IN CONTEXT

FOCUS
Employment law

BEFORE
1900 An average of 100 people die every day in industrial accidents across the US.

1909 Thousands of garment workers strike for improved conditions. Larger companies, such as the Triangle Shirtwaist Company, reject demands for increased workplace safety.

AFTER
1933 President Roosevelt's New Deal places social and workplace reform at the heart of government policy.

1940 The amended Fair Labor Standards Act cuts the work week in the US to 40 hours. Other US workers' rights won in the years after the Triangle Shirtwaist Factory fire include sick leave, safety precautions, and child labour laws.

U ntil the 9/11 terrorist attacks on the World Trade Center, the Triangle Shirtwaist Factory fire of 25 March 1911 was the single most serious loss of life in New York City. Almost all of the 146 who died were young immigrant women, predominantly Jewish and Italian, trapped when a fire spread through the top three floors of the Greenwich Village building where they worked. All were seamstresses, paid between $7 and $12 for a 52-hour, six-day week and forced to endure overcrowded and exploitative conditions. Their deaths were the result of a combination of municipal indifference and incompetence and

See also: The Trade Union Act 156–59 ▪ The Workers' Accident Insurance System 164–67 ▪ *Donoghue v. Stevenson* 194–95 ▪ The Universal Declaration of Human Rights 222–29 ▪ The European Convention on Human Rights 230–33

The late 19th-century **industrial boom** in the US is fed by a **ready workforce of easily exploited new immigrants**.

→

Fire regulations are flouted by businessmen, who bribe those entrusted with enforcing safety rules and actively **resist union calls for reform**.

↓

New legislation introduces much **stricter safety standards**, and there is recognition that labour laws should **serve the best interests of working people**.

←

The **Triangle Shirtwaist Factory fire shocks opinion across the US**, with the public outraged by **corporate callousness** over the safety of workers.

↓

The belief that society and economies as a whole benefit from fair standards of work is universally accepted.

---

of corporate corner-cutting. Fire regulations were routinely ignored, and firefighters were poorly equipped, with little understanding of how to tackle a fire in the upper storeys of an overcrowded building.

The tragedy highlighted a culture in which those enforcing safety regulations could be bribed by businessmen, and shocked the whole country. As a result, it led to a series of much more stringent fire regulations, and union membership was similarly boosted.

Blanck and Harris

The men who owned the Triangle Shirtwaist Company – Max Blanck and Issac Harris, themselves Russian immigrants – were typical profiteers of their era and class. There had been four earlier fires in factories they owned, and the pair had benefitted handsomely from insurance payouts each time. In 1909, they had conspired to break a strike by the International Ladies' Garment Workers' Association by paying the police to beat the women and politicians to look the other way. It has been suggested that the woefully inadequate fire precautions at the Triangle Factory were themselves a form of insurance: should the company falter, a fire could be advantageous. However, there is no suggestion the fire was started deliberately.

The fire

There were about 500 employees on the premises when the fire began, on the eighth floor, at about 4:40pm. It was almost certainly the result of a lit cigarette tossed into a steel bin containing several weeks' worth of scrap cotton and discarded tissue paper. The resulting flame ignited fabrics that were suspended from the ceiling. Somebody reached for the fire hose but found it had rotted, with its nozzle rusted shut. »

Firefighters douse the flames of the fire at the Asch Building's Triangle Shirtwaist Factory. The building was saved and still stands to this day, renamed the Brown Building.

> The emotions of the crowd were indescribable. Women were hysterical, scores fainted; men wept.
> **Louis Waldman**
> **Eyewitness to the Triangle Shirtwaist Factory fire (1892–1982)**

Those employees on the top floor, the tenth, made their way to the roof and to safety. Among them were Blanck and Harris. However, those on the eighth and ninth floors had no means of escape. Only one of the two small lifts was in use, and it could carry no more than 12 people at a time. After just three trips, it broke down.

There were two staircases, one leading to Greene Street, the other to Washington Place. Many people escaped to the roof via the former before the fire made it impassable. The Washington Place stairs were accessible but led to a locked door. A pile of bodies was later found behind it. The fire escape was equally useless – it buckled and disintegrated, causing 20 workers to fall to their death.

Those who were still trapped inside faced being burned alive or dying from smoke inhalation. To the horror of the crowds below, 62 sought a more desperate end still, throwing themselves to their

The fire at the factory destroyed much of the interior of the Asch Building. The youngest victims of the blaze were two teenaged girls who were both aged just 14.

deaths from windows in the blazing upper storeys. Several of them were on fire as they jumped, and many were seen to hold hands before leaping. Thirty-six also died after plunging down the lift shafts in a no-less-futile attempt at escape.

The city's fire services were helpless. Although almost every fireman in the city came racing to the building, their largest ladders could reach only to the sixth floor, and their most powerful hoses not much higher. Nets were stretched out to catch the falling and jumping workers, but they split apart from the pressure of the impact.

Public reaction

In December 1911, Blanck and Harris were tried for manslaughter but were acquitted, largely on technicalities. Their counsel, not denying that the Washington Place door was locked, successfully argued that there was no proof that the defendants knew the door was locked. In 1913, the families of the dead launched a civil suit, charging Blanck and Harris with causing "wrongful death". They succeeded only to the extent that compensation of $75 was awarded

> I know from my experience it is up to the working people to save themselves.
> **Rose Schneiderman**
> **Trade union activist (1882–1972)**

to each family. In the meantime, Blanck and Harris had already received an insurance payout of about $60,000 to help cover their "loss of revenue".

The fire burned for hardly 30 minutes, yet its social and political impact was enormous, despite the fact that Blanck and Harris later cleared their names. On 5 April 1911, a vast rally, estimated to have been 100,000 strong, marched through New York demanding improved working conditions. It was watched by a silent crowd of 400,000 people. Public outrage among all classes was palpable. In June 1911, the New York State Legislature sanctioned the creation of the Factory Investigating Commission, and an immense raft of reforms and recommendations followed.

Almost no kind of industrialized business escaped the commission's stringent recommendations, and chemical factories in particular were singled out. Among the most lasting reforms was the Sullivan-Hoey Fire Prevention Law, which made sprinkler systems compulsory and led to vastly improved means of access and exit, with all doors having to open outwards rather than inwards.

No less importantly, for the first time, factories were forced to provide sanitary provisions as basic as toilets for their workers. There had been none in the Triangle Company's premises. One reason that exits were locked was to prevent "interruption of work" if employees left the building to use a lavatory. As one young factory worker said of her work conditions, "Unsanitary. That's the word that is generally used, but there ought to be a worse one."

While the political response was partly one of self-interest – that political figures could boost their public standing if they were seen to be on the side of the workers rather than the bosses – it was also genuinely disinterested. There was a recognition that no country as forward-looking and enterprising as the United States could hope to

After organizing a march to protest against the loss of life in the Triangle Shirtwaist Factory fire, unions worked with reform-minded politicians to introduce tougher safety regulations.

prosper if it persisted with labour laws so obviously skewed against its working people. Roosevelt's 1933 New Deal was a direct result of the lesson learned from the Triangle fire: capitalism was best served if it genuinely had the interests of all at heart.

Modern parallels

The Triangle Shirtwaist Factory was manufacturing the shirts made popular by the rise of independent, adventurous young American women breaking free from the constraints of home and hearth, forging new careers in offices in cities across the United States. Their carefree garments and the new freedoms they symbolized were made possible only by forced labour that was scarcely any better than a form of slavery. The 1911 fire exposed the poor working conditions in garment factories at the time, but the parallels with 21st-century sweatshops in many parts of Asia that make fashion so cheap and fast-changing in the affluent West are striking. ■

Frances Perkins

A number of New York legislators actively responded to the challenge presented by the Triangle Factory fire. They stood in stark contrast to their predecessors at the New York-based political organization Tammany Hall. Among the most notable were Alfred E. Smith, Robert F. Wagner, and Charles F. Murphy. The most important, however, was a woman.

Frances Perkins, born in 1880, witnessed the Triangle fire, and it was perhaps the defining moment of her life. She had already campaigned fiercely for workers' rights, but her subsequent commitment to social justice was rewarded in 1933, when President Roosevelt made her secretary of labor – the first female member of any US cabinet. As much as anyone, Perkins can lay serious claim to be a prime shaper of the New Deal. She remained in office until the end of Roosevelt's presidency in 1945 and is known today not just as the longest-serving secretary of labor but also as an early champion of women's rights. She died in New York City in 1965.

THE WAR AGAINST MONOPOLY

THE FEDERAL TRADE COMMISSION (1914)

IN CONTEXT

FOCUS
Commercial law

BEFORE
1890 The US Sherman Antitrust Act outlaws price-fixing and monopolies.

1911 The US Supreme Court forces Standard Oil and American Tobacco to break up their monopolies.

AFTER
1914 The Clayton Antitrust Act forbids business mergers that might impair competition or create monopolies in the US.

1972 In *FTC v. Sperry & Hutchinson Co.*, the Supreme Court ruling confirms the FTC's power to define criteria for identifying unfair business practices.

1999 Microsoft is found to be an illegal monopoly by the Supreme Court. It escapes break-up upon appeal.

The **successful working of the free market** depends on **fair competition**.

↓

Giant monopolies and trusts **inhibit competition**.

↓

The free market is **unable to prevent the development** of monopolies and trusts.

↓

The government must have a powerful agency to **prevent anti-competitive practices**.

The creation of the Federal Trade Commission (FTC) by the 28th US president, Woodrow Wilson, in 1914 was a landmark event in American business. It was the first truly determined initiative to bring the overweening power of existing giant corporations under control.

The FTC's brief is to protect consumers, investors, and businesses from anti-competitive practices, such as bid-rigging, price-fixing, monopolies, and monopolistic mergers. There is an underlying assumption that the free market cannot guarantee the absence of these practices without being steered in the right direction.

Rapid economic growth in the US, partly due to a population increase, meant the necessity for legislation had become ever more pressing in the early 1900s. Many

See also: The Statute of Anne 106–07 ▪ The Sherman Antitrust Act 170–73
▪ The Whistleblower Protection Act 274 ▪ The WIPO Copyright Treaty 286–87

The Bosses of the Senate (1889).
This cartoon by Joseph Keppler depicts
corporate interests, such as copper, tin,
and coal, as huge money bags looming
over the Chamber of the US Senate.

key commodities were in the hands
of just a few huge businesses known
as trusts, which controlled entire
sections of the US economy, such as
oil, steel, railroads, and sugar. These
giant trusts were, in essence,
monopolies with complete control of
the market. Prices soared, service
dwindled, and the public demanded
action. President Theodore Roosevelt
proclaimed himself a "trustbuster"
and in 1904 he deployed the
Sherman Antitrust Act, which
outlawed price-fixing to force the
break-up of the Northern Securities
Company, a railroad conglomerate.

But Roosevelt's efforts were not
enough. Big business was booming,
and the rich were getting richer
while many workers were stuck on
low pay in dead-end jobs. People felt
capitalism was rigged – a belief
confirmed when both Standard
Oil and American Tobacco were
convicted of antitrust offences in
1911. Trustbusting became the
key issue in the 1912 presidential
elections that brought Woodrow
Wilson to power.

A new government agency

Wilson's administration passed the
Clayton Antitrust Act in 1914, which
created legal powers to curb trusts
by targeting mergers. However,

pursuing trusts through individual
cases would quickly clog up the
courts, so Congress also brought
in the Federal Trade Commission
Act. This bill outlawed "unfair
methods of competition" and
created a new government agency,
the FTC, with broad powers to
regulate business. To avoid political
influence, only three of the five
board members could be from
the same political party.

The FTC could investigate
evidence from consumers, media,
and businesses; review cases; and
issue rulings directly. Later Acts
extended its remit to cover "unfair
or deceptive acts or practices in or
affecting commerce". With the help
of new regulatory bodies such as
the Food and Drug Administration
(FDA), the FTC has played a huge
role in shaping US business over
the past century. ▪

Great corporations
exist only because
they are created
and safeguarded
by our institutions.
Theodore Roosevelt
26th US president (1901–09)

Ida Tarbell

Born in Pennsylvania in 1857,
Ida Tarbell was a pioneer
of investigative journalism.
She is best known for her
1904 book, *The History of
the Standard Oil Company*,
published as a series of
articles in *McClure's Magazine*
from 1902 to 1904, which
presented evidence that
Standard Oil was rigging the
prices that railroads paid for
oil. The book has been called
"the single most influential
book on business ever
published in the United
States" by American author
and historian Daniel Yergin.

A prolific and popular
writer during a 64-year career,
Tarbell was known for taking
complex subjects and breaking
them down into easy-to-
understand articles. She also
travelled across the US on
the lecture circuit to speak
on subjects including world
peace, politics, tariffs, labour
practices, and women's issues.
Tarbell died of pneumonia
in hospital, in Bridgeport,
Connecticut, in 1944.

ILLEGAL EVIDENCE IS FRUIT OF THE POISONOUS TREE
THE EXCLUSIONARY RULE (1914)

The unanimous ruling of the US Supreme Court in *Weeks v. United States* in 1914 was an unequivocal endorsement of the constitutional absolutes of the 1791 US Bill of Rights. Specifically, it upheld the Fourth Amendment of the Bill, which asserted that "The rights of the people to be secure in their persons, houses, papers, and effects, against unreasonable searches and seizures, shall not be violated." This was first time a US court had made a definitive ruling on the Fourth Amendment to clarify precisely what it meant in legal terms.

Weeks v. United States
The case had seemed humdrum at first. In 1911, Fremont Weeks had been convicted in Kansas City, Missouri, of breaking gambling laws by mailing lottery tickets over state lines. Yet the Supreme Court overturned his conviction on the grounds that the evidence had been obtained illegally. Weeks's house had been searched twice by

The **Bill of Rights guarantees** the **personal liberties** of all American citizens.

↓

Vague drafting makes the **interpretation** of some **Amendments unclear**, particularly the Fourth, which guards **against unreasonable search and seizure**.

↓

The exclusionary rule says that evidence obtained by an unlawful search or seizure is inadmissible in criminal trials.

See also: The US Constitution and Bill of Rights 110–17 ▪ The Declaration of the Rights of Man 118–19 ▪ The US Supreme Court and judicial review 124–29 ▪ *Miranda v. Arizona* 254–55

The Kansas City police department, some of its members shown here in around 1900, was assiduous in pursuing criminals, but it did not always follow the rule of law.

law-enforcement officers – on the second occasion by a US marshal. On both occasions, no search warrants were issued.

Weeks's constitutional right under the Fourth Amendment "to be secure" had been violated, so the evidence gathered was "excluded" from use in court, meaning it was ruled inadmissible. This principle was known as the exclusionary rule.

Clear parallels existed with later Supreme Court rulings that found constitutional rights had been violated, most obviously in *Miranda v. Arizona*, in 1966. In this case, rape and kidnapping convictions were overturned because the accused's constitutional rights – to remain silent and avoid self-incrimination (Fifth Amendment) and to legal counsel (Sixth) – had been ignored.

The exclusionary rule has always been controversial. The obvious criticism was that the guilty might

go unpunished – there was no question that Weeks was guilty. Defenders of the ruling said that, without the exclusionary rule, the Constitution itself was violated. More practically, it was in the wider interests of American justice to use the rule to hold law officers to the highest standards of evidence.

Exceptions to the rule

Later Supreme Court judgements have tended to water down strict interpretations of the exclusionary rule. For example, in *United States v. Leon*, a drug-trafficking case, the police conducted a search with a warrant later found to be invalid. The 1984 ruling maintained that the exclusionary rule did not apply, since evidence obtained by police "in good faith" with the search warrant was admissible; it also held that the "substantial social costs" of the guilty going free could be disproportionate.

An oddity of the exclusionary rule was that it applied only in federal cases. In *Wolf v. Colorado*, in 1949, the Supreme Court upheld

convictions by Colorado State, because it was up to state courts to decide whether or not they would implement the exclusionary rule in criminal cases.

It was only in the 1961 *Mapp v. Ohio* case, concerning a conviction of possession of obscene materials, that the exclusionary rule became mandatory in all US courts. The precedent cited was the Fourteenth Amendment, which guaranteed the right to "due process of law". ▪

The criminal goes free, if he must, but it is the law that sets him free.
Tom C. Clark
US Supreme Court justice (1949–67)

Edward Douglass White was chief justice of the eponymous White Court, the US Supreme Court that in 1914 in *Weeks v. United States* unanimously agreed on the exclusionary rule.

POWER IS THE BALLOT
THE REPRESENTATION OF THE PEOPLE ACT (1918)

IN CONTEXT

FOCUS
Electoral reform

BEFORE
1832 Mary Smith presents the first petition to the UK Parliament calling for women to be able to vote in local elections.

1893 New Zealand becomes the first country to give women the right to vote in parliamentary elections.

1894 The Local Government Act in the UK allows women to vote in county and borough elections.

AFTER
1920 The United States gives all women the right to vote.

1928 Universal suffrage in the UK is finally granted to all men and women aged over 21.

2015 Women in Saudi Arabia are granted the right to vote.

Before 1832, only 3 per cent of Britain's adult male population were entitled to vote. The law granted suffrage (the right to vote) only to men who earned a certain amount of money or held a large amount of property. As Parliament began slowly extending the franchise (the vote) to a larger proportion of the male population (with Acts passed in 1832, 1867, and 1884), women were questioning why they could not

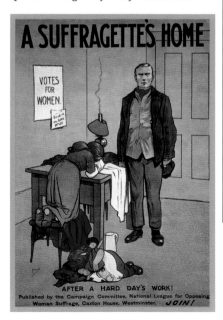

vote. Many men – as well as some women – were hostile towards the idea of women's suffrage, believing that women were too emotional to make rational political decisions, and that they didn't know about industry or commerce.

Deeds not words
Female campaigners started to organize themselves into groups. Some activists such as Millicent Fawcett, who formed the National Union of Women's Suffrage Societies (NUWSS) in 1897, believed in peaceful protest, using pamphlets, rallies, and petitions to Parliament to demand the vote. In contrast, Emmeline Pankhurst and the Women's Social and Political Union (WSPU, formed in 1903), with the motto "Deeds not words", favoured direct action: vandalism, hunger strikes, and chaining themselves to railings. The impetus for change was further crystallized by the Married Woman's Property Acts of 1870, 1882, and 1884, which

This anti-suffrage poster shows a husband arriving home after a hard day's work to find his tearful children left on their own while the mother is out campaigning.

See also: Magna Carta 66–71 ▪ The Glorious Revolution and the English Bill of Rights 102–03 ▪ The Declaration of the Rights of Man 118–19 ▪ The Universal Declaration of Human Rights 222–29 ▪ The Civil Rights Act 248–53

Voting rights are initially only extended to **rich land-owning men**, keeping power in the hands of the select few.

Working men successfully argue that they should be **represented in Parliament**.

During World War I, many **women leave the domestic sphere** to fill traditionally male jobs.

The Representation of the People Act gives women over 30 the right to vote.

allowed women to keep their own money and property on marriage. Women were now paying taxes on businesses they owned but had no say in how taxes were spent.

Since the 1860s, there had been repeated efforts by campaigners and sympathetic parliamentarians for legislation that would extend the right to vote to women, but they were continually thwarted. Things changed with the outbreak of World War I in 1914. With so many men sent off to war, women

Men ... have decided that it is entirely right and proper for men to fight for their liberties and their rights, but that it is not right and proper for women to fight for theirs.
Emmeline Pankhurst
My Own Story, **1914**

Suffragettes took to the streets campaigning for women's votes and publicizing forthcoming meetings, as in this photograph taken in Manhattan in around 1913.

were required to take on traditionally male jobs and responsibilities. Arguments against giving women the vote – such as them being the "weaker sex" – seemed absurd when around 2 million women had taken jobs previously held by men.

In 1918, Parliament finally passed the Representation of the People Act, which extended the vote not only to all men aged over 21 but also to women aged over 30.

Votes for all
The Act enfranchised an estimated 8.5 million women, who were able to vote for the first time in an election in December that year. And because the Parliament (Qualification of Women) Act had passed just weeks earlier, they were also able to vote for female candidates for the first time.

By then, women's suffrage had become a key issue around the world. New Zealand had already

forged ahead and, in 1893, became the first country to extend the right to vote to women. In 1920, the Nineteenth Amendment to the US Constitution allowed women to vote, and in 1928 Britain passed the Equal Franchise Act, giving all Britons over the age of 21 the right to vote, regardless of class, wealth, and gender. ▪

HE SHALL NOT EAT WHO DOES NOT WORK
THE RUSSIAN CONSTITUTION (1918)

IN CONTEXT

FOCUS
Constitutional law

BEFORE
1791 In France, revolutionaries proclaim a new constitution.

1871 The Paris Commune, based on radical, socialist ideals, rules the city briefly, for three months.

1905 The Russian Revolution leads to a new constitution and an elected legislature, the State Duma.

AFTER
1924 The 1918 Constitution is revised to consolidate the power of the Russian Communist Party (which later becomes the Communist Party of the Soviet Union).

1936 The Stalin Constitution gives total control to Stalin and the Communist Party.

1991 The Soviet Union (USSR) is dissolved, and with it the Communist Constitution.

The **revolution of the proletariat**, the working class, must **survive**.

↓

The **bourgeoisie** will do anything to **overturn the revolution**.

↓

The proletariat masses are **too fickle to sustain the changes** needed.

↓

The **revolutionary leaders** of the proletariat must **take firm control**.

↓

The constitution agrees a blueprint for society and excludes the bourgeoisie.

In 1917, during the February Revolution, Russian soldiers weary of World War I drove Tsar Nicholas II from St Petersburg to clear the way for a provisional government. Following the tsar's abdication in March, liberals had hoped to see a move towards representative democracy. However, a failed attempt in September by imperial Russian general Lavr Kornilov to overthrow the provisional government provoked Vladimir Lenin, who was then in exile in Finland, to rally his Bolshevik followers.

Bolshevik takeover
Lenin decided the time was right for his return to Russia, where he would play a leading role in the October Revolution. Influenced by German founder of communism Karl Marx, Lenin embraced the idea of the "dictatorship of the proletariat", so called because the power of the proletariat, or working class, should not be limited by laws created by the bourgeoisie.

On 25 October (7 November, Gregorian calendar), the Bolsheviks seized power and quickly formed both the Red Army and the Cheka – ruthless enforcers who went on to

See also: The Glorious Revolution and the English Bill of Rights 102–03 ■ The US Constitution and Bill of Rights 110–17 ■ The Declaration of the Rights of Man 118–19 ■ The Treaty of Versailles 192–93

become the Soviet secret police, or KGB. The following spring, as civil war continued to rage, they created a new constitution. The Constitution of 1918 was the first to recognize rule by the working class, making Russia the first-ever socialist state.

The constitution

When Lenin drew up a constitution, agreed in 1918, it was not intended to ensure stability with checks and balances, but was a revolutionary blueprint for changing society.

The constitution's aim was "the abolition of the exploitation of men by men, the entire abolition of the division of the people into classes, the suppression of exploiters, the establishment of a socialist society". An alliance of workers and peasants would rule the country through soviets – councils of workers' and soldiers' deputies that had sprung up all over Russia.

Initially, soviets had been open to all, but the constitution excluded the bourgeoisie from soviets and all other organs of government. It also forbade anyone from supporting the

anti-revolutionary White Army (led by the former imperial military) and made it the duty of workers and soldiers to join the new Red Army.

The Bolsheviks' attachment to power lasted beyond the Civil War; the 1918 Constitution replaced the tsar's despotism with the state despotism of what would become

This striking Soviet poster, issued to commemorate the 1917 Revolution, depicts a worker smashing the chains of oppression to win peace, freedom, socialism, and democracy.

the Russian Communist Party. Significantly, it did not include a guarantee of human rights for individuals.

The Russian Congress of Soviets, which had formed in 1917, was filled with soviet deputies, elected workers, peasants, and soldiers, but in reality it was just a rubber stamp for the Party. The "supreme organ of power", the Central Executive Committee, selected the head of state, and issued decrees. Commissars elected by Congress also issued decrees and saw to administration.

The Constitution of 1918 laid out the principles for constitutions that would later be adopted throughout the communist world – in Belarus, China, Cuba, Turkmenistan, North Korea, and Vietnam. It also provided a framework for the USSR government for 73 years. ■

Democracy for an insignificant minority, democracy for the rich – that is the democracy of capitalist society.
Vladimir Lenin
The State and Revolution, 1917

Vladimir Ilich Lenin

Vladimir Ulyanov, better known as Lenin, was born in Simbirsk (now Ulyanovsk) in 1870. Lenin turned his thoughts towards revolution in part due to the hanging of his elder brother in 1887 for his role in a plot to assassinate Tsar Alexander III.

Lenin, inspired by the French revolutionary constitution, the Paris Commune, and Karl Marx, went on to shape the Russian Revolution. He was determined to make the Revolution last by founding a party. As he had said

in 1902, "Give us an organization of revolutionaries and we will overturn Russia!" However, the Russian Social-Democratic Workers' Party (RSDWP) split into hard-line Bolsheviks and more moderate Mensheviks.

Lenin's dynamism and inspirational leadership took the Bolsheviks into power in Russia by the end of 1917 and ensured that there was no way back for Tsar Nicholas II. The Bolsheviks became the Russian Communist Party and Lenin became the first head of the Soviet state, until his death in 1924.

WE WANT A PEACE WHICH WILL BE JUST

THE TREATY OF VERSAILLES (1919)

IN CONTEXT

FOCUS
International law

BEFORE
1907 The Triple Entente sets Britain, France, and Russia in an alliance to confront the Central Powers – Germany and Austria-Hungary.

1918 Germany and Austria-Hungary agree to an armistice. Fighting ends with perhaps 9 million servicemen killed and 11 million civilians dead.

1918 Revolutions convulse Germany after it surrenders.

AFTER
1923 The fledgling Weimar Republic, the government of Germany, falters under the strain of hyperinflation.

1929–33 During the Great Depression, unemployment in Germany soars to six million.

1933 Adolf Hitler is confirmed as German Chancellor: Nazi one-party rule soon follows.

The Treaty of Versailles was signed on 28 June 1919 between the victorious Allied powers of World War I and the defeated German Empire. Over the following 14 months, four more treaties were concluded with Austria, Bulgaria, Hungary, and Turkey. Further treaties were signed with Turkey in 1923 and Germany in 1925.

The treaties remade the map of Europe. The Austro-Hungarian and Ottoman empires were dismantled; the former Russian Empire, now convulsed by civil war, was dramatically reduced.

Eight new nation states were also created: Czechoslovakia, Estonia, Finland, Hungary, Latvia, Lithuania, Poland, and Yugoslavia.

The 1919 Treaty had been drafted at the Versailles Peace Conference, attended by 27 nations, but led by Britain, France, Italy, and the US. The prime impetus for the conference had come from US president Woodrow Wilson. His ideal was a democratic, open, and equal league of nations (see box, opposite) based on "self-determination", forging a new, peaceful and prosperous world.

Wilson's vision for Europe was undermined by the impossibility of creating coherent nation states out of multi-ethnic peoples, and by other Allies' political imperatives.

Punishing Germany

British prime minister David Lloyd George and French premier Georges Clemenceau were set on a "war guilt clause". The logic was simple: since Germany was responsible for

Germany is shackled, in this 1932 protest poster by Heinz Wever, by the weight of reparations, as a result of the "war guilt" ascribed to the country in Article 231 of the Treaty of Versailles.

See also: The Geneva Conventions 152–55 ▪ The Nuremberg trials 202–09
▪ The United Nations and International Court of Justice 212–19

> Europe's **nations** are **prostrated** by **World War I**:
> another great **war** is **unthinkable**.

⬇

> The **US briefly emerges** as the **world's peacemaker**,
> championing democracy and a **league of nations**.

⬇

> **France and Britain insist** that **Germany's might**
> must be **curtailed**, to stop it starting another war, and that
> **Germany must pay** for the **damage** that it has done.

⬇

> The **Treaty of Versailles** formally ends the war and
> **compels Germany** to **disarm**, **surrender territory**, and
> make **huge reparations** to the Allied powers.

the war, it should bear the burden. So the Treaty of Versailles imposed two major conditions on Germany.

The first condition of the treaty was financial. Germany was to pay reparations of 132 billion marks. This was on top of its vast war debts of *c.* 150 billion marks. It also had to surrender almost all of its iron-ore and coal resources, as well as 13 per cent of its territory, where about 10 per cent of its people lived.

Germany also had to disarm: its armies, 3.8 million strong in 1914, were to be cut to 100,000; and it had to give up most of its navy and all of its larger merchant ships. The Rhineland, in the west of Germany, was to become a demilitarized zone, policed by Allied troops, and all of Germany's overseas colonies were to be given up.

Forced to sign the treaty, Germany was left both humiliated and impoverished, its economy ruined, its emperor exiled, and its people starving. Even at the time, it was recognized that such punitive demands on a defeated people could only provoke bitterness.

Dire consequences

Germany's punishment proved to be disastrous for the long-term success of the peace treaty. The country might have recovered if the Great Depression had not plunged it into further economic misery, to the benefit of Hitler. He was not an inevitable product of the Treaty of Versailles, but his rise would have been unthinkable without it. Aiming to end the war to end all wars, the Versailles Treaty paved the way for World War II and the Holocaust. ▪

The League of Nations

The world's determination to make impossible any future conflict on the scale of the World War I was epitomized by the creation in Geneva in 1920 of the League of Nations. It was to be an international force for cooperation and security between nations.

Although inspired by US president Woodrow Wilson, the League was undermined from the start by the refusal of the US, reverting to isolationism, to join it, and by the perception that it was a Franco-British attempt to justify colonial dominance.

The League of Nations soon proved toothless, a well-meaning body with no effective means of imposing its judgements and frequently unable to agree a collective course of action. At its peak in 1935, it could claim only 58 members, many of whom were ambivalent; some joined the League for only a few years.

False start or not – it was officially disbanded in 1946 – the League was the template for the United Nations in 1945.

This is not a peace,
it is an armistice for
twenty years.
Marshal Ferdinand Foch
French general (1851–1929)

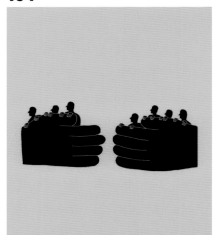

A DUTY OF CARE

DONOGHUE V. STEVENSON (1932)

IN CONTEXT

FOCUS
Tort law

BEFORE
1842 In the *Winterbottom v. Wright* case in the UK, judges rule against a coach driver who claims he is injured because of negligent maintenance by the coach provider.

AFTER
1943 The House of Lords holds that a duty of care does not extend to those traumatized after witnessing accidents. The 1982 *McLoughlin v. O'Brian* case recognizes such a duty.

1951 The duty of care principle is applied to a woman who is hit on the head by a cricket ball in a case that clarifies what a defendant needs to foresee.

1970 *Donoghue v. Stevenson* is cited in a landmark case involving damage to boats by young offenders in the care of the Home Office.

Damage occurs to an individual allegedly as a result of **carelessness** on the part of **another person**.

⬇

The **defendant** could have **reasonably foreseen** that their conduct was **likely to injure someone**.

⬇

The **"love thy neighbour" principle** extends to anyone bound to be affected by **careless acts**.

⬇

It is fair to impose a responsibility on the defendant for their actions.

On 26 August 1928, May Donoghue and a friend stopped at a café in Paisley, Scotland, where the friend ordered drinks for the pair. Donoghue had a Stevenson's ginger beer, which came in an opaque brown glass bottle that obscured the liquid inside. She poured and drank some of the ginger beer, but then noticed that a decomposing snail had fallen out of the bottle. She was shaken by this and became ill shortly afterwards.

The owner of the café was clearly not to blame since the sealed bottles had been delivered to him by the manufacturer, David Stevenson, and he couldn't see the contents within. Crucially, May Donoghue was not Stevenson's customer – her friend was, because

It would seem little short of outrageous to make [the defendants] responsible ... for the condition of the contents of every bottle which issues from their works.
Lord Buckmaster
Dissenting judge, 1932

An opaque bottle was at the heart of the *Donoghue v. Stevenson* case, with the final ruling based on the fact that the café owner could not be held responsible for what was not visible.

she had paid for the drinks. Under the law as it stood at the time, Mrs Donoghue was not entitled to compensation for her illness, since she had not entered into a contract with the drink's producer. She sued Stevenson anyway, and in 1931 her case ended up at the House of Lords, which was then the UK's highest court.

"Love thy neighbour"
The following year, Lord Atkin, speaking for the majority of judges who found in favour of Donoghue, said that Stevenson owed a broad duty of care to anyone who drank his product. If a claim for damages was made, it was important to establish whether someone could reasonably foresee that their actions would be likely to injure another person. The Bible's commandment to

"Love thy neighbour", Atkin said, raised the legal issue of "Who is my neighbour?" Atkin went on to say that a person should take into account not just people who are physically close to them but anyone who was bound to be affected by careless acts. In outlining a person's duty to others – what came to be known as a duty of care – he was setting a standard by which courts could assess whether someone should be held responsible for their careless conduct. This assessment

Who, then, in law is my neighbour?
Lord Atkin
House of Lords, 1932

was straightforward in the example of May Donoghue's ginger beer; the manufacturer had made a product designed to go into the wider world, so he should have foreseen that people consuming it would be harmed if it was contaminated.

Donoghue v. Stevenson was important in the field of tort law, which deals with compensation for harm to people's rights to safe products, a clean environment, and protection of their property and wider economic interests. The case clarified the existence of a general duty of care, not just a duty confined to situations such as the relationship between a doctor and a patient, between an employer and an employee, or a contract between a manufacturer and someone buying their product.

As courts later defined concepts such as foreseeability and proximity in more detail, the case came to be considered a landmark in personal injury and consumer law around the world, laying the foundation of the modern law of negligence. ▪

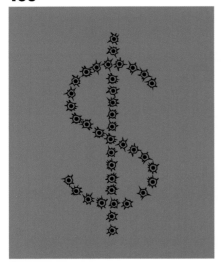

DEADLY WEAPONS MUST BE REGULATED
THE NATIONAL FIREARMS ACT (1934)

IN CONTEXT

FOCUS
Gun control

BEFORE
1791 The Second Amendment confirms the right to bear arms on the grounds of self-defence.

1929 In the St Valentine's Day Massacre, seven gang members are brutally murdered in Chicago.

1933 Giuseppe Zangara attempts to assassinate President-elect Roosevelt; he fatally wounds Chicago mayor Anton Cermak, and the call for gun control grows louder.

AFTER
1993 The number of American firearm homicides per year peaks; after soaring in the 1960s, it declines sharply from 1993 to 2000, then rises again.

2000–19 A total of 710 people are killed in mass shootings across the US.

The Second Amendment to the US Constitution makes it explicit that "the right of the people to keep and bear Arms shall not be infringed". It was intended to safeguard the citizens of the newly independent republic from attack, potentially even from their own government, by allowing for "a well-regulated militia". The debate as to whether this right is an incitement to violence or a cornerstone of American liberties has raged ever since.

Despite ambiguous Supreme Court rulings in 1875 and 1886 – both, in effect, watering down the Second Amendment – the National Firearms Act of 1934 was the first federal attempt at gun-control legislation. It was passed soon after the repeal of Prohibition, largely in response to public disquiet at the unchecked gang warfare during that era, when criminals gained control of the alcohol trade.

The Act applied to only two types of weapons: machine guns and short-barrelled guns. Neither was banned. The intention was to tax them out of existence, with a $200 levy imposed on all sales. In addition, owners of such weapons were required to register them. The Act did not apply to handguns.

The results of the Firearms Act were mixed. It mainly penalized the law-abiding; doing little to deter the criminal, who were unlikely to be swayed by legal directives. Further Supreme Court rulings in 2008, 2010, and 2016 have failed to provide a resolution to this deep ideological fault line in American society. ∎

The deadliest mass shooting in the US took place on 1 October 2017 in Las Vegas, when Stephen Paddock opened fire at a music festival. He killed 58 people and injured a further 413.

See also: The US Constitution and Bill of Rights 110–17 ▪ The Declaration of the Rights of Man 118–19 ▪ The US Supreme Court and judicial review 124–29

FROM A DEMOCRACY TO A DICTATORSHIP
THE NUREMBERG LAWS (1935)

Nazi racism towards Jewish
people was apparent even
before Adolf Hitler became
chancellor in January 1933. Jews
were seen as *Untermenschen*
("subhuman"), defiling racial purity.
In the early 1930s, they were
scapegoated and mistreated in
an attempt to drive them out of
Germany. Then, in 1935, the racial
discrimination was made into law.

There were two Nuremberg
Laws: the Law for the Protection of
German Blood and German Honour,
and the Reich Citizenship Law.
They went much further than the
many anti-Jewish decrees that had
been passed since 1933, such as
banning Jews from government
positions and restricting their
participation in key professions.

The German Blood and German
Honour Law banned marriage
between Jews and Germans,
and "extramarital" relations were
likewise outlawed. Jews could also
no longer employ female Germans
under 45 as domestic servants. The
Citizenship Law gave a convoluted
series of definitions of racial

Everything we have
done flows from the
Nuremberg Laws.
Reinhard Heydrich
Nazi SS official
(1904–42)

identity. Those with one-eighth
Jewish blood or less were deemed
German and citizens of the Reich;
those with three-quarters or
entirely Jewish blood were stripped
of all rights. Those in between were
Reich citizens but not members
of the German race.

The Nuremberg Laws were a
key stepping-stone to the Final
Solution itself, authorized in 1941:
Europe's Jews were no longer
merely to be victimized – they
were to be exterminated. ∎

See also: The Geneva Conventions 152–55 ▪ The Nuremberg trials 202–09 ▪ The
Genocide Convention 210–11 ▪ The Universal Declaration of Human Rights 222–29

A NEW INTERNA ORDER 1945–1980

TIONAL

The **United Nations Charter** aims to foster world peace and protect human rights.

↑

1945

An international tribunal is set up in **Nuremberg**, Germany, to try Nazi leaders on charges of war crimes and crimes against humanity.

1945

↓

The International Criminal Police Commission, founded in 1923, is revived. It adopts the name **INTERPOL** in 1956.

↑

1945

The UN adopts the **Genocide Convention**, making genocide a crime under international law.

1948

↓

The UN passes the **Universal Declaration of Human Rights**.

↑

1948

The **European Convention on Human Rights** becomes the first enforceable international treaty protecting human rights.

1950

↓

The **European Court of Justice** is established to complement the European Coal and Steel Community, a forerunner of the EU.

↑

1952

The Nordic Council, formed in 1952, passes the **Helsinki Treaty**, facilitating integration of the Scandinavian countries.

1962

↓

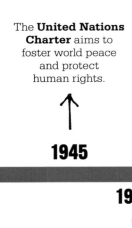

The decades following World War II saw a dramatic change in the global political landscape, and in attitudes towards international cooperation. Two devastating global conflicts separated by less than a generation had created an unprecedented desire for peace and justice, and the horrors of the Nazi Holocaust underlined the need for international legislation. However, it wasn't long before the opposing ideologies of East and West began to cast the long shadow of the "Cold War", made more menacing by the threat of nuclear weapons.

Although attempts had been made after World War I to set up truly international organizations, such as the League of Nations, these had ultimately failed in the turbulent economic and political atmosphere that saw both the global Great Depression and the rise of the Nazis in Germany. Towards the end of World War II, however, international leaders were more open to the idea of such an organization, and the United Nations was founded in October 1945.

Retribution and institutions

In the immediate aftermath of the war, the huge scale of the Nazi atrocities, especially the Holocaust, prompted a strong international response, which came first in the form of a series of military tribunals to try the surviving German military and political leaders. These trials were held in Nuremberg in 1945–46, with a panel of judges from the US, UK, Soviet Union (USSR), and France. They were the first international military tribunals

of their kind, and they defined three new types of crime: crimes against peace, including starting an unprovoked war; war crimes, such as breaking the international rules of war as set out in the Hague Conventions of 1899 and 1907; and crimes against humanity, including mass murder, forced labour, and religious persecution.

The UN recognized genocide as a crime in 1946 and outlawed it in 1948, the same year that it codified a general statement of its objectives in the Universal Declaration of Human Rights. Within a few years, the UN had brought together the world's major powers in numerous international agencies.

In Europe, which had suffered heavily from the ravages of both world wars, there was a widespread desire for peaceful cooperation,

The US, USSR, and UK sign the **Partial, or Limited, Test Ban Treaty**, a first step towards nuclear disarmament.

1963 ↑

In the case of **Miranda v. Arizona**, the US Supreme Court rules that suspects in police custody must be told of their right to remain silent.

1966 ↑

California introduces the principle of the **no-fault divorce**.

1969 ↑

In the **Roe v. Wade** case, the Supreme Court rules in favour of a woman's legal right to abortion in the US.

1973 ↑

1964 ↓

The **Civil Rights Act** outlaws discrimination on grounds of race in the US.

1966 ↓

The **International Covenant on Civil and Political Rights** (ICCPR) is drafted, to complement the Universal Declaration of Human Rights.

1970 ↓

The **Federal Witness Protection Program** is introduced to combat organized crime in the US.

1973 ↓

The US government introduces the **Endangered Species Act**.

not least to rebuild industries and foster economic regeneration. Lessons had been learned from the consequences of the punitive settlement imposed on Germany after World War I. In place of retribution, reconciliation – in particular, between France and Germany – led to the creation of new European institutions.

The 12 member nations of the Council of Europe agreed a Convention on Human Rights in 1950, and the European Coal and Steel Community, which later grew into the European Union (EU), established the European Court of Justice in 1952. A similar spirit of cooperation led to the creation of the Nordic Council in 1952. A decade later, this body agreed the Helsinki Treaty, which paved the way for closer integration of the Scandinavian countries. In stark contrast, tensions grew either side of the "Iron Curtain", with the "communist" bloc of the USSR, its allies, and China on one side, and the US and the capitalist West on the other. Each camp increased its nuclear arsenal, with things coming to a head during the Cuban Missile Crisis of 1962. In its wake came international talks to restrict the proliferation of nuclear weapons, resulting in the Partial, or Limited, Test Ban Treaty in 1963.

Social change
As well as international efforts to promote and protect human rights, there were growing movements, especially in the US, pressing for social change with legal reinforcement. The civil rights movement grew out of African American anger against the discriminatory "Jim Crow" laws, leading eventually to the Civil Rights Act of 1964. Women's rights were also forcibly put on the agenda by the rise of feminism, and changes were brought about in the laws on such issues as abortion and divorce.

There was also a growing concern for environmental issues, as the effects of human interference with nature became more apparent. In 1973, both the Convention on International Trade in Endangered Species of Wild Fauna and Flora (CITES) and the US Endangered Species Act were enacted. They began to address the need to protect the natural world, but they did not yet deal with the deeper ecological implications of the loss of biodiversity. ■

NEW EVILS REQUIRE NEW REMEDIES

THE NUREMBERG TRIALS (1945–49)

IN CONTEXT

FOCUS
Military law

BEFORE
1474 Burgundian knight Peter von Hagenbach is the first commanding officer to be convicted of war crimes.

1920 The League of Nations sets up the first international court, the Permanent Court of International Justice (PCIJ).

1943 Leaders of the Allied powers resolve to put Nazi war criminals on trial.

AFTER
1961 Nazi Adolf Eichmann is caught in Argentina, tried in Jerusalem, and executed.

1987 Klaus Barbie is tried and convicted of deporting Jews.

2017 The Yugoslav war crimes tribunal closes after convicting Yugoslav president Slobodan Milošević, Radovan Karadžić, and General Ratko Mladić.

A new charge of **"crimes against humanity"** is created for the **Nuremberg trials**.

Lawyers for the Nazis argue that they cannot be tried for **crimes that didn't exist when they were committed**.

There is a **precedent for trying war criminals** in the **Hague Conventions** of 1899 and 1907.

The Nazis' actions are so appalling that justice would not be served if they went unpunished.

The Nuremberg trials were a series of 13 court cases held in Nuremberg, Germany, between 1945 and 1949. Their purpose was to bring the leaders of the defeated Nazi regime to internationally recognized justice in the aftermath of World War II. Other similar trials followed, including a series held in Tokyo against Japanese war leaders, but the Nuremberg trials set the precedent.

Nazi leader Hermann Göring, one of the defendants, dismissed the Nuremberg trials as "victor's justice" – but they were an important landmark in the establishment of an international system of justice. They set a precedent for dealing with crimes of genocide and crimes against humanity across national borders and became a symbol of victory over warmongering and atrocity.

Coming retribution
Before the war had even come to an end, the Allied leaders began discussing what to do with the Nazi leaders. There was a widespread desire to bring justice and punishment to those who had caused so much suffering and death. Even more pressing was the need for retribution for the horrors of the Holocaust. As

The emaciated survivors discovered in Nazi concentration camps at the end of the war fuelled the need to punish the architects of the Holocaust.

evidence of the appalling fate of Jews under the Nazis came to light, the Allies resolved, under the four-part Moscow Declarations of 1943, to punish those responsible. One document, the Declaration on Atrocities, was signed by US president Franklin D. Roosevelt,

British prime minister Winston Churchill, and Soviet premier Joseph Stalin; it determined to return Germans to the scene of their crimes, judge them, and punish the guilty appropriately.

Trial or execution?

While Churchill was in favour of summarily shooting the high-ranking officers to avoid what he believed would turn out to be a show trial, the Russians were keen to do things right. Churchill wrote, "U.J. ["Uncle Joe", meaning Stalin] took an unexpectedly ultra-respectable line. There must be no executions without trial; otherwise the world would say we were afraid to try them."

After Roosevelt's death in April 1945, the Americans came to agree with the Russians, and US assistant secretary of war John McCloy expressed surprise that the British would object. In the end, the British agreed, and a site was chosen for the leading figures to be tried in Nuremberg, both for its good court and prison facilities

and because Hitler had held his largest rallies there, which gave a symbolic power to the process of punishing his regime for the atrocities it committed.

New court, new crimes

The court was set up as an International Military Tribunal under the London Charter that was signed on 8 August 1945 by the four leading Allies – the US, UK, Soviet Union (USSR), and France. Although there would be no jury, there was to be equal national representation among the judges and prosecution. The US and UK prosecutors Robert H. Jackson and Sir Hartley Shawcross would achieve prominence through their relentless cross-examination of the accused. The defence was largely in the hands of German lawyers.

At each of the 13 trials, judges, prosecutors, and defendants spoke four different languages: English, French, German, and Russian. Translating everything four ways in writing would have dramatically slowed proceedings, so for the first

[The Nazis] have been given the kind of a trial which they, in the days of their pomp and power, never gave to any man.
Robert H. Jackson
Summation for the prosecution, 26 July 1946

time, the trials were conducted in four languages with simultaneous translations transmitted through headphones to all participants.

Each interpreter had to translate into their target language in real time. That meant for each of the four languages, there had to be one interpreter for each of the other three languages. The stress on interpreters relaying instantly »

Robert H. Jackson

Born on a farm in Pennsylvania in 1892 and raised in New York, Robert H. Jackson grew up to become one of the most famous US Supreme Court justices in history and an ardent defender of the rule of law against the overreach of federal agencies. He was one of the last people to serve on the Supreme Court without having a law degree. Before joining the Supreme Court, he also, uniquely, held the posts of both US solicitor general and US attorney general.

As a Supreme Court justice, Jackson objected to the wartime internment of Japanese Americans and to segregation but ruled that communist plotters were not afforded protection by the constitutional right to freedom of speech and movement. Jackson is best known for his role as the chief US prosecutor at the Nuremberg trials, where his incisive style of questioning made a huge impact. He died in 1954 in Washington, DC.

often very harrowing testimony was immense, and some had to be replaced mid-trial. There was also criticism of the system because of the high possibility of mistranslation under pressure, as well as interpreters giving their own take on the statements, either consciously or inadvertently. Meanwhile, lawyers complained that the translation process gave defendants crucial thinking time under cross-examination. Despite all of this, the system proved successful and has since become the norm in international trials.

The London Charter defined three new kinds of crime. First were crimes against peace, defined, in essence, as planning for and starting wars of aggression. Second were war crimes, defined as breaking the conventions of war in the treatment of civilians and prisoners. And finally, there were crimes against humanity,

The Nazi leaders put on trial
included (pictured front row of the dock, from left) Hermann Göring, Rudolf Hess, Joachim von Ribbentrop, Wilhelm Keitel, and Ernst Kaltenbrunner.

which included murder, forced labour, forced movement of civilians, and persecution on political, religious, or racial grounds.

During the trials, prosecutors identified the Nazis' crimes against humanity as genocide, using a term coined in 1944 by Polish lawyer Raphael Lemkin. The word was his response to the Holocaust, as well as to other historic instances of the destruction of whole nations or groups defined by their ethnicity or religion. The United Nations outlawed genocide in the 1948 Convention on the Prevention and Punishment of the Crime of Genocide, which came into force in 1951, after the Nuremberg trials had concluded.

The accused
In October 1945, 24 Nazi leaders and several Nazi organizations, including the Gestapo, were indicted and ordered to appear before the main tribunal in what was called the Trial of the Major War Criminals. Some of the main players – notably Adolf Hitler himself, Heinrich Himmler, and Joseph Goebbels – were missing,

Reichsmarschall Hermann Göring was behind the implementation of the so-called Final Solution, the plan that was intended to completely annihilate Europe's Jewish population.

having either committed suicide in the closing stages of the war or fled without trace.

The tribunal considered that it was legitimate to try commanders for crimes that were committed by their troops, under the doctrine of "command responsibility", a concept that had been established by the Hague Conventions of 1899 and 1907. Although not everybody was in agreement, there was a precedent. In 1921, after World War I, German captain Emil Müller had been convicted under this directive by the German Supreme Court for the cruelty of his troops at the Flavy-le-Martel prison camp.

The most prominent among the accused at Nuremberg was Hermann Göring, the former air force chief and the man responsible for the implementation of a plan of mass murder called The Final

International Military Tribunal structure				
Participants	**French**	**British**	**American**	**Soviet**
Judges — Main	Professor Henri Donnedieu de Vabres	Lord Justice Colonel Sir Geoffrey Lawrence	Francis Biddle	Major General Iona Nikitchenko
Judges — Alternative	Robert Falco	Sir Norman Birkett	John J. Parker	Lieutenant Colonel Alexander Volchkov
Chief prosecutors	François de Menthon, later replaced by Auguste Champetier de Ribes	Attorney General Sir Hartley Shawcross	Associate Justice Robert H. Jackson	Lieutenant General Roman Andriyovych Rudenko
Defence	Mostly German One for each defendant, including Otto Stahmer (for Hermann Göring), Hans Flächsner (Albert Speer), Günther von Rohrscheidt and Alfred Seidl (Rudolf Hess), and Rudolf Merkel (the Gestapo)			

Solution to the Jewish Question. He was boldly unapologetic, lying outrageously and insisting that the Nazi leadership had only done what all war leaders do to ensure their country's survival.

On the other hand, Albert Speer, Hitler's armaments minister, was charming and debonair, skilfully offering all the information the court asked for. He apologized profusely for the terrors the Nazis had committed with such apparent sincerity that he was given just a 20-year prison sentence and spared the death penalty – unlike Göring. It was only later that the true depth of Speer's involvement came to the fore.

Legal defence
The Nazi leaders attempted several defences. One was that the crimes of which they were accused were *ex post facto*, or retroactive, laws –

that is, the crimes were only identified as crimes for the first time in the London Charter, which laid out the guidelines for the trials long after the crimes had been committed. Another was that the trials were not fair and impartial but were victor's justice brought by the Allies against the Germans, while ignoring similar crimes committed by their own troops. A third was that they had been acting under orders.

The tribunal dismissed the *ex post facto* argument by following the precedent for war crimes set by the Hague Conventions of 1899 and 1907, which prohibited certain methods of warfare. In relation to crimes against peace, they referred to the 1928 Kellogg–Briand Pact (or the Pact of Paris), by which signatory states promised not to attempt to solve disputes through

waging war. Crucially, though, it was argued that even if there was no precedent in law – as with crimes against humanity – the Nazi crimes were so appalling that justice would not be served if they were to go unpunished.

Condemnation and execution
In the end, the tribunal found all but three of the 24 accused men guilty. Twelve of them were sentenced to death, and the rest were given prison sentences ranging from ten years to life. On 16 October 1946, ten of the men condemned to death were taken to the prison gymnasium and hanged. As he was led to the gallows, Fritz Sauckel shouted, "I die innocent. The verdict was wrong."

Hermann Göring had escaped his fate by committing suicide by taking a cyanide pill the night » before he was due to be executed. The 12th man, Martin Bormann, who was Hitler's closest aide in the last years of the war, had been tried and condemned in his absence. It was long believed he had fled to South America, but in the 1970s, a skeleton was dug up in the ruins of Berlin; DNA testing in 1998 confirmed that it was Bormann.

Follow-up trials

After the Trial of the Major War Criminals, there was a series of follow-up trials at Nuremberg between December 1946 and April 1949. However, growing differences among the Allies undermined cooperation, so these were not international courts but US military tribunals, even though they were held in the same place. There were trials against doctors who had experimented on prisoners and trials against industrialists who had used forced labour. In all, a further 185 individuals were indicted, and 12 were condemned to death.

Meanwhile in Japan, between April 1946 and November 1948, another international tribunal was bringing 28 Japanese military leaders to trial. US general Douglas MacArthur had launched the process by arresting Japanese leaders in September 1945, when Japan's surrender brought World War II to an end. The following January, he approved the Charter of the International Military Tribunal for the Far East, called the Tokyo Charter. Like the London Charter, this laid out the way the trials would work.

The charter specified a similar system to Nuremberg, with three broad categories of crime. The charge of crimes against peace (class A charges) was brought against Japan's top leaders who had steered the war. War crimes and crimes against humanity (classes B and C) were brought against lower ranks. But unlike in Nuremberg, to be prosecuted for any of these latter two crimes, individuals first had to be charged with crimes against peace.

One other key difference from Nuremberg was that instead of four countries, there were 11 nations represented in Tokyo. Australia, Canada, China, France, British India, the Netherlands, New

Why don't you just shoot us?
Unknown Nazi war criminal, 1946

Zealand, the Philippines, the USSR, the United Kingdom, and the United States – all of which had been drawn into Japan's war – provided judges and prosecutors.

After two years, all 28 Japanese leaders tried were found guilty. Seven were condemned to death and hanged. The rest were given long prison sentences.

The aftermath

Many people found the experience of the Nuremberg and related trials a dispiriting one. All those attending had been through many weeks of listening to the horrors of the German crimes unfold.

Some continued to argue that it was indeed victor's justice. The Soviets were soon found to have massacred 22,000 captured Polish officers at Katyn in 1940, while hundreds of thousands of German civilians had been killed by the Allied bombing of Hamburg, Dresden, and other German cities. Harlan Stone, chief justice of the US Supreme Court at the time,

A total of 419 witnesses gave evidence at the International Military Tribunal for the Far East. The three defendants shown here are General Iwane Matsui, Colonel Kingoro Hashimoto, and General Kenji Doihara.

said the whole affair was a "sanctimonious fraud" and a "high-grade lynching party".

Despite the criticism, later there was a widespread belief that the trials had achieved something of great importance. They had formally recorded many of the crimes of the Nazi regime. Moreover, they left nobody in any doubt over who was responsible for starting the war. Crucially, though, the Nuremberg trials re-established the importance of the rule of law and set a precedent for dealing with disputes by legal means rather than resorting to arms. They were part of the determination, along with the creation of the United Nations, to build a future world that would be governed by international agreement rather than warfare.

The legacy

Robert H. Jackson, the leading judge at the Nuremberg trials, argued that it was not the fate of the individual Nazi leaders that was important but the affirmation of law as the final arbiter. In 1948, the Genocide Convention outlawed genocide, and the Universal Declaration of Human Rights was adopted by the United Nations. The Geneva Conventions, updating earlier standards for humanitarian treatment in war, followed in 1949.

Calls for the creation of an International Criminal Court to follow up on the Nuremberg trials were dogged by disagreement. It was finally established in The Hague, the Netherlands, in 2002, but without the agreement of several nations, including the United States, China, Iraq, India, Israel, Libya, Qatar, and Yemen. To date, the Hague court has tried and convicted eight individuals, as well as having acquitted four.

The Hague was also the location for the International Criminal Tribunal for the former Yugoslavia (ICTY), set up by the UN in 1993 to prosecute the serious war crimes that had been committed during the Yugoslav wars. The tribunal convicted more than 80 people including former Serbian president Slobodan Milošević; Radovan Karadžić, former president of the Republika Srpska; and Bosnian Serb commander Ratko Mladić.

The legal principles set in motion at the Nuremberg trials have failed to protect people

[An] international Magna Carta for all mankind.
Eleanor Roosevelt
Chair of the Universal Declaration of Human Rights' drafting committee (1884–1962)

against terrible war crimes and genocide, and there are many horrors that have gone unpunished or unrecorded. It also seems unlikely that the major powers will ever allow themselves to come under the scrutiny of such international courts and tribunals for their own crimes. And yet the principle of finding an international legal solution for the punishment of war criminals seems firmly in place, with the three categories of crimes set up for Nuremberg – crimes against peace, war crimes, and crimes against humanity – central to the pursuit of justice. ∎

Peter von Hagenbach

The first commanding officer to be convicted of war crimes was the Burgundian knight Peter von Hagenbach. Born c. 1420, von Hagenbach was the bailiff for the Upper Alsace region on what is now the French–German border. Between 1469 and 1474, he led an uprising with such brutality that a tribunal of 28 judges from across the Holy Roman Empire was called to try him for crimes including murder and rape. He defended himself by saying he was acting on the orders of Charles the Bold, Duke of Burgundy – the first but by no means the last time the defence of acting under orders has been used by war criminals.

This defence was rejected, and von Hagenbach was beheaded in 1474 after being convicted of murder, rape, and perjury. Some modern scholars suggest it may have been just a show trial to discredit Charles the Bold, but there seems little doubt that von Hagenbach did conduct a reign of terror.

GENOCIDE IS A VIOLATION OF THE LAWS OF HUMANITY
THE GENOCIDE CONVENTION (1948)

IN CONTEXT

FOCUS
International law

BEFORE
1899 The first of the Hague Conventions on the proper conduct of warfare is issued.

1915 The genocide of up to 1.5 million Armenians at the hands of the Turks begins.

1942 The Nazis agree the details of the Final Solution at the Wannsee Conference.

AFTER
1993 The UN sets up an international criminal tribunal (ICTY) to investigate crimes in the former Yugoslavia.

1995 An investigation by a UN international criminal tribunal (ICTR) begins into the Rwandan genocide of 1994.

2018 The UN warns that genocide remains "a threat and a reality", citing atrocities against the Rohingya, Yazidi, Syrians, and others.

Mass killing has always been a tragic part of history. But genocide reached a horrifying scale in World War II, as Germany murdered with industrial efficiency some 6 million Jews, as well as many Romany people and others in the Holocaust. After the war, there was a strong drive to reassert the rule of law in the face of these atrocities. To bring Nazi leaders to justice, the 1945 Charter of the International Military Tribunal, setting out a framework for the Nuremberg trials, identified the charge of crimes against humanity.

The Nazis' crime was on such a scale that it needed an entirely new structure to define it. Moreover, it was a crime committed by an entire state, not an individual, so it was crucial to find ways to identify who should be held responsible.

International law
In 1946, the United Nations (UN) passed a resolution recognizing genocide as a crime. The UN accepted the Convention on the Prevention and Punishment of the Crime of Genocide (known as the Genocide Convention) two years later and it came into force in 1951.

Much of the groundwork had been done by Dr Raphael Lemkin, who had escaped the Holocaust to reach the US. In 1944, he published his account of Nazi occupation,

Before the 20th century, **mass killing** of **targeted groups** of people is **not recognized as a crime** in international law.

After the Holocaust, the Nuremberg trials expose a **need to define and name the crime**, so guilty parties can be prosecuted.

In 1948, the UN adopts a Convention to **define, prevent, and punish genocide**.

See also: The Declaration of the Rights of Man 118–19 ▪ The Geneva Conventions 152–55 ▪ The Hague Conventions 174–77 ▪ The Nuremberg trials 202–09 ▪ The Universal Declaration of Human Rights 222–29

Axis Rule in Occupied Europe. British prime minister Winston Churchill had commented in a 1941 BBC broadcast that: "We are in the presence of a crime without a name." Lemkin named it genocide.

The Convention's Article 2 defines genocide as "any of the following acts committed with intent to destroy, in whole or in part, a national, ethnical, racial or religious group, as such: (a) killing members of the group; (b) causing serious bodily or mental harm to members of the group; (c) deliberately inflicting on the group conditions of life

Dr Raphael Lemkin, a Polish-Jewish international lawyer, campaigned vigorously after World War II for international legislation on genocide.

calculated to bring about its physical destruction in whole or in part; (d) imposing measures intended to prevent births within the group; and (e) forcibly transferring children of the group to another group."

The Convention was soon ratified by 130 countries, but the US, despite early involvement, did not ratify until 1988. The Convention has often faced obstacles, including the requirement to prove intent. For example, Saddam Hussein (Iraqi president, 1979–2003) claimed his assault on Iraqi Kurds, which killed many thousands in the 1980s, was an attempt to restore order. Campaigners argued that the Convention should include patterns of actions that indicate purpose.

Early tribunals

The Genocide Convention was first applied in the 1990s: the international criminal tribunals for Yugoslavia (ICTY) and Rwanda

Rape is no longer a trophy of war.
Navanethem Pillay
South African judge on the International Criminal Tribunal for Rwanda (1995–2003)

(ICTR) refined the definition of genocide. In Rwanda's case, it now included sexual violence and rape, after Hutus targeted Tutsi women for rape by HIV-infected men. The Yugoslavia tribunal meant targeting even a small part of a group could be a sign of genocidal intent.

While it continues to be refined, the Genocide Convention has already been crucial in enabling the international community to bring perpetrators of appalling crimes to justice by fair and legal process. ▪

Rwandan refugees fled in 1994 to camps in neighbouring states, such as Zaïre, but thousands died from diseases such as cholera.

Rwandan genocide

In just three months, between April and July 1994, up to a million Rwandans were massacred. The killers used machetes, clubs, and other blunt objects. Many people were herded into buildings that were doused with kerosene and set alight. Up to half a million women were raped.

The perpetrators were mainly Hutu, from the *Interahamwe* and *Impuzamugambi* youth militias, and most of the victims were Tutsi. The response of the international community was

thought to have failed badly. In the same year, the UN set up an investigative tribunal (ICTR) in Arusha, Tanzania. The entire process of investigation and trials took more than 20 years.

The trial of former Hutu mayor Jean-Paul Akayesu set the precedent for prosecuting genocidal rape. Hutu diplomat Jean-Bosco Barayagwiza and government minister Ferdinand Nahimana were convicted of genocide and sentenced to life imprisonment, reduced on appeal. In total, 93 people were put on trial, with 62 convicted.

THE ARCHITECTS OF THE BETTER WORLD

THE UNITED NATIONS AND INTERNATIONAL COURT OF JUSTICE (1945)

IN CONTEXT

FOCUS
International law

BEFORE
1899 The International Peace Conference at The Hague sets up the Permanent Court of Arbitration.

1920 The League of Nations sets up the Permanent Court of International Justice (PCIJ).

1944 The International Monetary Fund and the World Bank are set up at Bretton Woods, New Hampshire, US.

1944 At Dumbarton Oaks, Washington, DC, the Allies decide to establish the UN.

AFTER
1948 The UN issues the Universal Declaration of Human Rights.

1992 The Earth Summit is held by the UN in Rio de Janeiro, Brazil.

When the United Nations (UN) Charter was signed in San Francisco in June 1945, World War II still had three months to run, and the nations that came together wanted to prevent such a terrible conflict happening again.

The UN Charter contained two fundamental pledges: first, that it would rid the world of "the scourge of war"; and second, that it would rebuild "faith in fundamental human rights". The UN's record in fulfilling those pledges has proved to be more chequered than hoped, but they remain core to its mission today – to preserve peace and human rights by international agreement and discussion, and to solve disputes between nations – and between nations and individuals – by arbitration and legal process, not force of arms.

International cooperation

The UN's most visible department is its international Peacekeeping Force, which aims to achieve the first of the UN's five key targets – maintaining international peace and security. But peace very much depends on the UN's success in its

I believe at some future day, the nations of the Earth will agree on some sort of congress which will take cognizance of international questions of difficulty.
Ulysses S. Grant
18th US president (1869–77)

other four targets: to protect human rights, deliver humanitarian aid, promote sustainable development, and uphold international law. The UN also has a brief to strive to bring nations together to work towards these goals.

The beginning of international cooperation lay in the Hague Conventions of 1899 and 1907. The Hague peace conferences were the first real attempts by nations to come together and set agreed

Franklin D. Roosevelt

Born in New York in 1882, Franklin D. Roosevelt (FDR) won four consecutive terms as US president. After first being elected in 1933, he is best known for implementing the New Deal programme of public works to lift the US out of the Great Depression (1929–33). However, he considered his most important work to have been laying the foundations of the United Nations (UN). FDR drafted the text of the Declaration by United Nations, which was signed by delegates from 26 nations in January 1942. It

pledged to jointly fight the Axis powers of Germany, Italy, and Japan.

Plans to create a new organization for international cooperation grew out of this agreement. In April 1945, FDR was working on a speech he planned to deliver at the UN Conference on International Organization (UNCIO) when he collapsed and died. The UNCIO, which opened less than a fortnight after his death, agreed to establish the UN, and FDR's wife Eleanor later helped draft its Declaration of Human Rights.

See also: Vattel's *The Law of Nations* 108 ▪ The Hague Conventions 174–77 ▪ The Treaty of Versailles 192–93 ▪ The Universal Declaration of Human Rights 222–29 ▪ The International Criminal Court 298–303

President Roosevelt talks with Prime Minister Churchill after they had signed the Atlantic Charter aboard the USS *Augusta* in the Atlantic Ocean on 14 August 1941.

standards for what was acceptable in war, what was not, and what constituted a war crime. The ideas that the Conventions embody emerged originally from the American Civil War, when in 1863 President Abraham Lincoln issued the Lieber Code, laying out rules for the protection of civilians in wartime, as well as what constituted a truce, how spies and dissenters should be treated, and more.

The UN's roots

One of the key aims of the Hague Conventions was a system for settling disputes between nations. The 1899 conference saw the creation of the Permanent Court of Arbitration, which began work in 1902 to resolve differences on issues such as boundaries, sovereignty, and human rights. The court sat in the specially built Peace Palace in The Hague, which now houses the International Criminal Court.

The Hague Conventions were soon disrupted when Germany broke the rules with its invasion of Belgium in 1914. World War I saw many more violations, including the widespread use of poison gas.

The League of Nations

When the mayhem of World War I was over, some of the victorious Allies came together in Paris in 1919 determined that such a war should never happen again – that this should be "the war to end all wars". The Paris Peace Conference established the League of Nations with the avowed aim "to promote international cooperation and to achieve peace and security". The idea was to solve disputes between countries before they erupted into open warfare.

World War I marked the end of the age of empire. Instead, the victors wanted to build a world of independent nations coming together in open forums rather than through secret deals made behind closed doors, as had been the case in the 19th century. In this way, the victors hoped they could de-escalate tensions and disarm.

In the event, crucially, the United States, which was still wedded to its isolationist ideal, decided not to involve itself, and the League therefore had no power to enforce its will. As British prime minister David Lloyd George put it, "It had weak links spreading everywhere and no grip anywhere." When Nazi Germany built up its military and invaded Austria, Czechoslovakia, and Poland, the League of Nations was unable to stop Germany's actions triggering another world war. Yet even as the League collapsed, Allied leaders were beginning to think of a new organization that might prevent a third conflagration.

In August 1941, with the German–Italian Axis seemingly growing in power, US president Franklin D. Roosevelt and UK prime minister Winston Churchill met to frame what came to be called the Atlantic Charter, an affirmation "of certain common principles in the »

A world government must be created which is able to solve conflicts between nations by judicial decision.
Albert Einstein
Toward World Government, 1948

national policies of their respective countries on which they based their hopes for a better future for the world". Churchill and Roosevelt were soon joined by Russia and the governments of occupied Europe: Belgium, Greece, the Netherlands, Czechoslovakia, Luxembourg, Norway, Poland, Yugoslavia, and representatives from France.

Although the Atlantic Charter had no legal standing, it pledged cooperation to ensure peace in

times to come and to abandon the use of force. This pledge right at the height of the war, with support from the US for the first time, was a great inspiration for occupied countries.

At a meeting in the White House in December that year, just days after Japan's attack on Pearl Harbor, Roosevelt suggested to Churchill that the Allies call themselves the United Nations. Churchill agreed, noting that the phrase came from Lord Byron's

poem *Childe Harold's Pilgrimage*. As the war progressed, more countries signed up to the Declaration of United Nations, agreeing to the principles set out by the Atlantic Charter. By 1945, the total number had risen to 47 nations. At a conference at Dumbarton Oaks near Washington, DC, in 1944, delegates from China, Russia, the US, and the UK worked through proposals to build an organization to succeed the League

The structure of the UN

SECURITY COUNCIL

The Security Council makes decisions on the maintenance of international peace and security. It is the only body of the United Nations with the authority to issue binding resolutions to member states. There are five permanent members with the power of veto (China, Russia, France, the US, and the UK), and 10 non-permanent members are elected for two-year terms. A veto from just one member of the permanent Security Council overrules everyone else. The Security Council controls the Peacekeeping Force and establishes international sanctions.

PEACEKEEPING FORCE

Once a mission is approved by the Security Council, an operation is organized to help war-torn countries create the conditions necessary for lasting peace.

SECRETARIAT

The Secretariat comprises the secretary general and thousands of UN staff who carry out the day-to-day work of the UN, as mandated by the General Assembly and the United Nations' other main organs.

GENERAL ASSEMBLY

The General Assembly's primary role is to discuss issues and make recommendations, though it has no power to enforce its resolutions. The only body in which all 193 members have equal representation, it oversees the UN budget and appoints the secretary general.

ECOSOC

The Economic and Social Council is responsible for coordinating the UN's economic, environmental, and social policies.

ICJ

The International Court of Justice settles disputes between states. It sits at the Peace Palace in The Hague (the Netherlands).

SPECIALIZED AGENCIES

Examples of agencies:

FAO The Food and Agriculture Organization leads international efforts to beat hunger.

UNESCO The United Nations Educational, Scientific, and Cultural Organization promotes collaboration in education, sciences, and culture.

WHO The World Health Organization monitors public wellbeing.

UN PROGRAMMES

Examples of programmes:

UNDP The United Nations Development Programme helps countries eradicate poverty and reduce inequalities.

UNEP The United Nations Environment Programme promotes the wise use and sustainable development of the environment.

WFP The World Food Programme aims to eradicate hunger and malnutrition, feeding almost 80 million people every year.

ICC

The International Criminal Court prosecutes crimes against humanity. It is not part of the UN but cooperates and exchanges information with it.

of Nations that would maintain peace and security in the world. At the Yalta Conference in February 1945, Roosevelt, Churchill, and Russian premier Joseph Stalin agreed to the establishment of the United Nations and affirmed that it would meet for the first time in San Francisco in April.

The UN inherited several structures from the League of Nations, including the Secretariat, the departments led by the UN secretary general that would carry out the organization's basic administration. But there were two crucial additions: the General Assembly and the Security Council.

The General Assembly

Although it has no actual power, the General Assembly is the UN's parliament, where members meet to discuss important issues and make recommendations, so it has considerable influence. Each of the 193 members is represented and has one vote. There are also non-members such as the Vatican and Palestine, which can participate but have only observer status.

Most ordinary decisions depend on a simple majority vote. But some – such as the admission of new members, budgetary matters, and peace and security issues – require a two-thirds majority. Because of the assembly's large size, voting often tends to be in blocs – five groups of member states that are put together on a regional and geopolitical basis. The General Assembly meets once a year and also has special sessions, such as electing a new president for the year from each bloc.

The main session opens each year with a general debate, where members can raise concerns. But most of the assembly's work is done in the six committees:

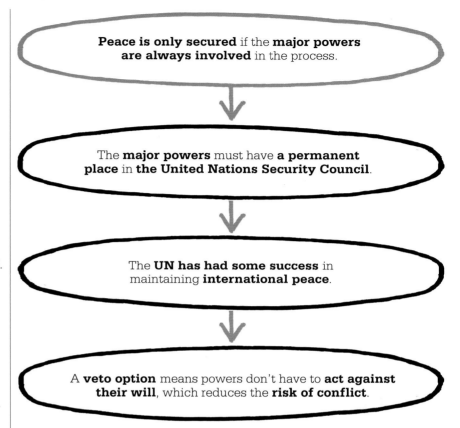

Peace is only secured if the **major powers are always involved** in the process.

The **major powers** must have **a permanent place** in **the United Nations Security Council**.

The **UN has had some success** in maintaining **international peace**.

A **veto option** means powers don't have to **act against their will**, which reduces the **risk of conflict**.

Disarmament and International Security (also known as the First Committee); Economic and Financial; Social, Humanitarian, and Cultural; Special Political and Decolonization; Administrative and Budgetary; and Legal.

The Security Council

In many ways, the real power of the UN lies with the Security Council. The original idea behind the Security Council was that the "big four" powers – the United States, Britain, the Soviet Union (USSR), and China, later joined by France – would be permanent members and steer all major decisions. Initially, they were joined by six non-permanent members, each serving for two years. An amendment to the UN Charter in 1965 added a further four non-permanent members, boosting membership of the Security Council to 15.

Generally speaking, the non-permanent members are selected in a bid to represent the different geographic regions fairly, with five members coming from Africa or Asia, one from Eastern Europe, two from Latin America, and two from western Europe or other areas. The membership continually rotates, with five of the 10 non-permanent members being elected each year by the General Assembly for two-year terms, and with five retiring. The presidency is also rotated, each member standing for one month at a time. »

Each member has one vote, and it takes nine votes to decide a policy. All members are obliged to abide by the council's rulings, but there is a crucial exception. At Yalta, Stalin insisted that each of the five permanent members had the power of veto. Roosevelt was reluctant to accept this at first, but it did fix a fatal flaw of the League of Nations, which could theoretically order its members to act in defiance of their own governments.

The veto remains a bone of contention. In the 1950s and '60s, the US had so much global influence that it never had to use the veto, but council decisions were continually blocked by the USSR, especially Andrei Gromyko whose frequent vetoes earned him the nickname Mr Nyet (Mr No). More recently, the US has used its veto to block any resolutions on the Israeli–Palestinian conflict. There has been much criticism of

Armoured UN vehicles accompany Congolese people fleeing from Kibumba Internally Displaced Persons camp, following an outbreak of violence in 2008 between rival political factions.

the Security Council's membership. In particular, the dominance of the five original permanent members, the P5, is seen as outmoded, reflecting the global politics of 1945 rather than today. Other countries, such as Brazil, Germany, India, and Japan (the so-called G4), have campaigned to be given permanent membership.

Peacekeeping

The Security Council's principal task is to maintain international peace. While it has achieved some success, most notably in El Salvador and Mozambique, its efforts to keep peace in Syria have been a conspicuous failure.

The creators of the UN realized that, without any armed forces, the League of Nations was unable to intervene effectively to keep the peace even in minor disputes. Consequently, the Security Council was quick to set up multinational peacekeeping forces. The first was deployed to oversee the ceasefire during the 1948 Arab–Israeli War in Palestine. They were intended to act as police forces, only ever responding with weapons in self-

There is no alternative to the UN. It is still the last best hope of humanity.
Kofi Annan
UN secretary general (1997–2006)

defence. Over the decades, these ad hoc international forces became more fully established, especially after 1992, when the United Nations Department of Peacekeeping Operations (DPO) was set up. Now they are a key part of the UN, but there is no standing army or permanent structure; the peacekeeping force is assembled afresh for each mission.

The Court of Justice

One of the key bodies carried over to the UN from the League of Nations was the Permanent Court of International Justice. The PCIJ's UN successor, the International Court of Justice (ICJ, or World Court) was set up in San Francisco in 1945. Unlike the UN, which had to find a new home in New York, the ICJ already had one at The Hague, in the Netherlands.

The ICJ's purpose is to settle disputes between nation states, but cases can only go ahead when the states involved consent to the Court having jurisdiction to consider the dispute. After the ICJ ruled in 1986 that the United States' covert war against Nicaragua was a violation of international law, the US withdrew its consent and agreed only to recognize the Court's

jurisdiction on a discretionary basis. The Security Council is authorized by the UN Charter to enforce the Court's rulings, but any of the P5 can veto such a move, which is what the US did over Nicaragua.

In 2002, an International Criminal Court was established to work with the ICJ to try individuals, not nations, for crimes such as genocide.

One world?

Through the ages, countless great thinkers – such as 16th-century Spanish philosopher Francisco de Vitoria – have wondered if all problems might be solved if there was just one government for the entire world. The logic is simple: wars seem to be fought at the behest of governments and rulers, so if there was just a single government or ruler, there would be no wars.

In 1943, one-time US presidential candidate Wendell Willkie wrote the bestselling book *One World*, in which he proposed a global federation. In 1945, in *The Anatomy of Peace*, Hungarian Emery Reves argued that an association of states such as the United Nations could never prevent war and that it should therefore be replaced by a federal

world government. The horror of the atomic bombs dropped on the Japanese cities of Hiroshima and Nagasaki in 1945 gave further impetus to the idea of a world government. German physicist Albert Einstein was one of the many high-profile campaigners who were deeply disturbed by the unprecedented destructive power of nuclear weapons.

More and more people began to call for the new United Nations to be transformed into a universal federation of states with the power

Swedish schoolgirl Greta Thunberg has made headline news all over the world with her no-nonsense environmental activism voiced at high-profile UN events.

to control arms. But any such vision rapidly evaporated in the postwar descent into a new "Cold War" between the USSR, driven by Lenin's vision of the Bolshevik World State, and the US-led West, which believed in a world dominated by democratic nation states and global capitalism.

The UN became accepted as the best compromise. In many ways, it turned out to be more of a success than commentators had feared, and it has provided a forum that has given a voice to a lot of rising nations. Yet in the 21st century, it seems unable to deal with conflicts in the Middle East, global terrorism, refugees, and trafficking. Additionally, as teenage climate activist Greta Thunberg so powerfully pointed out in her address to the General Assembly in 2019, the UN appears toothless in the face of the biggest crisis of all, global climate change and its impact on all of humanity. ∎

The 1989 Convention sets out a child's rights, including those concerning child labour – such as at this open-cast mine in Jharia, India.

The UN Convention on the Rights of the Child

One of the major successes of the United Nations is in relation to human rights. Over the decades, a comprehensive body of human rights law has been set up to act as a benchmark for people seeking to protect rights, including civil, cultural, economic, political, and social rights.

A landmark achievement was the UN Convention on the Rights of the Child, which was agreed in 1989. Every signatory must report regularly to the UN committee on their progress in this area. The

Convention insists every child must have basic human rights, including the right to life; to their own name and identity; to an education that enables them to fulfil their potential; to be raised by, or have a relationship with, their parents; and to express their opinions and be listened to. Under two special protocols, it also prohibits the involvement of children in warfare, the trafficking of children, child prostitution, and child pornography.

A SAFER WORLD
INTERPOL (1945)

Based in Lyon, France, INTERPOL is an international organization with a brief to coordinate efforts by different nations' police forces to fight crime that crosses national borders. Its work has become especially significant in tackling the drug trade, sex trafficking, and terrorism. It also has important day-to-day tasks such as notifying relatives of deaths abroad.

Foreign getaways
The idea of international law-enforcement cooperation began in the mid-19th century. In the 1850s, Prussian detectives, with British support, kept tabs on German philosopher and socialist revolutionary Karl Marx in London. In the 1870s, the Pinkerton detective agency in the United States shared information with Britain's Scotland Yard and France's Sûreté – all three agencies were keen to catch Adam Worth, an American bank robber who had moved to Europe and established a crime network in London and Paris.

The first concerted effort to formally establish a degree of police cooperation across borders came in 1914, when delegates from 24 countries met in Monaco. They wanted to pool identification techniques and work out how to catch fugitives. Although the Monaco Congress may have been limited in its achievements because it was arranged between legal experts and politicians, not

The 1898 assassination of Empress Elisabeth of Austria was one of several crimes that underscored the need for international police cooperation. She was stabbed by Italian anarchist Luigi Lucheni while in Geneva, Switzerland.

See also: The Metropolitan Police Act 140–43 ▪ The United Nations and International Court of Justice 212–19 ▪ The European Convention on Human Rights 230–33 ▪ The European Court of Justice 234–41

> Our collective goal
> must be to turn corruption
> into a high-risk,
> low-profit activity.
> **Jürgen Stock**
> **INTERPOL secretary general, 2016**

police professionals, it set out 12 key wishes that would later help lay the groundwork for the creation of INTERPOL.

The ICPC

Progress was interrupted by World War I, but police officials from 15 countries met at the International Criminal Police Congress in Vienna in 1923. This conference set up the International Criminal Police Commission (ICPC) to implement the 12 wishes, but cross-border cooperation on identification of criminals was at its heart. Original members included Austria, Germany, Belgium, China, France, Italy, and Yugoslavia. The UK joined in 1928, but the US did not join for another 15 years.

In 1933, the ICPC was officially recognized by the League of Nations. But by this time, politics was already influencing who was targeted as international criminals by the ICPC. For example, during the first half of the 1930s, many nations in the West thought that the chief fight was against communists. When Nazi Germany

annexed Austria in 1938, most countries withdrew from the ICPC and it became dominated by high-ranking SS officers. Its headquarters moved from Vienna to Berlin in 1942, where it was used by the Gestapo to target Jews, gypsies, and other minorities.

INTERPOL and Europol

After World War II, police officials from 17 countries met to revive the organization, which was tainted by Nazism and had lost most of its records. It moved to Paris in 1946 and started from scratch: Article 1 of its new constitution stressed fighting "ordinary" crime, aiming to exclude any offences with a political, religious, or racial basis. The name INTERPOL was adopted in 1956. While it has no policing power in any participating countries, its work to provide investigative support and aid cooperation between law-enforcement agencies has helped raise membership to 194 by the early 21st century.

In 1975, European police forces boosted their cooperation to combat terrorism with the TREVI group. (This French acronym stands for "terrorism, radicalism, extremism, and international violence".) When the Schengen agreements allowed freedom of movement between signatory countries, European police forces began to work even more closely, and in 1992, the European Police Office (Europol) was set up in The Hague. Originally intended as a drugs unit, it has expanded its brief, particularly towards organized crime that crosses national borders, including people trafficking, money laundering, and child exploitation.

Many countries fiercely guard their borders and their own way of dealing with offenders. INTERPOL's powers remain limited, and extraditions (sending citizens to another country to face trial) are often the subject of disputes. But the principle of cooperation between police forces worldwide is now widely accepted. ∎

Categories of crime pursued by INTERPOL

Terrorism and crimes against people and property
Includes crimes against children, people trafficking, terrorist plots, illegal immigration, automobile theft, and art theft.

Economic, financial, and computer crimes
Includes banking fraud, money laundering, corruption, counterfeiting, and fraud involving travel documents.

Illegal drugs and criminal organizations
Includes offences carried out by international drug cartels, the Mafia, and terrorist organizations.

ALL ARE EQUAL BEFORE THE LAW

THE UNIVERSAL DECLARATION OF HUMAN RIGHTS (1948)

IN CONTEXT

FOCUS
Human rights

BEFORE
1776 The US Declaration of Independence articulates "certain unalienable Rights".

1789 The Declaration of the Rights of Man and of the Citizen is agreed by the National Constituent Assembly of revolutionary France.

AFTER
1950 The European Convention on Human Rights (ECHR) is drafted.

1965 The International Convention on the Elimination of All Forms of Racial Discrimination is adopted by the United Nations (UN).

1979 The Convention on the Elimination of All Forms of Discrimination Against Women is opened for signature.

At the formation of the United Nations (UN) in 1945, protecting **human rights** is cited as one of the organization's **main objectives**.

⬇

To **define what human rights are**, the UN Commission on Human Rights **drafts a Declaration of Rights**.

⬇

The UN General Assembly votes on the Universal Declaration of Human Rights in 1948.

⬇

The Declaration – along with the International Covenant on **Civil and Political Rights** and the International Covenant on **Economic, Social, and Cultural Rights** – makes up the International Bill of Human Rights in 1966.

Prior to 1948's Universal Declaration of Human Rights (UDHR), there was no general statement in international law on what protections people were entitled to by virtue of simply being human. At the end of the 18th century, the French and American revolutions fought against the established institutions of power and, inspired by works such as Thomas Paine's *Rights of Man* in 1791, began to advance the idea of human rights. The 1807 abolition of the slave trade in the British Empire and advances in the rights of working people in the late 18th and early 19th centuries were important in creating the idea that everyone was entitled to a basic standard of fair treatment. In the aftermath of World War I, the Treaty of Versailles and the establishment of the League of Nations made further contributions through recognizing the idea of minority rights.

It is worth pointing out here that human rights law should not be confused with humanitarian law, which focuses on the conduct of warfare and the treatment of civilians. Before World War II, major international humanitarian treaties included the Geneva Conventions of 1864, 1906, and 1929, and the Hague Conventions of 1899 and 1907. Although the two categories of law share concerns about the treatment of people, today they are separate branches of law.

The UDHR was the most significant moment in the creation of human rights as a form of international law. By 2020, it had been translated into 523 languages and, while not legally binding, it was to reshape international law. It set out a series of protections that all countries ought to provide for their citizens. It was a key factor

See also: The US Constitution and Bill of Rights 110–17 ▪ The United Nations and International Court of Justice 212–19 ▪ The European Convention on Human Rights 230–33 ▪ The International Covenant on Civil and Political Rights 256–57

in the creation of human rights treaties, including the International Covenant on Civil and Political Rights (ICCPR) and the International Covenant on Economic, Social, and Cultural Rights (ICESCR), both signed in 1966. The UDHR also influenced many international and regional organizations, and has been cited in countless political campaigns around the world.

Origins of the UDHR

In 1941, in the midst of World War II, US president Franklin D. Roosevelt's "Four Freedoms" speech set out the idea that every human being was entitled to freedom of speech and religion, as well as freedom from fear and want. The idea that the postwar world should be founded on the promotion of human rights was contained in the 1942 Declaration by United

World War II created millions of refugees like these Jewish survivors of Nazi persecution in 1945. Globally, there were almost 71 million refugees in 2019, the highest number ever.

Nations, which was drafted by Roosevelt and UK prime minister Winston Churchill. In 1944, at the Dumbarton Oaks conference in Washington, DC – which set out the framework for the creation of the United Nations (UN) – human rights were mentioned without any real definition of what these would mean. But when the Charter of the United Nations was signed in 1945, it contained several specific references to human rights. For example, Article 1 of the Charter said that one of the UN's key functions was "promoting and encouraging respect for human rights and for fundamental freedoms for all without distinction as to race, sex, language, or religion".

The UN's Economic and Social Council set up the Commission on Human Rights in 1946. Its first meeting, in February 1947, was attended by representatives of 15 nations and was tasked with producing a bill of rights. The drafting committee of nine was drawn from those nations and reflected a diverse range »

Eleanor Roosevelt

Born in New York City in 1884, Anna Eleanor Roosevelt was the first lady of the US for the four terms that her husband Franklin Delano Roosevelt (FDR) was in office as US president, from 1933 to 1945. She lobbied for human rights around the world during the 1940s and 1950s and campaigned against poverty and racism in the US, as well as chairing the committee that drafted the UDHR.

The niece of President Theodore ("Teddy") Roosevelt, Eleanor married her fifth cousin Franklin in 1905 and persuaded him to stay in politics after he was disabled by polio in 1921. She often gave campaign speeches and travelled around the US on his behalf. Eleanor remained active in politics after her husband's death in 1945. She died in 1962 and was posthumously among the first group of winners of the UN human rights prize six years later for her work on human rights and women's rights.

The 30 provisions of the UDHR

1:	All humans are born free and equal.
2:	Everybody is entitled to rights without discrimination.
3:	All people have the right to life, liberty, and safety.
4:	No one should be kept as a slave or in servitude.
5:	There should be no torture or other inhuman treatment.
6:	Everyone has the right to be recognized as a person in law.
7:	The law should be the same for everybody.
8:	Everyone may access legal help to protect their rights.
9:	No one can arrest or exile anyone without good reason.
10:	People have the right to a fair, impartial public trial.
11:	Everyone is innocent until they are proved guilty.
12:	No one should attack a person's privacy or reputation.
13:	People have freedom of movement in their own country.
14:	Everyone has the right to seek asylum abroad.
15:	We all have the right to a nationality.
16:	Men and women can marry and have children.
17:	All people have the right to own property.
18:	Freedom of thought is everybody's right.
19:	People should have freedom of opinion and expression.
20:	Everyone has the right to freedom of peaceful assembly.
21:	Government authority should be based on free elections.
22:	State social security should be provided when needed.
23:	All people have a right to work and to fair pay.
24:	Everyone should get leisure time, including paid holidays.
25:	Adequate food and shelter are a basic human right.
26:	Access to education is everyone's right.
27:	We should be able to protect our artistic creations.
28:	All these freedoms should be available worldwide.
29:	We have a duty to protect other people's rights.
30:	No state or persons can take away these rights.

of backgrounds and expertise. Among the nine were René Cassin, a French lawyer who had fled the Nazis; Charles Habib Malik, a Lebanese philosopher; Peng Chung Chang, a Chinese academic; Hernán Santa Cruz, a judge from Chile; and Charles Dukes, a British trade unionist. It was chaired by Roosevelt's widow, Eleanor. The final draft of the UDHR was completed in 1948. On 10 December that year, the UN General Assembly sitting in Paris (the UN's New York headquarters was not yet built) voted on resolution 217, entitled "the International Bill of Human Rights". The resolution was passed with 48 states voting in favour, none voting against, and eight choosing to abstain, including South Africa (see box, right). Every year, World Human Rights Day is marked around the globe on 10 December.

A declaration of principles

The UDHR is not a legal document and, unlike a treaty, countries are not obliged to follow its terms as a matter of international law. Rather it is a declaration of principles about what rights ought to be protected globally. The UDHR was a response to the tragedy of World War II, during which, as the Declaration states, "disregard and contempt for human rights have resulted in barbarous acts which have outraged the conscience of mankind". In this respect, the advocacy of human rights also has the practical purpose of promoting peace between nations: as the UDHR's preamble notes, this helps support "the development of friendly relations between nations".

Human rights are also justified as being universal on the grounds of natural law, which the ancient Greek philosopher Aristotle explained as a body of unchanging

Apartheid and international human rights

A National Party government came to power in South Africa in 1948, pledging to establish apartheid ("separateness") laws in the country. The same year, South Africa abstained in the UDHR vote because Article 2 explicitly stated that everyone is entitled to all of its rights, regardless of race. In the years that followed, South Africa enacted laws, such as the 1950 Population Registration Act, that explicitly discriminated against people on the basis of their race.

After decolonization in the 1960s, newly independent African and Asian states spearheaded the drafting of the 1965 Convention on the Elimination of All Forms of Racial Discrimination. During the 1970s, the issue of apartheid in South Africa regularly came before the UN Commission on Human Rights and the UN General Assembly. Eventually, president F.W. de Klerk was compelled by a combination of trade and cultural sanctions and internal opposition to release African National Congress leader Nelson Mandela from prison in 1990. And between then and 1994, the government scrapped the apartheid laws.

This apartheid-era sign on a bench in Cape Town, South Africa, is a poignant reminder of the racial segregation that existed in every public place in apartheid South Africa.

moral principles independent of the laws of any nation. The UDHR preamble states that human rights are necessary to protect "the dignity and worth of the human person". Article 2 of the UDHR makes this concrete, stating that "everyone is entitled to all the rights and freedoms set forth in this Declaration without distinction of any kind".

In 1949, Hannah Arendt, a German-American philosopher and political theorist, and herself a stateless refugee from Nazi

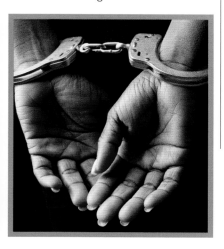

Germany but also highly sceptical of the UDHR, succinctly summed this up when she wrote, "The right to have rights, or the right of every individual to belong to humanity, should be guaranteed by humanity itself." Some other provisions in the UDHR also aimed to protect the right to have rights. Article 28 talks about "entitlement to a social and international order in which the rights and freedoms set forth in this Declaration can be fully realized", while Article 30 makes it clear that no states or individuals should engage in activities aimed at the destruction of any of the rights and freedoms set out in the Declaration.

Article 3 states that everyone has the right to life, liberty, and security of person, while Articles 4 and 5 focus on the prohibition of slavery and torture respectively. Articles 6 to 11 concern legal

Article 9 states that "no one should be subject to arbitrary arrest or detention", such as dissidents who are locked up in psychiatric hospitals – as many were in the Soviet Union (USSR).

rights governing the way a person is treated by courts and criminal justice systems. The UDHR also includes the right to own property (in Article 17), the right to an education (Article 26), and the right to seek political asylum (Article 14).

Indivisibility

Many analysts distinguish between first- and second-generation human rights. The former relate to liberty and political expression. Sometimes called natural rights, they include the rights to life, freedom of speech, »

To deny people their human rights is to challenge their very humanity.
Nelson Mandela
Address to the Joint Session of the US House of Congress, 1990

and a fair trial. They are covered by Articles 3–21 of the UDHR, and prohibit state interference in the freedoms of an individual.

Second-generation rights largely tend to deal with economic and social rights, such as the right to food, housing, and healthcare. They are covered by Articles 22–28 of the UDHR. These rights impose upon governments a duty to promote them – but whether they are enacted depends on the availability of resources.

Third-generation human rights go beyond basic civil and social rights and include the right to a healthy environment and the right to participate in cultural heritage. They are not yet included in the UDHR. Neither, explicitly, are the right not to fight and the abolition of the death penalty.

Some observers criticize the distinction between first- and second-generation rights as academic: all rights require state commitment (whether funding criminal courts or health clinics), and should be seen as universal, interdependent, and indivisible.

Bill of Human Rights

When the UN Commission on Human Rights came to turn the UDHR into international law, some

> We cannot let cultural relativism become the last refuge of repression.
> **Warren Christopher**
> **US secretary of state (1993–97)**

American medical students protest against the repeal of the Affordable Care Act (2010), which made health insurance more affordable, insisting that healthcare is a human right.

delegates in the Commission, led by the representative from the United States, supported the creation of two separate human rights treaties in 1966: the International Covenant on Civil and Political Rights (ICCPR), which had been ratified by 173 countries as of 2020; and the International Covenant on Economic, Social, and Cultural Rights (ICESCR), which had 170 state parties by 2020.

The UDHR had treated these rights as equally important, but there were some major differences between the two. Article 2 of the ICCPR requires signatories to "take the necessary steps" in order to "adopt such laws or other measures as may be necessary to give effect to the rights" protected in the treaty and to ensure that remedies are available for violations of those rights.

In contrast, the ICESCR only requires countries to use its "available resources, with a view to achieving progressively the full realization of the rights" contained in the treaty. This is generally considered to be a weaker legal requirement, and some observers see it as evidence of economic

and social rights not being treated seriously enough in international human rights law.

Relativism and rights

The UDHR was drafted at a time when large parts of Africa and Asia were still under colonial rule. The UDHR drafting committee was careful to recognize the different cultural and political traditions of rights. Yet, in 1947, the American Anthropological Association warned about the UDHR's alleged "intolerance" of cultural differences and questioned whether it was even possible to come up with a truly universal declaration of human rights.

Saudi Arabia was one of the eight nations that abstained in the UDHR vote in 1948. It was concerned about the references to religious freedom in the Declaration, which it felt was incompatible with Saudi society because of its strict adherence to Islam and Sharia law.

At the First International Conference on Human Rights in Tehran in 1968, some countries questioned whether the idea of human rights was inapplicable to societies in Africa, Asia, and the Middle East. At 1993's Second World Conference on Human Rights in Vienna, the conference's declaration and programme of action cautioned that "the significance of national and regional particularities and diverse historical, cultural, and religious backgrounds must be borne in mind" when promoting and protecting human rights.

This has led to concerns that relativism could undermine human rights by allowing countries to claim that their own traditions supersede all human rights claims. Some scholars, such as Abdullahi Ahmed An-Na'im, a Sudanese-American expert on Islamic law and human rights, have identified how rights such as the prohibition on torture have their origins in many different cultural and religious traditions around the world and argue it is wrong to dismiss human rights as simply a Western idea.

The UDHR was the starting point for many other human rights instruments that applied and extended the principles contained in the Declaration. In 1976, for example, the UN Commission on Human Rights set about drafting a treaty on women's rights, which became the 1979 Convention on the Elimination of all forms of Discrimination Against Women (CEDAW). The preamble to this Convention noted that "the Universal Declaration of Human Rights affirms the principle of the inadmissibility of discrimination against women", but went on to note that despite this, "extensive discrimination against women continues to exist". This was an acknowledgment that the UDHR needed to be set within a new legal framework to deal with the complex nature of discrimination against women.

Similarly, in 1989, the UN Convention on the Rights of the Child (UNCRC) noted that the UDHR had proclaimed that children were entitled to "special care and

Let us remember our roots as one human family, forever dedicated to upholding the central tenets of the Universal Declaration of Human Rights.
Barack Obama
44th US president (2009–17)

assistance", before going on to outline a specific legal framework for protecting their human rights.

The African Charter on Human and People's Rights (1981) – a regional human rights treaty for countries who are members of the African Union – stated in its preamble that the Charter sought to build on the UDHR with the "historical tradition and the values of African civilization".

Future challenges
For more than 70 years, the UDHR has been used by a wide variety of movements to help define their claims to basic human rights. Campaigners argue that to keep pace with a rapidly changing world, its scope needs to be extended. The right to a healthy environment and free internet access are just two such areas. The UDHR has achieved much, yet many millions are still denied their basic rights. ■

To mark the 70th anniversary of the UDHR, Chinese artist and activist Ai Weiwei designed a new flag, which depicts a footprint – symbolizing all those who have been forced to flee, often barefoot.

THE RIGHT TO LIBERTY AND SECURITY

THE EUROPEAN CONVENTION ON HUMAN RIGHTS (1950)

IN CONTEXT

FOCUS
Human rights

BEFORE
1945 Europe is devastated after World War II. No court exists to protect human rights anywhere in the world.

1948 The UN issues the Universal Declaration of Human Rights.

AFTER
1960 The European Court of Human Rights (ECtHR) delivers its first judgement, in the case of *Lawless v. Ireland*, which involves the detention of a terrorist suspect.

1998 Protocol No. 11 compels all member countries to let individuals access the ECtHR.

2017 The ECtHR delivers its 20,000th judgement.

The European Convention on Human Rights (ECHR) is a treaty on human rights between the 47 member states of the Council of Europe – not to be confused with the entirely separate European Union (EU). The ECHR was rooted in western Europe's resolve to rebuild after World War II and to protect itself against the rise of communism in Eastern Europe.

In 1948, 750 delegates at the Congress of Europe studied ideas for uniting and legally integrating Europe. When the newly formed Council of Europe met in 1949, its focus had become more modest in scope: the creation of a human rights treaty that, by protecting

See also: The Glorious Revolution and the English Bill of Rights 102–03 ▪ The US Constitution and Bill of Rights 110–17 ▪ The Universal Declaration of Human Rights 222–29 ▪ The International Covenant on Civil and Political Rights 256–57

Former British prime minister
Winston Churchill was the honorary president of the Congress of Europe at The Hague, in the Netherlands, in 1948.

democracy, could be used to guard the region against communism and totalitarianism.

The 10 founding states of the Council of Europe were Belgium, Denmark, France, Ireland, Italy, the Netherlands, Luxembourg, Norway, Sweden, and the UK. Delegates debated issues such as whether the emergency powers within the new Convention might be used to abuse human rights. Britain and France also worried that some independence movements in their respective colonies might use the Convention against them.

There was much debate about whether to create a court to enforce the new human rights convention.

Some nations did not understand how such a court would work, while others were more concerned about the scope of its powers.

The final text of the Convention was completed in 1950. It opened for signature in the same year and came into force in 1953, after being ratified by the Council of Europe's 10 founding states; other states signed up over the next 50 years. Once a sufficient number of member states had ratified the ECHR, the European Court of Human Rights (ECtHR) was set up in Strasbourg, France. The Court consists of a lower court and an appeals chamber, and it heard its first case in 1959.

When states sign up to the Convention, they must, under Article 1, protect the Convention rights for everyone in their country or otherwise under their control. If they do not, a person living in that »

You are living in the **territory** of a country that has **signed** the **European Convention on Human Rights**.

You are a victim of a **human rights abuse** because a **government** has **denied you a Convention right**.

You have **tried to resolve** your **complaint** in your **own country**, without success.

Your **complaint** is **of a sort** that has **not previously** been **resolved** by the European Court of Human Rights.

You are eligible to have your case heard in the European Court of Human Rights.

signatory state who suffers a rights violation, or the government of another signatory state, can take the offending state to the ECtHR.

The Convention rights

Inspired in part by the 1948 UN Declaration of Human Rights, Articles 2–13 of Europe's 1950 Convention list 12 substantive human rights that every individual is entitled to expect from their government (see below). Each set of rights is often referred to by its Convention article; for example, the prohibition of slavery is called "Article 4 rights". Other articles cover procedural mechanisms, such as derogations and permitted restrictions in the application of Convention rights.

In 1959, when the ECtHR was set up, signatory nations could choose whether or not to accept the Court's jurisdiction. Over the years, however, the original Convention has been repeatedly updated. Some amendments, known as Protocols, concern procedure – for example, in 1998, Protocol No. 11 required all ECHR signatory states to allow cases to go to the ECtHR. Other protocols added new rights, such as the rights to property and education, laid down in Protocol in 1954.

Interpreting rights

Some rights are absolute under the Convention. Article 3 rights, which prohibit torture, cannot be limited by governments or be suspended in an emergency. In 2006, the ECtHR blocked the Italian government from deporting Nassim Saadi on grounds of his suspected ties to terrorist groups, because he was held to be at risk of torture in Tunisia.

Other articles qualify some rights. In the 1950s, most nations still retained the death penalty for

> The European Court of Human Rights ... exerts a profound influence on the laws and social realities of its member states.
> **Dame Rosalyn Higgins**
> **British president, International Court of Justice (2006–09)**

murder. So Article 2 allowed a person to be intentionally killed by "sentence of a court following his conviction of a crime for which this penalty is provided by law". In 1983, however, the death penalty was abolished by Protocol.

The right to life often sparked a debate about whether there should be a right to die, with terminally ill people being offered assisted suicide. Recognizing that cultures and practices vary across Europe, the ECtHR has been careful to say that such questions are best dealt with by national courts.

The second paragraph of Article 10 (freedom of expression, conscience, and opinion) sets out where a government may limit the right to free speech. The ECtHR's task is to assess whether any government limitations are justified. In 1997, Swiss journalist Martin Stoll had published correspondence from confidential Swiss–US negotiations on the reparations to Holocaust victims from banks used by Nazis in World War II. The Swiss authorities convicted and fined Stoll. In 2007,

Key rights in the 1950 Convention	
Article 2:	The right to life
Article 3:	Freedom from torture and degrading treatment
Article 4:	Freedom from slavery and forced labour
Article 5:	The right to liberty and security of person
Article 6:	The right to a fair trial
Article 7:	The right to no punishment outside the law
Article 8:	The right to privacy and family life
Article 9:	Freedom of thought and religion
Article 10:	Freedom of expression, conscience, and opinion
Article 11:	The right to peaceful assembly and to join trade unions
Article 12:	The right to marry
Article 13:	The right to effective remedy to rights violations

Migrants' rights to liberty and family life have been upheld in cases judged by the European Court of Human Rights, but not all governments agree.

in *Stoll v. Switzerland*, the ECtHR found that the fine, although it had restricted Stoll's right to free expression, was justified, in order to protect confidential negotiations.

Some rights, such as Articles 5 and 6, affect a person's interaction with state courts and criminal justice systems. Article 2, the right to life, has also been interpreted as requiring countries to ensure their police forces investigate suspicious deaths. After British Special Forces (SAS) killed three suspected IRA terrorists in Gibraltar in 1988, the ECtHR in 1995 criticized the British investigation into their deaths as being flawed and secretive.

Article 3, amended in 2008, now requires police forces actively to prevent certain types of crime involving inhuman or degrading treatment. In 2018, victims of the serial sex offender known as the "black cab rapist" successfully argued at the UK Supreme Court that Article 3 of the Convention placed a responsibility on London's police to investigate, and attempt to prevent, sex crimes.

Controversial decisions
The right to participate in elections, as set out in 1954 in Article 3 of Protocol No. 1, has been interpreted by the ECtHR as not allowing countries to completely ban their prisoners from voting. This has proved controversial in some countries; the UK and Russia both strongly objected to this decision.

Some rights in the Convention protect personal interests, such as the rights to privacy (Article 8) and religious freedom (Article 9). In 2011, France banned the wearing of face coverings, including the burqa and other religious attire, anywhere in public. In the 2014 case *S.A.S. v. France*, the ECtHR ruled that the ban had not violated Article 9, but the judgement was criticized for being too deferential to the French government's policy of secularism and not protecting the rights of the women affected by the ban.

Advancing human rights
The Council of Europe is the body responsible for applying political pressure on countries to implement ECtHR decisions. Most states comply, even with decisions that they lose, but in the mid-2010s, concerns arose about long-term non-compliance with some decisions. Only one state has formally left the Convention – Greece, in the late 1960s after a military coup, though it later rejoined after the restoration of democracy. In 2015, Russia passed a law allowing its own courts to ignore ECtHR decisions.

Despite these setbacks, the decisions of the European Court of Human Rights are still cited around the world and have been important in advancing human rights issues, from abolition of the death penalty to protection of LGBTQ rights. ∎

Amal Clooney, an international human rights lawyer, successfully represented the Republic of Armenia in a 2015 ECtHR case about a denial of Armenian genocide.

A COURT WITH UNPARALLELED POWER

THE EUROPEAN COURT OF JUSTICE (1952)

IN CONTEXT

FOCUS
International law

BEFORE
1693 William Penn advocates a European parliament.

1806 Napoleon Bonaparte proposes a customs union for mainland Europe.

1927 French mathematician Émile Borel establishes the French Committee for European Cooperation.

AFTER
1957 The Treaty of Rome creates the European Economic Community.

1992 The Maastricht Treaty establishes the European Union, a big step towards political integration.

2009 Under the Treaty of Lisbon, new EU constitutional systems are set in place.

2020 The UK exits the EU, leaving 27 member states.

The **European Parliament** and the **Council of the European Union** agree **new EU legislation**.

The European Court of Justice (ECJ) **interprets** the legislation and **advises the national courts** of member states how to apply it.

The ECJ **enforces** the legislation if national courts are **not complying** with it. It can **impose fines** for non-compliance.

The ECJ can also take action against the EU Parliament, Council, or Commission on behalf of member states.

I n 1693, English-born William Penn – Quaker, democratic idealist, and founder of the Province of Pennsylvania in America – proposed a parliament for the whole of Europe, as a means to end its constant warring: "[so] that by the same Rules of Justice and Prudence by which Parents and Masters Govern their Families, and Magistrates their Cities, and … Princes and Kings their Principalities and Kingdoms, Europe may Obtain and Preserve Peace among Her Sovereignties". Nothing came of Penn's plan, though many others had the same dream – including Tsar Alexander I of Russia when the Napoleonic Wars engulfed Europe in 1803–15. In 1946 – after two world wars had torn Europe apart, convincing many that only a unified Europe could guarantee peace – former UK prime minister Winston Churchill appealed for a "United States of Europe".

Building on that vision, Europe today has two fundamental international organizations, the Council of Europe and the European Union (EU). The aim of the EU is to promote peace and prevent the resurgence of nationalism, by means of integration of its member states. It is based on the rule of law, and the European Court of Justice (ECJ) plays an important role in ensuring that EU regulations are observed and applied consistently in every EU country. In 2018, for example, the UK was referred to the Court for being in breach of EU law with regard to the Air Quality Directive. The Council of Europe (CoE) was set up in 1949, when representatives of 10 countries – France, Italy, the Netherlands, Belgium, Luxembourg, Denmark, Norway, Sweden, Ireland, and the UK – met in London to establish a forum for dialogue and

The Rule of Justice [ensures] that Power might not vanquish or oppress Right, nor one Neighbour act an Independency and Sovereignty upon another.
William Penn
"Essay Towards the Present and Future Peace of Europe", 1693

See also: Vattel's *The Law of Nations* 108 ▪ The Napoleonic Code 130–31 ▪ The European Convention on Human Rights 230–33 ▪ The Helsinki Treaty 242–43 ▪ *Google Spain v. AEPD and Mario Costeja González* 308–09

cooperation. The stated purpose of the CoE was then (and remains today) to uphold human rights, democracy, and the rule of law in Europe. The CoE now has a total of 47 member states.

The CoE is sometimes confused with the EU, and it has the same flag and anthem. However, the CoE has no power to make laws, though it does have the power to enforce agreements made by European states. Its emphasis is on the rights of European citizens, and it has spawned many subsidiary organizations and Conventions that focus on specific areas. Notable among these are the European Convention on Human Rights (ECHR), the European Committee for the Prevention of Torture (CPT), and the CoE Convention on the Protection of Children from Sexual Exploitation and Sexual Abuse. Crucially, in 1959, the CoE set up the European Court of Human Rights (ECtHR), which enforces the ECHR.

Economic ties

Among the subjects discussed by the CoE in its early days was the possibility of greater economic

[When] nations and men accept the same rules … their behaviour towards each other changes. This is the process of civilization itself.
Jean Monnet
A Ferment of Change, 1962

and political integration of member countries. Various ideas were put forward, but none could secure majority support.

In 1945, however, French political economist Jean Monnet had urged France to take over Germany's coal-producing regions in the districts of the Ruhr and the Saar – to weaken Germany's industrial might and help France's postwar economic recovery. The Monnet Plan was adopted: with US backing, in 1947 the Saar became a French protectorate, and in 1949

the Ruhr Agreement was imposed on western Germany, allowing the US, the UK, France, and the Benelux countries (Belgium, the Netherlands, and Luxembourg) to take control of the Ruhr's coal mines. This was a precondition for the establishment of the Federal Republic of Germany, which was formed by the merger of the western sectors of Allied-controlled Germany. (Soon after, the eastern sector became the Soviet-dominated German Democratic Republic.)

Tensions between former enemies France and West Germany over control of the Saarland spurred Monnet on with his vision of an integrated European community. In 1950, in a declaration drafted partly by Monnet, French foreign minister Robert Schuman proposed a plan to combine all French and German coal and steel production into a common market, governed by a single High Authority (HA) – a »

The Saar River was a key industrial corridor in the 1950s, connecting the Saarland coalfields with Saarbrücken, the regional capital city. Canals form links to France and to the Netherlands.

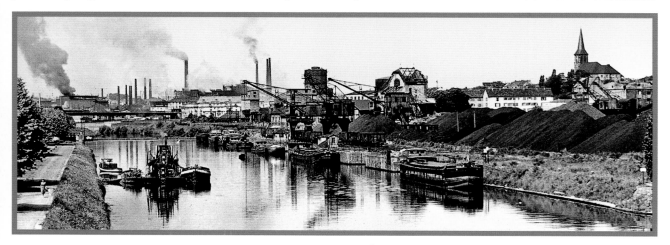

body that would, in time, evolve into the European Commission. Membership of this European Coal and Steel Community (ECSC) would be open to all other western European countries, and the HA would be composed of government-appointed representatives of each member state.

It was hoped that, in due course, greater political integration would follow. "Europe will not be made all at once," Schuman declared. "It will be built through concrete achievements which first create a de facto solidarity. The coming together of the nations of Europe requires the elimination of the age-old opposition of France and Germany." The pooling of coal and steel industries would mean that "any war between France and Germany becomes not merely unthinkable but materially impossible". It would be the "first concrete foundation of a European federation, indispensable to the preservation of peace".

German chancellor Konrad Adenauer was enthusiastic, as were the leaders of Italy and the Benelux countries, though the UK demurred. Importantly, the idea also had the

> Common foundations for economic development ... will change the destinies of those regions which have long been devoted to the manufacture of munitions of war.
> **Robert Schuman**
> **The Schuman Declaration, 1950**

backing of US secretary of state George C. Marshall, whose Marshall Plan, enacted in 1948, poured billions of American dollars into postwar Europe, to rebuild infrastructure and foster trade.

The Treaty of Paris
In June 1950, delegates from France, West Germany, Italy, and the Benelux countries began the negotiations that would lead to the creation of the ECSC. The

Treaty of Paris was finally signed in April 1951 and came into force in July 1952. The talks were complex. Not all parties shared the same vision as Monnet, and hopes of an overarching political union were quickly dashed.

Monnet was sure that the HA was the key to integration: countries could appeal to the HA to review any decision they did not like. But for the Benelux countries, this was not enough, and as a democratic safeguard to stop the HA taking dictatorial control, they proposed a Special Council of Ministers. This would be made up of representatives of each national government, and it could challenge the HA's decisions or hear appeals itself. More significantly, some delegates also proposed a Court of Justice, believing that a strong court could help build the constitutional system that Europe would need in order to achieve full integration.

Monnet was sceptical about the proposed court, believing that it would impede cooperation. But both ideas – of the Special Council of Ministers and of a Court of Justice – had support. The Benelux delegates wanted the court to be

Jean Monnet

French political adviser Jean Monnet was a pioneer of European integration and the brains behind the Schuman Plan, which merged western European heavy industry to form the European Coal and Steel Community (ECSC).

Born in 1888 in the Cognac region, the young Monnet travelled the world for the family cognac business, and became a respected international financier. During World War I, he gained distinction as an economic intermediary between France and its allies,

and in 1919 he was made deputy secretary general of the League of Nations. In 1952, he became the first president of the ECSC.

Monnet worked tirelessly towards realizing his dream of a fully integrated European community. In 1955, he set up the Action Committee for the United States of Europe, which was a driving force behind subsequent achievements, such as the creation of the Common Market and, ultimately, the European Union. Monnet died in 1979.

The European Court of Justice (ECJ) now has jurisdiction over the 27 states of the European Union. It was established in 1952 as the Court of Justice of the European Coal and Steel Community. In 1993, when the 12 nations of the European Communities created the European Union, the ECJ – formerly the court of just an economic union – became the supreme court of this political union.

List of countries:
1. Belgium (1958)
2. Italy (1958)
3. France (1958)
4. Luxembourg (1958)
5. Netherlands (1958)
6. Germany (1958)
7. Denmark (1973)
8. Ireland (1973)
9. Greece (1981)
10. Portugal (1986)
11. Spain (1986)
12. Finland (1995)
13. Austria (1995)
14. Sweden (1995)
15. Hungary (2004)
16. Slovakia (2004)
17. Poland (2004)
18. Cyprus (2004)
19. Czech Republic (2004)
20. Estonia (2004)
21. Latvia (2004)
22. Lithuania (2004)
23. Malta (2004)
24. Slovenia (2004)
25. Bulgaria (2007)
26. Romania (2007)
27. Croatia (2013)

Key:
EU member (since year shown)
Non-EU country

able to review not just the legality of an HA decision but also its policies – yet they were determined that this should be a matter between states. The Germans, however, advocated private access, while the French worried that if the court had the power to review policy, it would lead to undemocratic government by judges. A compromise was reached. The court would have the power to annul HA decisions that violated the terms and spirit of the Treaty of Paris, while the HA would avoid decisions that would disturb member countries.

Limitations on powers
When it became clear that the HA would be the executive of the ECSC, and the Court of Justice its judiciary, the French ensured the Court remained an administrative one. It would have powers to ensure the observation of ECSC law and to interpret the Treaty of Paris, but not the power of constitutional review

to examine policy. The new court was based in Luxembourg, with one judge from each of the six member states, plus a seventh from one of the three large countries – West Germany, France, and Italy – a position held in rotation. (Today, the European Court of Justice has 27 judges, one from each EU state.)

By the time the Treaty of Paris was signed in 1951, some of the enthusiasm for supranational bonds had already waned, and plans for a political union and a defence union were dropped. Yet the strong legal framework gave momentum to the European project.

The ECSC was overseen by four institutions: the HA, which was a nine-member executive; the Common Assembly, made up of 78 representatives appointed from the parliaments of the member states; the Special Council of Ministers, composed of representatives of national governments; and the Court of Justice. Modelled on the Council

of Europe, the Common Assembly was designed to provide democratic legitimacy; it first met in September 1952 in Strasbourg.

Three communities
Gradually, European politicians began to discuss the idea of a common market. The European Economic Community (EEC), also known as the Common Market, was formed by the six founding member states of the ECSC, under the Treaty Establishing the European Economic Community – commonly known as the Treaty of Rome. It was signed in 1957 and came into force on 1 January 1958.

The treaty also created a third community: the European Atomic Energy Community (EAEC), soon known as Euratom. Conceived to oversee the development of the European market for atomic energy, it now covers all aspects of nuclear power, including the safe disposal of nuclear materials. »

The EEC and Euratom had their own councils and executive bodies. But due to reservations among some states about the supranational powers of the HA, these executives had more limited powers, and their councils greater powers, than in the case of the ECSC. Rather than "high authorities", the new executives were "commissions". The remit of the Court of Justice of the ECSC was expanded to include both the EEC and Euratom. The Common Assembly was also shared across the three communities and became the European Parliament.

A condition of the success of [the European] experiment is that there should be a body whose task is to ensure that the rules are the same for everyone.
Judge David Edward
European Court of Justice (1992–2004)

The Treaty of Rome, creating the European Economic Community, was signed on 25 March 1957 by delegates of France, West Germany, Italy, Belgium, the Netherlands, and Luxembourg.

Further integration

The creation of the EEC was a watershed moment. Never before had a major group of nations pooled resources so freely. Members were still hesitant about further political integration, but legal integration proceeded apace, with the ECJ making many key decisions throughout the 1960s.

In 1965, the Merger Treaty (also known as the Treaty of Brussels) was signed, coming into force in 1967. It merged the executives and councils of the ECSC, EEC, and Euratom: collectively, the three were now known as the European Communities (EC). The executive became the Commission of the European Communities.

The UK had previously declined to join any of the communities but had a change of heart after fearing economic isolation. It first applied to join the EEC in 1963, then again in 1967, but both attempts were blocked by French president Charles de Gaulle, who saw the economic union from a firmly nationalist point of view – as a vehicle for French economic interests – and wanted no further integration or expansion.

When de Gaulle resigned in 1969, French opposition to UK membership softened. Germany was going through a remarkable economic recovery, and the UK, then in a contrastingly poor state, was finally admitted to the EC in 1973, along with Denmark and Ireland. However, this expansion came just before a massive oil price hike initiated by OPEC (Organization of the Petroleum Exporting Countries) in the autumn of 1973, creating a

dramatic downturn in Europe's economic fortunes. Many Europeans felt that the only way to counter the two global superpowers – the US and the Soviet Union (USSR) – was to build a more connected Europe.

The European Parliament first held direct elections in 1979 and made Simone Veil of France its president. Greece joined the EC in 1981, with Spain and Portugal following in 1986. In 1985, five of the 10 member countries agreed at Schengen in Luxembourg to abolish border checks. Other countries signed up later, and by 1997, 26 European states were party to the Schengen Agreement.

The UK remained aloof from Schengen, and Prime Minister Margaret Thatcher opposed further economic integration. But change occurred in 1985, when Englishman Arthur Cockfield became vice president of the Commission of the European Communities, under its French president Jacques Delors.

Van Gend en Loos v. the Netherlands

One landmark ruling made by the European Court of Justice (ECJ) was in the case of *Van Gend en Loos v. Nederlands Inland Revenue Administration* in 1963. Van Gend en Loos, a Dutch company, transported formaldehyde from Germany to the Netherlands. The Dutch charged a tariff on this import, in breach of Common Market rules. The ECJ ruled that Van Gend en Loos could recover the tariff. This established the key principle of "direct effect", whereby courts of member states are bound to recognize the rights conferred by the European Community.

LES RESULTATS COMPLETS

Libération

LE TRAITE DE MAASTRICHT EST RATIFIE A UNE COURTE MAJORITE

OU..i

50,9% 49,1%

La revue des éditoriaux européens

Cockfield became a convert to the idea of a "single market", which would guarantee the free movement of goods, capital, services, and labour (the "four freedoms") between member states. His white paper on the subject, which was well received by the other EC states, led to the Single European Act of 1986. This would create a single market in 1993, and also gave the European Parliament greater legislative powers in order to achieve this.

Meanwhile, a move to pick up the failed dream of a European political community, first mooted in 1952, had gained support in the European Parliament. In 1984, under the Spinelli Plan, drafted mainly by Italian political theorist Altiero Spinelli, the Parliament resolved to proceed from economic union to full political union. As negotiations continued, other dramatic events unfolded: the Berlin Wall fell in 1989, the USSR collapsed, and East and West Germany were unified. So it was in a buoyant mood that the 12 member states of the EC met at Maastricht in the Netherlands in December 1991 to draft a new treaty.

French newspaper *Libération* ran a hesitant-looking headline announcing the marginal result of the referendum on the Maastricht Treaty in 1992. The result became known as the "petit oui".

European Union

One key formal objective of the Maastricht Treaty was the adoption of a universal currency. Economic and monetary union (EMU) was intended to promote the gradual convergence of member states' economies. But before the treaty could be ratified, the law in France, Denmark, and Ireland required it to be put to a referendum. In Ireland, it was approved by a large majority, but in France the majority in favour was tiny. In Denmark, it was rejected by an equally small margin. Only after four opt-outs for Denmark were negotiated did another referendum give its approval.

The Maastricht Treaty was signed in February 1992, and in November 1993 the EC became the EU. It inherited the institutions of its predecessor: the Commission, the Council, the Parliament, and the ECJ, which was renamed the Court of Justice in 2009, while its lower court, formerly the Court of First Instance, was renamed the General Court. Combined, they are known as the Court of Justice of the European Union. The Commission develops overall policy and strategy and proposes new laws, while the Council of the EU – made up of ministers from each member state – coordinates policies. Together, the Council and the Parliament – which is directly elected by the public – agree and adopt new EU legislation.

Maastricht was a logical step in the 40-year process of convergence, but achieving it had not been easy. The tensions that flared between EU states in the 21st century, over economic and migrant crises, tested the hopes of federalist politicians. They could no longer assume that ordinary people shared their dream of progressive integration. ∎

The European Court of Justice is based in Luxembourg City. Although the Court has 27 judges, one from each EU member state, cases are usually heard by panels of three, five, or 15.

THE SISTER NATIONS HAVE GROWN TOGETHER

THE HELSINKI TREATY (1962)

IN CONTEXT

FOCUS
International law

BEFORE
1814 The integrated state of Denmark–Norway breaks apart, and Norway forms a union with Sweden.

1845 Danish and Swedish students champion the pan-Scandinavian movement, but it collapses in 1864.

1905 The Norway–Sweden union dissolves, and Norway becomes fully independent.

1907 The Nordic Inter-Parliamentary Union of five countries starts holding annual meetings.

AFTER
1996 Norway and Iceland, as members of the Nordic Passport Union, are accepted into the European Schengen Area.

2000 The Øresund Bridge opens, connecting Denmark and Sweden.

Nordic countries are under pressure to form alliances with **powerful blocs** such as NATO and the USSR.

→

Neutrality in military alignments seems the **safest option**.

↓

Cooperating with one another is the best way for Nordic countries to **preserve neutrality**.

←

Strengthened by cooperation, Nordic countries can build stable links with **other nations**.

Created in 1952, the Nordic Council is an assembly of Members of Parliament from each Nordic country: Scandinavia's Norway, Denmark, and Sweden, plus Finland and Iceland. The involvement of active Members of Parliament, rather than delegates, is unusual in international assembly, and it fosters a rare degree of cooperation. There are 87 MPs in the Nordic Council – 20 each from Norway, Sweden, Denmark, and Finland, and seven from Iceland. Denmark's total includes two from the Faroe Islands and two from Greenland; Finland's includes two from the Åland Islands. The Council meets once a year, in autumn, with further "theme sessions" held in spring. The assembly is linked to the Nordic Council of Ministers, made up of ministers from each government.

While the ties between the Nordic countries are ancient, the direct impetus for inter-Nordic cooperation was World War II. Both Denmark and Norway were occupied by the Nazis, and Finland was under constant threat from the Soviet Union

See also: Vattel's *The Law of Nations* 108 ▪ Scandinavian cooperation 160–61 ▪ The United Nations and International Court of Justice 212–19 ▪ INTERPOL 220–21 ▪ The European Court of Justice 234–41

(USSR). Sweden remained neutral but vulnerable, as war raged all around it.

Postwar alignments

After the war ended, Sweden put forward to Norway and Denmark a plan for a Scandinavian defence union, but initial talks broke down. There were significant pressures in different directions from the major world blocs. European countries were forming the economic ties that would lead to the European Union. The US, eager to establish bases in Scandinavia, insisted that the Nordics were too weak to defend themselves and must join the emerging North Atlantic Treaty Organization (NATO). The USSR coveted Finland.

Disadvantaged by their war-ravaged economies, Denmark and Norway, along with Iceland, joined NATO as founding members in 1949. Sweden maintained its neutrality. And Finland, anxious for stable relations with its powerful land neighbour and erstwhile enemy, signed the Finno-Soviet

Treaty – which was an agreement of "friendship, cooperation, and mutual assistance" – in 1948.

The Nordic Council

Despite the failure of the defence union idea, in 1952 Danish prime minister Hans Hedtoft proposed a Nordic Council, intended simply as a consultative inter-parliamentary body rather than as a stronger union. Norway, Sweden, and Iceland quickly agreed, and the first session was held the following year, in the Danish Parliament, with Hedtoft as president. Within a few years of its inception, the Council introduced

The Øresund Bridge, linking Sweden and Denmark, is 7.85 km (almost 5 miles) long. It spans the sea between Malmö and the island of Peberholm, then continues by tunnel to Copenhagen.

practical dimensions to Nordic cooperation: a joint labour market and a passport union enabled citizens to travel freely and to work and reside anywhere in the region.

The Council proved remarkably resilient. After Stalin died, relations between Finland and the USSR softened, and in 1955 Finland joined the Council. Representatives from Greenland, and from the Faroe and Åland Islands, joined later.

In 1962, the five Nordic countries bonded even more closely, with the signing of the Helsinki Treaty – a formal agreement of cooperation. Nine years later, this led to the creation of the Nordic Council of Ministers, which is responsible for intergovernmental cooperation. Its vision is for the Nordic region to become the most environmentally sustainable and integrated region in the world. ■

Legal harmonization

There has been a tradition of legislative cooperation in the Nordic region since 1872, when lawyers from all the nations convened in Copenhagen. Later, the desire for judicial harmonization formed a key part of the Helsinki Treaty, which sought "cooperation in the field of law with the aim of attaining the greatest possible uniformity in the field of private law". One of the Treaty's stated aims was to achieve uniform rules for penalizing criminal offences. Article 5 states that the aim should be to allow a crime committed in one Nordic nation to be prosecuted in another.

Although there has been cooperation between the countries, political differences have been an obstacle to complete harmonization. In recent years, EU harmonization has taken priority over Nordic aims. That has proved problematic, since Denmark, Finland, and Sweden are EU members, but Iceland and Norway are not.

LET US STEP BACK FROM THE SHADOWS OF WAR

THE PARTIAL TEST BAN TREATY (1963)

IN CONTEXT

FOCUS
Arms control

BEFORE
1945 The US drops atomic bombs on the Japanese cities of Hiroshima and Nagasaki.

1946 The UN Atomic Energy Commission (UNAEC) is created to address the risks of the use of atomic energy.

1952 The US carries out the first hydrogen bomb test.

1961 The USSR tests its Tsar Bomba, the most powerful hydrogen bomb ever tested.

AFTER
1998 India and Pakistan each test several atomic or hydrogen bombs, in a race to become nuclear-armed states.

2006–17 North Korea conducts six underground nuclear tests.

On 5 August 1963, the US, Soviet Union (USSR), and the UK signed the Partial, or Limited, Nuclear Test Ban Treaty (PTBT or LTBT). The treaty did not slow the nuclear arms race directly, but banned nuclear weapons tests in the atmosphere, underwater, or in outer space, marking a vital first step in control of nuclear weapons.

MAD arms race
In the 1950s, tensions escalated between the West and Soviet bloc, during the Cold War. The US and USSR pursued a headlong nuclear arms race, driven in part by a game-theorist strategy of mutual assured destruction (MAD). On the

See also: The Geneva Conventions 152–55 ▪ The Hague Conventions 174–77 ▪ The Chemical Weapons Convention 276–77 ▪ The Anti-Personnel Mine Ban Convention 288–89

The Tsar Bomba ("king of bombs") was secretly detonated by the Soviets on an Arctic island. The explosion was c.1,500 times greater than those of Hiroshima and Nagasaki combined.

basis that full-scale use of nuclear weapons would completely destroy both attacker and defender, MAD suggests both sides build enough nuclear weapons to guarantee each side would be utterly annihilated if it launched its weapons. That way, neither side would ever dare strike first. Stanley Kubrick's 1964 film *Dr. Strangelove* brilliantly satirized the dangers of this strategy.

The public was terrified by the possibility of an all-out nuclear war and the ensuing global destruction. Protest movements sprang up, most notably the Campaign for Nuclear Disarmament (CND), and, in 1961, up to 50,000 from Women Strike for Peace marched against nuclear weapons in 60 US cities.

The Cuban Missile Crisis

International negotiations on nuclear disarmament had begun in 1958, and the United Nations (UN)

formed the Ten Nation Committee on Disarmament (TNCD) in 1960, which became the Eighteen Nation Committee (ENCD) in 1961, but progress was limited. The tipping point came after a series of nuclear near-misses: in 1961, for example, the US accidentally dropped nuclear bombs on Goldsboro, North Carolina, that were a whisker away from detonating. However, it was the 13-day Cuban Missile Crisis of October 1962 that provided the final wake-up call. The USSR was building nuclear launch sites on Cuba, just 145 km (90 miles) from the US coast. When US air forces spotted them, President John F. Kennedy retaliated with a naval blockade around Cuba. Nuclear war seemed imminent.

Kennedy and Soviet Premier Nikita Khrushchev pulled back from the brink: the USSR dismantled its Cuban sites and the US removed

President John F. Kennedy in 1962 addresses the American public on television, to explain the threat from Soviet missile sites in Cuba and why the US Navy was blockading the island.

its naval blockade. Horror at what might have happened pushed Kennedy and Khrushchev to the negotiating table. Khrushchev argued for a comprehensive ban on nuclear tests, but Kennedy could not get the US military to agree. His advisers wanted Soviet troops to withdraw from Cuba as a precondition of talks, while the USSR feared that the proposed verification inspections were »

We will not ... risk worldwide nuclear war ... in which even the fruits of victory would be ashes in our mouth.
John F. Kennedy
35th US president (1961–63),
Address to the nation, 1962

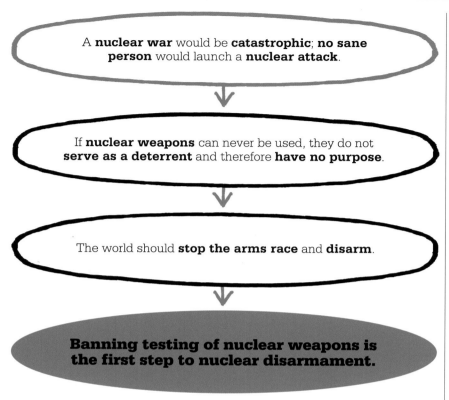

A **nuclear war** would be **catastrophic**; **no sane person** would launch a **nuclear attack**.

If **nuclear weapons** can never be used, they do not **serve as a deterrent** and therefore **have no purpose**.

The world should **stop the arms race** and **disarm**.

Banning testing of nuclear weapons is the first step to nuclear disarmament.

A nuclear war cannot be won and must never be fought.
Ronald Reagan
40th US president (1981–89), State of the Union address, 1984

pretexts for spying by the West. In June 1963, President Kennedy made an impassioned plea for "a treaty to outlaw nuclear tests [and] check the spiralling arms race".

The first test ban

In July 1963, W. Averell Harriman, former US ambassador to the USSR, and Andrei Gromyko, Soviet foreign minister, resumed negotiations in Moscow. After ten days, they initialled a draft treaty, hoping the other three nuclear powers of the time (the UK, France, and China) would join, but only the UK signed along with the US and USSR.

The Partial Nuclear Test Ban Treaty (PTBT) banned nuclear-weapons tests in the atmosphere, in outer space, and underwater, but permitted underground testing. The treaty did nothing to cut stockpiles of nuclear weapons, halt production, or limit their use, but it was a major step forward.

Within three months, a total of 100 governments had signed up, although France and China stayed out. Since then, 25 more nations have joined. Under the treaty, the US, UK, and USSR can veto treaty amendments. Also, a majority, including all three original parties, must approve any amendment.

Non-proliferation

Efforts to limit the spread of nuclear weapons beyond the original five nuclear powers began in the 1960s, alongside the PTBT. In 1961, the UN unanimously passed Ireland's resolution to ban nuclear powers from giving the technology to other states. Sweden proposed also that non-nuclear countries pledge not to make or host nuclear weapons; the proposal had good support, but many states abstained, including the US. The Irish and Swedish proposals sought to create a regime that everyone could adhere to, and it came to fruition in the Treaty on the Non-Proliferation of Nuclear Weapons (NPT) of 1968.

In the NPT, non-nuclear-armed nations agreed never to acquire or develop nuclear weapons, while nuclear states agreed to eliminate their nuclear arsenals over time and share technology for nuclear energy.

Comprehensive ban

In 1977, work began on a treaty to end nuclear testing. Progress was slow, partly because American weapons developers felt testing was vital to keep nuclear weapons up to date; under pressure from them, US president Ronald Reagan halted negotiations in 1982. The Soviets' 1979–89 occupation of Afghanistan also soured relations with the US.

In 1991, Soviet general secretary Mikhail Gorbachev announced that the USSR would unilaterally stop its nuclear weapons testing. The US Congress responded warmly, urging that negotiations quickly reopen. Even so, discussions were hampered by concerns of the military on both sides, until the dissolution of the USSR in December. The UN then took the lead, forming the Conference on Disarmament in 1994 to draw up a Comprehensive Nuclear-Test-Ban Treaty (CTBT) that banned all nuclear-weapon and peaceful-nuclear test explosions.

The US was the first country to sign the CTBT in 1996, and most states have since joined. Yet the treaty cannot come into effect until it is not only signed, but ratified, by all 44 members of the Conference, including all the nuclear powers. By 2019, 168 countries had ratified the CTBT, and another 17 countries had signed but not ratified it. Crucially, five of the original 44 Conference members (China, Egypt, Iran, Israel, and the US) have not yet ratified the treaty, and three more (India, North Korea, and Pakistan) have not even signed it.

Stand-off

Although the CTBT has not come into effect, there has been progress. The US and Russia greatly reduced their nuclear warhead numbers, under the Intermediate-Range Nuclear Forces Treaty (INF Treaty)

of 1987. The NPT was renewed indefinitely in 1995 and had 191 signatories by 2020.

Since the PTBT, only Pakistan, India, North Korea, and probably Israel, are known to have acquired nuclear weapons. However, Iran has been accused of illegally enriching uranium to make bombs. The International Atomic Energy Agency (IAEA) demanded access for verification, and international sanctions were imposed from 2006. Intense diplomatic negotiations continue, in an attempt to deter Iran from creating a nuclear arsenal.

North Korea, too, has ploughed on with its nuclear programme, despite international sanctions. Between 2006 and 2017, it held six major underground nuclear tests (detected by US Geological Survey seismographs), and in 2017 it claimed to have perfected a hydrogen bomb. Meanwhile, the five main nuclear powers, especially the US and China, still seem no nearer to eliminating their nuclear arsenals. In 2019, the US backed out of the INF Treaty.

There is now a complex body of international law reflecting 70 years of intense negotiation to keep the

All nations should declare … that nuclear weapons must be destroyed. This is to save ourselves and our planet.
Mikhail Gorbachev
Soviet general secretary (1985–91), BBC interview, 2019

threat of war at bay. The IAEA upholds these treaties, monitoring nuclear activity in more than 140 countries, but many states do not give the inspectorate free access. The International Court of Justice adjudicates treaty infringements, but some states have refused to abide by its judgements. As long as nuclear and other weapons of mass destruction exist, the danger remains, and efforts to uphold and extend disarmament treaties continue. ■

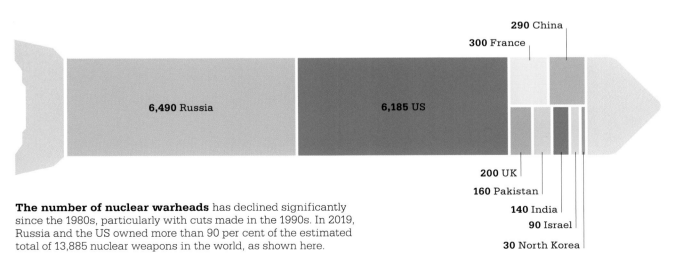

The number of nuclear warheads has declined significantly since the 1980s, particularly with cuts made in the 1990s. In 2019, Russia and the US owned more than 90 per cent of the estimated total of 13,885 nuclear weapons in the world, as shown here.

6,490 Russia
6,185 US
300 France
290 China
200 UK
160 Pakistan
140 India
90 Israel
30 North Korea

MY CHILDREN WILL NOT BE JUDGED BY THE COLOUR OF THEIR SKIN

THE CIVIL RIGHTS ACT (1964)

IN CONTEXT

FOCUS
Human rights

BEFORE
1866 America's first Civil Rights Act guarantees civil but not political and social rights.

1880s Jim Crow laws segregate the white and black populations in the Southern states.

1896 The Supreme Court allows segregation on the "separate but equal" principle.

AFTER
1965 The Voting Rights Act outlaws discriminatory obstacles that prevent black people voting.

1968 The Fair Housing Act bans discrimination in housing.

2019 A white supremacist shooter in El Paso, Texas, kills 22 and injures 24.

All US citizens are born equal, and **all US citizens** should have **equal rights**.

⬇

The **Thirteenth and Fourteenth Amendments** were not initially seen to outlaw **racial discrimination**.

⬇

The **Civil Rights Act** prohibits **segregation in public** and outlaws **discrimination based on race**.

I n 1776, the US declared with forthright zeal in its Declaration of Independence, "We hold these truths to be self-evident, that all men are created equal … " And yet this did not prevent black Africans from being kept as slaves for almost a century more. Even after the Civil War of 1861–65 ended with slaves being given their freedom, black people continued to suffer. In the early 1960s, a century after the end of slavery, there was still racial segregation in the US.

In 1866, the first Civil Rights Act gave equal legal protection to all citizens. The Civil Rights Act of 1875 went further, affirming that all people are equal in law and prohibiting racial discrimination in public places, such as on trains and in restaurants and lodging houses. However, five cases treated together in the Supreme Court in March 1883 nullified this, asserting that neither the Thirteenth Amendment to the US Constitution (which banned slavery) nor the Fourteenth (which guaranteed equal protection by the law) could prevent racial discrimination by private individuals, and that this could not be prohibited by law. Essentially, the Court declared that the Civil Rights Act of 1875 was unconstitutional, which was a huge blow to the rights of African Americans.

Segregation

After the Civil War had ended, the Republican armies had protected the civil rights of freed slaves in the South, but in 1877 a political compromise withdrew those armies and gave Southern states "the right to deal with blacks without northern interference". Named after a black caricature from American theatre, the Jim Crow laws of the Southern United States came into force in the 1870s and 1880s and were every bit as racially divisive as South Africa's apartheid laws.

In theory, black people had the same rights under the Constitution as white people, but the Jim Crow laws gave racial segregation legal force. White and black Southerners

It shall be unlawful for a negro and white person to play together … in any game of cards or dice, dominoes or checkers.
Jim Crow law
Birmingham, Alabama, 1930

See also: The Representation of the People Act 188–89 ▪ The Universal Declaration of Human Rights 222–29 ▪ The European Convention on Human Rights 230–33 ▪ The International Covenant on Civil and Political Rights 256–57

had mixed fairly freely until the 1880s, when some state legislatures then required railroads to provide separate carriages for "Negro" and "colored" passengers.

Protests began immediately, and in 1892, train passenger Homer Plessy refused to sit in the carriage reserved for black people. Plessy, who described himself as "seven-eighths Caucasian and one-eighth African blood", was arrested. The case went to the Supreme Court, which, in 1896, ruled that state governments could indeed separate people racially, as long as all races were given equal facilities. It was a hammer blow. This "separate but equal" principle gave states freedom to continue segregation, and this division lasted for almost 60 years.

Black people were sent to separate schools, they worked separately, travelled separately on trains and buses, and were seated separately in restaurants. The facilities for black people were far inferior to those for white people, despite the equality

Separate waiting rooms, dining areas, water fountains, and entrances were commonplace, while some establishments didn't even permit black people on the premises at all.

principle – for example, school buses were provided for white children, while black children had to walk to school.

Continued discrimination

America's entry into World War II in 1941 saw a million black men and women serve their country in defence of democracy and freedom. Yet they still faced discrimination when they returned. In 1948, President Harry Truman outlawed discrimination in the military, and the civil rights movement began to gain momentum.

In the 1950s, civil rights activists made their first real breakthrough. Founded in 1909,

the National Association for the Advancement of Colored People (NAACP) was patiently developing its legal challenges to segregation laws in public schools. In Topeka, Kansas, the board of education refused to allow Linda Brown, daughter of black resident Oliver Brown, to attend her local school, instead insisting she take a bus to the black elementary school across town. The NAACP stepped in and filed a case against Topeka on behalf of Oliver Brown.

The NAACP argued that schools for black children were not as good as the white schools. It also stated that segregation violated the clause in the Fourteenth Amendment, which holds that no state can "deny to any person within its jurisdiction the equal protection of the laws." The case went with four others to the Supreme Court as *Brown v. Board of Education of Topeka*. The »

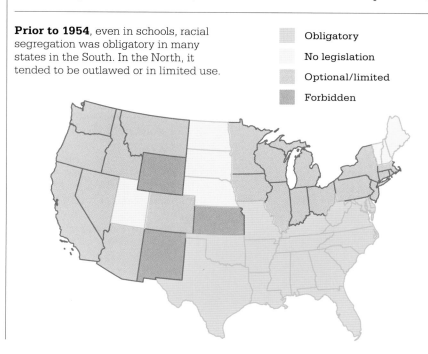

Prior to 1954, even in schools, racial segregation was obligatory in many states in the South. In the North, it tended to be outlawed or in limited use.

Obligatory

No legislation

Optional/limited

Forbidden

With her defiant stance over bus seating in Montgomery, Alabama, in 1955, Rosa Parks began an unstoppable movement towards equal rights and the end of segregation.

Supreme Court agreed too, with Chief Justice Earl Warren ruling in 1954 that "in the field of public education the doctrine of 'separate but equal' has no place," as segregated schools are "inherently unequal." However, it would take decades for the decision to be fully implemented. Meanwhile, there was another challenge to segregation.

Rosa Parks

On 1 December 1955, Rosa Parks, a woman of mixed heritage in Montgomery, Alabama, quietly refused the bus driver's insistence that she give up her seat in the "mixed" middle section of the bus she was travelling on. Like Plessy 63 years earlier, she was arrested, but this time there was resistance in the form of public protests. On the day of her trial, black civil rights activists led by pastor Dr Martin Luther King Jr called for a boycott of all the buses in Montgomery. The day's boycott turned into one of

the longest and most determined civil rights actions the US has seen. The boycott went on for 381 days, during which 90 per cent of black people refused to travel on the buses. It proved highly effective and ended only when the Supreme Court ruled that segregation on buses was illegal.

White backlash

The court ruling triggered a vicious reaction, with someone firing a shotgun through Martin Luther King's door, bombings at black churches, and a young black man, Willie Edwards, being killed by the Ku Klux Klan (a white supremacist hate group) for dating a white woman. Black people soon returned to riding separately on the buses.

To reduce tension, President Dwight D. Eisenhower put a new Civil Rights Act in place in 1957, enabling the prosecution of anyone who tried to stop someone voting. However, segregation was still an ugly fact. In 1960, four students in Greensboro, North Carolina, staged a sit-in at the Woolworth's lunch counter where they had been refused service because only white people could sit at the bar. Soon

People always said that I didn't give up my seat because I was tired, but that isn't true … No, the only tired I was, was tired of giving in.
Rosa Parks
Rosa Parks: My Story, **1992**

student sit-ins were being staged across the South. Protesters were often beaten and jailed, but they persisted until Woolworth's relented and the segregated counters ended.

In October 1960, Martin Luther King had been arrested in Atlanta, Georgia, for leading one such civil rights sit-in at a lunch counter. Presidential candidate John F. Kennedy offered his support to King and assisted with his release. Grateful for this display at a difficult moment, King endorsed Kennedy for president, and as a result,

Native American civil rights

Unlike black people, Native Americans sought to limit the damage of discrimination not by inclusion but by the protection of tribal lands. The brutal 1830 Removals Act had robbed them of much, but there was a fraction left to provide some homeland. There was tension within the civil rights movement in the 1950s and '60s between black people, who were campaigning for recognition in the Constitution, and Native Americans who thought this

was a naive hope. The Indian Civil Rights Act (ICRA) of 1968 was intended by Congress to recognize that the policy of assimilation had been a failure. But not all Native Americans were happy with the bill. By guaranteeing the constitutional rights of individuals, the ICRA allowed them to challenge tribal governments. Various US administrations have since shifted gradually towards recognizing tribal sovereignty but it remains a thorny issue.

70 per cent of black people voted for him in the November election, contributing to his victory.

In 1961, seven black and six white youngsters became known as "Freedom Riders" touring the South together on a bus to protest against the segregation laws. When the bus reached Anniston, Alabama, a mob ambushed it and threw in a firebomb. The Freedom Riders forced their way out but were beaten by the mob. Pictures of the burning bus served to add impetus to the civil rights movement.

"I have a dream"

On being publicly pressured by King, President Kennedy made a decisive move. On 11 June 1963, he broadcast the urgent moral case for legislation to end segregation, saying, "This nation was founded on the principle that all men are created equal" and "Race has no place in American life and law."

In August, to put pressure on Congress to pass Kennedy's legislation, King led a march of 250,000 in Washington, DC, where he delivered his famous "I have a dream" speech and promised "An oasis of freedom and justice".

The March on Washington for Jobs and Freedom, led by Martin Luther King, was held in August 1963. Some 250,000 people took part in this huge civil rights protest.

Kennedy was assassinated three months later, before his legislation had passed through all its stages. However, his successor, President Lyndon B. Johnson, using the tide of emotion from Kennedy's death, was able to push the Civil Rights Act through and it became law in July 1964.

The new law guaranteed equal employment rights for all, outlawing discrimination in any business exceeding 25 people, and an Equal Employment Opportunity Commission was created to review complaints. The Act also protected black people against discrimination in voter qualification tests, and outlawed segregation in hotels, motels, restaurants, theatres, and all other public places. Additionally, desegregation in public schools was enforced, and federal funds would be withdrawn from any programmes that practised discrimination.

A key battle had been won in the fight against discrimination, but the long war continues. Martin Luther King was assassinated in Memphis, Tennessee, in 1968, aged 39, sparking a wave of race riots. Gradually things improved for black people, and with the election of Barack Obama as president in 2009, it looked as if a corner might have been turned. However, it is clear that there is still a long way to go before true equality is achieved. ■

Martin Luther King Jr gave his emotional, historic "I have a dream" speech to the assembled crowds at the Lincoln Memorial during the March on Washington, 1963.

THE RIGHT TO REMAIN SILENT

MIRANDA V. ARIZONA (1966)

IN CONTEXT

FOCUS
Constitutional law

BEFORE
1791 The Fifth Amendment makes it clear that no one "shall be compelled to be a witness against himself".

1911 American magazine *The Atlantic* complains that US legal processes are biased in favour of criminals.

1914 The exclusionary rule upholds the rights of all citizens to be "secure" against evidence obtained during an illegal search or seizure.

AFTER
2000 The Supreme Court rules in *Dickerson v. United States* that "Miranda warnings are constitutionally required".

2010 The Supreme Court's ruling in *Berghuis v. Thompkins* asserts that any suspect under interrogation must actively assert his or her right to silence or actively waive it.

Complaints mount about **US law enforcement** using threatening methods while **interrogating suspects**.

Courts often overlook the **Fifth Amendment** to the US Constitution, which gives defendants **the right not to self-incriminate**.

The Miranda decision upholds the right to silence and to a lawyer.

Despite **claims** that justice is undermined, the **Miranda decision** helps to guard **against police misconduct**.

The Miranda decision, more properly known as *Miranda v. Arizona*, was a landmark Supreme Court ruling in June 1966 that reinforced one of the most famous amendments of the 1791 Bill of Rights, the Fifth – the right to remain silent. The decision was simultaneously hailed as a victory for personal rights and denounced as an unwarranted restriction on law enforcement that would tie the hands of the police in the interests of Constitutional propriety.

The Fifth Amendment
The central ruling of the Miranda decision went beyond the Fifth Amendment's assertion that "No person shall be compelled in any criminal case to be a witness against himself". Instead it made it plain that any suspect in police custody must be explicitly informed not only of their right to remain silent but also of their right to refuse to answer questions. At the same time, as allowed for under the Sixth Amendment, any

See also: The US Constitution and Bill of Rights 110–17 ▪ The Declaration of the Rights of Man 118–19 ▪ The exclusionary rule 186–87

Richard Nixon, when running for president in 1968, promised to crack down on crime. Central to his bid was a vow to overturn the Miranda decision, which he vehemently opposed.

suspect's right to a lawyer was affirmed, the lawyer to be provided at public expense if necessary. The Miranda warning has since become a routine introduction to all police questioning of suspects.

Background and decision

The decision's name comes from the case of Ernesto Miranda, a vagrant with a long history of criminal offences. He had been arrested in Phoenix in 1963 on charges of rape and kidnapping. Three other cases were also considered by the Supreme Court. In each of them, the suspects, all tried and convicted, had not been explicitly advised of their rights under the Fifth Amendment.

The ruling, a majority decision, with five judges in favour and four against, sparked instant controversy. Many people saw it as a charter for criminals, with the obviously guilty being freed essentially on a technicality. Supreme Court justice James Harlan, who opposed the ruling, claimed, for example, that it amounted to a "hazardous

experimentation". North Carolina Democrat senator Sam J. Ervin complained that "self-confessed criminals are turned free … because the arresting officer failed to tell the criminal something he already knew". New York Democrat senator Robert Kennedy countered with the question, "You think that additional warning in some way infringes upon effective law enforcement?"

Later developments

The issue of "additional warning" was pertinent. In all four cases, the suspects were described as men of "limited education" who were unlikely to have been aware of their rights under either the Fifth or Sixth Amendments. In addition, police interrogations were often hostile and frequently threatening. Although a later Supreme Court judgement in 2000, *Dickerson v. United States*, emphatically backed the Miranda decision, that of *Berghuis v. Thompkins* in 2010 significantly weakened it, ruling that the right to silence be held only if the suspect explicitly invoked it. ▪

A serious problem in the enforcement of our criminal law will occur [if the right to silence is not observed].
Gary K. Nelson
Miranda's defence lawyer (1935–2013), to the Supreme Court

Ernesto Miranda

Born in Mesa, Arizona, in 1941, Ernesto Miranda was almost the archetypal drifter. Even as a young teenager his life was given over to petty crime followed by inevitable incarcerations in various penal institutions. His arrest in 1963 was another in a litany of such run-ins with the law, and he didn't deny his guilt. In fact, it was precisely because he confessed under interrogation without having been made aware of his right to silence and to legal representation that the Supreme Court overturned his conviction, despite the Arizona supreme court having supported the original decision to find him guilty.

He was then re-tried for the same crime, but with his confession withheld as evidence. The same guilty verdict and 20- to 30-year sentence was returned. After parole in 1972, he reverted to his former indigent life. Further arrests and periods in prison followed. He died in a knife fight in a Phoenix bar in 1976.

THE FOUNDATION OF FREEDOM, JUSTICE, AND PEACE

THE INTERNATIONAL COVENANT ON CIVIL AND POLITICAL RIGHTS (1966)

IN CONTEXT

FOCUS
Human rights

BEFORE
1948 The UN adopts the Universal Declaration of Human Rights.

1965 The UN's International Convention on the Elimination of All Forms of Racial Discrimination is adopted.

AFTER
1979 The UN adopts the Convention on the Elimination of All Forms of Discrimination against Women.

1989 The UN's Convention on the Rights of the Child deals comprehensively with the rights of those under the age of 18.

1989 The Second Optional Protocol of the ICCPR aims to abolish the death penalty.

1992 The United States ratifies the ICCPR.

Any state signing up to the International Covenant on Civil and Political Rights (**ICCPR**) must implement **agreed-upon rights** ...

↓ ↓ ↓

by passing **new laws** protecting rights,

enforcing **existing laws** protecting rights,

and providing **local remedies** for human rights **abuses**.

↓ ↓ ↓

Failure to implement rights means the state is not complying with the Covenant.

↓

A victim of a **violation of the rights** in the ICCPR may take a case to the UN's **Human Rights Committee**.

The International Covenant on Civil and Political Rights (ICCPR) is one of the two big international treaties created by the United Nations (UN) in 1966 – the other being the International Covenant on Economic, Social, and Cultural Rights (ICESCR) – that turned the 1948 Universal Declaration of Human Rights into binding international law. These two treaties together make up the International Bill of Human Rights.

After the UN Commission on Human Rights drafted the ICCPR and opened it for signature in 1966, it came into force in 1976. Countries that sign up to it are

See also: The Declaration of the Rights of Man 118–19 ▪ The United Nations and International Court of Justice 212–19 ▪ The Universal Declaration of Human Rights 222–29 ▪ The International Criminal Court 298–303

> Freedom of opinion and freedom of expression are indispensable conditions for the full development of the person.
> **Human Rights Committee**
> General Comment No.34

also required to adopt laws that protect the rights contained in the Covenant and to use government resources to ensure that the rights are protected.

Among the rights enshrined in the Covenant are freedom of thought, religion, expression, and assembly; the right to a fair trial; freedom from torture and other inhuman or degrading treatment; and equality of treatment before the law. Discrimination on grounds of race, gender, language, religion, or social class is outlawed. Article 25 guarantees the right of citizens to vote and be elected at free elections held at regular intervals, leading some to criticize the ICCPR for representing only a Western tradition of democracy. Some signatories have ignored parts of the Covenant when it suits them. For example, Indonesia's blasphemy laws have been used against non-Muslims.

Scrutinizing states

Currently, 173 states have ratified the ICCPR. Each is required to submit a report to the UN's Human

Chilean politician Michelle Bachelet was appointed to the role of UN's high commissioner for human rights in 2018, charged with ensuring that the ICCPR and other human rights treaties function properly.

Rights Committee (HRC) every four to five years on what progress the country is making to implement the rights contained within the Covenant. The HRC is a body of 18 experts from signatory nations, empowered to scrutinize states and issue recommendations on their human rights compliance. Although not formally a court, the decisions of the HRC have been vital in shaping human rights law.

Taking action against states

The First Optional Protocol to the 1966 ICCPR allows individuals in the 116 states that have ratified the Protocol (which include France, Germany, Russia, and Brazil) to refer their country to the HRC if they believe it has violated their rights under the ICCPR. In

> … the ideal of free human beings enjoying civil and political freedom … can only be achieved if conditions are created whereby everyone may enjoy his civil and political rights …
> **ICCPR preamble**

1994, Nicholas Toonen used this Protocol to take the Australian government to the HRC on the grounds that Tasmanian laws criminalized sexual relationships between men. He successfully argued that this was a violation of Article 17, the right to privacy.

The HRC has also helped in cases where a victim of human rights violations has nowhere else to turn. Jehovah's Witnesses have brought a series of cases against the government of South Korea, objecting to the punishments imposed on those who refused to be conscripted into the army. They successfully argued that this was a violation of Article 18 of the ICCPR, which protects freedom of conscience and belief.

Despite its many successes, the HRC does not have the power to force states to follow the provisions of the Covenant. Furthermore, its resources are limited, so it struggles to keep pace with the influx of complaints and reports it receives. As a result, some states continue to flout the Covenant. ▪

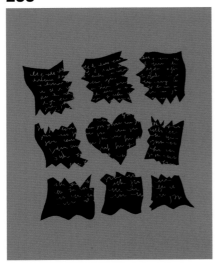

END THE BLAME GAME

NO-FAULT DIVORCE (1969)

IN CONTEXT

FOCUS
Civil law

BEFORE
1794 Prussia's General State Laws permit couples without children to divorce.

1917 Bolshevik Russia loosens divorce laws on the grounds that marriage is a bourgeois construct.

AFTER
1975 Australia permits no-fault divorce on the grounds only of the "irretrievable breakdown" of a marriage.

2010 New York becomes the last US state to introduce no-fault divorce.

2019 Britain commits to introducing no-fault divorce, with a Bill entering Parliament in 2020.

In almost all Western societies, divorce was once universally presumed the most desperate of remedies, and was socially shaming. Since marriage was the bedrock of Christian belief in the primacy of the family, divorce was more or less unthinkable. It was made more so by its complexity and the need to prove "fault", whether adultery, cruelty, or abandonment. Its impact on the victims – children above all – weighed just as heavily.

It ... mystifies me that the spouses could ... be forced to stay married to someone who refuses to let go.
L.M. Fenton
American divorce lawyer,
Salon magazine, 2010

By the late 1960s, attitudes had changed. It was in the US state of California in 1969 that a new legal belief emerged: that a couple who had suffered "irreconcilable differences" had sufficient grounds for divorce. No "fault" needed to be demonstrated. Since 2010, no-fault divorces have been legal in every US state.

The arguments for and against have been fierce. No-fault divorce has been hailed as a liberation, a rational means of ending any doomed marriage, with painful disputes avoided. It has no less been criticized as a cheapening of what should be a lifelong commitment, with liberalized divorce laws invariably leading to more divorces. It cannot be said whether children benefit or not from their parents' more ready separation.

Either way, Western opinion has since accepted no-fault divorce as the least harmful way to end a marriage. However, while the law can moderate and reason, it cannot legislate for the full complexity of human relationships. ∎

See also: The Universal Declaration of Human Rights 222–29 ▪ The European Convention on Human Rights 230–33 ▪ Same-sex marriage 292–95

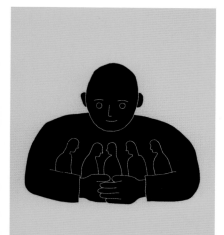

THE SAFETY AND WELFARE OF WITNESSES
THE FEDERAL WITNESS PROTECTION PROGRAM (1970)

Often known simply as the Witness Security Program, or WITSEC, the Federal Witness Protection Program began under the terms of the Organized Crime Control Act of 1970. It is administered jointly by the US Department of Justice and the US Marshals Service, and was the brainchild of Gerald Shur of the Department of Justice's Organized Crime and Racketeering Section.

The program was sparked by the case of Joe Valachi, who in 1963, already serving life for murder, was the first senior member of the Mafia to detail its inner workings. In return, even in prison, he was accorded official protection. Valachi's case highlights an important fact: the program is intended to protect criminals who become informers, rather than aiding the innocent victims of crime.

Those who are protected are cut off not just from their past but from everything bar immediate family. Granted new identities, spirited away from everywhere familiar, their lives are turned upside down.

In effect, the price of their safety is a double life, an elaborate lie rigorously enforced. To date, about 18,000 people have been given protection. The US Marshals boast that not a single person who has adhered to its demanding dictates has been the victim of a revenge killing. With a conviction rate of those testifying against former associates of 89 per cent, it has proved a major weapon in the fight against organized crime. ∎

Joe Valachi, the first to break the Mafia code of *omertà* (silence). Shur claimed that Valachi "could discuss spaghetti sauce and the killing of a close friend with the same lack of emotion".

See also: INTERPOL 220–21 ∎ The Universal Declaration of Human Rights 222–29 ∎ DNA testing 272–73

THE RIGHT OF A WOMAN TO DECIDE

ROE V. WADE (1973)

The right to vote aside, no issue has more obviously defined the struggle for women's rights in the modern world than abortion. But whereas the demand for votes for women was fought (and won in many countries) in the early years of the 20th century, the legal right to abortion only came to the fore in the 1960s. It would become an absolute touchstone of what was originally called Women's Liberation and is now known as feminism. To this day, abortion remains possibly the prime focus of all assertions of female equality.

Throughout history, women confronted with unwanted or unexpected pregnancies faced the prospect of a blighted life, especially if they lacked financial support. If disowned by the child's

See also: The Representation of the People Act 188–89 ▪ The Universal Declaration of Human Rights 222–29 ▪ The European Convention on Human Rights 230–33 ▪ The Dickey–Wicker Amendment 284 ▪ Equal pay certification 314–15

Margaret Sanger

American campaigner Margaret Sanger was a champion of family planning and contraception in the early 20th century. Born in 1879, she opened the first birth control clinic in the United States in 1916. She established several birth control organizations, and she served as the first president of the International Planned Parenthood Federation, which became the world's largest non-governmental international women's health, family planning, and birth control body. In the early 1950s, Sanger encouraged funding for biologist Gregory Pincus to develop the birth control pill.

The success of Sanger, and also that of British campaigner Marie Stopes, in confronting almost the greatest social taboo of their age remains unmatched. Their impact on the struggle of women in the 1960s for abortion as a fundamental right cannot be underplayed. That said, Sanger essentially opposed abortion, considering birth control to be a far more effective method of preventing unwanted pregnancies. She died in 1966.

father, as often happened, women faced a lifetime of abject poverty unless they gave up the child for adoption, since they could not look after a child and work. So-called "illegitimate" children did not have the same rights of inheritance as those born "within wedlock", and their mothers were often treated as social pariahs.

After World War I, the efforts of Margaret Sanger in the US and Marie Stopes in the UK forced some public discussion of the hitherto taboo subjects of contraception and family planning, but this had little impact for women of all classes who found themselves pregnant, since contraception and abortion were still illegal – even Sanger's advocacy of contraception resulted in her being arrested several times.

In 1920, the Soviet Union (USSR) became the first European government to legalize abortion, though its totalitarian ruler Joseph Stalin reversed the policy in 1936 to boost a population that had been decimated by purges and famine. In most countries, abortion was viewed as a desperate last remedy, a source of shame and horror. Those women who nonetheless chose abortion not only faced the emotional trauma of being stigmatized by those around them but also risked endangering their own lives through botched procedures performed by unqualified practitioners – so-called "back-street abortions".

By the time of the liberalizing 1960s, a groundswell of opinion in much of the world held that anti-abortion laws were antiquated and should be swept away. When the contraceptive pill was legalized (in the UK in 1961 and across the whole of North America by 1972), denying women the right to abortion seemed illogical and discriminatory. In the US, that right finally gained legal force in 1973, with *Roe v. Wade*.

A groundbreaking case

In 1969, 21-year-old Texan, Norma McCorvey, found herself pregnant with her third child and wanted an abortion, but this was illegal in Texas. McCorvey's cause was taken up by two feminist lawyers, Sarah Weddington and Linda Coffee, who recognized her case had the capacity to prove groundbreaking. They filed a lawsuit for McCorvey (who for the purposes of the legal hearing adopted the name Jane Roe to protect her identity), alleging that the Texan abortion laws were unconstitutional. The defendant in the case was Dallas County district attorney Henry Wade, who represented the State of Texas. »

Enforced motherhood is the most complete denial of a woman's right to life and liberty.
Margaret Sanger
"Suppression", published in
***The Woman Rebel*, 1914**

Thanks to **decades of campaigning**, the belief grows that **legal abortion is a fundamental right** of women.

⬇

The **Ninth and Fourteenth Amendments** are judged to cover the right of a woman to **abort a pregnancy**.

⬇

The **US Supreme Court** rules that women have a **constitutional right to choose abortion**.

⬇

Roe v. Wade **legalizes abortion in the US.**

⬇

Despite some **opposition on moral grounds**, abortion remains legal in most countries as a **woman's right to choose**.

An initial court case ruled in McCorvey's favour but when Texas appealed against that decision, the case moved to the Supreme Court in 1970. After more than two years of legal wrangling, a majority decision of seven to two finally ruled in McCorvey's favour in January 1973.

Enshrining personal rights and the right to privacy, the Ninth and Fourteenth Amendments of the US Constitution provided the legal basis for the ruling. The Supreme Court ruled that these encompassed a woman's right to make her own decision on whether or not to have an abortion. But at the same time, the Court made clear that this right was not "absolute" because it had to be balanced against the need to protect the mother's life (late-term abortion carries serious risks) and that of the foetus. The Court sought to resolve this potential conflict by considering pregnancy in each of its three trimesters. It ruled that, unless there were compelling medical reasons, a decision on abortion in the first trimester (up to 12 weeks) should be the mother's alone; during this period, abortions generally pose less of a threat to a woman's health than childbirth. During the second trimester, there could be grounds for not allowing an abortion if it posed a threat to a woman's health. Although the judgement largely side-stepped the contentious question of when a foetus becomes a viable human, it accepted that it was by the start of the third trimester, so the state should prohibit abortion then (unless the woman's life is at risk).

Even on strictly legal terms, the ruling has been questioned by many commentators. One of the two dissenting judges, Bryon White, said, "I find nothing in the language or history of the Constitution to support the Court's judgement", calling it "an improvident and extravagant exercise of the power of judicial review". Even Edward Lazarus, a clerk to the Supreme Court and firm supporter of women's right to choose abortion, said, "As a matter of Constitutional interpretation and judicial method, [the ruling] borders on the indefensible [and] provides essentially no reasoning in support of its holding."

Pro-choice
The impact of the judgement was immediate. Any state law that conflicted with this ruling was automatically overturned, but

Norma McCorvey's pregnancy was at the heart of the *Roe v. Wade* case. After converting to Catholicism later in life, she opposed abortion and regretted her part in its legalization.

abortion remains a moral and political issue that still divides opinion. The feminist case is that abortion is fundamentally a question of women's rights – that abortion is as much a right as free speech – and a critical weapon in the fight for women's equality.

Feminists ask why only women should suffer the consequences of an unwanted pregnancy, with not just their lives but those of their child potentially blighted. They point, too, to the undeniable fact that there will always be unwanted pregnancies and so there will always be abortions, regardless of whether abortion is lawful or not – and illegal abortions are far more likely to go wrong and, therefore, are far more likely to place the mother's life at risk.

Pro-life

The classic counter is that abortion is murder – that from the moment of conception, a foetus is a unique human life. In 2017, American conservative commentator Ben Shapiro made the case simply: "It is a violation of moral law to kill another human being. Which is why we have murder laws." Both sides of the debate claim to have the science on their side. Those against abortion say that the DNA signature of any foetus is immediately clear from conception and that ultrasound technology makes it clear that a foetus is a human being capable of feeling pain. Other clinicians say that the foetus cannot feel pain until 24 weeks of pregnancy. In 2018, American journalist Jennifer Wright insisted, "A foetus's right to life is debatable. A woman's is not."

The political divide

When the *Roe v. Wade* ruling was made, it highlighted a clear divide between pro-abortion Democrats and anti-abortion Republicans. The ruling is still in effect but, in 2017, there were howls of Democrat outrage when President Donald Trump nominated conservative Brett Kavanaugh for the Supreme Court. Democrats suspected Kavanaugh was appointed to help fulfil the president's 2016 election campaign pledge to reverse the ruling.

Despite attempts made by several states to reintroduce anti-abortion legislation, including Alabama in 2019, all efforts to date have been blocked, with all Supreme Court judgements since 1973 backing the original ruling. Although the Hyde Amendment enacted by Congress in 1976 barred federal funding for abortions, two key judgements by the Supreme Court – *Planned Parenthood v. Casey* in 1992 and *Whole Woman's Health v. Hellerstedt* in 2016 – emphatically reinforced the 1973 ruling of *Roe v. Wade*.

Around the world, as of 2020, about 60 per cent of women of reproductive age live in countries where abortion is legal. For the remainder, it is either banned entirely or practised only when a woman's life or health are at risk. The divisions highlighted by the abortion debate remain essentially irreconcilable. ■

Alabama's abortion ban … diminishes the capacity of women to act in society and to make reproductive decisions.
Judge Myron Thompson
commenting on the Human Life Protection Act, 2019

NOTHING IS MORE PRICELESS THAN ANIMAL LIFE

THE ENDANGERED SPECIES ACT (1973)

IN CONTEXT

FOCUS
Environmental law

BEFORE
1900 America's Lacey Act prohibits commercial hunting and interstate trade of certain animals and plants.

1966 The Endangered Species Preservation Act leads to the first list of threatened and endangered species.

1972 The US bans the capture of marine mammals in its waters.

AFTER
1988 Scientists argue that a sixth mass extinction on Earth is under way.

2004 California condors reproduce in the wild for the first time in 17 years.

2007 The bald eagle is delisted following recovery.

2008 The polar bear is listed as threatened due to habitat loss in the Arctic.

The ESA's two aims are to **prevent extinction** and **increase numbers** of endangered species.

Section 4 requires the designation of species as **threatened or endangered**.

One of the **main threats** to endangered species is the **destruction of their habitat**.

If a species is **listed as endangered**, the ESA gives its key habitat **special protection**.

Throughout history, humans have directly caused the extinction of many species of wildlife, such as the dodo, great auk, passenger pigeon, and Tasmanian tiger. Right now, it seems the threat we pose to other animals is accelerating, with 50 per cent of species in real danger of disappearing and many biologists talking of extinctions on a massive scale. Hunting is partly to blame, but the principal reason is the loss of natural habitat through farming, deforestation, and urbanization.

Americans began to be aware of the threat to native wildlife in the late 1800s, and in 1900 the US introduced the Lacey Act to ban trafficking in certain species of wildlife and plants. Originally intended to stop the hunting of wild and game birds and their sale across state lines, today it is used primarily to prevent the importing of invasive species.

The steep rise in human population and activity in the 20th century put many more animals under threat, and by the 1960s, environmental movements were exerting pressure on the US and other governments to act. In 1966, the Endangered Species Preservation Act led to the first list of endangered species, and in 1969, Congress amended the Act to provide additional protection to

See also: The Cruelty to Animals Act 146–47 ▪ The "Vivisection Act" 163 ▪ The World Network of Biosphere Reserves 270–71 ▪ The Kyoto Protocol 305

CITES and international conservation

By the mid-20th century, the world began to recognize that the international trade in wild animals and plants was driving some species to extinction, exploited for food, medicine, or other purposes. In 1963, the International Union for the Conservation of Nature (IUCN), which monitors global diversity, began work on an international agreement to restrict this trade. These efforts came to fruition in Washington, DC, in 1973 with CITES, the Convention on International Trade in Endangered Species of Wild Fauna and Flora. CITES regulates or bans international trade in species under threat and is now one of the cornerstones of international conservation. CITES currently has 183 signatory countries and regulates trade in more than 5,000 animal and 30,000 plant species. The parties to the Convention meet regularly and develop plans to protect endangered plants and animals from commercial exploitation.

The ESA is the strongest and most effective tool we have to repair the environmental harm that is causing a species to decline.
Norm Dicks
US congressman (1977–2013)

species in danger of worldwide extinction by prohibiting their importation and subsequent sale in the US. Inspired by regulations agreed by the 1973 Convention on International Trade in Endangered Species of Wild Fauna and Flora (CITES), the groundbreaking Endangered Species Act (ESA) went even further to protect the natural heritage of the US.

Coordinated efforts

The ESA allows individuals and organizations to petition to have a species listed as endangered or threatened. There is then a rigorous scientific evaluation and public review before a final decision is made to put the species on the list. If a species is listed, critical habitat areas are given special protection, and a Species Recovery Plan is put in place, outlining how the numbers of the endangered species will be increased.

Populations are monitored over time to see whether a species has recovered enough to be removed from the list. This long-term commitment is a key part of the Act. Most wildlife experts consider the ESA a huge success in preventing extinctions. It is credited with the comeback of several species – including the American bald eagle, the California condor, and the grizzly bear – and it set a global standard for protection of endangered species.

In 2019, in a bid to satisfy the demands of commercial interests, President Trump's administration made revisions to the ESA that weakened it significantly. One of the proposed revisions is to restrict the protected critical habitat to the area the endangered species now survives in, rather than the area it would inhabit if it recovered. With the climate crisis and other environmental threats accelerating species loss at an alarming rate, the changes to the ESA defy calls for stronger, not weaker, protection. ∎

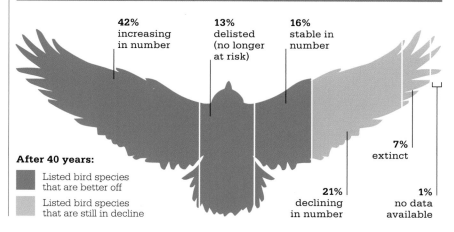

Bird species threatened under the ESA

42% increasing in number

13% delisted (no longer at risk)

16% stable in number

7% extinct

21% declining in number

1% no data available

After 40 years:
Listed bird species that are better off
Listed bird species that are still in decline

LAW IN T

MODERN

1980–PRESENT

THE
AGE

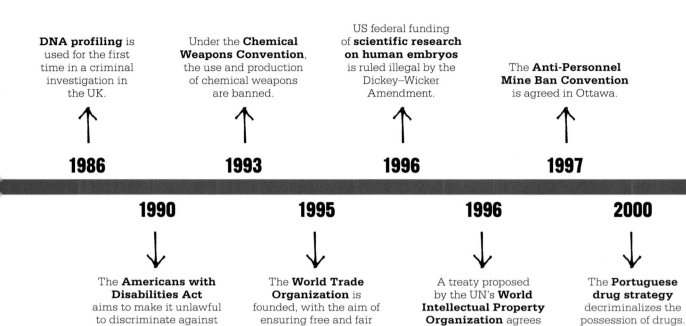

DNA profiling is used for the first time in a criminal investigation in the UK.

↑

1986

Under the **Chemical Weapons Convention,** the use and production of chemical weapons are banned.

↑

1993

US federal funding of **scientific research on human embryos** is ruled illegal by the Dickey–Wicker Amendment.

↑

1996

The **Anti-Personnel Mine Ban Convention** is agreed in Ottawa.

↑

1997

1990

↓

The **Americans with Disabilities Act** aims to make it unlawful to discriminate against people with disabilities.

1995

↓

The **World Trade Organization** is founded, with the aim of ensuring free and fair international trade.

1996

↓

A treaty proposed by the UN's **World Intellectual Property Organization** agrees rules to protect digital copyright.

2000

↓

The **Portuguese drug strategy** decriminalizes the possession of drugs.

B y the closing decades of the 20th century, the threat of new world wars had retreated, thanks to international cooperation and the work of the UN and its agencies. But these organizations could not stop the relentless loss of life in regional conflicts, from Kosovo and Sudan to Afghanistan and Syria. The effects of chemical weapons and the deadly legacy of landmines led to international Conventions imposing bans on both: the 1993 Chemical Weapons Convention and the Anti-Personnel Mine Ban Convention in 1997.

The world was rapidly becoming more interconnected. The growth in international trade and the burgeoning power of multinational corporations led to the founding of the World Trade Organization in 1995, its aim being to create a global

framework for free trade. Yet it was not just the economic landscape that was changing; technological advances on a scale never seen before were ushering in a new era, as well as new legal challenges. In 1996, the World Intellectual Property Organization – an agency of the UN dedicated to defending trademarks, patents, and copyrights – turned its attention to the issues presented by a digital revolution. The need for regulation to safeguard intellectual property rights and ensure the security of data is evident, but as fast as technological solutions are introduced, determined hackers find ways of overcoming them. The law has struggled to keep pace.

Public access to digital data has also highlighted problems regarding privacy and individuals' ownership of information about themselves.

In 2014, the European Court of Justice ruled that the "right to be forgotten" trumps that of freedom of speech – but even this has been challenged.

Human rights
Public attitudes towards human rights and discrimination shifted fundamentally in some parts of the world. Campaigners brought pressure to bear on governments to enact laws protecting the rights of people with disabilities and recognizing the right of same-sex couples to marry. The US led the way with the former in 1990; the Netherlands with the latter in 2000, and other countries followed suit. In Iceland, equal pay certification obliges employers to undergo a regular audit to show that they offer equal pay for work of equal value.

The Netherlands becomes the first country to legalize **same-sex marriage**.

2000

The **International Criminal Court** opens in The Hague in the Netherlands.

2002

The **Kyoto Protocol** comes into force to reduce greenhouse gas emissions and slow the pace of climate change.

2005

The European Court of Justice rules that people have the **"right to be forgotten"** – to have negative data about them removed from internet searches.

2014

2001

Euthanasia is legalized in the Netherlands, subject to strict conditions and under medical supervision.

2005

UNESCO oversees the **International Convention Against Doping in Sport**.

2011

INTERPOL establishes the **Match-Fixing Task Force** to tackle organized crime in sport.

2017

Iceland's **equal pay certification** ensures that companies are obliged to pay women and men the same for equivalent work.

The law is also grappling with new ethical issues, including those raised by human embryo research and by the suffering of terminally ill people.

The fight against crime

Advances in science can often pose ethical problems, but science has also been invaluable in securing the evidence to ensure justice is served. DNA profiling to identify criminals proved to be as crucial a forensic tool as fingerprinting, while digital technology became indispensable in every aspect of law enforcement, especially given the increasing sophistication and international scope of organized crime.

The world of sport experienced significant change, too, with the increase in global sponsorship, live television coverage, and online gambling multiplying the financial stakes. As the industry expanded, corruption increased – the rewards of cheating lured individuals, crime rings, and rogue nations alike. UNESCO moved to stem the tide with the International Convention Against Doping in Sport in 2005, and in 2011 INTERPOL set up a task force to combat match-fixing.

In 2000, alarmed at the rate of new HIV/AIDS cases – half of which arose from injecting drugs – the Portuguese government put in place a new drug strategy, decriminalizing the possession of drugs as part of wider health and social reforms whose impact other countries are now studying.

Protecting the planet

By the 1980s, the damaging effects of human activity on the natural world were clear, and the issue won space on the international agenda. In 1983, UNESCO led the way in environmental protection, with the creation of a network of Biosphere Reserves to foster conservation and sustainable development.

An even bigger problem is the potentially catastrophic effects of global climate change. In 1992, the Rio Earth Summit agreed international goals for the reduction of greenhouse gas emissions, but a reluctance to implement change and adopt sustainable energy policies prevented any legally binding agreement until the 21st century. In 1997, the Kyoto Protocol defined targets for the reduction of emissions, which came into force in 2005. Given our failure to enact reduction policies, the challenge for law is to find new ways to ensure everyone does their part. ■

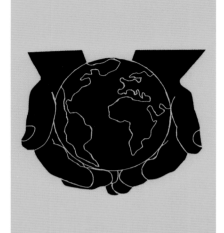

BOUNDLESS, PRICELESS, AND THREATENED
THE WORLD NETWORK OF BIOSPHERE RESERVES (1983)

The biosphere is the surface "skin" around Earth that supports mankind and all other forms of life. In 1971, UNESCO launched its Man and the Biosphere Programme (MAB), with the aim of encouraging economic development that would be environmentally sustainable while protecting the natural world. In 1972, in Stockholm, the Conference on the Human Environment was the first forum aimed at addressing international environmental issues. Among its recommendations was the setting up of "biological reserves" to protect threatened flora and fauna.

At the time, concerns were growing about deforestation, air and water pollution, overfishing, and population declines in many wild animals. The first 57 Biosphere Reserves (BRs) were selected in 1976. In the years that followed, more were designated and a plan for a World Network of Biosphere Reserves (WNBR) arose from a UNESCO-sponsored conference in Minsk, Belarus, in 1983.

Mutual benefits
According to the UN's 1992 legally binding international Convention on Biological Diversity (ratified by 193 nations as of 2020), "Ecosystems, species, and genetic resources should be used for the benefit of humans, but in a way that does not lead to the decline of biodiversity". Recognizing that

A Biosphere Reserve's zones

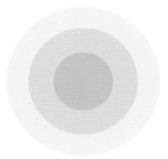

■ **The core zone** is a strictly protected area where human activity is limited, and lifeforms and ecosystems (communities of interacting species and the environment on which they depend) are conserved.

■ **The buffer zone** is used for monitoring, scientific research, training, and education.

■ **The transition zone** is where people live and work, and where sustainable cultural and economic activity is allowed.

See also: The United Nations and International Court of Justice 212–19
▪ The Endangered Species Act 264–65 ▪ The Kyoto Protocol 305

Yellowstone National Park, in the American states of Wyoming, Montana, and Idaho, was designated a Biosphere Reserve in 1976.

species diversity is crucial to sustain our planet's web of life, the WNBR now aims to show how biodiversity and human cultural diversity are mutually beneficial.

Environmental sustainability rests on the premise that if people have an economic or cultural stake in their environment – for example, they rely on harvesting its fish for food or its timber for building – they are more likely to protect it, and ensure that stocks are not depleted. In many BRs, local people also benefit from ecotourism.

Building the network
A global network is important to truly reflect Earth's biodiversity. Governments can nominate new BRs. If MAB's governing body agrees that they meet the required criteria, they are added to the WNBR. Each BR is protected by the environmental laws of the country in which it is situated.

In the 50 years since the MAB programme was launched, the threats facing the biosphere have intensified. One million species face extinction in the next few decades, including 40 per cent of amphibians and 30 per cent of marine mammals. Human-induced climate change will exacerbate the decline, which some scientists describe as Earth's sixth mass extinction.

In 2020, there were 701 BRs in 124 countries, ranging in size from the enormous Central Amazon BR in Brazil to Biosffer Dyfi BR, a small estuary in south Wales. Globally coordinated and legally enforceable measures such as the WNBR programme offer the best way of meeting the huge environmental challenges facing the planet. ▪

Russia's *zapovedniks*

Russia was a world leader in creating wildlife sanctuaries. Its first state-organized *zapovednik* (Russian for nature reserve) was set up in Barguzinsky, near Lake Baikal, in 1916, to conserve its population of sables – small mammals valued for their fur. In 2020, there were more than 100 *zapovedniks*, covering about 1.4 per cent of the country's total area. Some are vast: the Great Arctic Zapovednik, for example, covers 4 million ha (almost 10 million acres) of tundra and supports polar bears, snowy owls, seals, whales, and more.

Russian soil scientist Vasily Dokuchaev first put forward the idea for *zapovedniks* in the 1890s, proposing that people other than scientists should be excluded from them. Russian botanist Ivan Borodin later argued that they should not be established piecemeal, but should be planned to include every main ecosystem. These reserves provide research environments where scientists can see nature unaffected by human influence.

We should preserve every scrap of biodiversity as priceless while we learn … what it means to humanity.
E.O. Wilson
American biologist, 1992

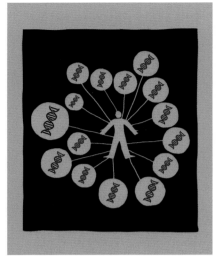

IT IS TO JUSTICE WHAT THE TELESCOPE IS FOR THE STARS
DNA TESTING (1986)

IN CONTEXT

FOCUS
Criminal law

BEFORE
c. **1900** Fingerprinting is adopted as the first scientific way to identify crime suspects.

1953 The structure of DNA, the genetic code governing life, is revealed by scientists James Watson, Francis Crick, Rosalind Franklin, and Maurice Wilkins in the UK.

AFTER
1994 The FBI coordinates DNA profiling across the US.

2002 The INTERPOL DNA database is established: 84 countries participate.

From 2010 Increasingly complex software programs are developed to analyse and identify DNA samples.

2017 The Rapid DNA Act in the US boosts further research into DNA as a policing tool.

Scientists show that **DNA samples** can exactly **identify any individual**.

⬇

Law-enforcement agencies around the world routinely adopt DNA profiling.

⬇

DNA databases provide a rapidly growing resource: millions of records are assembled and their applications grow.

⬇

Concerns remain that DNA testing is not always stringently applied: the **potential for misuse** is clear.

DNA (deoxyribonucleic acid) profiling was the most important breakthrough in forensic crime-solving since the widespread introduction of fingerprinting in the early 20th century. The value of the DNA molecule in forensics relies on the fact that although 99.9 per cent of the DNA of every human who has ever lived is identical, the 0.1 per cent difference provides irrefutable identification of any individual (apart from identical twins). DNA can be sampled from saliva, skin, blood, hair, or cells. To be of value, however, it is essential that both the sampling and analysis are performed to exacting standards.

The first use of DNA testing in a criminal investigation was to establish innocence rather than

See also: INTERPOL 220–21 ▪ The Universal Declaration of Human Rights 222–29 ▪ The European Convention on Human Rights 230–33 ▪ The International Convention Against Doping in Sport 304

Alec Jeffreys carried out research on genetics at Leicester University, in the UK, from 1977 to 2012. His work has been useful in paternity and immigration disputes, as well as in crime detection.

> People have unrealistic perceptions of the meaning of scientific evidence, especially when it comes to DNA.
> **EUROFORGEN**
> **(European Forensic Genetics Network of Excellence), 2017**

guilt. In 1986, Richard Buckland, a youth with learning difficulties, was arrested for the rape and murder of 15-year-old Dawn Ashworth in the UK. The case came to the attention of British geneticist Alec Jeffreys. He examined DNA taken from semen found on Ashworth's corpse and showed that it was not Buckland's. Jeffreys also demonstrated that whoever killed Ashworth had killed another girl, Lynda Mann, three years earlier. Buckland was released from custody, and after a long investigation, serial sex offender Colin Pitchfork was found to have a DNA match with the semen samples. He was found guilty on two counts of murder and sentenced to life imprisonment.

Advances in DNA testing

Quick to exploit DNA as a major advance, law-enforcement agencies around the world set up databases to store and share information. The US Federal Bureau of Investigation (FBI) launched its Combined DNA Index System in 1998; by 2020, it held DNA profiles of more than 14 million offenders, gathered from

crime scenes. Similarly, the UK's National DNA Database (NDNAD), created in 1995, had 6.5 million profiles by 2020.

Since DNA profiling was first used, advances in technology have made it possible to analyse tiny samples very quickly. The clear success of DNA profiling has led to an assumption that it is infallible, but human error has led to several miscarriages of justice. In 1998, for example, 16-year-old Josiah Sutton from Houston, Texas, was given a 25-year jail sentence for rape, based on DNA evidence. This was later shown to have been mishandled in the forensics laboratory, and Sutton was exonerated.

Shortcomings

In reality, as the number of stored DNA samples increases, the risk of blunders – of files muddled or

testing techniques misapplied – also grows. "Secondary transfer", where DNA is transferred to an object or person through an intermediate, has proved to be a difficulty. Also, most everyday objects carry tiny traces of multiple people, and it can be almost impossible to distinguish the DNA of those in frequent contact. As a UK government report explained, "Our ability to analyse [DNA] may outstrip our ability to interpret." ▪

The Green River Killer

The Green River Killer serial murder case – one of the worst in US history – spectacularly vindicated the use of DNA profiling. Gary Ridgway raped and strangled at least 49 young women in Washington State between 1982 and 2001, when he was finally arrested. He dumped their bodies in or near the Green River. The police had no leads.

In 2001, improved DNA sampling techniques led to a crucial breakthrough for the

police investigation. DNA samples taken from semen found on some of the victims were compared with one taken from Ridgway in 1987, when, suspected of the killings, he had been interviewed but not charged. The samples proved to be an exact match; Ridgway was found guilty of murder, and he was sentenced to 48 consecutive life sentences. He later claimed to have killed as many as 80 women, and the true total may have been more.

EMPOWER THE WATCHDOGS OF WRONGDOING
THE WHISTLEBLOWER PROTECTION ACT (1989)

IN CONTEXT

FOCUS
Employment law

BEFORE
1863 The False Claims Act is probably the world's first whistleblowing law, to curb fraud by defence contractors in the American Civil War.

1966 The US Freedom of Information Act aims to make government business "open to public scrutiny".

AFTER
1998 In Britain, the Public Interest Disclosure Act protects whistleblowers in public or private institutions, if the disclosed information is in the public interest.

2010 The US Dodd–Frank Act includes protection for whistleblowers in its regulation of financial institutions.

2015 Concerns mount that the Dodd–Frank Act harms smaller banks and lenders.

Employees who highlighted misconduct, deliberate or not, in any US federal agency were first given protection by 1989's Whistleblower Protection Act. The Act offered guarantees to whistleblowers that retaliation, such as demotions or suspensions, would not be taken against them.

Although the US was leading the world with this legislation, and despite it being fortified by the Whistleblower Protection

Protecting employees who disclose government illegality, waste, and corruption is a major step toward a more effective civil service.
Whistleblower Protection Act

Enhancement Act in 2012, the legislation has rarely achieved its intended impact. Its protections do not include immunity from legal action by an employer – a fact that dissuades other workers from speaking up.

A 2006 US Supreme Court ruling, in *Garcetti v. Ceballos*, was discouraging, with even the First Amendment guarantee of freedom of speech deemed inapplicable for whistleblowing public employees such as Richard Ceballos, a Los Angeles deputy district attorney.

The 1989 Act also excluded US intelligence-agency employees. The 1998 Intelligence Community Whistleblower Protection Act (ICWPA) gave them only limited rights; the Act was amended in 2014 to extend their immunity.

The Dodd–Frank Act, passed after the financial crisis of 2007, aimed to curb excessive risk-taking by financial institutions and protect consumers. This proved successful, partly because 10–30 per cent of any money recouped may be paid to the whistleblower. ∎

See also: The Universal Declaration of Human Rights 222–29 ▪ The International Covenant on Civil and Political Rights 256–57 ▪ Megan's Law 285

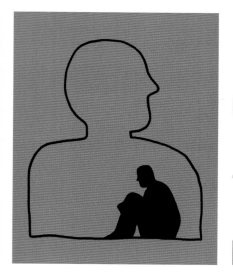

TOGETHER WE HAVE OVERCOME. TOGETHER WE SHALL OVERCOME

THE AMERICANS WITH DISABILITIES ACT (1990)

IN CONTEXT

FOCUS
Equal rights

BEFORE
1964 The Civil Rights Act aims to end segregation in the US on the basis of race.

1965 The Voting Rights Act bans discriminatory practices that prevent some American citizens from exercising their right to vote.

1973 The Rehabilitation Act outlaws discrimination against the disabled in any federally funded programme in the US.

AFTER
1992 The Equal Employment Opportunity Commission begins enforcing employment protections that are laid down in the ADA.

2000 The EU's Framework for Equal Treatment in Employment and Occupation includes protections for disabled workers.

The 1990 Americans with Disabilities Act (ADA) aimed to guarantee "the full civil and human rights of people with disabilities". The government wanted to make it clear that society should encourage and enable people with disabilities to make the fullest possible contribution to American life. The ADA outlawed employment discrimination against those with disabilities; and every employer with more than 15 workers had to "accommodate" any such employee's "reasonable" needs – unless it caused the company undue hardship.

The ADA also required that any building or business open to the public – such as schools, hotels, health clubs, and shops – had to provide easier access and could not discriminate against those with disabilities. Telecommunications and transportation – buses, trains, planes, even cruise ships – faced similar obligations. In 2008, the ADA Amendments Act broadened the ADA's scope, and the definition of disability, to protect more people.

President George H.W. Bush signed into law the Americans with Disabilities Act – the first comprehensive civil rights law for people with physical and mental disabilities – on 26 July 1990.

Although the legislation showed that the US was in the vanguard of disability legislation, the results have been mixed. Many smaller businesses complained about the high costs of compliance. In 1990, 70 per cent of "significantly" disabled citizens were unemployed; by 2010, the figure was unchanged. Organizations that fail to comply with the employment sections of the ADA face no sanctions beyond making good on their breaches. ∎

See also: The Universal Declaration of Human Rights 222–29 ▪ The European Convention on Human Rights 230–33 ▪ The Civil Rights Act 248–53

A WORLD FREE OF CHEMICAL WEAPONS

THE CHEMICAL WEAPONS CONVENTION (1993)

IN CONTEXT

FOCUS
Arms control

BEFORE
1899, 1907 The Hague Conventions propose the international outlawing of chemical weapons.

1925 The Geneva Protocol proposes more enforceable prohibitions but its impact is limited.

1975 The Biological Weapons Convention comes into force.

1990 An agreement between the US and the Soviet Union commits both to halting the production of new chemical weapons and to destroying stockpiled weapons.

AFTER
2013 Civil war breaks out in Syria. There are multiple chemical weapons attacks – including a sarin gas attack on a Damascus suburb that kills more than 1,400 civilians.

One of the most ambitious international treaties governing warfare, the Chemical Weapons Convention (CWC) aims to outlaw the use of these weapons everywhere. It was approved by the UN's General Assembly and made available for signature in 1993. By 2020, it had been ratified by 193 countries, and only three UN members – Egypt, South Sudan, and North Korea – were not party to it.

There is a long history of treaties to outlaw chemical weapons. The first was signed in Strasbourg in 1675 when France and various German states agreed to ban "poisoned bullets". More tellingly, in the Brussels Declaration of 1874, the Laws and Customs of War prohibited "poison or poisoned weapons". Further restrictions were placed on the use of chemical weapons at the Hague Peace Conferences of 1899 and 1907.

Following the extensive use of chemical weapons in World War I, Germany was forbidden to use chemical weapons under the Treaty of Versailles. Then, in 1925, the Geneva Protocol outlawed the use

The **Chemical Weapons Convention** (CWC) agrees measures to **ban their use** in warfare.

The CWC **prohibits** all **manufacture and use** of any chemical weapons.

It orders the **destruction** of existing chemical weapons and the **decommissioning** of all manufacturing facilities.

Nations must give access to **independent verifiers** to ensure destruction and decommissioning have been **carried out**.

See also: The Geneva Conventions 152–55 ▪ The Hague Conventions 174–77 ▪ The United Nations and International Court of Justice 212–19 ▪ The Partial Test Ban Treaty 244–47 ▪ The Anti-Personnel Mine Ban Convention 288–89

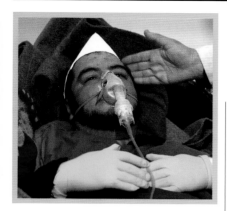

A victim of a chemical weapons attack in Syria in April 2017. Syrian president Bashar al-Assad blamed "terrorists" for this and other attacks, but his armed forces were implicated.

of chemical weapons, although not their manufacture. Japan used them widely against the Chinese during the Sino-Japanese War of 1937–45. At the start of World War II, both Nazi Germany and the Allies had stockpiles though they were rarely used on the battlefield, chiefly for fear of retaliation.

International agreements

In 1975, after several years of preparatory work, the Biological Weapons Convention came into force. This was the first multilateral disarmament treaty to ban the

production of an entire category of weapons, but its effectiveness was limited by the absence of the means to verify compliance.

Real progress came only with the thawing of US–Soviet relations after 1985. By 1990, both countries had agreed to halt production and destroy existing chemical weapons, paving the way for the global agreement that followed in 1993.

Provisions and abuses

The CWC's provisions were clear: every signatory agreed to produce no further chemical weapons, eliminate any they already held, and allow mandatory inspections by the Organisation for the Prohibition of Chemical Weapons (OPCW), carried out if necessary with only 12 hours notice. In 2007, Albania became the first country to comply fully, and by late 2018, 97 per cent

The use in war of asphyxiating, poisonous or other gases, and of all analogous liquids, materials or devices, has been justly condemned.
Geneva Protocol, 1925

of the stockpiles declared by their possessor states had been verifiably destroyed. Implementation of the ban has been hard to police, however. Syria signed up to the CWC in 2013 and claimed to have destroyed all its chemical weapons, but repeated attacks with chemical weapons have been reported in the civil war that erupted that year. Despite denials, Syrian state forces have been strongly implicated. ▪

Iraq's chemical weapons

Born in c. 1941, Ali Hassan al-Majid (better known as "Chemical Ali") was a cousin of the Iraqi dictator Saddam Hussein. He held some of the most important government posts during the 1980s and 1990s, and during the later stages of the Iran–Iraq War (1980–88) he commanded all the state agencies in the Kurdish-populated north of the country.

Iraq had deployed chemical weapons against Iranian forces since 1980, but in 1987–88, al-Majid authorized their use

against Kurdish civilians. The Al-Anfal ("Spoils of War") genocide against the Kurds may have resulted in as many as 180,000 deaths. In the most notorious incident, on 16 March 1988, Iraqi planes dropped mustard gas and sarin canisters on the town of Halabja, killing at least 5,000 and inflicting injury and long-term illness on thousands more. Chemical Ali was arrested by US forces in 2003 and, after a lengthy trial, was executed in 2010.

Ali Hassan al-Majid ordered the use of deadly chemical weapons against Kurdish civilians in northern Iraq in 1987–88.

TO OPEN TRADE FOR THE BENEFIT OF ALL

THE WORLD TRADE ORGANIZATION (1995)

IN CONTEXT

FOCUS
International free trade

BEFORE
1929–39 The Great Depression creates mass unemployment around the world.

1947 The General Agreement on Tariffs and Trade (GATT) is established; 23 countries are founder members.

1986 The Uruguay Round of GATT talks begin – the most ambitious international trade talks yet attempted.

AFTER
1999 Violent protests take place outside the WTO talks in Seattle.

2001 The Doha Development Round attempts to introduce greater trade liberalization but makes only limited progress.

2015 Doha talks are officially abandoned by the WTO.

The Bretton Woods Conference of 1944 attempts to create a global **economic regulatory system** for the postwar world.

The UN-sponsored **GATT** (General Agreement on Tariffs and Trade) is signed in 1947.

The agreement's **stated aims** are free trade and the **abolition of high tariffs**, which penalize imports.

The WTO becomes the most powerful legislative and judicial body in the world.

However, the WTO's goal of **trade liberalization** is consistently hampered by **competing national interests**.

T he creation of the World Trade Organization (WTO) in 1995 arguably represents the most forward-looking of all international agreements. It grew out of the General Agreement on Tariffs and Trade (GATT), which had been established by the United Nations in 1947. Both GATT and the WTO were informed by a single ethos: free trade between nations on terms that are both equitable and transparent produces only benefits. This was essentially an extension of the arguments put forward by Scottish economist Adam Smith in the 18th century:

that enlightened self-interest, if harnessed to individual enterprise, was the surest possible way to increase wealth.

As World War II drew to a close, such a global dream began to seem possible. For US president Franklin D. Roosevelt, British economist John Maynard Keynes, and others, one of the main lessons of the 1930s was that high import tariffs had helped destabilize international relations without improving the global economy. They believed that free trade promoted prosperity and peace, and to that end the Bretton Woods Conference of 1944 set up

the International Monetary Fund (IMF) and World Bank to help secure global financial stability and provide loans for the governments of nations that were struggling. It also agreed to put in place a system to regulate the rules of trade, and GATT followed three years later, sponsored by the newly created UN.

Reconciling interests
The Cold War that followed World War II produced a seemingly unbridgeable barrier between the world's two dominant powers, the US and the Soviet Union (USSR), underlined by the nuclear arms

See also: The Sherman Antitrust Act 170–73 ▪ The Federal Trade Commission 184–85 ▪ The WIPO Copyright Treaty 286–87

African commerce was given a boost in 2019 by the establishment of the African Continental Free Trade Area, enabling tariff-free trade between most of the continent's nations.

race, a stand-off with no obvious solution. At the same time, divisions between what were becoming known as the First and Third Worlds – the economically "developed" and "developing" countries – made the prospect of establishing any common means of commerce even less likely. The problem was not simply how such a variety of interests could be reconciled. It was that narrower national interests were always more likely to prevail than lofty aspirations. It is a contradiction that has never been resolved.

The multilateral trade talks that led to the creation of the WTO were known as the Uruguay Round since they began at Punta del Este in Uruguay. They took place within the framework of GATT from 1986 to 1993, with 123 nations taking part. Trade negotiations are

notoriously complex and slow moving – China, for example, only signed up to the WTO in 2001 after 15 years of talks. That said, by 2020, the WTO had 164 member nations, who between them accounted for 98 per cent of all global trade.

Basic mechanisms

The stated aim of the WTO is to ensure trade flows as smoothly, predictably, and freely as possible. It strives to eliminate protectionist, high import tariffs and so create »

The WTO has one of the most impressive records in global economic governance.
Anna Lindh
Swedish politician (1957–2003)

Seattle, 1999

The WTO is no stranger to internal disputes, often over matters of complex economic policy. From the late 1990s, external opposition emerged to any organization held to advance the exploitative, capitalist interests that were pushing a global neoliberal agenda – including the IMF, the World Bank, and the European Union, as well as the WTO. The WTO meeting in Seattle, Washington, in December 1999 saw this opposition reach a new pitch. In excess of 50,000 demonstrators descended on the city, protesting against environmental degradation, cheap imports, democratic unaccountability, unsafe work practices, or the existence of capitalism in general. Peaceful protests spiralled into violence, made worse by hamfisted attempts by the police to clear the streets. A new form of disruptive civic protest was born, whose offspring included the Occupy movement and Extinction Rebellion.

"The Battle of Seattle" occurred on 30 November and 1 December, drawing attention to the effects of global trade.

The structure of the World Trade Organization

Ministerial Conference

This is the highest policy-making body and usually convenes every two years. Every member nation is represented, and it can make decisions on any aspect of the WTO's multilateral trade agreements.

Dispute Settlement Body

When disputes arise, members of the General Council convene as this committee to establish dispute settlement panels.

General Council

Between conferences, this is the supreme decision-making body. It meets regularly and has delegates from every member country.

Trade Policy Review Body

General Council members sometimes convene as the Trade Policy Review Body to oversee proposed changes in national trade policies.

Council for Trade in Goods

This committee oversees GATT, which covers international trade in goods. Ten subgroups cover specific areas such as agriculture, market access, and government subsidies.

Intellectual Property Rights Council

The Council for Trade-Related Aspects of Intellectual Property Rights (TRIPS) is responsible for monitoring the elimination of the trade in goods that infringe intellectual property rights.

Council for Trade in Services

This body oversees a number of subcommittees and is responsible for the General Agreement on Trade in Services. This agreement covers trade in financial services.

stable trading conditions that will encourage investment and job creation. This, it is hoped, will boost developing nations, lifting their people from poverty and allowing them to compete equally with the developed world.

The WTO coordinates its efforts with the IMF and World Bank, and has used trade sanctions against countries deemed to have abused its rules. Generally every two years, a ministerial conference convenes to make big decisions. Committees overseeing trade in goods and services, and the contentious issue of intellectual property rights, meet more regularly, and subcommittees negotiate the minutiae of trade

policy. The Appellate Body, an independent committee of seven trade law experts, was established in 1995. It considers reports from dispute settlement panels, which it has the power to overturn.

Varied criticisms

The WTO is ponderous and slow to react because it has to consider a very large number of conflicting interests. Critics accuse it of being in thrall to the interests of its most powerful members. They also question the transparency of the WTO's decisions and argue that it discriminates against developing nations. One consistent criticism is that in seeking to

defend intellectual property rights (especially proprietary rights of a business over any product it has created), the WTO has denied the potential benefits of medicines, in particular, to countries unable to afford them. For example, companies that invested in developing "patented" original HIV medicines forced cheaper, but equally effective, generic medicines out of many markets in the developing world. In such cases, profits and shareholders' dividends seem to have taken preference over patients.

Further criticisms have been levelled against trade blocs that have successfully used their economic muscle to impose tariffs that are

> What countries must do to join the WTO is … accept the rule of law, reduce corruption, and become open, accountable, and democratic.
> **Richard Haass**
> US diplomat, July 2018

much higher than those allowed for other countries. For example, agricultural imports into the EU face average tariffs of 11.5 per cent. Under exactly the same WTO rules, Russia has never been able to levy tariffs higher than 6.5 per cent. So EU farmers enjoy a level of WTO-sanctioned protection that is denied to their counterparts in Russia.

Any such international body is vulnerable to manipulation by its most powerful members. Every WTO member or bloc – such as the EU, ASEAN (Association of Southeast Asian Nations), or Mercosur (Latin America's "southern market") – has to have agreed "schedules" with the WTO that make clear their tariffs, quotas, and subsidies. These are then subject to approval by the WTO. Yet not only is it possible to trade without this form of certification, but the EU's WTO schedules, for example, have remained uncertified since 2004.

US president Donald Trump and his Chinese counterpart Xi Jinping shake hands after talks in 2017. The following year, relations between the two nations deteriorated over the issue of trade.

Although the WTO is the ultimate arbiter of tariff and subsidy disputes, resolving them requires the unanimous consent of all 164 WTO members, and there is no means of knowing how such decisions are reached. Global or not, the WTO can hardly claim to be democratic. That said, since the late 1990s, the number of trade disputes under the WTO has consistently declined. There were 50 in 1997, but only 18 in 2017, for example. This suggests that, given sufficient time, most such difficulties can be untangled under WTO jurisdiction. So the organization does seem to offer the hope of equitable global trade.

An imposed ideal?

The quest for multilateral trade agreements will always take second place to national interests. Every nation has sought to bend the WTO's rulings to its own advantage. The US has long resented countries or blocs that have sought to extract favourable trading terms from the WTO while the US has sought to do exactly the same. The WTO's critics argue that, in effect, it has become simply another means for those with economic muscle to impose their own agendas. When

> If the last 25 years have taught us anything about the WTO, it is that this organization is resilient and resourceful.
> **Roberto Azevêdo**
> WTO director general, 2020

Donald Trump called the WTO "a disaster" in 2018, and threatened to pull the US out of it, it was the first step in a high-stakes negotiation. His administration had just slapped tariffs on Chinese imports, with China imposing counter-tariffs.

GATT was born from a postwar belief that the world should and could be remade. The WTO is its direct descendent. It may be compromised, but it has nudged the world in the direction of greater prosperity and fairness based on free trade. However clumsy, its underlying vision remains essentially optimistic. ∎

WHEN DOES LIFE BEGIN?

THE DICKEY–WICKER AMENDMENT (1996)

IN CONTEXT

FOCUS
Family law

BEFORE
1976 In the US, The Hyde Amendment outlaws federal funding for abortions, except in cases of medical emergency.

1978 Louise Brown, the first "test-tube baby", is born in the UK; the potential of embryo research is clear.

1979 A federal Ethics Advisory Board recommends that embryo research is acceptable for the treatment of infertility; its advice is disregarded.

AFTER
2009 President Obama issues an executive order removing the restriction on federal funding of stem-cell research.

2011 The US Court of Appeals for the District of Columbia Circuit upholds Obama's order with reservations; the essential provisions of the Dickey–Wicker Amendment remain in force.

Since 1996, the Dickey–Wicker Amendment has prohibited the use of federal funding for the creation of human embryos for research purposes, or for research in which human embryos are destroyed or injured. The bill, which is attached to US appropriations (government spending) bills, had already been approved by the House Committee on Appropriations, in 1995, before it was put to the vote in Congress in 1996.

The Amendment – which never prohibited human-embryo research itself, only federal funding of such research – strikes at the heart of the ethical questions that similarly fuel the abortion debate. At what point can a human life be said to begin, and what laws should be in place to protect it? The work on human embryos that began in the 1970s opened up new horizons in medical science. It offered the possibility of conception for infertile couples, as well as the potential for pioneering treatments for serious diseases using stem cells. But the issue has always been controversial.

Congress often legislates without understanding the full scope of its enactments.
Cathryn Smeyers
Oncofertility Consortium, 2013

In 2009, the Amendment was partially watered down by President Barack Obama, and in 2011 the Court of Appeals conceded that the Amendment was "ambiguous" and did not prohibit the funding of research that uses embryonic stem cells. Medical opinion is substantially opposed to the Amendment, claiming that vital research is being hampered by an obsolete law enacted by those unqualified to make such a decision. ∎

See also: The Universal Declaration of Human Rights 222–29 ▪ The European Convention on Human Rights 230–33 ▪ *Roe v. Wade* 260–63

EVERY PARENT SHOULD HAVE THE RIGHT TO KNOW
MEGAN'S LAW (1996)

IN CONTEXT

FOCUS
Criminal law

BEFORE
1947 California becomes the first US state to compile a register of sex offenders.

1994 The Jacob Wetterling Crimes Against Children and Sexually Violent Offender Registration Act is passed.

AFTER
1996 The Pam Lychner Sexual Offender Tracking and Identification Act leads to a federal database of offenders.

2006 The Adam Walsh Child Protection and Safety Act sets new conditions for the frequency at which offenders must update the authorities as to their whereabouts.

2016 International Megan's Law (a US Act) requires registered sex offenders to be identified on their passports.

M egan's Law is a US federal law that requires state authorities to make information about registered sex offenders available to the public. It was passed as an amendment to the Jacob Wetterling Act of 1994, which required states to create registers of those convicted of sexually violent crimes or crimes against children. States can decide how much information to release to the public, and via what medium.

The new law was enacted as a result of the rape and murder in July 1994 of seven-year-old Megan Kanka in New Jersey. She was killed by a neighbour, 33-year-old Jesse Timmendequas, who had already been convicted of two sex crimes against children and had served six years in prison. Megan's parents, Maureen and Richard Kanka, launched a campaign for mandatory community notification of sex offenders, arguing that if they had known of Timmendequas's history, they would have protected their daughter from him. Within months of the murder, New Jersey enacted

Megan's Law, which became a model for the law of the same name passed in Congress two years later.

No one has ever doubted the good intentions of Megan's Law, but it has not reduced the number of offences, and has been denounced as a violation of the privacy rights that are guaranteed by the Fourth Amendment. It has also encouraged some to take the law into their own hands, meting out vigilante punishments against convicted sex offenders. ∎

President Bill Clinton signs Megan's Law in the presence of Megan's mother and brother; New Jersey representative Dick Zimmer; and John Walsh, host of TV's *America's Most Wanted*.

See also: The US Constitution and Bill of Rights 110–17 ▪ The Universal Declaration of Human Rights 222–29 ▪ The European Convention on Human Rights 230–33

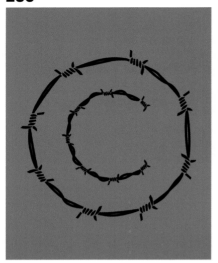

IF CREATIVITY IS A FIELD, COPYRIGHT IS A FENCE

THE WIPO COPYRIGHT TREATY (1996)

The Berne Convention of 1886 was the first attempt to regulate copyright internationally. Initially, just 10 nations signed up to it but now, administered by the UN's World Intellectual Property Organization (WIPO), it has 178 signatories.

The very first copyright law had been the Statute of Anne, passed by the British Parliament in 1710, but it did not apply outside Britain. The Berne Convention extended copyright protection to authors and artists in an ever-growing number of countries – recognizing both that they are the legal owners of the work they produce and that they should be the main beneficiaries of their labour. The Convention also stated that copyright did not need to be asserted but was vested

Internet service providers (ISPs) host art, music, films, photographs, articles, and books online.

Much of this **online content** infringes copyright, with the result that the **original creators** are **not paid royalties**.

The **WCT** extends the Berne Convention to cover **digital content**, and the **Music Modernization Act** deals with **streamed music**.

Despite legislation, enforcing the principle of **content ownership** across the internet **remains challenging**.

See also: The Statute of Anne 106–07 ▪ The Universal Declaration of Human Rights 222–29 ▪ The European Convention on Human Rights 230–33 ▪ *Google Spain v. AEPD and Mario Costeja González* 308–09 ▪ The Open Internet Order 310–13

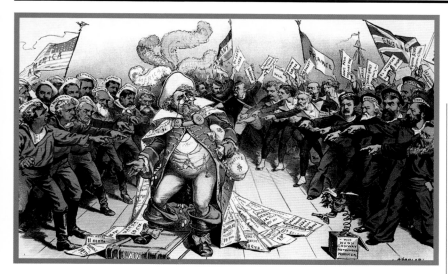

The "Pirate Publisher" flaunting copyright was satirized in this cartoon in the American magazine *Puck* in 1886, the year of the Berne Convention, which sought to defend copyright.

automatically in the creator. Several updates to the Convention followed. For example, in 1908, it was agreed that copyright would last for 50 years (later extended to 70) after the creator's death.

A digital world

Since the 1990s, there has been an exponential growth in digital media, with music, books, journals, photographs, film, and art available online at the touch of a key. As it became ever easier to copy and upload content, so it proved harder to determine its provenance. Artists, authors, and others regularly found their creations hosted online, with no attribution and no hope of receiving royalties. The big challenge facing legislators was in applying the provisions of the Berne Convention to the digital world.

To meet that challenge, in 1996, a conference arranged by the World Intellectual Property Organization adopted the WIPO Copyright Treaty (WCT), which came into effect six years later. The WCT outlined the importance of copyright protection

in encouraging creative activity. After all, why would anyone create anything if it was going to be copied and passed off online as someone else's work?

Protection of creative content and ownership was sorely needed. The US Chamber of Commerce said in 2018 that online video piracy alone was costing the American economy almost $30 billion a year, in addition to up to 560,000 job

losses in the country's film and television industry. The law also protects industrial design. Alongside patent and trademark laws, it was a legal weapon in the battle against counterfeit goods. Global trade in these fake items was worth $509 billion by 2016, according to the Organisation for Economic Cooperation and Development (OECD).

Further copyright legislation has followed, including, in the US, the Digital Millennium Copyright Act (1998), which increased penalties for those infringing copyright on the internet, and the Music Modernization Act (2018) to protect the copyright and royalties of artists whose music is streamed online.

The problem remains, however, that legal mechanisms, though well intentioned, are still finding it hard to police digital copyright. ▪

Kim Dotcom

One of the most shameless exploiters of the almost limitless possibilities of the internet, Kim Dotcom was born Kim Schmitz in 1974. After operating lucrative scams in Germany, he moved to Hong Kong, where he launched the file-sharing website Megaupload in 2005. In its heyday, Megaupload possibly accounted for four per cent of all internet traffic. Anyone could register and anyone could upload. A vast repository of illegal, downloadable files

was the result, with Dotcom profiting from the huge advertising revenue. As the money flooded in, he bought cars, houses, planes, and yachts.

However, the spending spree came to an end in 2012 with Dotcom's arrest in New Zealand after he was charged in the US with copyright infringement, money-laundering, and other offences. He has denied these charges. By March 2020, he was still attempting to prevent his extradition to the US.

THE LANDMINE DOES NOT RECOGNIZE PEACE

THE ANTI-PERSONNEL MINE BAN CONVENTION (1997)

By the early 1990s, an estimated 110 million anti-personnel landmines (APLs) were buried in the ground across the globe. Most were left over from former conflicts in Africa, the Middle East, and Southeast Asia. Detonated by people stepping on them, they caused horrific injuries or death. The exact number of casualties is unknown, but up to 25,000 people were being killed or maimed every year as they went about regular activities such as herding animals or collecting firewood. Those who trod on the mines were not the only ones to suffer: the consequences were also devastating for families deprived of breadwinners. In conflict zones around the world, these weapons were used in such large numbers because they are easily deployed and very cheap. On the other hand, getting rid of them is dangerous and expensive. An APL bought for $3 (£2.50) can cost $1,000 (£815) to remove. This was clearly an urgent and growing humanitarian crisis.

The Ottawa Treaty

A solution came in the form of the Anti-Personnel Mine Ban Convention (or Ottawa Treaty), which was agreed by 122 countries in Ottawa, Canada, in December 1997 and came into force in March 1999. By 2020, the number of countries signed up to it had increased to 164. All signatory nations made a commitment not to produce or use APLs, to destroy all stockpiled APLs within four years of signing, and to eliminate all minefields "under their jurisdiction or control" within 10 years of signing. The treaty encouraged international cooperation in mine clearance and medical support.

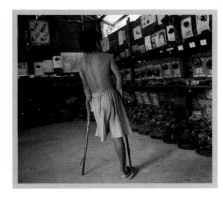

Most victims (71 per cent) of anti-personnel mines are civilians. Children account for half of those. An injury that can be devastating for an adult is more often fatal for a child.

See also: The Geneva Conventions 152–55 ▪ The Universal Declaration of Human Rights 222–29 ▪ The Chemical Weapons Convention 276–77

Unexploded weaponry of all types is a **legacy of World War II**.

→

Later conflicts, in Africa and Asia especially, see widespread use of **cheap landmines**.

↓

Russia, China, and the US offer **support for the ban** despite **refusing to sign the Ottawa Treaty**.

←

As deaths and injuries mount, so do calls to **ban and destroy landmines**.

↓

A consensus emerges that the destruction of landmines is a humanitarian good.

The results have generally been encouraging. By 2014, 70 million APLs had been removed and more than 4,000 sq km (1,544 sq miles) of mined areas cleared. The numbers killed or injured fell by an estimated two-thirds, although there were still more than 130,000 casualties between 1999 and 2018. And nearly 20 civilians were still being killed or injured every day by landmines and other devices in 2018.

Non-signatories

Thirty-two nations have refused to sign, including the US, China, and Russia – all permanent members of the UN Security Council. India, Iran, Syria, and Libya are also notable non-signatories. Reasons for not signing vary. The US, for example, has produced no APLs since 1997 and has donated almost $2 billion to mine-clearance programmes, but it has always maintained that APLs are essential for the defence of South Korea, menaced by its neighbour North Korea. In 2014, the US did pledge not to use such weapons anywhere except to protect South Korea, but in early 2020, President Donald Trump's administration lifted the restriction on the deployment of anti-personnel landmines by American forces, saying that the ban could put US troops at a "severe disadvantage". ▪

Civilians should not be killed or maimed by weapons that strike blindly and senselessly.
Arms Control Association

The Diana effect

A number of high-profile campaigners have lent their support to the fight against APLs, including British actor Daniel Craig, a UN-appointed advocate for mine removal, but none has influenced public opinion more than Diana, Princess of Wales. In January 1997, before the Ottawa Treaty had been agreed, as patron of the HALO Trust (the world's largest anti-mine charity) and as a guest of the International Red Cross, she visited a minefield in Angola, just one of hundreds that were planted during the country's civil war. Reported in media headlines around the globe, Diana's identification with – and very public support for – the victims of Angola's landmines sparked the world's outrage and helped build support for a ban on mines. In early August 1997, three weeks before her death, she visited landmine survivors in Bosnia and Herzegovina, which was also littered with minefields.

Diana, Princess of Wales, visits a minefield in Angola. Her son, Prince Harry, is now the patron of the HALO Trust.

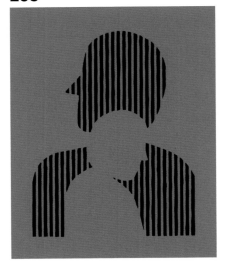

PATIENTS, NOT CRIMINALS
THE PORTUGUESE DRUG STRATEGY (2000)

IN CONTEXT

FOCUS
Decriminalizing drug use

BEFORE
1868 Under the UK's Pharmacy Act, only qualified pharmacists are allowed to buy and sell dangerous drugs and poisons.

1912 The International Opium Convention, the first international drug control treaty, is agreed. It comes into force globally in 1919.

1971 US president Richard Nixon calls for a "war on drugs" to combat rising drug abuse.

AFTER
2012 Washington and Colorado become the first two US states to decriminalize the personal use of cannabis.

2014 The World Health Organization calls for drug use to be decriminalized.

2019 Thirty-one UN agencies endorse the decriminalization of drug use.

I n 2000, Portugal passed legislation to decriminalize the use of previously illegal drugs, such as heroin and cocaine. The aim was to tackle a spiralling addiction problem by treating rather than punishing drug users – a radical move in a nation famed for its conservatism.

During the 1800s, Western views of drug use had hardened as opium addiction levels increased. Although in 1839 and 1856, the UK had twice gone to war with China to protect the lucrative opium trade, it had been the first country (in 1868) to pass a modern law restricting the sale of drugs and poisons. In the

There is no correlation between the harshness of drug laws and the incidence of drug-taking.
The Economist
Leader, 5 May 2009

20th century, despite a succession of international drug control treaties and ever harsher national laws that criminalized drug use as well as drug trafficking, both continued to proliferate worldwide.

Tackling the problem
Under the authoritarian regime of António de Oliveira Salazar, its prime minister from 1932 to 1968, Portugal missed the explosion in drug use that other countries experienced in the 1960s. In 1974, three years after his death, the regime collapsed in a bloodless revolution that opened up the country to international trade, and cannabis and heroin flooded in.

Portugal initially reacted with a crackdown that punished drug users and traffickers, but had little effect. In 1983, however, a new law gave drug users the option to accept treatment and suspend criminal punishment. In 1987, the Taipas Centre, funded by the Ministry of Health and led by public health campaigner Dr João Castel-Branco Goulão, opened in Lisbon, serving as a model for other treatment centres across Portugal. As drug use continued to rise, a 1998 government report backed

See also: The Poor Laws 88–91 ▪ INTERPOL 220–21 ▪ Euthanasia 296–97 ▪ The International Convention Against Doping in Sport 304

a comprehensive drug strategy, drawn up by Goulão, that focused on support for users, rather than continuing criminalization. Law 30, setting out the legal framework for the treatment of drug users and provision for their welfare, was passed in the year 2000 and came into force in July 2001.

The law decriminalized drug use but did not legalize it. Drug use remains an administrative violation in Portugal, and distributing and selling drugs is still a serious crime. But possession and use is seen as a public health problem, not a criminal offence. Anyone caught with less than 10 days' supply of drugs is brought before a local commission and steered towards psychiatrists, health workers, and counsellors – not the police.

Between 1999 and 2003, as more drug treatment centres opened in Portugal, drug-related deaths more than halved, rates of HIV/AIDS infection from contaminated needles fell dramatically, and far fewer teenagers were using hard drugs. The trend has largely continued. Despite a small peak in drug-induced deaths in 2015,

Drug-induced deaths per million in population:

More than 40 ▪ 10–40 ▪ Fewer than 10 ▪ Data unavailable

List of countries:

1. Portugal
2. Spain
3. Ireland
4. United Kingdom
5. France
6. Belgium
7. Luxembourg
8. Netherlands
9. Italy
10. Germany
11. Denmark
12. Norway
13. Croatia
14. Slovenia
15. Austria
16. Czech Republic
17. Hungary
18. Slovakia
19. Poland
20. Sweden
21. Greece
22. Bulgaria
23. Romania
24. Lithuania
25. Latvia
26. Estonia
27. Finland
28. Turkey

© EMCDDA, 1995–2019

Drug-induced deaths – overdoses and poisonings directly attributed to taking illegal drugs – averaged 22.6 per million people in Europe and Turkey in 2017. Portugal had only four such deaths per million of its population. Of all 8,238 deaths recorded, 34 per cent occurred in the UK.

Portugal's average has remained lower than that of any other European country.

An example to follow

The Netherlands, Germany, Italy, the Czech Republic, and Spain had decriminalized some drug use by statute or in practice by the year 2000, and Estonia, Croatia, Poland, and Switzerland have since followed suit. However, Portugal was the first European country to decriminalize all drug use, and it has seen a more dramatic fall in drug-related deaths than any of these countries.

Portuguese drug users wait beside a treatment van in Lisbon to receive their daily doses of methadone. Two of these vans operate each day in the city, serving around 1,200 patients a year.

Portugal's winning strategy seems to have been its decision to back decriminalization of all drug use with generous funding for initiatives such as drop-in centres, syringe-exchange schemes, and opioid substitution programmes. Lifting criminal sanctions for drug use has freed up resources to treat users and pursue dealers and traffickers.

Globally, more than 20 nations now have some kind of drug-use decriminalization laws, as have the Virgin Islands, 18 US states, and three Australian states. In 2019, representatives of 31 UN agencies all endorsed decriminalization of possession and use of drugs. While criminalizing drug use is still the status quo in most countries, more now acknowledge that, like Portugal, they must find a better way. ▪

MARRIAGE SHOULD BE OPEN TO ALL
SAME-SEX MARRIAGE (2000)

IN CONTEXT

FOCUS
Civil rights

BEFORE
1791 Revolutionary France declares homosexuality legal.

1969 The Stonewall Riots in New York highlight the plight of homosexuals in the US.

1996 The Defense of Marriage Act allows US states not to recognize same-sex marriages.

AFTER
2004 The UK passes the Civil Partnership Act.

2015 The US Supreme Court upholds the right to same-sex marriage in every US state.

2017 Anti-homosexual purges are launched in the Russian republic of Chechnya.

2019 The Iranian Minister of Foreign Affairs openly defends execution for homosexuality.

In a blaze of publicity that included live television coverage, the world's first legal same-sex marriages took place in the Netherlands on 1 April 2001, after legislation was passed in 2000 to allow them. The weddings of four couples – three male, one female – demonstrated a historic embrace of gay rights by one of the most tolerant countries in the world.

The campaign for same-sex partnerships to be recognized in law reached a milestone in 1989, when Denmark became the first country to introduce civil unions. A civil union confers similar or identical rights as marriage in areas such as tax benefits, pensions, and inheritance,

See also: The Representation of the People Act 188–89 ▪ The Universal Declaration of Human Rights 222–29 ▪ The Civil Rights Act 248–53 ▪ The International Covenant on Civil and Political Rights 256–57 ▪ *Roe v. Wade* 260–63

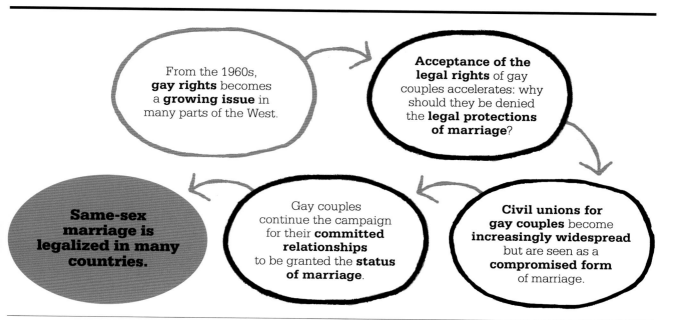

From the 1960s, **gay rights** becomes a **growing issue** in many parts of the West.

Acceptance of the legal rights of gay couples accelerates: why should they be denied the **legal protections of marriage**?

Civil unions for **gay couples** become **increasingly widespread** but are seen as a **compromised form** of marriage.

Gay couples continue the campaign for their **committed relationships** to be granted the **status of marriage**.

Same-sex marriage is legalized in many countries.

although laws vary across different countries, especially regarding the adoption of children. But a civil union lacks what might be called the spiritual status of marriage – its essence of profound commitment – which is reflected in the fact that the ceremony cannot contain any religious element, and no vows are exchanged. Pointing to a range of ceremonial, legal, and constitutional differences between civil unions and marriages, campaigners for equal rights highlighted that imposing a separate arrangement on same-sex couples treated them as inferior to their heterosexual counterparts. This distinction was criticized as "separate but equal" – a reference to a doctrine in US constitutional law invoked in the 19th century to justify racial segregation.

Cultural changes

The struggle for gay rights has gathered pace since the 1960s, and prejudice against homosexuality is increasingly perceived to be a form of abuse – as unreasonable as it is self-defeating. The argument that civil union implies a lesser status than marriage has gained ground, and same-sex marriage has become an indicator of cultural tolerance and progression. Gradually, other nations have followed the Netherlands' lead; by 2020, 29 countries had legalized gay marriage.

Marriage should be between a spouse and a spouse, not a gender and a gender.
Hendrik Hertzberg
American journalist (1943–)

However, the acceptance of what has come to be known as LGBTQ (lesbian, gay, bisexual, and transgender) rights is an almost exclusively Western phenomenon. Of the 29 countries where same-sex marriage is legal, sixteen are in Europe, seven in Latin America, two in North America, two in Australasia, one in Africa, and one in Asia. Across the vast majority of the world, gay marriage – and homosexuality – remains illegal.

Even in Europe, there is a clear split in attitudes, mostly along east–west lines. Public opinion polls in 2019 showed France, Germany, Belgium, the Netherlands, the UK, Italy, Spain, Portugal, and the Nordic countries to be resolutely in favour of same-sex marriage, while Greece, Hungary, Romania, Bulgaria, Poland, Latvia, Lithuania, and Slovakia were as resolutely opposed – despite an EU ruling in 2018 that same-sex marriages performed in one EU country must be recognized in EU » countries where they are not legal. Russia too is a particular opponent of gay rights, despite decriminalizing homosexual acts in 1993.

North America

The subject of gay rights also proved deeply divisive in the United States. In Canada, homosexuality was decriminalized in 1969 and same-sex marriage made legal in 2005, but in the US, the issue exposed a cultural rift. The country became both a hotbed of gay rights activism and a bastion of traditional values, with some determined to outlaw homosexuality as an offence against God and America itself. In 1962, homosexuality – defined by law as sodomy – was illegal in every US state bar Illinois. By 2003, it was still illegal in 13 states; in Idaho, it carried a sentence of life imprisonment. American gay rights campaigners, whether in California or New York, faced an unforgiving Middle America.

Legal precedents

Same-sex marriage was a peculiarly unstable legal minefield in the US. As early as 1971, the US Supreme Court had refused to rule on the

matter, dismissing it "for want of a substantial federal question". A series of later cases were no more illuminating, but a decisive moment appeared to have been reached in 1996, with the passing of the Defense of Marriage Act (DOMA). This was the product of a series of state-initiated actions that collectively made clear that any US state had the right "not to recognize same-sex marriages". Even as he signed it into law, US president Bill Clinton described the DOMA as "divisive and unnecessary".

The first same-sex couple to marry legally in the US, Marcia Kadish (left) and Tanya McCloskey exchanged rings at the city hall in Cambridge, Massachusetts, on 17 May 2004.

Clarity came with two further Supreme Court rulings. In 2013, in *United States v. Windsor*, the Court decreed that much of the DOMA was unconstitutional. Those states that had already declared same-sex marriage to be legal (Massachusetts was the first) were joined by a flood of others. In 2015, in *Obergefell v.*

Roy Jenkins, the British home secretary in 1967, championed the Sexual Offences Act as part of reforms of what he called "civilized society".

The Sexual Offences Act

In 1885, the UK Parliament passed the Criminal Law Amendment Act, which made all homosexual acts between men illegal. But by the mid-1950s, despite continued social prejudice against homosexuality, there was increasing recognition that its criminalization was an anachronism. The Wolfenden Report of 1957, commissioned by the government, stated that what consenting adults did in private was "not the law's business". But the report was sidelined by the government, which feared a public

outcry. It was not until the mid-1960s that a cross-party initiative was launched to decriminalize homosexuality.

In 1967, the reform became law with the passing of the Sexual Offences Act. Tellingly, however, the homosexual age of consent was set at 21: only in 2000 was it lowered to 16, the same as for heterosexual consent. The Act applied only to England and Wales. Homosexuality finally became legal in Scotland in 1981, and in Northern Ireland in 1982.

Hodges, the Supreme Court, citing the Fourteenth Amendment, obliged all states to perform and recognize same-sex marriages. At a stroke, gay marriage, with every legal right and obligation enjoyed by and conferred on heterosexual marriage, had become a fact of American life. It was a fundamental shift. In 1996, only 27 per cent of Americans were in favour of same-sex marriage; in 2019, the figure was 61 per cent.

Religious objections

While progressive attitudes to gay rights and same-sex marriage appeared to represent a new norm in the West, in reality they were outliers. In 2005, Pope John-Paul II, an otherwise noted champion of human freedoms, claimed that homosexual marriages were part of "a new ideology of evil … insidiously threatening society". "Homosexual acts", he stated in 2000, "go against natural law."

Catholic teaching found its most ready ally in the Muslim world. In 2019, Iran may have been extreme in still declaring homosexuality to be punishable by death, but in most Muslim countries it remained illegal. The extent to which gay people were persecuted varied across the Islamic world, but the essential point was the same: homosexuality was a deviance from Sharia law. The persecutions of homosexuals in Chechnya from 2017 were not unrepresentative in presuming homosexuality to be a perversion.

Across much of Africa and Asia, homosexuality remained a more or less unmentionable subject. While it was decriminalized in China in

Campaigners for same-sex marriage celebrated outside the US Supreme Court on 26 June 2015 – the day it ruled that same-sex marriages were legal across the whole of the United States.

> Marriage as a union of man and woman uniquely involving the procreating and rearing of children within the family is as old as the Book of Genesis.
> **Minnesota Supreme Court, 1971**

1997, in India it was decriminalized only in 2018. In both cases, almost no other civil rights were extended to homosexuals. South Africa is the only African country to have made same-sex marriage legal (in 2006), while Taiwan is the only country in Asia to have done so (in 2019).

Trans rights

Since at least 2000, many in the West have also embraced a belief in transgender rights: that a person's biological gender is less important than their identification with either gender. A biological male can identify as a female, and a biological female can identify as a male. This idea rests on the belief that societies too readily force boys and girls into predetermined gender-based roles, resulting in alienation and confusion for some individuals. But the concept left the rest of the world bemused, and some westerners thought it was pushing the liberated sexual agenda too far. Even some stalwart defenders of women's rights drew the line: in 2015, Germaine Greer, Australian intellectual and author of *The Female Eunuch*, said that in her opinion, transgender women were "not women".

Human values

A core truth has remained. For all that the championing of non-heterosexual rights has been a near-exclusively Western concern, the principle that drove it was a defence of the values that inform humanity as a whole. Any human being has the right to be judged on their own terms. Sexuality can never be dismissed; it remains a fundamental of human existence. But it is no guide to the morality of any person. ■

COMPASSION IS NOT A CRIME
EUTHANASIA (2001)

IN CONTEXT

FOCUS
Criminal law

BEFORE
1997 Oregon becomes the first US state to legalize assisted suicide.

1998 Dignitas, the world's first provider of euthanasia services, opens in Switzerland.

AFTER
2002 Belgium follows the Dutch by legalizing euthanasia and assisted suicide.

2005 France's Leonetti law allows limitation of treatment for patients at the end of life.

2017 Belgium reports 2,309 legal deaths from euthanasia – two of which are of minors.

2019 Italy's highest court rules that assisted suicide is not always a crime.

2019 The controversial case of Vincent Lambert ends with the French court ruling that his life support can be turned off.

Euthanasia remains one of the most contentious issues of the 21st century. Many ask if the deliberate taking of a human life is ever justified. Medical ethics are intended to preserve human life, not to end it, and almost every religion is similarly opposed to so-called mercy killings. There is also concern that legalized euthanasia could lead to sanctioned killing of the elderly, disabled, and vulnerable without their consent. On the other hand, there are circumstances of such incurable suffering that extending life amounts to a form of torture.

At the centre of this debate is modern medical science, which can sustain life but cannot always stop the suffering of those it keeps alive. For patients who hope only for an end to their agonies, why should their desire for the right to die be overridden by the scruples of others? The point is thrown into sharper relief when the means to a painless, medically administered death are so readily available.

Clarifying the debate
Definitions are key in understanding the debate. Euthanasia is when a doctor is legally able to bring about the death of a patient who is suffering from an incurable or terminal disease. It is subdivided into voluntary euthanasia, which is carried out with the consent of the patient, and non-voluntary, where the patient is being kept alive artificially on life support and is unable to give their consent, so a third party, invariably a close family member, provides consent.

Euthanasia can be either active – brought about by the doctor, by means of an injection – or passive, in that life-sustaining medicines are withheld. The latter is not to be confused with palliative sedation, when terminally ill patients are kept under sedation until they die. In contrast to euthanasia, assisted

Reject the temptation …
to use medicine to support
a possible willingness
of the patient to die.
Pope Francis, 2019

See also: The Universal Declaration of Human Rights 222–29 ▪ The European Convention on Human Rights 230–33 ▪ *Roe v. Wade* 260–63 ▪ The Dickey–Wicker Amendment 284

suicide (sometimes called physician-assisted suicide or assisted dying) means deliberately offering help to someone who wants to kill him- or herself – for example, when a physician gives the patient lethal drugs to take. Some see the term "assisted dying" as different, since it specifies that the patient must have a terminal illness and be in the last six months of life, but in practice the two phrases tend to be used interchangeably.

Moves to legalization

Opinion in the West has begun to tilt in favour of euthanasia. The Netherlands was the first country to legalize it, in 2001, with effect from 2002, followed by Belgium in 2002 and by Luxembourg and Colombia in 2020. Assisted suicide was legalized in Canada in 2016, in nine US states and Washington, DC, between 1997 and 2020, and in the Australian states of Victoria and Western Australia in 2019. The Netherlands, Belgium, and Luxembourg all made assisted suicide legal at the same time as euthanasia. Although euthanasia

is prohibited in Switzerland, the country has allowed assisted suicide since 1942 and is unique in that it offers assisted suicide to foreign nationals. In each of these countries where it is legal, permitted circumstances vary widely, such as the condition of the patient and the age requirement. In 2014, for example, Belgium dropped all age restrictions.

Further guidelines

In all cases, strict legal guidelines have been put in place. In Belgium, for example, which permits both

British author Terry Pratchett, best known for his fantasy novels such as the *Discworld* series, became an advocate for assisted dying after he was diagnosed with Alzheimer's.

euthanasia and assisted suicide, the patient must be suffering from "an incurable disorder", they must be "conscious and competent", and they must supply a written request. If death is not imminent, there must be a second medical opinion to back the original decision in favour of euthanasia, and there must be a delay of at least one month between the formal request and the act itself. Almost exactly the same conditions are in place in the Netherlands.

Public opinion

Euthanasia remains illegal in most Western nations, but in Britain, where it is also a crime, public opinion polls in 2019 showed a shift in support for euthanasia at 84 per cent. Medical opinion, however, remains divided over a legal means of ending life for those in intolerable pain. ▪

If an adult who is suffering and dying has requested euthanasia, why should others have the right to deny them?
Carmenza Ochoa
Right to a Dignified Death Foundation, 2015

Fabiano Antoniani

Almost no case more exactly highlighted the arguments over assisted suicide than that of Italian DJ and music producer Fabiano Antoniani. In 2014, a car crash left him tetraplegic and blind – in essence, physically helpless but still mentally alert. His case was taken up by Italy's leading campaigner for assisted suicide, Marco Cappato. In 2017, Cappato arranged for Antoniani to be taken to Switzerland, where, on 27 February, at the age of 40, he died from assisted suicide. Cappato was then charged with complicity in Antoniani's death, facing 12 years in prison. In September 2019, Italy's highest court declared him not guilty, saying that, in certain circumstances, anyone who "facilitates the suicidal intention ... of a patient kept alive by life-support treatments and suffering from an irreversible pathology" should not be punished.

THE CAUSE OF ALL HUMANITY

THE INTERNATIONAL CRIMINAL COURT (2002)

IN CONTEXT

FOCUS
International law

BEFORE
1950 The Fourth Geneva Convention becomes the foundation of global humanitarian law.

1998 The Rome Statute creates the International Criminal Court (ICC).

AFTER
2005 The ICC issues its first indictment against three Ugandan rebel commanders for war crimes and crimes against humanity.

2009 The trial begins of Thomas Lubanga, a rebel fighter in the Democratic Republic of Congo. He is later convicted of war crimes, the ICC's first conviction.

2019 The ICC authorizes an investigation into alleged crimes against humanity in Myanmar (Burma).

The ICC's logo is clearly visible on a glass wall in front of its headquarters in The Hague, the Netherlands. This, the Court's first permanent premises, was opened in 2015.

The idea of an international tribunal to prosecute war crimes dates back to the period after World War I and arguments over trying Kaiser Wilhelm for starting the conflict. It wasn't until after World War II, however, that the world's first international criminal tribunal was created. The Nuremberg and Tokyo tribunals prosecuted the senior political and military leaders of Germany and Japan for the actions of their troops during the war, the Holocaust, and their responsibility for starting the war. But these tribunals were not permanent, and after they had delivered their final judgements they ceased to operate.

During the Cold War, tensions between the Soviet Union (USSR) and the United States meant that there was no consensus at the United Nations (UN) on tackling international crimes. It was only after the end of the Cold War in 1991 that the idea of a permanent international criminal court was examined. The outbreak of civil wars in which horrific crimes were committed in the former Yugoslavia and Rwanda led to the creation of war crimes tribunals (1993–2017, Yugoslavia; 1994–2015, Rwanda) to deal with those specific conflicts. In the late 1990s, the UN General Assembly set up a series of meetings to create a new international court. At the final meeting in Rome in 1998, a treaty known as the Rome Statute of the International Criminal Court was agreed and, as of 2019, it had 123 signatories. The International Criminal Court (ICC) opened in The Hague in 2002 and issued its first indictments in 2005.

The ICC deals with four types of international crime, all of which are contained in the Rome Statute: war crimes, crimes against humanity, genocide, and the crime of aggression. The Rome Statute also clarifies how trials are to be conducted, the rights of defendants in ICC trials, and other aspects of the Court's administration.

International crimes

War crimes relate to the conduct of armed hostilities either between states or in situations where there are organized armed groups of rebels fighting the government of a state. War crimes originated with the 1899 and 1907 Hague Conventions relating to the methods of permissible warfare and were later developed in the Geneva Conventions, which regulate both

See also: The Geneva Conventions 152–55 ▪ The Hague Conventions 174–77 ▪ The Nuremberg trials 202–09 ▪ The Genocide Convention 210–11 ▪ The United Nations and International Court of Justice 212–19

the way that armies fight and other issues around a conflict, such as the treatment of prisoners of war. War may involve killing, but engaging in conduct such as ordering troops to kill enemy soldiers running away or surrendering – as Rwandan commander Bosco Ntaganda did in eastern Congo – is a war crime.

In 2016, the ICC convicted Ahmad al-Mahdi for the war crime of intentionally targeting religious and cultural sites in Timbuktu during fighting between insurgents and government forces in Mali.

Crimes against humanity differ from war crimes in that their target is civilians, not soldiers. Murder, enslavement, torture, deportation, and a number of other practices are considered a crime against humanity if they are perpetrated in an organized armed attack against a civilian population, and if the commanding officer of the group carrying out that armed attack had knowledge, or ought to have known, of the attack. Sexual violence and the punishment of civilians are classified as crimes against humanity.

Since 2016, more than one million Rohingya people of western Myanmar have been forced out of their country in what the UN has called an act of ethnic cleansing.

In both Kenya (2007–08) and the Ivory Coast (2010–11), organized violence in election campaigns – including mobs murdering political rivals and opposition supporters being beaten up – was deemed to constitute a crime against humanity. Prior to his death in 2011, the ICC was investigating Colonel Muammar Gaddafi for ordering armed retaliation against protestors. In 2019, the ICC agreed to open an investigation into whether the forcible deportation of the Rohingya people from the north of Myanmar is a crime against humanity.

Genocide is an attempt to destroy in whole or in part an ethnic or religious group. It was originally codified in the Genocide Convention in 1948. People have been prosecuted for genocide in the special tribunals in Rwanda and the former Yugoslavia. The ICC has only charged one person with genocide to date – former Sudanese president Omar al-Bashir, who was charged in 2010.

The crime of aggression is the use of armed force by one state against the "sovereignty, territorial integrity, or political independence" of another. Unlike the other crimes, aggression deals with the process of starting wars. It was not included in the original draft of the Rome Statute, but in 2010 the Statute was modified to include it. It was only activated in 2017, when enough states agreed to the definition.

Who the ICC can prosecute

Since the ICC does not have the capacity to prosecute every single international crime, it focuses on the most serious cases and on those who have what it terms "superior responsibility". Article 28 of the Rome Statute makes a military commander responsible for the crimes of the soldiers under their command and makes political leaders responsible for controlling the police and military in their country. When a country signs up to the ICC, it is expected to incorporate all of the definitions of international crimes within the Rome Statute »

Jurisdiction of the court shall be limited to the most serious crimes of concern to the international community as a whole.
Article 1 of the Rome Statute of the ICC, 1998

We can always do more. We can always do better. And we should not rest as long as there is one perpetrator that did not answer for his crimes.
Judge Song Sang-hyun
Former president of the ICC (1941–)

If a crime prosecutable by the ICC is committed, there are three ways to bring a case.

The government of the country in which that crime is committed **refers the case to the ICC** for prosecution.

The prosecutor of the ICC can authorize an investigation into a situation in **a country that is signed up** to the ICC.

The UN Security Council instructs the ICC to **investigate the case**.

into its own domestic law. People who commit international crimes can then be dealt with in their own country. The ICC only prosecutes someone when a country is unwilling or unable to do so. This is known as the complementarity principle, but it has been criticized as skewed, since it is easier for richer countries with more developed and stable legal systems to carry out prosecutions than those where, for example, the legal system may have collapsed.

The president of Kenya, Uhuru Kenyatta, was charged with crimes against humanity in relation to incidents of post-election violence in Kenya in 2007 and was referred to the ICC three years later. He was one of six suspects considered responsible for instigating the violence, but the charges against him were later dropped due to a lack of evidence. In 2009, the ICC issued an arrest warrant for Omar al-Bashir, the then president of Sudan, for crimes against

humanity, war crimes, and genocide in the Darfur region of Sudan. He was the first head of state to be indicted by the ICC. The Court followed the principle that even heads of state cannot expect legal immunity from prosecution in the context of such serious charges.

Criticism of the ICC

To date, the US, Russia, and China have refused to join the ICC. Since these countries are permanent members of the United Nations Security Council, there is no effective way to prosecute any crimes committed by them on their own territory, since they can simply veto any UN Security Council Resolution involving the ICC. However, that evasion does not apply with alleged crimes they commit on the territory of an ICC member. Both the UK and France are permanent members of the UN Security Council and the ICC. The ICC conducted an investigation into the conduct of British forces in Iraq in the mid-2000s, but this

Sudanese president Omar al-Bashir (centre, holding up his cane) was charged with instigating the Darfur genocide, the first of the 21st century, in which up to 400,000 people died.

Don't be vague.
Go to The Hague.
Kenyan politicians
Referring to
election violence cases, 2007

ended without any indictments. The ICC has recently tried to expand its scope by ruling that it can hear cases relating to countries that are not ICC signatories if the cases concern refugees who have fled from a non-signatory nation to a signatory one. In 2019, lawyers filed a case on behalf of Syrian refugees (Syria is not a signatory to the Rome Statute) who fled to Jordan (which is).

The majority of cases that have come before the ICC are from Africa, which has led to the

In 2016, the ICC convicted former Congolese vice president Jean-Pierre Bemba Gombo of murder, rape, and pillaging. However, the conviction was overturned in 2018.

Court being criticized as a neo-colonial institution and some countries threatening to withdraw from the ICC. Other countries have tried to withdraw in protest at the ICC beginning an investigation in their country. In 2018, when the ICC began investigating the government of the Philippines for crimes against humanity committed during its "war on drugs", it officially withdrew from the Court.

Only a handful of people are serving sentences as a result of convictions by the ICC. Canadian professor of international criminal law William Schabas described the progress of the ICC as "glacial" in its early years. Even where cases have resulted in a conviction, there have been some high-profile appeals. In 2016, Jean-Pierre Bemba Gombo, former vice president of the Democratic Republic of Congo, was convicted for war crimes and crimes against humanity when the militia he commanded was found to have carried out massacres in the Central African Republic in 2003. The conviction was later overturned on appeal because of procedural errors in his trial.

Despite these criticisms, the ICC remains an important forum for investigating some of the deadliest atrocities taking place around the world. ■

There must be justice.
There must be fairness.
Fatou Bensouda
Chief prosecutor of the ICC

Fatou Bensouda

Former lawyer and Gambian justice minister Fatou Bom Bensouda was born in 1961, and has served as the ICC's prosecutor since 2012. As such, she is responsible for making decisions on which suspects to investigate and then which to prosecute for international crimes. The prosecutor's office is independent of the Court, so to open an investigation, the prosecutor needs to apply for permission to a panel of judges at the ICC.

During her term in office, ending in 2021, Bensouda has broadened the focus of the ICC, launching investigations into possible war crimes in Afghanistan, Israel, and Myanmar and Bangladesh. She has also tried to increase the number of prosecutions for rape and the exploitation of women in armed conflict.

DOPING DESTROYS FAIR PLAY
THE INTERNATIONAL CONVENTION AGAINST DOPING IN SPORT (2005)

The use of performance-enhancing drugs in sport was widespread long before the adoption of the UNESCO anti-doping convention in October 2005. In 1967, the International Olympic Committee (IOC) published a list of prohibited substances, and in 1988 Canadian sprinter Ben Johnson was stripped of his gold medal at the Seoul Olympics after testing positive for anabolic steroids.

The scale of the problem was such that, by the early 21st century, it was deemed necessary to invoke the legal authority of the United Nations to deal with it. As the UN's Educational, Scientific, and Cultural Organization (UNESCO) considered sport to be "an educational tool", it took on the role. Its convention was ratified in 2007, and signatory nations are bound by international law to its provisions. Much of the practical work falls within the remit of other bodies, including the World Anti-Doping Agency (WADA), established by the IOC in 1999. It cooperates closely with national organizations and is party to the World Anti-Doping Code, first issued in 2004 and regularly updated.

In many cases, the motive for doping in sport (namely, cheating) is a simple matter of an individual's ambition. But the practice also occurs as part of deliberate state-sponsored initiatives. East Germany was the first country to introduce systematic doping, in the 1970s. In 2016–17, WADA cited Italy, France, and the US as having the most athletes violating the Code, and bodybuilding, athletics, and cycling as having the most violations. ∎

Marion Jones (centre) won three gold and two bronze medals for the US at the 2000 Olympics. She initially denied accusations of doping but seven years later admitted to steroid use.

See also: DNA testing 272–73 ▪ The Portuguese drug strategy 290–91 ▪ The Match-Fixing Task Force 306–07

THE BATTLE AGAINST CLIMATE CHANGE

THE KYOTO PROTOCOL (2005)

IN CONTEXT

FOCUS
Environmental law

BEFORE
1988 The Intergovernmental Panel on Climate Change (IPCC) is established.

1992 At the Earth Summit in Rio de Janeiro, Brazil, the first international goals for emissions reduction are agreed.

1997 The US Senate refuses to ratify the Kyoto Protocol, on the basis that developing countries are exempt from compliance.

AFTER
2009 The Copenhagen Summit ends in stalemate: no legally binding commitments are made.

2015 The Paris Agreement sets non-binding targets to limit the global temperature rise to 2°C (3.6°F) by 2100.

2017 President Donald Trump withdraws the US from the Paris Agreement.

The Kyoto Protocol, adopted in 1997 and enacted in 2005, was the first agreement between industrialized nations to make defined reductions in their emissions of greenhouse gases. The Protocol built on the United Nations Framework Convention on Climate Change (UNFCCC), adopted at the Rio Earth Summit in June 1992. The signatories to the UNFCCC have met annually since 1995 at Conferences of the Parties (COPs). The targets of the Kyoto Protocol are binding under international law.

In signing the Protocol, parties acknowledged that emissions from burning fossil fuels are leading to potentially catastrophic increases in the world's temperature, with predicted consequences including rising sea levels; species extinction and biodiversity loss; and increases in extreme weather events such as floods, droughts, and wildfires. The goal of limiting the increase in global temperature to less than 2°C (3.6°F) by 2100, as set out in the Paris Agreement at the 2015 COP, would demand unprecedented efforts.

Given the monetary cost of the reforms needed, not to mention the lifestyle changes required, results have been mixed. While some countries have met their targets, political leaders have clashed over the complex issue of the relative responsibilities of developed (signatory) nations and of major emerging economies. Meanwhile, global emissions and temperatures have continued to rise. ∎

Stabilization of greenhouse gas concentrations in the atmosphere [to] prevent dangerous anthropogenic interference with the climate system.
Objective (Article 2) of the UNFCCC

See also: The United Nations and International Court of Justice 212–19 ∎ The Endangered Species Act 264–65 ∎ The World Network of Biosphere Reserves 270–71

IT'S SPORT AGAINST THESE PEOPLE

THE MATCH-FIXING TASK FORCE (2011)

IN CONTEXT

FOCUS
Sports law

BEFORE
1919 Baseball team Chicago White Sox are bribed to throw the World Series, sending shockwaves across the US.

2010 A confidential FIFA report leaked to the press suggests some friendly games were fixed in the run-up to the World Cup.

2011 Istanbul police arrest 60 people on suspicion of match-fixing in Turkey.

AFTER
2013 Alleged match-fixing syndicate leader Dan Tan is arrested by Singapore police.

2014 The Council of Europe Convention on the Manipulation of Sports Competitions is signed; it comes into force in September 2019.

2016 Tennis star Novak Djokovic claims he was asked to throw a match in 2007.

Sport in all its forms has long been associated with betting. And the potential for illegal gambling activities to damage the integrity of sport has always been a threat.

However, attempts to tackle that threat took a new turn in 2011 when INTERPOL (the International Criminal Police Organization) established its Match-Fixing Task Force (IMFTF). The reason was simple: sport had become a vast global business that was increasingly vulnerable to systematic efforts to cheat. One long-standing method of cheating was to induce competitors to deliberately "throw" (lose) a game, so that the result of any sporting event could be determined in advance. Criminal gambling organizations could reap vast rewards in this way, placing bets on the basis of inside information. INTERPOL described such match-fixing as a trillion-dollar industry. If sport were to retain its integrity, eradicating such corruption had become essential.

Global networks

The epicentre of illegal betting syndicates is Southeast Asia, where many sports are accused of corruption, with team owners, referees, and players all implicated.

From about 2010, the Asian syndicates turned their attentions to the global stage. Although sports played by individuals are easier to fix than team sports, the latter are prime targets because their global popularity generates so many bets. One example was the Pakistan cricket team, with two of its players found guilty of deliberately bowling no-balls at predetermined moments during a Test match in 2010. This practice of fixing a specific aspect

The involvement of organized crime in the manipulation of sports competitions makes this phenomenon a global threat to the integrity and ethics of sport.
The Council of Europe, 2019

See also: INTERPOL 220–21 ▪ The International Criminal Court 298–303
▪ The International Convention Against Doping in Sport 304

> Sport is a target for **betting syndicates** everywhere, and the **possibilities for match-fixing** are clear.

As sport becomes a **global industry**, the **rewards for illicit betting** grow.

Southeast Asia sees a huge expansion in match-fixing **crime syndicates**.

Law-enforcement agencies worldwide **share intelligence** to help battle criminal organizations.

Cross-border investigation has achieved some success against match-fixing.

The Kelong King

Born in Singapore in 1964, Tan Seet Eng, also known as Dan Tan, was once described by INTERPOL as "the leader of the world's most notorious match-fixing syndicate". Widely known as the "Kelong King" ("Cheating King"), Tan is alleged to have started match-fixing in Singapore in the early 1990s, working with an associate, Wilson Raj Perumal, and was briefly jailed for illegal bookmaking. By 2010, Italian football had allegedly become his target, with games fixed in conjunction with crime rings in Eastern Europe.

Tan and Perumal were also alleged to have fixed matches in Hungary, Nigeria, and Finland. In 2011, Perumal was arrested in Finland and denounced Tan, claiming that he was the ringleader of a global match-fixing network. In 2013, Tan was arrested by Singapore police under the terms of a local law, and detained with no formal charges. Released in December 2019, he still faces charges in Italy and Hungary. He has denied any wrongdoing.

of a game – unrelated to the final result – is called spot-fixing and can involve huge sums of money.

Working with a global network of law-enforcement agencies, the IMFTF shares intelligence and provides a platform for cross-border investigations. In one success story, Dan Tan (see box, right) was arrested and detained in Singapore. In 2011, FIFA, the international governing body of football, agreed to grant millions of euros to INTERPOL for an anti-corruption training programme. But FIFA was itself rocked by scandal, with charges of corruption against many of its top officials, including its president, Sepp Blatter, and allegations of bribery

focused on the bidding process that led to FIFA awarding the hosting of the 2022 World Cup to Qatar.

The extent to which any organization could hope to end corruption on such a scale is limited, and online betting has made gambling even more attractive to criminals. Yet, by reaching across borders, INTERPOL has had some success in stemming the problem. ▪

South African cricket captain "Hansie" Cronje (foreground) was barred from the sport for life in 2000 after admitting match-fixing. He died in a plane crash in 2002.

THE RIGHT TO BE FORGOTTEN

GOOGLE SPAIN V. AEPD AND MARIO COSTEJA GONZÁLEZ (2014)

IN CONTEXT

FOCUS
Privacy law

BEFORE
1995 The EU creates its Data Protection Directive aiming to safeguard any individual's personal information.

AFTER
2003 American singer/actor Barbra Streisand attempts to suppress online images of her home, giving rise to the "Streisand effect" of creating even more interest in them.

2015 France's regulatory body CNIL (National Commission on Informatics and Liberty) tries to force Google to apply EU rules on privacy worldwide.

2016 The General Data Protection Regulation (GDPR) is approved by the EU Parliament.

2019 The ECJ concedes that its attempt to legislate for a global enforcement of the right to be forgotten has to be restricted to Europe.

In 2009, Spanish businessman Mario Costeja González was searching for his name on the Google search engine when he came across two legal notices that had appeared in a Spanish newspaper 11 years earlier – official acknowledgments that his house had been forcibly sold to clear a debt. When the newspaper digitized its old editions, Google had created a link to the notices. The issue was a matter of public record, but it meant that González's former financial woes were now available for anyone to access online. Since he worked as a financial adviser, this was potentially damaging for his career. The newspaper refused

Mario Costeja González refused to disclose how much money he spent on his legal battle with Google, insisting that it had been a fight for ideals, and those ideals had won.

to take down the notices, pointing out that it had been legally obliged to print them, and Google was similarly uncooperative. González went to court.

The Spanish Data Protection Agency agreed that Google should "delist" the links to González's earlier financial misadventures, but it had no means of compelling the company to obey. A Spanish court found itself unable to rule on the matter, so it was referred to the EU's highest court, the European Court of Justice (ECJ). The case raised two fundamental questions. First, is there a legal "right to be forgotten", with the past deemed legally irrelevant? And second, if such a right exists, how can it be applied to the internet?

Public interest

In its defence, Google argued that, as an American company, it was answerable only to US law; it was not the "data collector" and provided no more than a search engine to signpost information held by others; and since the information about González was demonstrably true, any attempt to suppress it represented an assault on freedom of expression –

See also: The US Constitution and Bill of Rights 110–17 ▪ The European Convention on Human Rights 230–33 ▪ The European Court of Justice 234–41 ▪ The WIPO Copyright Treaty 286–87 ▪ The Open Internet Order 310–13

The criteria used to impose the "right to be forgotten" were impossible to define from a legal point of view.
Enrique Dans
Spanish professor of information systems and innovation, 2019

in other words, the forced sale of González's house was a legitimate matter of public interest and should not be made to disappear.

The ECJ ruling

Any rulings by the ECJ are initially subject to a preliminary decision by an advocate general who, in 2013, dismissed Google's first argument, arguing that Google Spain was a Spanish company and so subject to European law. He supported the company's other objections, and it was assumed that the ECJ would follow suit.

In 2014, however, in a verdict that stunned many, the Court determined that Google is a "data collector" and so is responsible for whatever information its searches throw up. And it ruled that online data could be removed if it was deemed to be "inadequate, no longer relevant, or excessive … in the light of the time that had elapsed".

The 2014 ECJ ruling highlighted some of the key cultural and legal differences between countries. On the one hand, in the US the right

to freedom of expression (including freedom of the press) trumps all others. On the other hand, French law has enshrined *le droit à l'oubli* ("the right to be forgotten") since 2010, valuing privacy protection as a fundamental human right, one that should take precedence over the right to unfettered expression. A second issue is that internet content is effectively subject to no single law, national or international. One more impassioned critic of the ECJ ruling wondered why a law outlawing gravity had not been passed at the same time, since it would have had about as much effect.

Major climbdown

In 2019, the ECJ conceded that its strictures could only apply to Europe. A key objection to the ECJ's ruling had been that whatever Google may have been forced to "delist" was still available to anyone with internet access: the link could be removed, but not the content. Any legal judgement, however powerful, that sought to defend the "right to be forgotten" was

European data regulators should not be able to determine the search results that internet users around the world get to see.
Thomas Hughes
Executive director of privacy group Article 19, 2019

bound to be rendered irrelevant in a digital world driven by a desire for instantly available information. What was intended as a serious re-evaluation of legal rights to privacy in a new digital world ended in farce. González embarked on his campaign against Google to protect his privacy but ended up known around the world for the very thing he wanted to be forgotten. ∎

The role of an advocate general

In September 2019, when the ECJ reluctantly agreed that the right to be forgotten can only be applied to EU member states, it did so on the advice of Polish advocate general Maciej Szpunar. Five years earlier, when it ruled that Google was responsible for data thrown up by it, it did so against the advice of another advocate general, Finn Niilo Jääskinen.

The advocates general act independently of the ECJ's own judges, and they examine only those cases where the Court considers a new point of law is raised. An advocate general is allocated to each such case, and he or she has the authority to question the parties in dispute. Although their role is advisory, the "reasoned submissions" they produce are followed in most cases by the ECJ judges when they deliberate. There are 11 advocates general, who are nominated by EU member states, and they serve a term of six years.

A FREE AND OPEN INTERNET

THE OPEN INTERNET ORDER (2015)

IN CONTEXT

FOCUS
Internet law

BEFORE
1996 The Telecommunications Act regulates only existing cable-modem ISPs in the US; broadband ISPs are exempt.

2010 Chile is the first country in the world to enshrine net neutrality in law.

2014 In an FCC poll in the US, 99 per cent of replies support net neutrality.

AFTER
2015 EU Regulation 2015/2120 seeks to protect equal network access in Europe.

2017 The FCC reverses its 2015 ruling with a Restoring Internet Freedom Order.

2019 The District of Columbia Court of Appeals supports the FCC's decision to end net neutrality.

Almost no question about the internet and its future in the US has proved more contentious and troubled than that of net neutrality (a term coined in 2003 by Tim Wu, a law professor at Columbia University). Net neutrality is the principle that access to all content and services on the internet should be free from interference by internet service providers (ISPs). It concerns only the delivery mechanism of digital data; it does not alter the digital data itself.

However, net neutrality does determine not just how information can be accessed but, in practice, what information can be accessed. Given the ubiquity of the internet

See also: The US Constitution and Bill of Rights 110–17 ▪ The Universal Declaration of Human Rights 222–29
▪ The WIPO Copyright Treaty 286–87 ▪ *Google Spain v. AEPD and Mario Costeja González* 308–09

and, in consequence, the world's near-absolute dependence on it, this is a matter of vital importance.

ISPs and content providers

The internet is a digital interaction between content providers and consumers, allowing more or less limitless transfer (traffic) of digital data between content providers and consumers – everything from messages, emails, and online stores to video-streaming and social media services and search engines. The physical link between them is a vast, endlessly complex global network of cables and transmission towers, provided by ISPs. As well as building this costly infrastructure, each ISP designs a financial model for charging all the suppliers and consumers that use their network.

Any internet user (provider or consumer) must pay an ISP for using its network. If the ISP adhered to net neutrality, the user could be confident that their access to the internet would be entirely even-handed. The ISP

> We nurture and protect our information networks because they stand at the core of our economies, our democracies, and our cultural and personal lives.
> **Tim Berners-Lee**
> **Inventor of the World Wide Web, 2006**

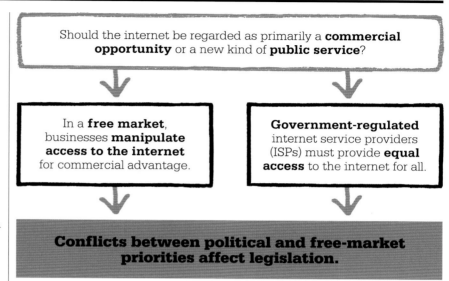

Should the internet be regarded as primarily a **commercial opportunity** or a new kind of **public service**?

In a **free market**, businesses **manipulate access to the internet** for commercial advantage.

Government-regulated internet service providers (ISPs) must provide **equal access** to the internet for all.

Conflicts between political and free-market priorities affect legislation.

would not give priority or lesser treatment to any content. Even the largest content providers with countless users, such as Google, YouTube, Facebook, and Twitter, would be treated in exactly the same way as the humblest, such as the website of a local sole trader or community.

In an unregulated market, ISPs could choose, for their commercial advantage, to block content or to "throttle" it, by deliberately slowing the transmission speed so that it downloads slowly or has to be of low quality. They could discriminate by pricing – for example, charging more to content suppliers for artificially speeded "fast lanes" (paid priority) or zero-rating access (limiting the content available to free users), which could leave other content suppliers at a disadvantage.

In 1996, when the internet was in its infancy, the first attempt to regulate ISPs in the US came with the Telecommunications Act. It classified ISPs that had existing

telephone networks (cable-modem or dial-up) as telecommunications services, or "common carriers" under the 1934 Telecommunications Act, to be regulated as public utilities. Broadband ISPs were classed as "information services" and exempt from regulation. The distinction was critical, as it governed whether ISPs were legally bound to provide equal access to content for all.

FCC policy

The Federal Communications Commission (FCC) is the regulatory body for all communication systems in the US, but over the years it has changed its policy several times. In 2002, the FCC reclassified even the cable-modem ISPs as "information services", not "common carriers". Its 2008 attempt to regulate ISPs was foiled (see box, p.312). Convinced that the advantages of net neutrality are overwhelming, and with strong public support, the FCC issued an Open Internet Order » in April 2015. This reinforced the idea that ISPs were basically no different from, for example, phone companies, by designating them as "telecommunications services" rather than "information services". ISPs were now obliged to provide equal internet access to all. The Order established clear guidelines, or "bright-line rules", that the ISPs had to abide by: no blocking, no throttling, increased transparency, and no paid prioritization.

Pros and cons

Before and after the 2015 Open Internet Order, debate raged over whether net neutrality should be protected by law. Should the US government treat the internet as a public good, subject to regulation as a public utility? Or should it allow the free market to set terms and conditions for internet access?

The supporters of legislation contend that benign government regulation is an essential condition for the advance of the internet, by giving the greatest benefits to the largest number. The internet is too important to be left to unfettered free markets. Almost any ISP has a vested commercial interest in

promoting or speeding certain sites and suppressing or blocking others. If ISPs favour those who pay most, those who pay least would be relegated to an internet hinterland. In addition, in rural areas where the choice of ISP is limited or non-existent, there is an obvious temptation for any ISP to abuse what is essentially a monopoly.

Another objection to self-regulation is that any two-track network (see diagram, right) amounts to a form of censorship, if ISPs determine what can and cannot be viewed purely on the basis of their own, short-term financial advantage. ISPs could also wield political influence – for example, by blocking websites.

Opponents of regulation no less forcefully argue that, since its sudden emergence in the 1990s, the internet has proved itself perfectly capable of self-regulation. ISPs argue for a two-track network governed by the free market. If, for example, a video-streaming service responsible for more than 30 per cent of all bandwidth use in the US crowds out other content providers who are all using the same ISPs, why should it not have to pay more

> This is no more a plan to regulate the Internet than the First Amendment is a plan to regulate free speech.
> **Tom Wheeler**
> **FCC chairman, 2015**

for its disproportionate use of limited bandwidth? In addition, any user of the internet, whether domestic or commercial, could then choose, if they want, to pay more for a faster, higher-quality service. Increased revenues to ISPs would result in greater investment in new infrastructure, to the long-term advantage of all.

Ironically, some competing corporations, using immense resources and each with their own commercial priorities, have clashed over the net neutrality issue. Google, for example, is a content provider but

Tom Wheeler, chairman of the FCC under President Obama, is a champion of net neutrality, and believes regulation is necessary.

Comcast and BitTorrent

One compelling argument against net neutrality is that it is difficult to enforce. Long before the FCC's 2017 reversal of net neutrality, ISPs had often illegally slowed traffic that they considered was consuming too much bandwidth.

The United States' most famous net neutrality case was in 2008. For several years, Comcast had systematically obstructed, or made effectively impossible, transfers of data via BitTorrent (a file-sharing service used to download large files such as

movies). Comcast claimed that they slowed BitTorrent transfers only during periods of high-density traffic, but they were slowing the transfers more or less permanently. Campaigners asserted this was "blocking free choice on the internet".

The FCC censured Comcast for violating net neutrality, by throttling BitTorrent, and in 2008 issued a cease-and-desist order. Comcast in turn sued the FCC in *Comcast Corp. v. FCC* and, in 2012, the District of Columbia Court of Appeals found against the FCC.

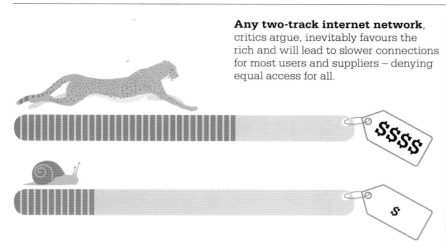

Any two-track internet network, critics argue, inevitably favours the rich and will lead to slower connections for most users and suppliers – denying equal access for all.

also has an ISP company, and has confronted heavyweight corporate ISP rivals, such as Comcast, Verizon, and AT&T – which have opposed net neutrality. As a search engine, sending huge amounts of data and therefore occupying an immense amount of bandwidth, Google has questioned why it should pay much higher prices for access, effectively subsidizing its rivals.

Political bias
There was a clear political element to the existing, often bitter, battle between the advocates of a

What is responsible for the phenomenal development of the internet? It certainly wasn't heavy-handed government regulation.
Ajit Pai
FCC chairman, 2017

regulated internet and those of a free-market internet. The five FCC commissioners responsible for the Open Internet Order in 2015 were all political appointees of President Barack Obama. By 2017, the mostly new FCC commissioners had been appointed by President Donald Trump. Their support for corporate interests was clear, and the FCC reversed its 2015 decision in December 2017, with a Restoring Internet Freedom Order, which also prohibited state or local regulation of ISPs.

The 2017 Order made inevitable legal battles with individual states that wanted to enact their own net neutrality. In early 2018, more than 20 states filed a lawsuit against the Order, but supporters of net neutrality suffered a significant setback in October 2019 when the District of Columbia Court of Appeals ruled that the FCC had acted within its rights in ending net neutrality. The Court's controversial ruling flew in the

Ajit Pai, made chairman of the FCC by President Trump in 2017, is a favoured target of net-neutrality campaigners. Ironically, he was first appointed to the FCC in 2012 by President Obama.

face of consistent public support for net neutrality: some polls showed 80 per cent of Americans were clearly in favour. The Supreme Court may be the ultimate arbiter of this otherwise unresolved and hugely controversial debate – a ruling by that court could have a direct impact on the position of the US as the dominant influence on the internet across the world.

Different approaches
The acute controversy around net neutrality in the US partly reflected the difficulty of legislating for a world where technology constantly evolves. The problem is not only confined to the US. In the European Union, for example, the preferred solution is strongly in favour of net neutrality, a position that even post-Brexit Britain endorses.

The European stance was partly driven by Finland, which in 2009 introduced a Universal Service Obligation (USO) that strongly supported net neutrality and made the provision of broadband a legal obligation. Broadband availability in rural areas in many countries is still frequently as pressing an issue as net neutrality. ∎

IT'S NOT ABOUT THE MONEY. IT IS ABOUT EQUALITY

EQUAL PAY CERTIFICATION (2017)

IN CONTEXT

FOCUS
Employment law, equal rights

BEFORE
1919 In the US, Michigan and Montana pass equal pay laws.

1951 The UN International Labour Organization's Equal Remuneration Convention states the principle of equal pay for men and women doing work of equal value.

1957 The Treaty of Rome lists equal pay for men and women as a key principle of the EEC.

1963 The Equal Pay Act is introduced in the US.

1975 Women in Iceland go on strike for a day, refusing to work, cook, or care for children.

AFTER
2019 New York governor Andrew Cuomo strengthens the state's 1944 legislation by forbidding potential employers to ask about previous salaries.

In June 2017, the parliament of Iceland passed legislation designed to close the gender pay gap. Like many countries, Iceland had long had equal pay laws, but employers still paid women less than men. The new laws were intended to make sure equal pay actually happened.

The legislation stated that every business in Iceland that employs more than 25 people must obtain a certificate that guarantees its pay structure complies with equal pay laws. Larger firms had to comply by the end of 2019; smaller firms between 2020 and 2022.

The change was heralded as a breakthrough for women, and led to calls for similar legislation in other countries. But critics insisted the law was unnecessary since Iceland already had laws that guaranteed women equal pay for equal work. They argued that research showing persistent gender wage gaps was

---

Women's pay remains **well behind men's pay** in almost every country.

Equal pay acts exist in most countries, but since they are **difficult to enforce**, they have only **narrowed the gap to a limited extent**.

But employers can still **sidestep equal pay legislation** by employing men and women in **different roles**.

In 2017, **Iceland passed legislation** forcing most employers to prove that their pay structure complies with a national **equal pay standard**.

See also: The Trade Union Act 156–59 ▪ The Workers' Accident Insurance System 164–67 ▪ The Representation of the People Act 188–89 ▪ The Civil Rights Act 248–53 ▪ *Roe v. Wade* 260–63 ▪ Same-sex marriage 292–95

The Ford machinists' strike

On 7 June 1968, women sewing machinists at Ford's car factory in Dagenham, UK, went on strike. They were making the covers for the cars' seats, and without their contribution, the production line soon ground to a halt. Led by Rose Boland, Eileen Pullen, Vera Sime, Gwen Davis, and Sheila Douglass, the machinists were protesting against the grading of their jobs as Grade B (less skilled), which meant they got less pay than most of the men, who were put in Grade C (more skilled).

They argued that sewing demanded a very high level of skill and so they should receive equal pay.

The strike attracted a lot of attention, since the factory was important to the UK's economy, and women in other jobs also began to campaign for equality. Eventually, Barbara Castle, the secretary of state for employment and productivity, negotiated a pay rise for the machinists, to within 8 per cent of the men's wage. The Equal Pay Act was introduced two years later.

Leaders of the machinists' strike protest outside the offices of Barbara Castle. Three weeks later, Castle agreed to listen to their grievances.

flawed, and that the new legislation would discourage employers from hiring women. They also pointed out that Iceland had been top of the World Economic Forum's Global Gender Gap Index – which monitors women's pay around the world – for nine years out of the previous 10.

The idea that women and men should be paid equally is an old one. In 1839, French author George Sand described in her play *Gabriel* "an impenetrable crystal vault" – what later feminists would call the "glass ceiling", the invisible barrier that stops women progressing as high in their careers as men.

Only after two world wars, when women had to take on jobs that had previously been done by men, were calls for equal pay widely heeded. In 1944, New York State legislated that women should be paid the same as men for the same work, which also became a key principle of the new European Economic Community (EEC), founded in 1957.

The US introduced its first national legislation with the Equal Pay Act of 1963, and the UK followed suit with its Equal Pay Act in 1970. Gradually, many other countries added their own laws.

Despite equal pay legislation, the gender pay gap – the average hourly percentage gap between the salaries received by men and women – has persisted. Women are paid on average just 77 per cent of what men are paid. The reasons for this are complex. More women than

In 99.6 per cent of all occupations, men get paid more than women. That's not an accident; that's discrimination.
Elizabeth Warren
American politician and lawyer (1949–)

men work in lower-paid jobs, such as nursing or teaching, so their overall pay rate is lower. Typically male sectors, such as engineering, by contrast, pay well. Women also have less time to do paid work – they carry out 76.4 per cent of domestic work and unpaid care globally. Even within companies women tend to occupy roles that pay less – and very few women rise to the top of the pay scale. Iceland is one of the more equal countries in the world, yet even there less than 20 per cent of CEOs are women.

Long road ahead

Iceland's legislation may not remove the differences between men and women in career needs and aspiration, but it is a clear step towards righting inequality. Even so, pay (along with education, health, and political representation) is just one aspect of an overall global gender gap of 68.6 per cent, which (based on the current rate of change across 153 countries) the World Economic Forum predicts will not close for 99.5 years. ▪

DIRECTO

RY

DIRECTORY

The legal milestones set out in this book have formed the backbone of modern law. These key developments owe a debt, not just to history's great legal scholars but also to monarchs, theologians, politicians, and campaigners who contributed to other initiatives, precedents, and pieces of legislation. Rulers such as Clovis and Genghis Khan imposed national civil law codes that influenced later governments. Islamic scholars produced the *Fatawa-e-Alamgiri* that inspired the codification of laws across South Asia, and President F.W. de Klerk took a step towards greater equality when he oversaw the dismantling of South Africa's apartheid laws. Each of the legal advances listed below has contributed to the evolution of modern lawmaking.

THE DRACONIAN CODE
621 BCE

In a bid to reduce arbitrary punishments and blood feuds, the Athenian aristocrat Draco was asked to compile the first written law code for the city-state of Athens. Draco's code favoured the powerful aristocrats and meted out severe punishments for even minor crimes. Athenians soon railed against the extreme penalties. In c. 594 BCE, the Athenian magistrate Solon repealed most of Draco's laws, retaining only his punishment of banishment for homicide. Today, anything that is perceived as overly harsh is called "draconian".
See also: Plato's *Laws* 31
▪ Aristotle and natural law 32–33

BOOKS OF PUNISHMENTS
536 BCE

The earliest known Chinese laws are the "books of punishments" (*hsing shu*), which Tzu-ch'an, prime minister of the state of Cheng, had inscribed onto a set of bronze tripod vessels. The vessels did not survive, but they are said to have listed 22 harsh punishments such as hard labour, mutilation, castration, and death. Evidence of their use and the opposition they aroused survives in a letter of protest from an official in a neighbouring state.
See also: Zhou dynasty China 24
▪ Confucianism, Daoism, and Legalism 26–29

THE TRIAL OF SOCRATES
399 BCE

The philosopher Socrates became a target when he positioned himself against Athenian democracy by arguing that, instead of rule by majority opinion, only the truly learned and wise should hold power. His teachings inspired many young Athenians to question the status quo, and in 399 BCE, three orators accused him of "impiety" and "corrupting the young". When a jury of 500 men, selected by drawing lots, found Socrates guilty, the philosopher was sentenced to death by the self-administration of poisonous hemlock.
See also: Plato's *Laws* 31
▪ Aristotle and natural law 32–33
▪ The trial of Galileo Galilei 93

KAPU
c. 500 CE

The ancient Hawaiian *kapu* system provided accepted codes for much of everyday life – religion, gender roles, lifestyle, and politics. Similar to the Polynesian tradition of taboo, *kapu* translates as "forbidden", but it can also mean "sacred". Breaking *kapu* invoked harsh penalties, even if the offence was unintentional. By the early 19th century, belief in the system had declined. In 1819, King Kamehameha II abolished it, publicly breaking *kapu* by allowing men and women to dine together.
See also: Confucianism, Daoism, and Legalism 26–29

THE LAWS OF ÆTHELBERT
600 CE

The earliest known piece of English law is a law code drawn up by Æthelbert, king of Kent, the first

Christian king in England. It survives in the 12th-century *Textus Roffensis* (*The Rochester Book*). As it is written in old English, rather than the customary Latin, it is also the first law code recorded in a Germanic language. It is based on German law and considers issues such as violent crime, rights and obligations, *wergeld* (compensation), and the status of the king.
See also: The Domesday Book 58–59 ▪ Magna Carta 66–71

THE TANG CODE
624 CE

China's long tradition of recording laws reaches back to the Western Zhou dynasty (*c.*1046–771 BCE). The Tang Code, with 502 articles and commentaries, is the earliest surviving complete legal code. It combines Confucian philosophy and the Legalist tradition of writing down laws, and consists of two parts: general rules and specific offences. The Tang Code influenced future legal codes in China and across East Asia.
See also: Zhou dynasty China 24 ▪ Confucianism, Daoism, and Legalism 26–29

THE BREHON LAW(S)
7th–17th century

The ancient Irish laws, known as Brehon law, or *Fénechas* (the law of the *Féni*, the free men of Ireland) were interpreted and preserved by wandering arbitrators called Brehons. Dating as far back as the Bronze Age but first written down in the seventh century CE, Brehon law was a hierarchical system, with harsher penalties imposed on those of lower rank. Its criminal

laws, however, discouraged violent and capital punishments, preferring fines and reparations. As England brought Ireland under its rule in the 1600s, Brehon law was banned and English common law enforced.
See also: Early legal codes 18–19 ▪ Gratian's *Decretum* 60–63

THE *LEX VISIGOTHORUM*
*c.*643 CE

Chindasuinth, ruler of the Kingdom of Visigoths (present-day Spain and southern France) introduced the Visigothic Code, revised in 654 CE by his son Recceswinth. The code marked the transition from Roman to Germanic law and covered the whole population for the first time; Romans living in the kingdom had earlier been subject to Roman law (*leges romanae*) and Visigoths to Germanic law (*leges barbarorum*).
See also: The Twelve Tables 30 ▪ Gratian's *Decretum* 60–63

MEDIEVAL LAW SCHOOLS
11th–13th century

The rediscovery, around 1070, of Justinian's *Digest*, a compilation of Roman law lost to scholars for more than 500 years, encouraged the study of law at Europe's first university, established in Bologna in 1088. During the 1100s, Gratian, a Bolognese jurist, wrote *Decretum*, his textbook on canon law, which the university also began to teach. It became a specialized law school – the first since antiquity – inspiring other European institutions to follow its example. By the end of the 12th century, universities in Oxford, Paris, and Montpellier also taught law.
See also: Ulpian the Jurist 36–37 ▪ Gratian's *Decretum* 60–63

THE GREAT LAW OF PEACE
12th century

In around the 12th century, the Iroquois Confederacy marked the coming together of five Native American nations (later six) known as the Haudenosaunee. Together with fellow chief Hiawatha, their leader – the Great Peacemaker – formulated the Great Law of Peace, an oral constitution conveyed by *wampum* (shell-bead) symbols, that sets out a binding social and ethical code for the nations. The unity that the Great Law achieved impressed Founding Father Benjamin Franklin; its articles influenced the US Constitution he helped to frame, as the US Senate formally acknowledged in 1988.
See also: The Peace of Westphalia 94–95 ▪ The US Constitution and Bill of Rights 110–117

THE ASSIZE OF BREAD AND ALE ACT
1202

The first English law to regulate the sale of food was the Assize of Bread and Ale Act. To protect the public from rogue traders, the Act ensured the public paid a fair price for their ale and laid out the standard weight for a loaf of bread sold for a farthing.
See also: The *Lex Mercatoria* 74–77 ▪ The Sherman Antitrust Act 170–73

GENGHIS KHAN'S *YASSA*
1206

Genghis Khan brought unity to the vast Mongol Empire in northeast Asia and imposed customary laws that only the ruling family could view and implement. No copies of

the *Yassa* survive, but secondary sources suggest that it promoted obedience to Genghis Khan and unification of the nomadic clans, and codified penalties for offences.
See also: Zhou dynasty China 24
■ Plato's *Laws* 31

THE *SIETE PARTIDAS*
1256

Compiled under Alfonso X of Castile in Spain, the *Siete Partidas* or Seven-Part Code provided legal, moral, and philosophical rules for all Castilians. Based on Roman law, it was designed to guide legislative judgements and offer a unified legal code for the whole kingdom. As the Spanish Empire grew in the 1500s, the *Siete Partidas* was exported to Latin America, where it remained influential until the 19th century.
See also: The Treaty of Tordesillas 86–87

THE TRIAL OF JOAN OF ARC
1431

The trial of Joan of Arc before a Church court in Rouen, France, is one of the best documented of the Middle Ages. After seeing visions, Joan became convinced that she could drive the English out of France and help the Dauphin to be crowned King Charles VII. She led many successful battles against the English, but was later captured by the Burgundians, French allies of the English. Joan was charged with 70 offences, largely based on her claim to have received divine revelations, which was judged to be blasphemous. Found guilty of heresy, she was burned at the stake.
See also: The trial of Galileo Galilei 93 ■ The Salem witch trials 104–05

THE TRIAL OF MARTIN LUTHER
1521

In 1517, Martin Luther nailed his Ninety-Five Theses, attacking the abuses of the Roman Catholic Church, to the door of a church in Wittenburg, Germany. The act is widely considered to mark the start of the Protestant Reformation – the movement challenging the Church's doctrines and practices. In 1521, the Pope excommunicated Luther, who was accused of heresy and put on trial in Worms before an imperial council of the Holy Roman Empire. Luther used the trial to defend and spread his ideas. An edict calling for his arrest ensued but was never enforced, as Frederick III of Saxony protected Luther, who continued his work, which ultimately contributed to the founding of Protestantism.
See also: The trial of Galileo Galilei 93

THE *SOBORNOYE ULOZHENIYE*
1649

Before Russia's introduction of the *Sobornoye Ulozheniye* (law code of the Zemsky Sobor parliament) in 1649, corruption was widespread in a period known as the "Time of Trouble". Following civil unrest, a group of Muscovites, impressed by the stabilizing effects of law codes in nearby countries, demanded that Russia follow suit. Statesman Nikita Odoyevsky was tasked with compiling the code from Russian precedents and from Byzantine law (the Roman law that was influenced by Christian beliefs and in use from the sixth century CE until the fall of Constantinople in 1453). The new

code was extremely thorough; its 25 chapters covered religion, property, landholding, inheritance, commerce, travel permits, military service, and criminal law. The code also classed peasants as serfs and limited the power of the Orthodox Church.
See also: Slave codes 98–101
■ The Russian Constitution 190–91

THE *HABEAS CORPUS* ACT
1679

England's Magna Carta, sealed in 1215, stated the concept of *habeas corpus* – that a person should not be unlawfully imprisoned – but in 1660, after the restoration of the monarchy, Parliament decided that it should be formally enshrined in law. *Habeas corpus* translates from Latin as "you shall have the body" and denotes in law that a person must be brought before a court to assess the lawfulness of their detention. A key tenet of common law today, *habeas corpus* has been suspended at various times in history, such as during World War II when "enemy aliens" were held without charge.
See also: Magna Carta 66–71
■ The Glorious Revolution and the English Bill of Rights 102–103

THE *FATAWA-E-ALAMGIRI*
Late 17th century

The Mughal Empire's Sharia-based legal code, the *Fatawa-e-Alamgiri*, was named for Alamgir, ("Conqueror of the World"), a title used by the emperor Aurangzeb who introduced the code. Compiled by scholars of the Hanafi School, one of four schools of jurisprudence of Sunni Islam, it formed the basis of judicial law for India's Mughal Empire, covering all aspects of life including family, slaves, taxation, war, and property. It later influenced the codification of laws across South Asia.

See also: The *Arthashastra* and the *Manusmriti* 35 ▪ The Koran 54–57

THE TRANSPORTATION ACT
1717

Largely to resolve the lack of space in UK prisons, the transportation of criminals to North America was introduced in 1717 by an Act of Parliament. Convicts were bound by a contract to work without pay for seven years for a lesser offence, and 14 or more years for serious crimes. After America became independent in 1776, Britain sent criminals to Australia instead.

See also: The Poor Laws 88–91

AIR LAW
1784

In 1783, the Montgolfier brothers launched the first manned hot-air balloon over Paris, France – an innovation that raised questions about the sovereignty of air space. A police ordinance banned balloon flights over Paris without a special permit. Belgium and Germany soon passed similar laws, marking the start of specialized aviation law.

See also: The Hague Conventions 174–77

THE PENAL SETTLEMENT OF AUSTRALIA
1788

In January 1788, 736 convicts transported from Britain arrived in Botany Bay, Australia, creating the continent's first penal colony. As transportation was less costly than

imprisonment in Britain, it was frequently imposed even for minor crimes. In the next 80 years, over 160,000 criminals were transported to Australia, helping Britain to populate its new colony, but severely depleting the Indigenous Australian population as a result of disease, conflict, and land seizures. Increasing numbers of new settlers, who arrived as the colony prospered, objected to the transportation of criminals, and the practice was ended in 1868.

See also: The Treaty of Tordesillas 86-87 ▪ The Poor Laws 88–91

THE TREATY OF WAITANGI
1840

As more British migrants arrived in New Zealand in the 1830s, the British government recognized the need to make a treaty with Māori chiefs to protect British interests and secure land rights. It was drafted and translated into Māori (but with discrepancies that obscured the extent of Māori rights ceded). The treaty gave the British sovereignty over New Zealand and the exclusive right to buy Māori lands. In return, the Māori were guaranteed rights of ownership of all their lands and gained the rights and privileges of British subjects.

See also: The Treaty of Tordesillas 86–87 ▪ The St Catherine's Milling case 169

THE BERN TREATY
1874

Postal systems expanded in the 18th and 19th century, but the lack of standard agreements controlling international mail impeded trade. In 1874, at a conference convened

by the Swiss government, delegates from 22 countries agreed the Treaty of Bern, which came into force in 1875. The treaty established the General Postal Union and created a single postal district across 19 European countries, plus the US and Egypt, allowing the exchange of mail under a uniform framework of rules and regulations. Membership grew to 55 within the first ten years. In 1878, the General Postal Union was renamed the Universal Postal Union and the treaty became the Universal Postal Convention. The treaty paved the way for future international agreements similarly based on the principle of reciprocity, such as the 1883 Paris Convention for the Protection of Industrial Property that included protection for patents and trademarks.

See also: The World Trade Organization 278–283 ▪ The Open Internet Order 310–13

THE TRADE MARKS REGISTRATION ACT
1875

The passing of the 1875 Trade Marks Registration Act created a system that, for the first time, allowed UK businesses to formally register and gain legal protection for their trademarks, preventing other companies from copying their product identity. The Act defined trademarks as devices, marks, or names of individuals or firms "printed in some particular and distinctive manner". The first UK trademark to be registered (on 1 January 1876) was the distinctive red triangle of Bass Breweries.

See also: The Venetian Patent Statute 82–85 ▪ The Statute of Anne 106–07 ▪ The WIPO Copyright Treaty 286–87

THE DREYFUS AFFAIR
1894

In 1894, Alfred Dreyfus, a French army captain of Jewish faith, was falsely accused of selling secrets to Germany, on the basis of flimsy evidence. He was court-martialled for treason and imprisoned on Devil's Island in French Guiana. Fresh evidence indicating that the true culprit was Major Ferdinand Walsin-Esterhazy came to light in 1896 but was not properly explored, and he was acquitted. Growing public unease over the miscarriage of justice was stoked by novelist Émile Zola, who wrote his open letter *"J'Accuse …!"* in support of Dreyfus. Although a document implicating Dreyfus was revealed as a forgery, a second court martial in 1899 again found Dreyfus guilty. The sentence was commuted and Dreyfus accepted a presidential pardon. He was finally exonerated by a court of appeals in 1906.
See also: The trial of Galileo Galilei 93 ▪ The Salem witch trials 104–05

THE *BÜRGERLICHES GESETZBUCH*
1900

After the unification of the German Empire in 1871, its former states initially retained their own varied civil laws, but the need for a single national German code of law was widely recognized. Based on Roman law, the *Bürgerliches Gesetzbuch* (*Civil Law Book*), also known as the BGB, was drafted in 1881, finally ratified in 1896, and came into law in 1900, establishing a national civil law across Germany. The BGB formed the foundation of modern German law and was used as a model for civil law in other nations including China, Italy, Japan, South Korea, and Switzerland.
See also: The Twelve Tables 30 ▪ The Napoleonic Code 130–131

THE SCOPES TRIAL
1925

After the passing of the Butler Act in Tennessee, US, in 1925, which made it illegal to teach evolution in schools, activists were keen to refute its validity. Physics teacher John Scopes volunteered to be accused of teaching human evolution. His trial pitted anti-evolutionist William Jennings Bryan for the prosecution against celebrated attorney Clarence Darrow, allowing both sides to pitch eloquent arguments. Scopes was found guilty and fined $100, but had achieved his and his supporters' aim of bringing debates about science vs. religion into the public sphere.
See also: The trial of Galileo Galilei 93

THE MOON TREATY
1979

In a bid to ensure the international community has some jurisdiction in space, the Moon Treaty, covering the Moon and other celestial bodies, was adopted by the UN General Assembly in 1979. It states that these areas of outer space are the "common heritage of mankind" and their environment should therefore be protected. The treaty, which came into force in 1984 when Austria became the fifth country to ratify it, asks that an international group be established to regulate any future exploitation of the natural resources of the Moon or other celestial bodies. Although 18 nations are parties to the treaty, no nation involved in human space flight has yet ratified the agreement.
See also: The World Network of Biosphere Reserves 270–71 ▪ The Kyoto Protocol 305

THE REPEAL OF THE APARTHEID LAWS
1991

The policy of apartheid – which segregated the South African population by race, discriminating against the black majority and favouring the white population – was put in place in 1948. In 1991, under increasing pressure from South African activists and the international community, President F.W. de Klerk repealed most of the remaining apartheid laws. These included the Land Acts of 1913 and 1936, which gave the best land to white people, and the Population Registration Act of 1950, which classified all babies by race at birth. The dismantling of the laws and the election of a government with a nonwhite majority in 1994 officially ended the apartheid system.
See also: The Nuremberg Laws 197 ▪ The Civil Rights Act 248–53

THE OSLO ACCORDS
1993, 1995

In a bid to secure a lasting peace between Israel and Palestine, the two Oslo Accords, negotiated initially in Norway, were signed by the Israeli government and the Palestine Liberation Organization (PLO) in 1993 (in Washington, DC) and 1995 (in Egypt). Earlier initiatives had included the UN Security Council Resolution 242 of 1967, adopted unanimously after the

Six-Day War between Israel and Arab forces from Egypt, Syria, and Jordan. The Oslo Accords met one key goal of Resolution 242; the PLO recognized Israel's right to exist, and was acknowledged in turn as Palestine's representative body. They also afforded the Palestinians a degree of self-governance in the occupied territories of Gaza and the West Bank, and required both sides not to incite violence against each other. The five-year interim period set out in the Accords ended in 1999 without agreement, violence resurfaced, and the provisions of the Accords were largely abandoned.
See also: The Peace of Westphalia 94–95 ▪ The Treaty of Versailles 192–93

THE UNDERLYING LAW ACT
2000

Until 1975, when Papua New Guinea became independent from Britain, the Papuan legal system had been based on English common law. The new Papuan constitution embraced both customary law and common law. The Act seeks to ensure that customary law is a key source of the nation's underlying law and is applied unless it is inconsistent with a written law or contrary to national interests and goals.
See also: The St Catherine's Milling case 169

THE USA PATRIOT ACT
2001

A month after the deadliest terrorist attacks in US history, carried out on 11 September 2001 by the Islamic extremist group al-Qaeda, President George W. Bush signed into law the USA PATRIOT Act (an acronym for

Uniting and Strengthening America by Providing Appropriate Tools Required to Intercept and Obstruct Terrorism). The Act expanded the surveillance powers of intelligence and law-enforcement agencies, among other measures facilitating searches of suspect individuals' homes, business premises, emails, telephone, and financial records – powers which have repeatedly raised civil rights concerns. From 2005, 16 sections of the Act were due to "sunset" (cease to have effect), but a modified Act passed in 2006 made 14 of the sunset provisions permanent and extended two others. In 2011, three major surveillance measures were extended until 2015. The USA FREEDOM Act of 2015 limited the US government's authority to collect data, but key surveillance powers of the USA PATRIOT Act were again restored and extended.
See also: The International Covenant on Civil and Political Rights 256–57

THE WORLD PRESS FREEDOM INDEX
2002

In a bid to counter the suppression of information, every year since 2002, Reporters Without Borders (RSF) has published the World Press Freedom Index, which ranks 180 countries according to the level of freedom afforded to journalists. RSF pools responses from experts and analyses abuses and acts of violence against journalists to determine the rankings. Norway topped the 2020 index for the fourth year in a row, while North Korea replaced Turkmenistan in last place.
See also: The Universal Declaration of Human Rights 222–29

THE INFECTIOUS DISEASE CONTROL AND PREVENTION ACT
2009

When the COVID-19 pandemic struck in 2020, South Korea could quickly take steps to combat the virus thanks to earlier legislation covering infectious diseases. As well as extensive testing, its government employed a measure added to the Act in 2015 when the country faced an outbreak of MERS–CoV, a similar coronavirus. The amendment allowed officials to collect mobile phone, emails, and other data revealing the movements of infectious patients in the period before they were diagnosed. This was then published on social media to alert, trace, and test possible contacts. While judged intrusive by some, the measure helped South Korea to contain infection levels.
See also: The International Covenant on Civil and Political Rights 256–57

THE MODERN SLAVERY ACT
2015

Under the UK Act, which enhances earlier legislation and reparations for victims, any organization that supplies goods or services in the UK and has a global turnover of more than £36 million must publish an annual statement outlining the measures it takes to ensure that no human trafficking, slavery, or forced labour occur in any part of its operations. A 2019 Home Office review has called for the Act to be further strengthened and extended to cover the public sector.
See also: The Abolition of the Slave Trade Act 132–39

GLOSSARY

In this glossary, terms defined within another entry are identified with *italic* type.

Absolute monarchy A monarchy in which the king or queen has complete control of the nation. See also *constitutional monarchy*.

Acquittal A *judgement* that a *defendant* is not guilty of a crime.

Act A *statute* or law that has been formally passed by a *legislature*.

Action A formal demand to a *court* of law to settle a dispute between two or more parties.

Act of Parliament A new law, or change to an existing law, made by the UK Parliament.

Advocate A lawyer who assists, defends, or argues the case for someone in a *court* of law.

Amendment An official addition or alteration made to a law, *statute*, or *constitution*. The US Bill of Rights consists of the first ten amendments to the US Constitution.

Appeal A request to a supervisory *court* to overturn the decision of a lower court.

Arbitration A process in which an impartial third party makes a binding decision regarding a legal dispute without it having to be resolved in *court*.

Assize A *court* that sat periodically in each county of medieval England.

Barrister A type of lawyer in the UK and some other countries with *common law* systems, who can appear as an *advocate* in both higher and lower *courts*.

Bill A proposal for a new law, or change to an existing law, that is presented for debate.

Bill of rights A formal declaration of the most important *rights* and freedoms that are common to all *citizens* of a country or *state*.

Canon law The body of law that regulates the organization of the Christian Church and *codifies* Christian beliefs.

Case law Law based on decisions made by *judges* in previous cases. See also *precedent*.

Citizen A person who belongs to a city or a bigger community such as a *state* or country.

City-state A city which, with its surrounding territory, is also an independent political *state*.

Civil law 1) A legal system based on *Roman law* and *codification* rather than *precedent*; used mainly in continental Europe and South America. 2) The branch of law that deals with disputes between private organizations or individuals, not crimes.

Civil rights The *rights* of people in a society to equal treatment and equal opportunities, whatever their gender, race, or religion. Examples of

civil rights include the right to vote, the right to a fair trial, and the right to use government services and public facilities.

Codification The process of arranging laws into a systematic form such as a *constitution* or a *law code*.

Common law The law of the land, derived from neither the *statute* books nor a written *constitution*, but from past *court* decisions based on *precedent*. Common law is the basis of legal systems in most English-speaking countries. See also *civil law*.

Comparative law The study of different legal systems by comparing and contrasting them.

Congress In the US Constitution, the body forming the legislative arm of the *federal* government. It consists of two elected assemblies, the House of Representatives (or Lower House) and the Senate (or Upper House).

Constitution The principles and laws concerning the way in which a country is governed.

Constitutional monarchy A monarchy in which the king or queen shares power with an elected *parliament*. See also *absolute monarchy*.

Contract A legally binding agreement between two or more parties in which an offer is made and accepted and each party benefits.

Copyright The exclusive legal right to reproduce, sell, or distribute an original creative work, usually for a fixed number of years.

Corporation An independent legal entity, owned by shareholders, that is authorized to conduct business.

Counsel 1) A *barrister*. 2) A lawyer appointed to give legal advice, or to represent a client in a *court* of law.

Court An institution or body of people with the authority to hear and resolve legal disputes. Also, a place where legal disputes are heard.

Covenant 1) A binding written agreement that can be enforced in a *court* of law. 2) (biblical) A binding agreement, based on faithful loyalty, between God and His people.

Crimes against humanity A deliberate, systematic, and widespread attack on a civilian population. Examples include murder, rape, and torture.

Criminal law The branch of law by which the *state* punishes those who have committed the most serious kind of wrong.

Cybercrime Criminal activities carried out using a computer or the internet.

Damages Money awarded by a *court* to a party that has suffered loss or injury as a result of another party's wrongful act.

Decriminalization Removing or reducing legal penalties for an act.

Defence The process of presenting *evidence* in an attempt to prove that a *defendant* is innocent.

Defendant A person or organization accused in a *court* of law.

Democracy A form of government in which supreme power is vested in the people or exercised by their elected representatives.

Direct democracy Government by the people in fact, rather than merely in principle – *citizens* vote on every issue affecting them.

Discrimination The unfair and prejudicial treatment of a person or group of people based on factors such as race, gender, religion, disability, social class, or sexuality.

Divine right of kings A doctrine that held that a monarch derived legitimacy from God, and was not subject to any earthly authority.

DNA Deoxyribonucleic acid. A large molecule that carries unique genetic information and can therefore be used to exactly identify any individual.

Due process The carrying out of legal proceedings according to established rules and principles that ensure people are treated fairly and their legal rights are respected.

Edict An official proclamation, command, or instruction issued by someone in authority.

Election A formal process in which a population (the electorate) of a country, *state*, or local area votes for an individual to hold a position of public office.

Embargo A government order to cease trade or other commercial activity with a particular country, often used as a diplomatic measure.

Enlightenment, The A period also known as the Age of Reason, spanning 1685–1815, when European thinkers questioned established ideas on religion and authority and promoted ideals such as liberty, progress, and tolerance.

Evidence Information presented at a *court*, *hearing*, or *trial* to help a *judge* or *jury* reach a *verdict*.

Executive The branch of government that is responsible for seeing that laws and policies are implemented and enforced.

Extradition The return of a person accused of a crime to the *state* or country where the crime was said to have been committed.

Federal Describes any political system where there is an overall central government (federal government), but with many areas of decision-making being carried out by regional governments – for example, governments of provinces or *states*; the division of powers between the federal and regional governments is normally guaranteed by a *constitution*.

Felony A crime regarded by many legal systems as more serious than a minor misdemeanour.

Feudal Describes a medieval political, social, economic, and military system where a country's monarch ruled at the top of a pyramid-like hierarchy. Each level of society was entitled to claim rights from those "below", but also obliged to undertake duties to those "above".

Fraud Criminal deception to secure financial or personal gain.

Genocide The deliberate, targeted killing of, or causing serious harm to, a large group of people, especially an entire religious group, race, or nation.

Habeas corpus (Latin for "you shall have the body".) The right of a person who is imprisoned or detained to appear before a *court* of law to establish whether their detention is lawful. A *writ* of *habeas corpus* orders the custodian to bring the detainee before the court.

Hearing A proceeding before a *court* or another legal decision-making body. A hearing is generally shorter and less formal than a *trial*.

Human rights Freedoms and *rights* that are inherent to all human beings and defined and protected by law. Examples of human rights include the right to life, liberty, and security.

Indictment A formal written accusation of a crime.

Intellectual property Creations or inventions that are protected by laws such as *patents*, *copyright*, and *trademarks*, enabling people to claim recognition for, or benefit financially from, what they create.

International law A system of laws covering the rights and duties of *sovereign* nations.

Judge A public official with the authority to preside over legal matters and *court* proceedings.

Judgement The final decision of a *court* or *judge* on a legal matter.

Judicial review The process whereby the *judiciary* can review the lawfulness of a decision or ruling made by the *legislature* or *executive*, providing an essential system of checks and balances. A key example of judicial review is the power of the US Supreme Court to decide whether a law violates the US Constitution.

Judiciary The branch of government that is responsible for administering justice and includes the *judges* and *courts* of law.

Jurisdiction The power of a *state*, *court*, or *judge* to make legal decisions and enforce laws. For example, a state may have jurisdiction over people, property, or circumstances within its territory.

Jury A body of people, known as jurors, who are sworn to give a *verdict* on a *court* case on the basis of *evidence* submitted to them.

Law code A comprehensive and systematic written collection of laws adopted by a nation or *state*.

Law enforcement The process of ensuring compliance with the law by means of arrests, punishment, rehabilitation, and deterrence.

Lawsuit In *civil law*, a *court* case in which a *plaintiff* claims to have suffered a loss as a result of a *defendant*'s wrongful actions.

Legislation A law or set of laws that is being prepared, enacted, or passed.

Legislature The branch of government that is responsible for making and passing laws.

Litigation The process of resolving a dispute between two or more opposing parties in *court*.

Magistrate A judicial official – or justice of the peace (JP) in England and Wales – who administers the law in *courts* that deal with minor crimes.

Magna Carta A charter of *rights* drafted in 1215 to limit abuses of power by the English monarchy.

Mandate A command or the authority to act in a certain way, given to a government representative by an electorate.

Martial law Military control that replaces the normal civilian government of a country, usually to maintain order in times of crisis.

Nation state An independent *state* in which the majority of the *citizens* share a common language and culture. These citizens identify as a nation and the state is ruled in their name.

Natural law A system of justice held to be common to all people and derived from the unchanging rules of nature rather than from the changing rules of society.

Papal bull An order or *edict* issued by the Pope on a matter of religious, legal, or political importance.

Parliament The law-making branch, or *legislature*, of a country's government, often made up of elected politicians.

Patent A form of legal protection that grants inventors ownership of their idea and ensures that other people cannot copy the invention without the inventor's permission. A patent protects an invention, whereas *copyright* protects the expression of an idea.

Plaintiff A person, organization, *state*, or country accusing a *defendant* in a *court* of law.

Precedent A principle or rule established by a *judgement* or ruling in a previous legal case. A precedent may be cited to justify a ruling in a subsequent case that deals with similar issues.

Prosecution The process of presenting *evidence* in an attempt to prove that a *defendant* is guilty of a crime.

Ratification The process of signing, or formally approving, a law, *treaty*, *contract*, *amendment*, or other agreement, making it legally valid.

Referendum A direct vote by the electorate on a specific issue, proposal, or policy.

Republic A *state* with no monarch, in which power resides with the people and is exercised by their elected representatives.

Revolution The sudden and often violent overthrow of a social order or political regime by the people.

Rights What a person is entitled to, either by law or as a matter of ethics.

Roman law The legal system of the ancient Romans, which still forms the basis of many modern-day systems of *civil law*.

Sentence The punishment given by a *judge* to a *defendant* found guilty of a crime in a *court* of law.

Separation of powers The division of government into three branches – the *executive*, *judiciary*, and *legislature* – that are separate, independent bodies, which ensures that no single branch gains too much power.

Sharia law The body of divine law in Islam that governs the religious and secular life of Muslims.

Sovereignty The authority held by a *state* – or by its ruler, leader, *parliament*, or government – that is not subject to any outside control or influences.

State 1) A *sovereign* political region and the people who live in it. 2) A member of a *federal* system. 3) A government and its institutions.

Statute A law that has been enacted by a *legislature* and formally written down. *Amendments* can be made to existing statutes.

Suffrage The right to vote in an *election* or *referendum*. Universal suffrage refers to the right to vote of *citizens* regardless of their gender, race, social status, or wealth. Women's suffrage describes the right of women to vote on the same basis as men.

Supreme court The highest judicial *court* in a country or *state*, which has *jurisdiction* over the lower courts. In the US, the Supreme Court is the highest *federal* court and has the power to interpret the US Constitution.

Tort law The branch of *civil law* that deals with wrongful actions of one party that cause another party to suffer loss or harm.

Trademark A word, phrase, sign, or symbol that distinguishes the goods or services of one enterprise from those of other enterprises. A trademark can be registered, which gives the owner an exclusive right to use the trademark.

Trade union An organized group of employees who negotiate with employers and the government to maintain and improve pay and working conditions.

Treaty A formal *contract* that sets out agreements – such as a trade agreement, an alliance, or the end of hostilities – between *states*.

Trial A formal examination of *evidence* by a *judge* in a law *court* in order to reach a *verdict* in a *criminal* or *civil law* case.

Universal jurisdiction In *international law*, the power of a national *court* to prosecute individuals for serious crimes such as *crimes against humanity*, *war crimes*, and *genocide*, regardless of where the crime was committed.

Verdict The conclusion of a *judge* or *jury* based on the *evidence* that is presented in *court*.

War crime An act carried out in the conduct of war that violates the international laws and customs of war. Examples of war crimes include taking hostages, using child soliders, and deliberately killing civilians or prisoners.

Warrant A legal document that allows someone to do something, particularly one that gives the police permission to make an arrest, seize goods, or search property.

Writ A formal legal document that orders a person to carry out, or stop carrying out, a specific action.

INDEX

QUOTE ATTRIBUTIONS

ACKNOWLEDGMENTS

Dorling Kindersley would like to thank Ira Sharma, Vikas Sachdeva, Shipra Jain, and Sampda Mago for design assistance; Chauney Dunford, Maisie Peppitt, Janashree Singha, and Tanya Singhal for editorial assistance; Miriam Kingston for advice on the contents list; Alexandra Beeden for proofreading; Helen Peters for indexing; DTP Designer Rakesh Kumar; Jackets Editorial Coordinator Priyanka Sharma; Managing Jackets Editor Saloni Singh; and Geetika Bhandari for picture research assistance.

PICTURE CREDITS

The publisher would like to thank the following for their kind permission to reproduce their photographs:

(Key: a-above; b-below/bottom; c-centre; f-far; l-left; r-right; t-top)

18 Alamy Stock Photo: Ivy Close Images (br). 19 Alamy Stock Photo: Science History Images (crb). Getty Images: DEA PICTURE LIBRARY / De Agostini (cla). 21 Alamy Stock Photo: Art Collection 2 (cla). 23 Alamy Stock Photo: Ira Berger. 25 Getty Images: API / Gamma-Rapho (cb). 27 Alamy Stock Photo: China Span / Keren Su. 29 Dreamstime.com: Mariusz Prusaczyk. 31 Dreamstime.com: Whirlitzer (cr). 33 Alamy Stock Photo: Janetta Scanlan (tl). 35 Alamy Stock Photo: Mark Markau (br). 37 Alamy Stock Photo: Chronicle (cr). iStockphoto.com: Nastasic (br). 40 Alamy Stock Photo: Lebrecht Music & Arts / Lebrecht Authors. 41 Alamy Stock Photo: Lebrecht Music & Arts / Lebrecht (tl); Historic Images (tr). 44 Alamy Stock Photo: Niday Picture Library. 46 Alamy Stock Photo: Classic Image. 47 Alamy Stock Photo: imageBROKER / hwo. 53 Alamy Stock Photo: Granger Historical Picture Archive / Granger, NYC. 55 Dreamstime.com: Yulia Babkina. 56 Bridgeman Images. 57 SuperStock: Universal Images. 59 Alamy Stock Photo: IanDagnall Computing. 61 Alamy Stock Photo: Aurelian Images. 62 Alamy Stock Photo: Glasshouse Images / JT Vintage. 63 SuperStock: Universal Images. 65 Alamy Stock Photo: Art Collection 2. 69 Alamy Stock Photo: Pictorial Press Ltd. 70 Alamy Stock Photo: World History Archive. 71 Alamy Stock Photo: Ian Dagnall. 73 Alamy Stock Photo: Granger Historical Picture Archive / Granger, NYC (tr). Getty Images: UIG / Prisma (bc). 75 Alamy Stock Photo: INTERFOTO / History. 76 Alamy Stock Photo: Timewatch Images. 77 Getty Images: UniversalImagesGroup / Prisma. 83 Alamy Stock Photo: Sergey Borisov. 84 Getty Images: Dea / A. Dagli Orti / De Agostini Editorial. 85 Alamy Stock Photo: Art Collection. 87 Alamy Stock Photo: Pictorial Press Ltd. 89 Alamy Stock Photo: Granger Historical Picture Archive / Granger, NYC. 90 Getty Images: Stringer / Fotosearch (br). 91 Alamy Stock Photo: The Print Collector / Heritage Images. 92 Alamy Stock Photo: Pictorial Press Ltd (cr). 94 Alamy Stock Photo: INTERFOTO / History (br). 97 Alamy Stock Photo: incamerastock. 100 Alamy Stock Photo: Virginia Museum of History & Culture. 101 Alamy Stock Photo: North Wind Picture Archives (tl, crb). 102 Alamy Stock Photo: GL Archive (cb). 103 Alamy Stock Photo: GL Archive. 105 Alamy Stock Photo: Pictorial Press Ltd. 106 Alamy Stock Photo: Chronicle (cb). 109 Alamy Stock Photo: Archive Images (cr). 112 Alamy Stock Photo: IanDagnall Computing. 115 The New York Public Library. 116 Alamy Stock Photo: Granger Historical Picture Archive / Granger, NYC. 117 Alamy Stock Photo: IanDagnall Computing. 119 Alamy Stock Photo: World History Archive. 127 Alamy Stock Photo: Granger Historical Picture Archive / Granger, NYC. 128 Alamy Stock Photo: © Aldo Liverani / Andia. 129 Dreamstime.com: Luckyphotographer. 130 Getty Images: Universal Images Group / Christophel Fine Art (br). 131 Alamy Stock Photo: Classic Image. 135 Alamy Stock Photo: incamerastock (t); Nic Hamilton Photographic (bl). 136 Alamy Stock Photo: Everett Collection / Everett Collection Historical (bc); World History Archive (tl). 137 Alamy Stock Photo: The History Collection. 141 Alamy Stock Photo: Chronicle. 142 Alamy Stock Photo: GL Archive. 143 Alamy Stock Photo: The Picture Art Collection. 145 Alamy Stock Photo: The Granger Collection. 147 Getty Images: Stringer / Hulton Archive. 149 Alamy Stock Photo: Archivah. 150 Alamy Stock Photo: Lebrecht Music & Arts / Lebrecht Authors. 153 Alamy Stock Photo: Pictorial Press Ltd (bl); The History Collection (cra). 154 Alamy Stock Photo: Shawshots. 158 Alamy Stock Photo: North Wind Picture Archives (tl); Prisma Archivo (br). 159 Getty Images: Stringer / Hulton Archive. 160 Alamy Stock Photo: Artokoloro (cr). 162 Alamy Stock Photo: Chronicle. 165 Alamy Stock Photo: GL Archive (tr); INTERFOTO / History (ca). 166 Alamy Stock Photo: Falkensteinfoto. 168 Alamy Stock Photo: 19th era 2 (cb). 171 Alamy Stock Photo: Glasshouse Images / JT Vintage (cla); Universal Images Group North America LLC / Encyclopaedia Britannica, Inc. / Library of Congress (tr). 173 Alamy Stock Photo: Craig Joiner Photography (crb). Dreamstime.com: Demerzel21 (tr). 175 Library of Congress, Washington, D.C.: Kurz & Allison LC-DIG-pga-01949 (digital file from original print) LC-USZC4-507 (color film copy transparency) LC-USZ62-1288 (b&w film copy neg.) LC-USZC2-1889 (color film copy slide). 176 Alamy Stock Photo: Historical image collection by Bildagentur-online. 177 Getty Images: Foto Frost / Ullstein Bild Dtl.. 179 Alamy Stock Photo: Painters. 181 Getty Images: Hulton Archive / Archive Photos. 182 Alamy Stock Photo: Granger Historical Picture Archive / Granger, NYC. 183 Alamy Stock Photo: Everett Collection Historical / Everett Collection (tr); WS Collection (tl). 185 Alamy Stock Photo: Granger Historical Picture Archive / Granger, NYC (cla). Getty Images: Bettmann (tr). 187 Alamy Stock Photo: Imago History Collection (clb). Missouri Valley Special Collections, Kansas City Public Library, Kansas City, Missouri: (cra). 188 Getty Images: Hulton Archive / Heritage Images (bc). 189 Getty Images: Bettmann. 191 Getty Images: Corbis Historical / Michael Nicholson. 192 Alamy Stock Photo: Sueddeutsche Zeitung Photo / Scherl (cb). 195 Dreamstime.com: Aliaksei Haiduchyk. 196 Getty Images: NurPhoto (crb). 204 Getty Images: Bettmann. 205 Getty Images: The LIFE Picture Collection / Thomas D. Mcavoy (bl); Library of Congress / Corbis Historical (tr). 208 Getty Images: Bettmann. 209 Alamy Stock Photo: The Picture Art Collection. 211 Getty Images: Bettmann (cla); Hulton Archive / Malcolm Linton (clb). 214 Alamy Stock Photo: Granger Historical Picture Archive / Granger, NYC. 215 Alamy Stock Photo: Pictorial Press Ltd. 218 Getty Images: AFP / Walter Astrada. 219 Alamy Stock Photo: UPI / Jemal Countess (ca). Rex by Shutterstock: Sipa / Dommergues (clb). 220 Alamy Stock Photo: Pictorial Press Ltd. 225 Alamy Stock Photo: Everett Collection Historical / Everett Collection (cra). Getty Images: GPO / Hulton Archive / Zoltan Kluger (bl). 227 Alamy Stock Photo: Shaun Higson / South Africa (tl). iStockphoto.com: E+ / Bill Oxford (bl). 228 Getty Images: NurPhoto / Ronen Tivony. 229 Getty Images: John Phillips. 231 Getty Images: Picture Post / Kurt Hutton. 233 Getty Images: Anadolu Agency / Anadolu (br); Christopher Furlong (tl). 237 Alamy Stock Photo: INTERFOTO / History. 238 Getty Images: Roger Viollet / Harlingue. 240 Getty Images: Keystone / Hulton Archive. 241 Alamy Stock Photo: Agencja Fotograficzna Caro / Eckelt (br); World History Archive (tl). 243 Alamy Stock Photo: mauritius images GmbH / Johannes Heuckeroth (ca). iStockphoto.com: E+ / KristianSeptimiusKrogh (bl). 245 Alamy Stock Photo: mccool (bl). SuperStock: Fine Art Images / A. Burkatovski (cra). 247 Federation of American Scientists: https://fas.org/issues/nuclear-weapons/status-world-nuclear-forces (b). 251 Alamy Stock Photo: IanDagnall Computing (cla). 252 Alamy Stock Photo: World History Archive. 253 Getty Images: Bettmann (tl); Rolls Press / Popperfoto (br). 255 Alamy Stock Photo: PictureLux / The Hollywood Archive (cla). Rex by Shutterstock: AP / Matt York (tr). 257 Getty Images: IP3 / Nicolas Kovarik. 259 Getty Images: Washington Bureau / Archive Photos (crb). 261 Getty Images: Bettmann. 262 Getty Images: The LIFE Picture Collection / Cynthia Johnson. 263 Getty Images: Julie Bennett. 265 American Bird Conservancy: Endangered Species Act: A Record of Success (br/Data). Dreamstime.com: Artof Sha (br/Bird). 271 Getty Images: Moment / James Forsyth. 273 Alamy Stock Photo: Science History Images (crb). 275 Getty Images: Fotosearch / Archive Photos (cr). 277 Getty Images: AFP / Mohamed Al-Bakour (cla); AFP (clb). 281 Getty Images: AFP / Khaled Desouki (cla); Sygma / Sion Touhig (crb). 283 Getty Images: Bloomberg. 285 Rex by Shutterstock: AP / Denis Paquin (crb). 287 Alamy Stock Photo: History and Art Collection. 288 Getty Images: LightRocket / Peter Charlesworth (cb). 289 Getty Images: Tim Graham Photo Library / Tim Graham. 291 European Monitoring Centre for Drugs and Drug Addiction: © EMCDDA, 1995–2019 (tr). Getty Images: Corbis News / Horacio Villalobos (bl). 294 Getty Images: Keystone-France / Gamma-Keystone (clb). Rex by Shutterstock: AP / Elise Amendola (tr). 295 Getty Images: Alex Wong. 297 Getty Images: Corbis Entertainment / Colin McPherson. 300 Dreamstime.com: Mikechapazzo. 301 Getty Images: AFP / Fred Dufour. 302 Getty Images: AFP. 303 Getty Images: AFP / Michael Kooren (clb). Rex by Shutterstock: Alan Gignoux (tr). 304 Getty Images: AFP / Jeff Haynes (cb). 307 Getty Images: ALLSPORT / Graham Chadwick. 308 Reuters: Vincent West (cb). 312 Getty Images: Mark Wilson. 313 Dreamstime.com: Simi32 (tl). Getty Images: Alex Edelman (br). 315 Alamy Stock Photo: Trinity Mirror / Mirrorpix

All other images © Dorling Kindersley
For further information see: www.dkimages.com